THE CHRISTIAN WRITERS

MARKET GUIDE

2022

THE CHRISTIAN WRITERS
MARKET GUIDE

Your Comprehensive Resource for Getting Published

STEVE LAUBE

THE CHRISTIAN WRITERS MARKET GUIDE 2022

ISBN – 978-1-62184-207-1 (paperback)
ISBN – 978-1-62184-208-8 (ebook)

Cover design by Five J's Design (*fivejsdesign.com*)
    and Hannah Linder (*hannahlinderdesigns.com*)
Typesetting by Jamie Foley (*jamiefoley.com*)
Edited by Lin Johnson

Printed in the United States of America.

Visit The Christian Writers Institute at *www.ChristianWritersInstitute.com*.

E-mail: *admin@christianwritersmarketguide.com*

TABLE OF CONTENTS

PART 5: SUPPORT FOR WRITERS 225

FOREWORD

GENERALISTS HAVE BECOME AS RARE AS UNICORNS
in the writing game. When I was a pup—admittedly a half century ago when
rainbows were black and white—we wannabe writers tried everything.
Fiction. Nonfiction. Newspapers, magazines, Sunday-school papers,
newsletters, you name it.

Nowadays, those of us who continue to write both fiction and nonfiction—
now adding blogs and ezine markets to our targets—are often urged to pick
one or the other. Agents, publishers, bookstore managers, everyone it
seems, wants to categorize us, brand us, let potential readers know what
to expect from us.

Well, I may be charging up the wrong hill; but I say let your identity
become quality. Yes, it may help—especially if you're a beginner—to home in
on one genre. But don't limit yourself. Worry less about speed and numbers
and branding and more about quality.

Become known as a trusted producer of accessible, readable prose; and
your horizons will expand. And when you have produced something with
which you're entirely happy—because you've become an aggressive self-
editor—do your homework, or what realtors and lawyers refer to as your
due diligence.

Peruse. Study. Examine.

You must immerse yourself in the markets, know them, understand
what they're looking for. And there's no better place to do that than right
here. This guide is designed to fully inform you. You'll learn who's who in
the industry, who's looking for what. You can avoid the embarrassment of
pitching a how-to-wash-your-dog piece to a theological periodical, a funny
take on family life to a purveyor of speculative fantasy.

There's enough within these pages to make you look like a credentialed
pro if you just invest in it the time your career deserves.

Welcome to the journey!

— Jerry B. Jenkins
www.JerryJenkins.com

INTRODUCTION

WRITING IS A SERIOUS BUSINESS. It is also a serious calling. The privilege of having your words influence other people's thinking or inspiring their spirit is a gift from God. A number of publication opportunities for great writing from great authors exist. Traditional methods for publication remain, but the diversity of online opportunities are seemingly endless. In addition, independent-publication options have made it easier to see your byline on a book, on a blog post, or in an online magazine.

Since many Christian bookstores have closed, it may seem like the Christian publishing industry is shrinking; but it is not. It is simply changing. Therefore, you must research more effectively to find the best place for your work. The problem with online search engines is the immense number of results you receive. Then the results depend on that site's search-engine optimization and those who have paid to have their sites show at the top. *The Christian Writers Market Guide* has curated the information for you. Now you can find what is targeted specifically for the Christian market and your areas of interest.

One of the biggest mistakes a writer can make is to ignore the guidelines of an agent, an editor, or a publisher. In the past, some publications dropped their listings in this guide because writers failed to follow the instructions in it. Editors are looking for writers who understand their periodicals or publishing houses and their unique approaches to the marketplace. This book will help you be such a writer. With a little time and effort, you can meet an editor's expectations, distinguish yourself as a professional, and sell what you write.

If you can, I recommend you attend a writers conference, whether virtual or in person. (We have many listed inside.) It is good to meet new people and become familiar with the best teachers in the industry. If you cannot get to a conference, consider exploring the courses available online at *ChristianWritersInstitute.com*. There are more than 110 to choose from, and you can enjoy them at any time on any device.

If this is the first time you've used this guide, read the "How to Use This Book" section. If you run into an unfamiliar term, look it up in the "Publishing Lingo" section in back and learn the terminology.

Please be aware that the information in this guide is provided by the companies or individuals through online questionnaires and email inquiries, as well as their websites and writers guidelines. The companies or individuals do not pay to be listed in the *Guide*. The entries are not endorsed by me or The Christian Writers Institute. We make every attempt to verify the accuracy of the information provided. The entries are for information only. Any transaction(s) between a user of the information and the individuals or companies listed is strictly between those parties.

May God bless your writing journey. We are on a mission to change the world, word by word. To that end, strive for excellence and make your work compelling and insightful. Great writing is still in demand. But it must be targeted, crafted, critiqued, edited, polished, and proofread until it shines.

My thanks go to Lin Johnson whose invaluable work makes this all possible. She keeps tabs throughout the year on market changes, so every listing is accurate to the best of our information at the time of publication. (Our online version of this guide, *ChristianWritersMarketGuide.com*, is updated regularly during the year.) As the administrator of the online and print editions, she is the genius behind the details. In addition, I would also like to acknowledge my wife, Lisa. Her love, support, and encouragement have been incalculable. We make a great team!

Steve Laube
President
The Christian Writers Institute
and
The Steve Laube Agency
24 W. Camelback Rd. A-635
Phoenix, AZ 85013
www.christianwritersinstitute.com
www.stevelaube.com

To update a listing or to be added to the next edition or online, go to *christianwritersmarketguide.com*. Click on the Get Listed tab, and fill out the form.

For direct-sales questions, email the publisher: *admin@christianwritersinstitute.com.*

For books and courses on the writing craft, visit The Christian Writers Institute: *www.christianwritersinstitute.com.*

HOW TO USE THIS BOOK

THE CHRISTIAN WRITERS MARKET GUIDE 2022 **IS DESIGNED** to make it easier for you to sell your writing. It will serve you well if you use it as a springboard to become thoroughly familiar with the markets best suited to your writing style and areas of interest and expertise.

As you look through this guide, you may run into words in the listings that you are not familiar with. If so, check "Publishing Lingo" at the back of the book.

GETTING ACQUAINTED WITH THIS BOOK

Start by getting acquainted with the setup of this guide.

Book Publishers
Part 1 lists traditional book publishers with information about what they are looking for. Notice that many houses accept manuscripts only from agents or through meeting with their editors at a writers conference. If you need a literary agent, check the agent listings in Chapter 16.

Independent Book Publishing
Since independent book publishing is a viable option today, Part 2 provides resources to help you. Chapter 2 lists independent book publishers, many of which provide all the services you need as packages or à la carte services. If you decide to publish on your own, Chapters 3 and 4 list design, production, and distribution services. You'll also want to hire a professional editor and proofreader, so see Chapter 19 for help in this area.

Periodical Publishers
Part 3 lists periodical–magazine, newspaper, and newsletter–publishers. Chapter 5 will help you find markets by topics (e.g., marriage, evangelism) and types (e.g., how-to, poetry, personal experience). Although these lists are not comprehensive, they provide a shortcut for finding appropriate markets for your ideas.

Cross-referencing may be helpful. For example, if you have an idea for a how-to article on parenting, look at the lists in both the how-to and parenting categories. Also, don't overlook writing on the same topic for different periodicals, such as money management for a general adult magazine, a teen magazine, a women's newsletter, and a magazine for pastors. Each would require a different slant, but you would get more mileage from one idea.

Specialty Markets

In Part 4, "Specialty Markets," you'll find nonbook, nonperiodical markets like daily devotionals and drama. Here you can explore types of writing you may not have thought about but can provide a steady writing income.

Support for Writers

As a writer, you'll need support to keep going. Part 5 provides information for various kinds of support.

One of the best ways to get published today is to meet editors at writers conferences. Check out Chapter 17 for a conference or seminar near you or perhaps in a location you'd like to visit. Before deciding which conference to attend, check the websites for who is on faculty, what houses are represented, and what classes are offered that can help you grow your craft and writing business. You may also want to factor in the size of the conference. Don't be afraid to stretch outside your comfort zone.

For ongoing support and feedback on your manuscripts, join a writers group. Chapter 18 lists groups by state and internationally. If you can't find one near you, consider starting one or join an online group.

Since editors and literary agents are looking for polished manuscripts, you may want to hire a professional editor. See Chapter 19 for people who offer a variety of editorial services, including coaching.

Whether you publish your book with a royalty house or go the independent route, you'll need to do most, if not all, of the promotion. If you want to hire a specialist with contacts, check out Chapter 20, "Publicity and Marketing Services." And if you need accounting or legal help, check out Chapter 21.

One way to promote your message and your books is through speaking. If you need help in this area—and most writers do—see Chapter 22, "Speaking Services." There you will find organizations and conferences that train speakers and/or connect them with groups looking for speakers.

Since writers who stagnate don't get published, check out Chapter 23 for education resources to help you improve your writing style, write different types of manuscripts, and learn the business of writing and publishing. You'll find a variety of free and paid resources, including podcasts and classes.

Entering a writing contest can boost your sales, supplement your writing income, lead to publication, and sometimes give you valuable feedback on your writing. Check out Chapter 24 for a list of contests by genre. Many of them are not Christian oriented, but you can enter manuscripts with a Christian worldview.

USING THIS BOOK

Once you get acquainted with this guide, start using it. After you identify potential markets for your ideas and/or manuscripts, read their writers guidelines. If these are available on the website, the URL is included. Otherwise, email or send (with a SASE) for a copy. Also study at least one sample copy of a periodical (information to obtain one is given in most listings) or the book publisher's website to see if your idea truly fits there. Never send a manuscript without doing this market study.

Above all, keep in mind that this guide is only a starting point for your research and change is the one constant in the publishing industry. It is impossible for any market guide to be 100 percent accurate since editors move around, publications and publishing houses close, and new ones open. But this guide is an essential tool for getting published in the Christian market and making an impact on God's Kingdom with your words.

PART 1

TRADITIONAL BOOK PUBLISHERS

1

TRADITIONAL BOOK PUBLISHERS

Before submitting your query letter or book proposal, it's critical that you read and follow a publisher's guidelines exactly. In many cases, the guidelines are available on the website and a direct link is given in the listing. If you do not have a literary agent—and even if you do—check out a publisher thoroughly before signing a contract.

Note: Not all the imprints listed in imprint entries below are in this book, primarily since they are focused for the general market. Also, some may be in other sections.

1517 MEDIA
Fortress Press, Beaming Books, Broadleaf Books, Augsburg

ABINGDON PRESS
2222 Rosa L. Parks Blvd., Nashville, TN 37228-1306 | 615-749-6000
www.abingdonpress.com
Constance Stella, senior acquisitions editor
- **Denomination:** United Methodist
- **Parent company:** United Methodist Publishing House
- **Submissions:** Publishes 120 titles per year; receives 2,000 submissions annually. First-time authors: fewer than 5%. Bible: CEB.
- **Royalty:** minimum 7.5%
- **Types and topics:** Christian living/spirituality, leadership, theology, academic, nonfiction
- **Guidelines:** *www.abingdonpress.com/submissions*
- **Tip:** Looking for "any young and new voices that have active speaking and

conference engagements, as well as blog and social-media followers."

AMBASSADOR INTERNATIONAL

411 University Ridge, Ste. B14, Greenville, SC 29601 | 864-751-4844
www.ambassador-international.com
Katie Cruice Smith, senior editor

Mission statement: To spread the gospel of Christ and empower Christians through the written word

Submissions: Publishes 50 titles per year; receives 750 submissions annually. First-time authors: 50%. Length: minimum 144 pages. Responds in one month. Bible: KJV, NIV, ESV, NKJV, NASB.

Royalty: 15-20% print, 25% ebooks, no advance

Types and topics: biography, business, Christian living/spirituality, finances, theology, Bible studies, children, devotionals, fiction, teen/YA

Guidelines: *ambassador-international.com/get-published/submission-guidelines*

Tip: "We're most open to a book which has a clearly defined market and the author's total commitment to the project. We do well with first-time authors. We have full international coverage. Many of our titles sell globally."

AMERICAN CATHOLIC PRESS

16565 State St., South Holland, IL 60473-2025 | 708-331-5485
acp@acpress.org | *www.acpress.org, www.leafletmissal.com*
Rev. Michael Gilligan, editorial director

Denomination: Catholic

Submissions: Publishes four titles per year; receives ten submissions annually. Responds in two months. Bible: NAS.

Payment: flat fee: $25-$100

Average first print run: 3,000

Types and topics: liturgy, nonfiction

Guidelines: *www.americancatholicpress.org/faq.html#faq5*

Tip: "We publish only materials on the Roman Catholic liturgy. No poetry or fiction."

AMG PUBLISHERS

6815 Shallowford Rd., Chattanooga, TN 37421 | 423-894-6060
amandaj@amgpublishers.com | *www.amgpublishers.com*
Amanda Jenkins, author liaison

Parent company: AMG International

Mission statement: to minister to people through the written word

Submissions: Publishes ten titles per year; receives 200 submissions annually. First-time authors: 60%. Length: 120 pages or more. Responds in three to six months. Bible: any. Looking for "strong biblical content that is doctrinally accurate, with little to no denominational slant/viewpoint."

Royalty: 14-16%, sometimes offers advance

Types and topics: African-American, apologetics, Bible study, Hispanic, Bible reference/commentaries, Bible studies, devotionals

Types of books: ebook, hardcover, offset paperback

Imprints: Living Ink (youth fiction), God and Country Press (historical and patriotic devotions and books)

Guidelines: *amgpublishers.com/index.php/author-guidelines*

Tip: "Most open to an interactive workbook Bible study geared for small groups that effectively taps into a largely female audience. We are currently placing priority on books with strong bibliocentric focus."

ANCIENT FAITH PUBLISHING

PO Box 748, Chesterton, IN 46304 | 800-967-7377
khyde@ancientfaith.com | www.ancientfaith.com/publishing
Katherine Hyde, editorial director
Jane Meyer, children's project manager, jmeyer@ancientfaith.com

Denomination: Orthodox Christian

Mission statement: to embrace the fullness of the Orthodox Christian faith, encourage the discipleship of believers, equip the faithful for ministry, and evangelize the unchurched

Submissions: Publishes 12-16 titles per year; receives 100 submissions annually. First-time authors: 50%. Length: 40,000-100,000 words. Responds in three months. Bible: NKJV.

Royalty: 10-15%, no advance

Average first print run: 2,000

Types and topics: biography, Christian living/spirituality, church history, contemporary issues, family, marriage, memoir/personal narrative, theology, worship, Bible reference/commentaries, children, fiction, teen/YA

Guidelines: *www.ancientfaith.com/publishing#af-resources*

Tip: "Read and follow the guidelines. Look through our website to see the kinds of books we publish. Do not submit material that is not intended specifically for an Eastern Orthodox audience."

ANEKO PRESS

PO Box 652, Abbotsford, WI 54405 | 715-223-3013
jeremiah@lspbooks.com | *www.anekopress.com*
Jeremiah Zeiset, president

> **Parent company:** Life Sentence Publishing, Inc.
> **Mission statement:** to publish books for ministry
> **Submissions:** Publishes 20 titles per year; receives 50 submissions annually. First-time authors: 20%. Length: 30,000-100,000 words. Responds in two weeks. Bible: KJV, ESV, NKJV. Niche is publishing ministry-related books.
> **Royalty:** 30%, no advance
> **Average first print run:** 1,000-5,000
> **Types and topics:** Christian living/spirituality, nonfiction
> **Types of books:** audiobook, ebook, hardcover, offset paperback
> **Guidelines:** *anekopress.com/write-for-us*
> **Tip:** "The majority of our authors are in ministry as missionaries or other similar ministries."

ARMOUR BOOKS

PO Box 492, Corinda, QLD 4075, Australia
words@armourbooks.com.au | *www.armourbooks.com.au*
Anne Hamilton

> **Mission statement:** to publish quality books with a "kiss from God at their heart"
> **Submissions:** Publishes five titles per year; receives 50-100 submissions annually. First-time authors: 50%. Length: maximum 50,000 words. Responds in two to four weeks.
> **Royalty:** 9-10%, sometimes offers advance
> **Types and topics:** Christian living/spirituality, fiction, nonfiction, fantasy, science fiction
> **Type of books:** POD
> **Guidelines:** by email or mail
> **Tip:** "The golden rule: Support other authors as you would like to be supported."

ASCENDER BOOKS

100 Missionary Ridge, Birmingham, AL | 888-811-9934
www.ironstreammedia.com

> **Parent company:** Iron Stream Media
> **Submissions:** Authors must come from the Spirit-led community.

Also includes online studies for churches and small groups. Note: Imprint will be discontinued and rolled into Iron Stream.

Types and topics: Bible study, spiritual growth, spiritual warfare

Guidelines: *www.ironstreammedia.com/submission-process*

ASHBERRY LANE

13607 Bedford Rd. NE, Cumberland, MD 21502 | 866-245-2211

r.white@whitefire-publishing.com | *AshberryLane.com*

Roseanna White, senior fiction editor

> **Parent company:** WhiteFire Publishing
>
> **Mission statement:** Ashberry Lane is a romance line that specializes in "heartfelt stories of faith."
>
> **Submissions:** Publishes five to ten titles per year; receives 50 submissions annually. First-time authors: 10%. Length: 60,000-110,000 words. Responds in three months.
>
> **Royalty:** 50% for ebooks, 10% of retail for print; sometimes offers advance of $500-$2,000
>
> **Types and topics:** fiction: historical romance, romance, romantic suspense
>
> **Type of books:** POD
>
> **Guidelines:** *ashberrylane.com/submissions*
>
> **Tip:** "Please be familiar with our titles and mission."

ASPIRE PRESS

PO Box 3473, Peabody, MA 01961 | 800-358-3111

info@hendricksonrose.com | *www.hendricksonrose.com*

Lynette Pennings, managing editor

> **Parent company:** Hendrickson Publishing Group/Tyndale House Ministries
>
> **Mission statement:** to publish books that are compassionate in their approach and rich with Scripture, giving godly insight and counsel for those personally struggling and for believers who have a heart to minister and encourage others
>
> **Submissions:** Need credentials in helping others.
>
> **Types and topics:** Christian living/spirituality, counseling

AVE MARIA PRESS

PO Box 428, Notre Dame, IN 46556 | 800-282-1865, ext. 1

submissions@mail.avemariapress.com | *www.avemariapress.com*

Heidi Hess Saxton, senior acquisitions editor

> **Denomination:** Catholic

Mission statement: to serve the spiritual and educational needs of individuals, groups, and the Church as a whole

Submissions: Publishes 40 titles per year; receives 350 submissions annually. First-time authors: 30%. Length: 20,000-60,000 words. Responds in three to four weeks. Bible: RSV2CE, NABRE. While many of the books address a wide ecumenical readership, primary interest is in books for Catholics and Catholic institutions.

Royalty: 10%, advance of at least $1,000

Types and topics: Advent, African-American, Christian living/spirituality, death and dying, evangelism, faith formation, family, grief, healing, Hispanic, marriage, ministry, parenting, prayer, theology, curriculum, ministry resources, small-group study guides

Types of books: ebook, hardcover, offset paperback

Guidelines: *www.avemariapress.com/manuscript-submissions*

Tip: "Our most successful books identify and address a specific felt-need for a potential reader. We are eager to work with authors who have robust platforms and direct connections to their potential readers. There are a number of areas in which we do not accept unsolicited manuscripts: fiction (for adults or teens), children's books (fiction or nonfiction), poetry, and accounts of personal conversion or private revelation. If your manuscript falls in one of these categories, we advise you to seek a publisher active in your area of interest."

B&H KIDS

1 Lifeway Plaza, Nashville, TN 37023 | 615-251-2000
michelle.freeman@lifeway.com | *www.bhpublishinggroup.com/categories/kids*
Michelle Freeman, publisher
Anna Sargeant, associate publisher, anna.sargeant@lifeway.com

Denomination: Southern Baptist

Parent company: B&H Publishing/Lifeway Christian Resources

Mission statement: to help kids develop a lifelong relationship with Jesus and to empower parents and church leaders to guide the spiritual growth of the next generation

Submissions: Publishes 18-24 titles per year; receives hundreds of submissions annually. First-time authors: 10-20%. Length: depends on age group. Responds in one to three months. Bible: CSB.

Royalty: 18-22%, gives advance

Types and topics: Bible stories, board books, devotionals, fiction, first-chapter, middle grade, nonfiction, picture books, teen/YA. Any book for children or teens with a Christian message. Themes include but are not limited to adventure, attributes of God, Bible story retellings, biblical virtues, church, community, diversity and inclusion, family, relationships, friendships, prayer, emotions, and theology.

Types of books: audiobook, board books, ebook, hardcover, offset paperback, picture books

Guidelines: by email

Tip: "We are a conservative Christian publishing house that publishes Protestant authors. Note that illustrations for children's books are not necessary or suggested."

B&H PUBLISHING GROUP

1 Lifeway Plaza, MSN 188, Nashville, TN 37234
www.bhpublishinggroup.com
Ashley Gorman, acquisitions and development editor

Denomination: Southern Baptist

Parent company: LifeWay Christian Resources

Submissions: Publishes 90 titles per year; receives thousands of submissions annually. First-time authors: 10%. Responds in two to three months. Bible: CSB.

Royalty: varies, advance

Types and topics: Bible study, Christian living/spirituality, church growth, evangelism, leadership, marriage, parenting, theology, women, worship, academic, Bible reference/commentaries, children

Imprints: B&H Publishing (trade books), B&H Kids (children), B&H Academic (textbooks), Holman Bibles, B&H Español (Spanish)

Guidelines: none

Tip: "Be informed that the market in general is very crowded with the book you might want to write. Do the research before submitting."

BAKER ACADEMIC

6030 E. Fulton Rd., Ada, MI 49301 | 616-676-9185
submissions@bakeracademic.com | bakerpublishinggroup.com/bakeracademic
Robert Hosack, senior acquisitions editor

Parent company: Baker Publishing Group

Submissions: Publishes 50 titles per year. First-time authors: 10%.

Royalty: advance

Types and topics: academic, professional

Guidelines: *bakerpublishinggroup.com/bakeracademic/contact/ submitting-a-proposal*

BAKER BOOKS

6030 E. Fulton Rd., Ada, MI 49301 | 616-676-9185
bakerpublishinggroup.com/bakerbooks
Rebekah Guzman, editorial director
Brian Vos, senior acquisitions editor
Stephanie Duncan Smith, acquisitions editor
Patnacia Goodman, acquisitions editor

> **Parent company:** Baker Publishing Group
> **Types and topics:** apologetics, biography, business, Christian living/ spirituality, church life, culture, family, leadership, marriage, memoir/ personal narrative, ministry, parenting, spiritual growth, theology, Bible reference/commentaries
> **Guidelines:** *bakerpublishinggroup.com/contact/submission-policy*

BAKER PUBLISHING GROUP

Baker Academic, Baker Books, Bethany House, BrazosPress, Chosen, Revell

BARBOUR PUBLISHING, INC.

PO Box 719, Uhrichsville, OH 44683 | 740-922-6045
submissions@barbourbooks.com | *www.barbourbooks.com*
Annie Tipton, senior acquisitions editor
Paul Muckley, senior acquisitions editor, Bible and reference
Rebecca Germany, senior editor and acquisitions, fiction

> **Mission statement:** to inspire the world with the life-changing message of the Bible
> **Submissions:** Takes fiction proposals only through agents. Responds only if interested.
> **Types and topics:** Christian classics, Christian living/spirituality, Hispanic, activities and puzzles, Bible reference/commentaries, Bible stories, children, devotionals, planners; fiction: Amish, contemporary, historical, romance, suspense/thriller
> **Imprints:** Barbour Books (nonfiction), Barbour Fiction, Barbour Reference, DayMaker (planners), Barbour Young Adult (nonfiction, devotionals), Barbour Kidz (children), Barbour Bibles, Casa Promesa (Spanish)
> **Guidelines:** *www.barbourbooks.com/frequently-asked-questions*

BEAMING BOOKS

510 Marquette Ave., Minneapolis, MN 55403 | 800-960-9705
www.beamingbooks.com
Naomi Krueger, acquisitions editor

Denomination: Evangelical Lutheran Church in America
Parent company: 1517 Media
Submissions: Publishes 24 titles per year; receives 250 submissions annually. First-time authors: 50%. Length: 500 words for picture books. Responds in three months. Bible: NIV, CEB.
Royalty: gives advance
Types and topics: activities and puzzles, devotionals, fiction, board books for ages birth-3, picture books for ages 3-8, activity books for ages 3-8, early-reader and first-chapter books for ages 5-9, nonfiction books for ages 5-9 and 8-12, fiction for ages 8-12, activity books for families, devotionals for children ages 0-12 and families
Tip: "Look at what we've published before. Read a few of our books."

BETHANY HOUSE PUBLISHERS

11400 Hampshire Ave. S, Bloomington, MN 55438 | 952-829-2500
bakerpublishinggroup.com/bethanyhouse
Andy McGuire, executive acquisitions editor
Raela Schoenherr, senior acquisitions editor
David Long, fiction acquisitions editor
Jeff Braun, nonfiction acquisitions editor
Jennifer Dukes Lee, nonfiction acquisitions editor

Parent company: Baker Publishing Group
Mission statement: to publish high-quality writings that represent historical Christianity and serve the diverse interests and concerns of evangelical readers
Submissions: Publishes 75-85 titles per year. Bible: NIV.
Royalty: varies, gives advance
Types and topics: Christian living/spirituality, family, prayer, relationships, theology, devotionals; fiction: Amish, biblical, contemporary, fantasy, historical, Regency, romance, romantic suspense
Types of books: ebook, hardcover, offset paperback
Tip: "The best opportunities for new authors come via literary agencies, conferences, writing communities, and author referrals. Get connected."

BLING! ROMANCE

100 Missionary Ridge, Birmingham, AL 35242 | 888-811-9934
editor@blingromance.com | *shoplpc.com/bling-romance*
Jessica Nelson, acquisitions and managing editor

Parent company: Iron Stream Media
Mission statement: to entertain and engage the contemporary reader

with stories that are simultaneously character- and plot-driven, written by seasoned and debut novelists with unique voices

Submissions: Publishes eight titles per year; receives 40 submissions annually. First-time authors: 50%. Length: 80,000 words. Responds in three months. Bible: NIV. Note: This imprint will be discontinued and rolled into Iron Stream Fiction.

Royalty: 40%, no advance

Types and topics: fiction, romance

Types of books: ebook, POD

Guidelines: *shoplpc.com/bling*

Tip: "At Bling! the first thing readers will notice is a solid, entertaining story. Think parables. We seek clean, wholesome stories with God's moral truths woven into the story. Please avoid sermons in stories."

BOLD VISION BOOKS

PO Box 2011, Friendswood, TX 77549-2011 | 832-569-4282
boldvisionbooks@gmail.com | *www.boldvisionbooks.com*
Karen Porter, managing editor
Rhonda Rhea, acquisitions editor

Mission statement: To publish compelling, creative, and beautiful books. Our goal is to change the world and further the message of Christ through the written word. We are small, but innovative, aspiring to be astute and progressive in this changing industry.

Submissions: Publishes 25 titles per year; receives 150 submissions annually. First-time authors: 85%. Length: 50,000-70,000 words. Responds in three to four months. Bible: any.

Royalty: 25-50%, sometimes offers advance of $1,000-$5,000

Average first print run: 2,000-10,000

Types and topics: arts, business, Christian living/spirituality, family, parenting, productivity, speaking, teaching, time management, writing, YA; fiction: adventure, contemporary, historical, humor, mystery, romance, teen/YA

Types of books: ebook, hardcover, offset paperback

Imprints: Nuts 'n Bolts (teaching, writing, speaking, painting, acting, business principles, productivity, time management), Optasia Books (fee-based for beloved pastors)

Guidelines: fiction: *www.boldvisionbooks.com/new-page-1;* nonfiction: *www.boldvisionbooks.com/new-page*

Tip: "To become a successful writer, learn the craft of writing and attend writers conferences and take courses to understand this industry. Keep your message firmly planted in the Word of God.

Know your audience and what they need. Read and follow our guidelines, and send a professional proposal. We want to see timeless truth told in fresh creative language."

BRAZOS PRESS

6030 E. Fulton Rd., Ada, MI 49301 | 616-676-9185
submissions@brazospress.com | bakerpublishinggroup.com/brazospress
Katelyn Beaty, senior acquisitions editor

Parent company: Baker Publishing Group

Mission statement: to draw upon the riches of the Christian story to deepen our understanding of God's world and inspire faithful reflection and engagement

Submissions: Publishes books that creatively draw on the riches of our catholic Christian heritage to deepen our understanding of God's creation and inspire faithful reflection and engagement. Authors typically hold advanced degrees and have established publishing platforms.

Types and topics: nonfiction

Guidelines: *bakerpublishinggroup.com/brazospress/submitting-a-proposal*

Tip: "We welcome book proposals from scholars, church leaders, activists, artists, and writers who have something to say and can write with both skill and passion, demonstrating that serious writing can also be lively and compelling."

BRIDGE LOGOS

17750 N.W. 115th Ave., Bldg. 200, Ste. 220, Alachua, FL 32615 | 386-462-2525
swooldridge@bridgelogos.com | www.bridgelogos.com
Peggy Hildebrand, acquisitions editor

Submissions: Publishes 40 titles per year; receives 200 submissions annually. First-time authors: 30%. Length: 250 pages. Responds in six weeks.

Royalty: 10%, advance: $500

Types and topics: African-American, apologetics, biography, business, Charismatic, Christian living/spirituality, church life, contemporary issues, cults, evangelism, family, finances, Hispanic, Jewish roots, leadership, marriage, parenting, relationships, spiritual warfare, theology, women, children, devotionals, fiction

Guidelines: *www.bridgelogos.com/Manuscript_Submission.html*

Tip: "Looking for well-written, timely books that are aimed at the needs of people and that glorify God. Have a great message, a well-written manuscript, and a specific plan and willingness to market your book. Looking for previously published authors with an active ministry who are experts on their subject."

BRIMSTONE FICTION

1440 W. Taylor St., Ste. 449, Chicago, IL 60607 | 224-339-4159
brimstonefiction@gmail.com | *www.brimstonefiction.com*
Rowena Kuo, CEO and executive editor

> **Submissions:** Publishes 8-12 titles per year; receives 60 submissions annually. First-time authors: 60%. Length: 60,000-100,000 words. Responds in six to eight weeks. Bible: NIV.
>
> **Royalty:** 30% of profits, no advance
>
> **Types and topics:** fiction: adventure, fantasy, historical, romantic suspense, science fiction, speculative, suspense/thriller, teen/YA, time travel, women's
>
> **Types of books:** ebook, POD
>
> **Guidelines:** *brimstonefiction.com/submission-guidelines*
>
> **Tip:** "We welcome new and multipublished authors and/or authors with or without agents. If you have a good story, come and meet us at writers conferences or through our website."

BROADLEAF BOOKS

PO Box 1209, Minneapolis, MN 55440-1209 | 800-328-4648
submissions@broadleafbooks.com | *broadleafbooks.com*
Lil Copan, senior acquisitions editor
Valerie Weaver-Zercher, acquisitions editor

> **Denomination:** Evangelical Lutheran Church in America
>
> **Parent company:** 1517 Media
>
> **Types and topics:** Christian living/spirituality, culture, social justice
>
> **Guidelines:** *www.broadleafbooks.com/info/submissions*
>
> **Tip:** "Please note that we receive a large volume of proposals. You will receive a response only if we see your proposal as a potential fit for our program."

BROADSTREET PUBLISHING

8646 Eagle Creek Cir., Ste. 210, Savage, MN 55378 | 855-935-2000
proposals@broadstreetpublishing.com | *www.broadstreetpublishing.com*
Tim Payne, editorial manager

> **Submissions:** Publishes 100+ titles per year.
>
> **Types and topics:** Bible promises, biography, Christian living/

spirituality, coloring books, devotionals, fiction, journals
Imprints: Belle City Gifts (journals and planners)
Guidelines: *broadstreetpublishing.com/contact*

CASCADE BOOKS

199 W. 8th Ave., Ste. 3, Eugene, OR 97401 | 541-344-152
proposal@wipfandstock.com | *wipfandstock.com/search-results-grid/*
?imprint=cascade-books

Parent company: Wipf and Stock
Submissions: Responds in one to two months.
Types and topics: religion, theology
Types of books: ebook, POD
Guidelines: *wipfandstock.com/submitting-a-proposal*

CASCADIA PUBLISHING HOUSE

126 Klingerman Rd., Telford, PA 18969
editor@CascadiaPublishingHouse.com | *CascadiaPublishingHouse.com*
Michael A. King, publisher and editor

Submissions: Looking for creative, thought-provoking, Anabaptist-related material.
Types and topics: nonfiction with Anabaptist/Mennonite leaning
Guidelines: *www.cascadiapublishinghouse.com/submit.htm*
Tip: "All Cascadia books receive rigorous evaluation and some form of peer or consultant review."

CATHOLIC BOOK PUBLISHING CORP.

77 W. End Rd., Totowa, NJ 07572 | 973-890-2400
info@catholicbookpublishing.com | *www.catholicbookpublishing.com*
Anthony Buono, editor

Denomination: Catholic
Submissions: Responds in two to three months.
Royalty: negotiable, no advance
Types and topics: Christian living/spirituality, liturgy, prayer, nonfiction
Imprint: Resurrection Press (popular nonfiction)
Guidelines: *catholicbookpublishing.com/page/faq#manuscript*

CHALICE PRESS

483 E. Lockwood Ave., Ste. 100, St. Louis, MO 63119 | 800-366-3383
submissions@chalicepress.com | *chalicepress.com*
Brad Lyons, publisher

Mission statement: to publish resources inviting all people into deeper relationship with God, equipping them as disciples of Jesus Christ, and sending them into ministries as the Holy Spirit calls them

Submissions: Particularly interested in publishing content by and for women, young adults (age 18 to 35), and racial/ethnic cultures for our academic, congregational leadership, and general audiences.

Types and topics: Christian education, Christian living/spirituality, discipleship, evangelism, leadership, ministry, missions, theology, academic, children, nonfiction, teen/YA

Guidelines: *chalicepress.com/pages/write-for-us*

Tip: "Our theological tradition is evangelistic (we share with others our experience of God), inclusive (we are guests at a table where everyone is welcome) and mission-oriented (our gratitude to God compels us to serve others)."

CHARISMA HOUSE

600 Rinehart Rd., Lake Mary, FL 32746 | 407-333-0600
charismahouse@charismamedia.com | *www.charismamedia.com*
Kyle Duncan, VP of acquisitions and content development

Mission statement: to inspire and equip people to live a Spirit-led life and walk in the divine purpose for which they were called

Types and topics: Christian living/spirituality, evangelism, Holy Spirit, missions, prayer, prophecy, theology, Charismatic

CHICKEN SOUP FOR THE SOUL BOOKS

See listing in the periodical section, "Adult Markets."

CHOSEN

6030 E. Fulton Rd., Ada, MI 49301 | 616-676-9185
bakerpublishinggroup.com/chosen
Kim Bangs, editorial director
David Sluka, acquisitions editor

Parent company: Baker Publishing Group

Mission statement: to help believers live Spirit-empowered lives, to better know and love the Lord Jesus Christ, to pray about the concerns that are on God's heart, to be empowered by his Spirit for ministry, to fulfill the Great Commission, and to transform their communities and their world

Submissions: Publishes 24-27 titles per year; receives 300 submissions annually. First-time authors: fewer than 10%. Length: 224 pages.

Responds in one month. Bible: any.

Royalty: varies, gives advance

Types and topics: African-American, Charismatic, Hispanic, prayer, prophecy, spiritual warfare, nonfiction

Types of books: audiobook, ebook, hardcover, offset paperback

Guidelines: *bakerpublishinggroup.com/chosen/contact/preparing-a-proposal-for-chosen-books*

Tip: "Be involved in the Spirit-empowered church and have a solid platform into your target audience engaged and established."

CHRISM PRESS

13607 Bedford Rd. NE, Cumberland, MD 21502 | 301-876-4876

www.chrismpress.com

Rhonda Ortiz, editor

Karen Ullo, editor

Marisa Deshaies, editor

Parent company: WhiteFire Publishing

Mission statement: to publish stories informed by Catholic and Orthodox Christianity that may not be able to find a home in either mainstream secular or Christian (evangelical) presses

Submissions: Publishes five to ten titles per year; receives 60 submissions annually. First-time authors: 25%. Length: 60,000-100,000 words. Responds in three months.

Royalty: 50% ebooks, 10% print, gives advance

Types and topics: all fiction for adults and YA

Types of books: audiobook, ebook, POD

Guidelines: *www.chrismpress.com/submissions*

Tip: "Chrism Press serves the Catholic and Orthodox Christian markets. We are open to submissions from authors outside these faiths, but please read our mission statement and submissions FAQ carefully to see if your work would be a good fit for us."

CHRISTIAN FOCUS PUBLICATIONS

Geanies House, Fearn, Tain, Ross-shire IV20 1TW, Scotland, UK | 01862-871011

submissions@christianfocus.com | *www.christianfocus.com*

Willie MacKenzie, director

Catherine.Mackenzie, children's editor, Catherine.Mackenzie@christianfocus.com

Types and topics: biography, Christian living/spirituality, church history, theology, academic, activities and puzzles, Bible reference/

commentaries, children, crafts, fiction, game books

Imprints: Christian Focus (popular adult titles), CF4K (children), Mentor (serious readers), Christian Heritage (classic writings from the past)

Guidelines: *www.christianfocus.com/about/adult-guidelines;* children's guidelines: *www.christianfocus.com/about/childrens-guidelines*

Tip: "Read our website please. Don't send us stuff we don't publish."

CHURCH PUBLISHING INCORPORATED

19 E. 34th St., New York, NY 10016 | 800-242-1918

nabryan@cpg.org | churchpublishing.org

Nancy Bryan, VP of editorial

Denomination: Episcopal

Types and topics: Bible study, biography, counseling, death and dying, finances, leadership, memoir/personal narrative, prayer, social justice, theology, worship

Guidelines: *churchpublishing.org/manuscriptsubmission*

Tip: "CPI's core publishing program is structured around *The Book of Common Prayer, The Hymnal 1982*, and the specialized books and resources used in the liturgy, faith formation, governance, life, and mission of the Episcopal Church."

CKN CHRISTIAN PUBLISHING

cknchristianpublishing.com

Parent company: Wolfpack Publishing

Mission statement: to publish books that will help readers to rise and develop their understanding of God's Word and to apply it more abundantly to their lives

Submissions: Responds in three months.

Royalty: up to 35%

Types and topics: fiction: Amish, historical, mystery, romance, westerns

Types of books: ebook, POD

Guidelines: *cknchristianpublishing.com/christian-manuscript-submissions*

Tip: "We enjoy seeing forgotten books come to life in a new and up-to-date way and watching the success. We will bring the book to life again with a new cover, marketing plan and promotion of the book in the best way we can. We will also work with you if you have a backlist that you have received the rights to."

CLADACH PUBLISHING

PO Box 336144, Greeley, CO 80633 | 970-371-9530
cathyl@cladach.com | *www.cladach.com*
Catherine Lawton, publisher and editor
Christina Slike, assistant editor

> **Submissions:** Publishes four titles per year; receives 50 submissions annually. First-time authors: 50%. Length: 120-300 pages. Responds in three months. Bible: NIV, NRSV.
> **Royalty:** 10-20%, advance: $100
> **Types and topics:** healing, memoir/personal narrative, nature, devotionals, poetry; fiction: frontier, literary
> **Types of books:** audiobook, ebook, offset paperback, POD
> **Guidelines:** *cladach.com/authors*
> **Tip:** "We are accepting very few unsolicited manuscripts."

CLC PUBLICATIONS

PO Box 1449, Fort Washington, PA 19034 | 215-542-1242
submissions@clcpublications.com | *www.clcpublications.com*
Jim Pitman, director
David Fessenden, editorial coordinator

> **Parent company:** CLC Ministries International
> **Mission statement:** books for the deeper life
> **Submissions:** Publishes 12 titles per year; receives 200 submissions annually. First-time authors: 30%. Length: 35,000-80,000 words, 144-320 pages. Responds in six to eight weeks. Bible: ESV.
> **Royalty:** 12-14%, gives advance
> **Average first print run:** 2,000-3,500
> **Types and topics:** Christian living/spirituality
> **Types of books:** audiobook, ebook, offset paperback
> **Guidelines:** *www.clcpublications.com/about/prospective-authors-submissions*
> **Tip:** "We prefer a book that speaks to an international audience, not only North America."

COLLEGE PRESS PUBLISHING

PO Box 1132, Joplin, MO 64801 | 800-289-3300
collpressbooks@gmail.com | *www.collegepress.com*

> **Denomination:** Church of Christ
> **Submissions:** Responds in two to three months.
> **Types and topics:** apologetics, biography, Christian living/spirituality, academic, Bible reference/commentaries, Bible studies
> **Guidelines:** *www.collegepress.com/pages/for-authors*

CONVERGENT BOOKS

crownpublishing.com/archives/imprint/convergent-books
Keren Baltzer, editorial director
Derek Reed, executive editor

Parent company: Penguin Random House/The Crown Publishing Group

Mission statement: to seek out diverse viewpoints and honest conversations that shed light on the defining challenges facing people of faith today

Submissions: Looking for books that help readers ask important questions, find paths forward in disagreement, and shape the way faith is expressed in the modern world.

Types and topics: Christian living/spirituality, memoir/personal narrative, self-help, social issues

Tip: Represents "a broad spectrum of Christian thought, both explicit and implicit."

CROSSLINK PUBLISHING

1601 Mt. Rushmore Rd., Ste. 3288, Rapid City, SD 57701 | 888-697-4851
publisher@crosslinkpublishing.com | *www.crosslinkpublishing.com*
Rick Bates, managing editor

Parent company: CrossLink Ministries

Submissions: Publishes 35 titles per year; receives 500 submissions annually. First-time authors: 85%. Length: 12,000-60,000 words. Responds in one week.

Royalty: 10% print, 20% ebooks, no advance

Average first print run: 2,000

Types and topics: Christian living/spirituality, Bible studies, children, devotionals, fiction

Imprint: New Harbor Press

Guidelines: *www.crosslinkpublishing.com/submit-a-manuscript*

Tip: "We are particularly interested in providing books that help Christians succeed in their daily walk (inspirational, devotional, small groups, etc.)."

CROSSRIVER MEDIA GROUP

4810 Gene Field Rd. #2, St. Joseph, MO 64506 | 816-752-2171
deb@crossrivermedia.com | *www.crossrivermedia.com*
Debra L. Butterfield, editorial director
Tamara Clymer, publisher, tamara@crossrivermedia.com

Mission statement: to glorify God by providing high-quality books and materials that ignite a woman's relationship with God and inspires her to lead a life that honors Him

Submissions: Publishes six to ten titles per year; receives 50 submissions annually. First-time authors: 50%. Length: 60,000-85,000 words. Responds in 12-16 weeks. Bible: any except NIV.

Royalty: 10-15%, no advance

Types and topics: Bible study, Christian living/spirituality, family, marriage, devotionals; fiction: biblical, contemporary, historical, romance, speculative, suspense/thriller

Type of books: ebook

Guidelines: *www.crossrivermedia.com/about/manuscript-submissions*

Tip: "Read our website."

CROSSWAY

1300 Crescent St., Wheaton, IL 60187 | 630-682-4300
submissions@crossway.org | *www.crossway.org*
Jill Carter, editorial administrator
Todd Augustine, senior acquisitions editor

Parent company: Good News Publishers

Mission statement: To publish gospel-centered, Bible-centered content that will honor our Savior and serve his Church. We seek to help people understand the massive implications of the gospel and the truth of God's Word, for all of life, for all eternity, and for the glory of God.

Submissions: Publishes 125 titles per year; receives 500 submissions annually. First-time authors: 2%. Length: 40,000-80,000 words. Responds in six to eight weeks. Bible: ESV.

Royalty: varies, gives advance

Average first print run: varies

Types and topics: Bible study, Christian living/spirituality, contemporary issues, academic, Bible reference/commentaries

Types of books: audiobook, ebook, hardcover, offset paperback

Guidelines: *www.crossway.org/submissions*

Tip: "Be sure to look at our guidelines and see if your project fits. A well-written proposal is vital."

CSS PUBLISHING GROUP, INC.

5450 N. Dixie Hwy., Lima, OH 45807-9559 | 419-227-1818
editor@csspub.com | *www.csspub.com*
David Runk, publisher

Submissions: Publishes 15 titles per year; receives 500-1,000 submissions annually. First-time authors: 50%. Length: 100-125 pages. Responds in three weeks to six months. Bible: NRSV. Looking for lectionary-based resources for worship, preaching, group study, drama, and use with children (but not children's books); sermons, preaching, and worship resources for special seasons and days of the church year and special themes or emphasis; children's object lessons and sermons; resources for working with youth; pastoral aids, such as materials to assist in counseling; easy-to-perform dramas and pageants for all age groups, primarily for Advent/Christmas/Epiphany and Lent/Easter (no full-length plays); parish-tested materials for use in education, youth ministry, stewardship, and church growth; a few general titles.

Royalty: outright purchase, no advance

Types and topics: Christian education, ministry, church resources, drama, nonfiction

Guidelines: *store.csspub.com/page.php?Custom%20Pages=10*

Tip: "We're looking for authors who will help with the marketing of their books."

DAVID C. COOK

4050 Lee Vance Dr., Colorado Springs, CO 80918 | 719-536-0100
www.davidccook.org
Michael Covington, VP of publishing and acquisitions for pastors and leaders
Susan McPherson, acquisitions editor, women and family
Stephanie Bennett, acquisitions editor, students and youth

Mission statement: to equip the Church with Christ-centered resources for making and teaching disciples

Submissions: Publishes 40 titles per year; receives 1,200 submissions annually. First-time authors: 10%. Length: 45,000-50,000 words. Responds in one month.

Royalty: 12-22%, gives advance

Types and topics: Christian living/spirituality, discipleship, family, leadership, marriage, men, parenting, women, Bible reference/ commentaries, Bible studies, church resources, devotionals, teen/YA

Types of books: ebook, hardcover, offset paperback, POD

Guidelines: *shop.davidccook.org/pages/frequently-asked-questions*

Tip: "We look for significant platform, excellent writing, and relevant content."

DIVINE MOMENTS BOOK SERIES

See listing in the periodicals section, "Adult Markets."

DOVE CHRISTIAN PUBLISHERS

PO Box 611, Bladensburg, MD 20710 | 240-342-3293
editorial@dovechristianpublishers.com | *www.dovechristianpublishers.com*
Raenita Wiggins, acquisitions editor

Parent company: Kingdom Christian Enterprises

Mission statement: to entertain, edify, equip and encourage people through products that glorify and honor Jesus Christ and His kingdom and to provide new and emerging Christian authors with a forum for their creative and Kingdom-building voices

Submissions: Publishes ten titles per year; receives 300 submissions annually. First-time authors: 95%. Length: 100-220 pages. Responds in four to six weeks. Bible: NIV.

Royalty: 10-25%, no advance

Types and topics: Christian living/spirituality, church life, discipleship, ministry, prayer, Bible studies, children, devotionals; fiction: fantasy, historical, humor, mystery, romance, science fiction, suspense/thriller

Types of books: ebook, hardcover, POD

Guidelines: *www.dovechristianpublishers.com/publish-with-us*

Tip: "Author should establish a platform and familiarize themselves with book marketing and promotion prior to submission."

EERDMANS BOOKS FOR YOUNG READERS

4035 Park East Ct. SE, Grand Rapids, MI 49546 | 800-253-7521
kmerz@eerdmans.com | *www.eerdmans.com/youngreaders*
Kathleen Merz, editorial director
Courtney Zonnefeld, assistant editor

Parent company: Wm. B. Eerdmans Publishing Co.

Mission statement: to engage young minds with books—books that are honest, wise, and hopeful; books that delight us with their storyline, characters, or good humor; books that inform, inspire, and entertain

Submissions: Publishes 12-18 titles per year; receives 1,500 submissions annually. First-time authors: 5-10%. Length: picture books, 1,000 words; middle-grade books, 15,000-30,000 words. Responds in four months if interested.

Royalty: advance

Types and topics: African-American, animals, history, multicultural, nature, social issues, humor, middle grade, picture books, teen/YA

Types of books: audiobook, ebook, hardcover

Guidelines: *www.eerdmans.com/Pages/Item/2237/EBYR-Guidelines.aspx*

Tip: "We are always looking for well-written picture books and novels for young readers. Make sure that your submission is a unique, well-crafted story, and take a look at our current list of titles to get a sense of whether yours would be a good fit for us."

WM. B. EERDMANS PUBLISHING CO.

4035 Park East Ct. SE, Grand Rapids, MI 49546 | 800-253-7521
submissions@eerdmans.com | *www.eerdmans.com*
Trevor Thompson, senior acquisitions editor
David Bratt, acquisitions editor
Andrew Knapp, acquisitions editor

> **Submissions:** Publishes 100 titles per year. Responds in two months.
> **Royalty:** advance sometimes
> **Types and topics:** biography, Christian living/spirituality, contemporary issues, ethics, history, ministry, theology, academic, Bible reference/commentaries, nonfiction
> **Imprints:** Eerdmans Books for Young Readers (children and teens)
> **Guidelines:** *www.eerdmans.com/Pages/Item/2068/Submission-Guidelines.aspx*
> **Tip:** "Review submission guidelines carefully and check recent catalogs for suitability. Target readerships range from academic to semipopular. We are publishing a growing number of books in Christian life, spirituality, and ministry."

eLECTIO PUBLISHING

4206 S. Mentor Ave., Springfield, MO 65804 | 972-987-0015
submissions@electiopublishing.com | *www.electiopublishing.com*

> **Submissions:** Publishes 60-100 titles per year; receives 1,000 submissions annually. First-time authors: 70-80%. Length: 25,000-100,000 words. Responds in nine months.
> **Royalty:** 20%, no advance
> **Types and topics:** African-American, Christian living/spirituality, Hispanic, memoir/personal narrative, Bible studies, teen/YA; fiction: historical, mystery, romance
> **Guidelines:** *www.electiopublishing.com/index.php/submissions/submission-guidelines*
> **Tip:** "Please read carefully the submissions guidelines listed on website."

ELK LAKE PUBLISHING, INC.

35 Dogwood Dr., Plymouth, MA 02360-3166 | 508-746-1734
Deb@ElkLakePublishingInc.com | *ElkLakePublishingInc.com*
Deb Haggerty, publisher and editor-in-chief

Mission statement: to captivate our readers and carry them to places of escape, encouragement, education, and entertainment—to broaden their horizons and urge them to new heights

Submissions: Publishes 70-100 titles per year; receives 350 submissions annually. First-time authors: 70%. Length: 80,000-90,000 words, 300 pages. Responds in two weeks. Bible: NASB, ESV.

Royalty: 40%, no advance

Types and topics: Bible study, Christian living/spirituality, fiction

Types of books: audiobook, ebook, hardcover, POD

Guidelines: *elklakepublishinginc.com/wp-content/uploads/2021/07/ELPI-Proposal_Guidelines-07192021.pdf*

Tip: Submit "letter perfect proposals, well-edited manuscripts."

EMANATE BOOKS

PO Box 141000, Nashville, TN 37214-1000 | 615-889-9000

www.thomasnelson.com/emanatebooks

Joel Kneedler, publisher

Parent company: Thomas Nelson Publishers/HarperCollins Christian Publishing

Mission statement: to reflect the work of the Holy Spirit, feed His church, and help a new generation hear from God and grow in their spiritual journey

Submissions: Agents only.

Types and topics: Christian classics, nonfiction, Charismatic focus

Types of books: audiobook, ebook, hardcover, offset paperback

ENCLAVE PUBLISHING

24 W. Camelback Rd. A-635, Phoenix, AZ 85013

acquisitions@enclavepublishing.com | *www.enclavepublishing.com*

Steve Laube, publisher and acquisitions editor

Mission statement: to publish out-of-this-world stories that are informed by a coherent theology

Submissions: Publishes 12 titles per year; receives 200 submissions annually. First-time authors: 20-30%. Length: 80,000 to 140,000 words. Responds in two to three months.

Royalty: varies, no advance

Average first print run: 1,500

Types and topics: fiction: fantasy, science fiction, speculative, supernatural

Types of books: audiobook, ebook, hardcover, offset paperback

Imprint: Enclave Escape (YA)

Guidelines: *www.enclavepublishing.com/guidelines*

Tip: "Keep word count above 80,000 words and below 140,000. Too often we are sent books that are either far too short or extremely long."

END GAME PRESS

PO Box 206, Nesbit, MS 38651 | 901-590-6584

victoria@endgamepress.com | *www.endgamepress.com*

Victoria Duerstock, publisher

Mission statement: to leverage all of its resources to make the greatest positive impact possible by holding a high standard for the books it publishes in both design and quality, while also making the experience a good one for each of the authors in the End Game Press family

Submissions: Publishes 20 titles per year; receives 300 submissions annually. First-time authors: 25%. Length: depends on the genre. Responds in two to three months. Bible: any.

Royalty: 20-25%, gives advance

Types and topics: Christian living/spirituality, faith, marriage, parenting, prayer, board books, fiction, middle grade, picture books, teen/YA

Types of books: audiobook, ebook, hardcover

Imprints: End Game Kidz (children and YA)

Guidelines: *www.endgamepress.com/submissions*

Tip: "Make a personal connection and have a clean manuscript/proposal with well-thought-out marketing ideas."

EXEGETICA PUBLISHING

312 Greenwich #112, Lee's Summit, MO 64082 | 816-269-8505

editor@exegeticapublishing.com | *www.exegeticapublishing.com*

Mission statement: to encourage Christians and non-Christians alike to engage with the Bible, to understand the world around them, and to "taste and see that the Lord is good," as Psalm 34:8 exhorts

Submissions: Publishes ten titles per year; receives 30 submissions annually. First-time authors: 10%. Length: 200-300 pages. Responds in three to four weeks. Bible: NASB, NKJV, ESV.

Royalty: 10%, no advance

Types and topics: Bible, Christian living/spirituality, theology, academic

Types of books: ebook, offset paperback

Imprint: Grace Acres Press

Guidelines: *exegeticapublishing.com/submit-a-proposal*

Tip: "Follow submission guidelines with solid biblical resources."

FAITHWORDS

1 Franklin Park, 6100 Tower Cir., Ste. 210, Franklin, TN 37067

615-221-0996

www.faithwords.com

Beth Adams, acquisitions editor

Karen Longino, acquisitions editor

Sean McGowan, editor and acquisitions

India Hunter, associate editor and acquisitions

Parent company: Hachette Book Group

Royalty: minimum 10%, advance

Types and topics: African-American, Christian living/spirituality, Hispanic, marriage, parenting, social issues

Types of books: ebook, hardcover, offset paperback

Guidelines: none

Tip: "Have a clear, well-written proposal and a solid platform."

FIREFLY SOUTHERN FICTION

100 Missionary Ridge, Birmingham, AL 35242 | 407-414-8188

fireflysouthernfiction@aol.com | *shoplpc.com/firefly*

Eva Marie Everson, managing editor

Parent company: Iron Stream Media

Mission statement: Firefly Southern Fiction is story-driven with distinctly Southern characters living within the realm of Southern tradition, both historical and contemporary.

Submissions: Publishes four titles per year; receives 20 submissions annually. First-time authors: 20%. Length: 75,000-95,000 words. Responds in three months. Note: This imprint will be discontinued and rolled into Iron Stream Fiction.

Royalty: 40%, no advance

Types and topics: Southern fiction

Types of books: audiobook, ebook, offset paperback

Guidelines: *shoplpc.com/firefly*

Tip: "Know your audience, Southern people, Southern lifestyle, Southern history."

FIRST STEPS PUBLISHING

PO Box 571, Gleneden Beach, OR 97388 | 541-961-7641

publish@firststepspublishing.com | *www.FirstStepsPublishing.com*

Suzanne Fyhrie Parrott, publisher

Submissions: Publishes three titles per year.

Types and topics: fiction: adventure, historical, mystery, suspense/ thriller

Guidelines: *www.firststepspublishing.com/get-published*

Tip: "We are looking for well-written books by new authors taking them from raw manuscript to a well-marketed and designed masterpiece people want to read."

FLYAWAY BOOKS

100 Witherspoon St., Louisville, KY 40202-1396

submissions@flyawaybooks.com | *www.flyawaybooks.com*

Jessica Miller Kelley, acquisitions editor

Denomination: Presbyterian

Parent company: Westminster John Knox Press/Presbyterian Publishing Corporation

Submissions: Responds in six weeks or not interested.

Types and topics: picture books

Types of books: picture books

Guidelines: *www.flyawaybooks.com/submissions*

Tip: "Flyaway Books embraces diversity, inclusivity, compassion, care for each other, and care for our world. Many of our books explore social justice and other contemporary issues. Some retell familiar religious stories in new ways, while others carry universal themes appealing to those with any, or no, religious background."

FOCUS ON THE FAMILY

8605 Explorer Dr., Colorado Springs, CO 80995 | 719-531-5181

www.focusonthefamily.com

Larry Weeden, editor in chief

Types and topics: family, marriage, parenting, nonfiction

Types of books: ebook, hardcover, offset paperback

Guidelines: none

Other information: Books are published with Tyndale House Publishers and Broadstreet Publishing.

FORTRESS PRESS

PO Box 1209, Minneapolis, MN 55440-1209

gaedeb@fortresspress.com | *www.fortresspress.com*

Beth Gaede, senior acquisitions editor, professional and ministry resources

Scott Tunseth, senior acquisitions editor, ministry, tunseths@fortresspress.com

Denomination: Evangelical Lutheran Church in America

Parent company: 1517 Media

Types and topics: Bible study, Christian living/spirituality, culture, history, ministry, social justice, theology, academic, Bible reference/commentaries

Types of books: hardcover, offset paperback

Guidelines: *www.fortresspress.com/info/submissions*

FORWARD MOVEMENT

412 Sycamore St., Cincinnati, OH 45202-4110 | 800-543-1813

editorial@forwardmovement.org | www.forwardmovement.org

Richelle Thompson, managing editor

Denomination: Episcopal

Mission statement: to offer resources that strengthen and support discipleship and evangelism

Submissions: Responds in four to six weeks.

Types and topics: Bible study, discipleship, evangelism, leadership, prayer, nonfiction

Types of books: ebook, offset paperback

Guidelines: *www.forwardmovement.org/Pages/About/Writers-Guidelines.aspx*

THE FOUNDRY PUBLISHING

PO Box 419527, Kansas City, MO 64141 | 800-877-0700

RMcFarland@thefoundrypublishing.com | www.thefoundrypublishing.com

René McFarland, submissions editor

Bonnie Perry, editorial director

Denomination: Nazarene

Mission statement: to empower people with life-changing ways to engage in the mission of God

Submissions: Responds in two months.

Types and topics: Christian living/spirituality, ministry, nonfiction

Guidelines: *www.thefoundrypublishing.com/book-manuscript-submission-faqs.html*

Tip: "Because we are a denominational publisher of holiness literature, our books reflect an evangelical Wesleyan stance in accord with the Church of the Nazarene. We seek practical as well as serious treatments of issues of faith consistent with the Wesleyan tradition."

FOUR CRAFTSMEN PUBLISHING

PO Box U, Lakeside, AZ 85929-0585 | 928-367-2076

info@fourcraftsmen.com | www.fourcraftsmen.com

CeCelia Jackson, editor in chief
Martin Jackson, publisher

> **Mission statement:** to publish truth that works for Christian readers
> **Submissions:** Publishes four to six titles per year; receives five submissions annually. First-time authors: 100%. Length: 40,000-80,000 words. Responds in two weeks. Bible: NASB, NKJV, TLB, TEV.
> **Royalty:** 10% print, 50-60% ebook, no advance
> **Average first print run:** 500
> **Types and topics:** Bible study, Christian living/spirituality, finances, spiritual warfare, testimony
> **Types of books:** ebook, hardcover, offset paperback, POD
> **Guidelines:** *fourcraftsmen.com/additional-info*
> **Tip:** "Original work, not compilation of source quotes. Necessary quotes correctly attributed and permissions provided."

FRANCISCAN MEDIA

28 W. Liberty St., Cincinnati, OH 45202 | 513-241-5615
proposal@FranciscanMedia.org | *www.FranciscanMedia.org*
Christopher Heffron, editorial director

> **Denomination:** Catholic
> **Submissions:** Publishes 20-30 titles per year. Responds in six to eight weeks. Bible: NRSV. Seeks manuscripts that inform and inspire adult Catholics, other Christians, and all who are seeking to better understand and live their faith. Goal is to help people "Live in love. Grow in faith."
> **Royalty:** 10-14%, advance: $1,000-$3,000
> **Types and topics:** Christian living/spirituality, spiritual growth, fiction, nonfiction
> **Guidelines:** *www.franciscanmedia.org/writers-guidelines*
> **Tip:** "Special consideration will be given to book proposals that show how the book relates to one or more of the teachings of St. Francis or the Franciscan charism."

GOOD & TRUE MEDIA

1520 S. York Rd., Gastonia, NC 28053 | 704-865-1256
info@goodwillpublishers.com | *www.goodwillpublishers.com*

> **Parent company:** Good Will Publishers
> **Mission statement:** to educate the imagination, move the heart, deepen the mind, strengthen the soul
> **Submissions:** Publishes 10-20 titles per year.
> **Types and topics:** children, picture books

Tip: Looking for books that "have a strong moral foundation and will also foster virtue in children while entertaining them and nurturing their imagination."

THE GOOD BOOK COMPANY

1805 Sardis Road N, Ste. 102, Charlotte, NC 28270 | 866-244-2165
submissions@thegoodbook.com | *www.thegoodbook.com*
Brian Thomasson, VP of editorial

Mission statement: to promote, encourage, and equip people to serve our Lord and Master Jesus Christ

Types and topics: Bible study, Christian living/spirituality, evangelism, children, devotionals, teen/YA

Guidelines: *www.thegoodbook.com/authors*

Tip: "Our aim with all our resources is to get people directly interacting with the Bible. So we expect our authors to facilitate that process, rather than just commenting on their own view of what the Bible says. A primary question we ask of any resource submitted to us is: does it handle the Bible well (i.e., taking note of the context of each passage), and is it helping people understand its message?"

GRACE ACRES PRESS

PO Box 22, Larkspur, CO 80118 | 303-681-9995
Anne@graceacrespress.com | *www.GraceAcresPress.com*
Anne R. Fenske, publisher

Parent company: Exegetica Publishing

Mission statement: to grow your faith one page at a time

Submissions: Publishes six titles per year; receives 20 submissions annually. First-time authors: 75%. Length: 100-300 pages. Responds in one month. Bible: NKJV, NIV.

Royalty: 10-15%, no advance

Average first print run: 500-2,000

Types and topics: Bible study, biography, discipleship, evangelism, missions, nonfiction

Types of books: ebook, hardcover, offset paperback, POD

Guidelines: by email

Tip: "Explain your contribution as a copartner in marketing your book."

GRACE PUBLISHING

PO Box 1233, Broken Arrow, OK 74013-1233 | 918-346-7960
editorial@grace-publishing.com | *www.grace-publishing.com*
Terri Kalfas, publisher

Parent company: The Jomaga Group, LLC

Mission statement: to develop and distribute—with integrity and excellence—biblically based resources that challenge, encourage, teach, equip, and entertain Christians young and old in their personal journeys

Submissions: Publishes six to eight titles per year. Length: 40,000 words. Responds in six months. Bible: any.

Royalty: varies, no advance

Types and topics: Christian living/spirituality, memoir/personal narrative, anthologies, Bible studies, devotionals

Types of books: ebook, POD

Imprints: Jomaga House (Christian worldview but not necessarily overtly Christian)

Guidelines: *grace-publishing.com/manuscript-submission*

Tip: "We're looking for material that is presented in a manner relevant to today's Christian without going outside the boundaries of orthodox Christianity. No fluff."

GROUP PUBLISHING, INC.

1515 Cascade Ave., Loveland, CO 80538 | 970-669-3836

submissions@group.com | *www.group.com*

Mission statement: to create experiences that help people grow in relationship with Jesus and each other

Submissions: Publishes 30 titles per year; receives 200 submissions annually. First-time authors: 10%. Length: 128-250 pages. Responds in three months. Bible: NLT.

Royalty: 8-10%, sometimes offers advance of $2,000

Average first print run: 3,000

Types and topics: Christian education, family, leadership, parenting, activities and puzzles, church resources, curriculum

Types of books: ebook, hardcover, offset paperback

Guidelines: *grouppublishingps.zendesk.com/hc/en-us/articles/211878258-Submissions*

Tip: "Most open to a practical resource that will help church leaders change lives; innovative, active/interactive learning. Tell our readers something they don't already know, in a way that they've not seen before."

GUIDEPOSTS BOOKS

110 William St., Ste. 901, New York, NY 10038 | 212-251-8100

bookeditors@guideposts.org | *www.guideposts.org*

Jon Woodhams, nonfiction editor

Caroline E. Cilento, editor

Jane Haertel, fiction editor

Submissions: Publishes 20-30 titles per year.

Types and topics: Christian living/spirituality, memoir/personal narrative; fiction: contemporary, women's

HARAMBEE PRESS

100 Missionary Ridge, Birmingham, AL 35242 | 888-811-9934

harambeepresslpcbooks@gmail.com | *shoplpc.com/harambee-press*

Edwina Perkins, managing editor

Parent company: Iron Stream Media

Mission statement: to raise up the ethnic voice, to give us a place to communicate, through publication, with each other and the world

Submissions: Publishes four to eight titles per year; receives 60 submissions annually. First-time authors: 50%. Length: 40,000-90,000 words. Responds in three months. Bible: NIV.

Royalty: 40%, no advance

Types and topics: African-American, Christian living/spirituality, marriage, memoir/personal narrative, parenting, devotionals; fiction: mystery, romance, suspense, women's

Types of books: audiobook, ebook, POD

Guidelines: *shoplpc.com/harambee*

Tip: "Whether through fiction or nonfiction, HP authors should carry a message of hope and redemption, because that is the message our ancestors wanted to give to us."

HARBOURLIGHT BOOKS

PO Box 1738, Aztec, NM 87410

customer@harbourlightbooks.com | *www.pelicanbookgroup.com*

Nicola Martinez, editor-in-chief

Parent company: Pelican Book Group

Mission statement: to publish quality books that reflect the salvation and love offered by Jesus Christ

Submissions: Length: 25,000-80,000 words. Responds in three to four months. Bible: NIV, NAB.

Royalty: 40% ebook, 7% print, sometimes gives advance

Types and topics: fiction: adventure, crime, family saga, mystery, suspense, westerns, women's

Types of books: audiobook, ebook, hardcover, offset paperback, POD

Guidelines: *pelicanbookgroup.com/ec/index.php?main_ page=page&id=55&zenid=06f25d411f1d61bfa008693b5b246c4*

HARPERCHRISTIAN RESOURCES

501 Nelson Pl., Nashville, TN 37214

www.harperchristianresources.com

> **Parent company:** HarperCollins Christian Publishing
> **Mission statement:** to equip people to understand the Scriptures, cultivate spiritual growth, and live an inspired faith with Bible study and video resources from today's most trusted voices
> **Types and topics:** Bible studies, ministry programs, small-group study guides
> **Types of books:** video curriculum based on existing books

HARPERCOLLINS CHRISTIAN PUBLISHING

HarperChristian Resources

Thomas Nelson: Nelson Books, W Publishing Group, Thomas Nelson Fiction, Emanate Books, Tommy Nelson, Thomas Nelson Gift

Zondervan: Zondervan Books, Zondervan Reflective, Zondervan Fiction, Zondervan Gift, Zondervan Academic, Zonderkidz

WestBow Press

HARPERONE

353 Sacramento St. #500, San Francisco, CA 94111-3653 | 415-477-4400

gideon.weil@harpercollins.com | *harperone.com*

Gideon Weil, editorial director

Michael Maudlin, executive editor, michael.maudlin@harperpercollins.com

> **Parent company:** HarperCollins Publishing
> **Mission statement:** to publish books for the world we want to live in
> **Submissions:** Publishes 75 titles per year; receives 10,000 submissions annually. First-time authors: 5%. Length: 160-256 pages. Responds in three months.
> **Royalty:** 7.5-15%, gives advance
> **Types and topics:** Christian living/spirituality
> **Types of books:** ebook, hardcover, offset paperback
> **Imprint:** Shelf-Seekers (millennials)

HARVEST HOUSE PUBLISHERS

PO Box 41210, Eugene, OR 97404-0322 | 800-547-8979

harvesthousepublishers.com

Kathleen Kerr, acquisitions editor, nonfiction

Steve Miller, acquisitions editor, nonfiction

Ruth Samsel, acquisitions editor, gifts

Kyle Hatfield, acquisitions editor, children and family

Types and topics: Christian living/spirituality, family, relationships, Bible reference/commentaries, Bible studies, children, gift

Imprint: Harvest Kids (children)

HENDRICKSEN PUBLISHERS

PO Box 3473, Peabody, MA 01961-3473 | 800-358-3111

editorial@hendrickson.com | www.hendricksonrose.com

Patricia Anders, editorial director

Jonathan Kline, academic editor, jkline@hendrickson.com

Amy Paulsen-Reed, acquisitions editor, apaulson-reed@hendrickson.com

Parent company: Tyndale House Ministries

Mission statement: to meet the publication needs of the religious studies academic community worldwide and to produce thoughtful books for thoughtful Christians

Submissions: Publishes 16 titles per year; receives 50-100 submissions annually. First-time authors: 40%. Length: trade, 75,000-100,000 words; academic, 100,000-200,000 words. Responds in two to three months. Bible: none.

Royalty: 12-14%, advance

Average first print run: varies

Types and topics: archaeology, church history, culture, marriage, ministry, parenting, theology, academic, Bible reference/commentaries, biblical studies, language studies

Types of books: audiobook, ebook, hardcover, offset paperback

Imprints: Hendrickson Publishers (trade books), Hendrickson Academic (academic), Rose Publishing (Bible reference for everyone), RoseKidz (children), Aspire Press (counseling), Hendrickson Bibles (Bibles)

Guidelines: by email

Tip: "Please be sure to look at our website to see what kind of books we publish."

HERITAGE BEACON HISTORICAL FICTION

100 Missionary Ridge, Birmingham, AL 35242 | 888-811-9934

editor@smittenromance.com | shoplpc.com/heritage-beacon-historical-fiction

Denise Weimer, managing editor

Parent company: Iron Stream Media

Submissions: Publishes six titles per year; receives 20 submissions annually. First-time authors: 75%. Length: 65,000-80,000 words.

Responds in one to two months. Bible: NIV. Note: This imprint will be discontinued and rolled into Iron Stream Fiction.

Royalty: 40%, no advance

Types and topics: historical fiction

Types of books: audiobook, ebook, POD

Guidelines: *shoplpc.com/heritage-beacon*

Tip: "Romance should be a subplot, rather than the main plot."

ILLUMINATE YA

100 Missionary Ridge, Birmingham, AL 35242 | 888-811-9934
illuminateYAsubmissions@gmail.com | *shoplpc.com/illuminateYA*
Tessa Emily Hall, acquisitions editor

Parent company: Iron Stream Media

Mission statement: to touch teens' deepest needs, answer their life questions, sweep them away in a can't-put-me-down adventure, and portray their world with a thread of hope

Submissions: Publishes four titles per year; receives 25 submissions annually. First-time authors: 50%. Length: 50,000-95,000 words. Responds in one to three months. Bible: NIV. Note: This imprint will be discontinued and rolled into Iron Stream.

Royalty: 40%, no advance

Types and topics: fiction: contemporary, fantasy, historical, romance, science fiction, speculative

Types of books: audiobook, ebook, POD

Guidelines: *shoplpc.com/illuminate-ya*

Tip: "Our YA novels are clean reads; no vulgar language or sex scenes. IlluminateYA seeks to change our culture by publishing books with strong moral values. We will consider inspirational themes but prefer stories that can reach the young, general-market reader."

IMAGE BOOKS

1745 Broadway, New York, NY 10019 | 212-782-9000
imagebooks@randomhouse.com | *crownpublishing.com/imprint/image-catholic-books*
Gary Jansen, senior editor

Denomination: Catholic

Parent company: Crown Publishing Group/Penguin Random House

Mission statement: to publish solid, unswerving, admirable Catholic resources

INTERVARSITY PRESS (IVP)

430 Plaza Dr., Westmont, IL 60559 | 630-734-4000
mail@ivpress.com | ivpress.com
Cindy Bunch, editorial director
Al Hsu, senior editor and acquisitions
Ethan McCarthy, editorial assistant and acquisitions
Jon Boyd editorial director, IVP Academic
Elissa Schauer, managing editor and IVP Kids editor

Parent company: InterVarsity Christian Fellowship

Mission statement: to serve those in the university, the church, and the world by publishing resources that equip and encourage people to follow Jesus as Savior and Lord in all of life

Submissions: Publishes 110 titles per year; receives 1,200 submissions annually. First-time authors: 20%. Length: 20,000-90,000 words. Responds in three months. Bible: NIV.

Royalty: 12-18%, gives advance

Average first print run: 5,000

Types and topics: African-American, Asian, Bible study, Christian living/spirituality, counseling, Hispanic, justice, ministry, psychology, theology, academic, Bible reference/commentaries, Bible studies, children, nonfiction

Types of books: audiobook, ebook, hardcover, offset paperback

Imprints: IVP Academic (textbooks, academic, scholarly resources), IVP (Christian living, current issues, Bible studies), IVP Formatio (spiritual formation), IVP Praxis (church leadership), IVP Kids (children)

Guidelines: *www.ivpress.com/submissions*

Tip: "We accept submissions only from agents or from authors who have had direct contact with an editor."

IRON STREAM MEDIA

Note: Many of these imprints will be discontinued and books rolled into the main imprint.

Iron Stream Books: New Hope Publishers, Ascender Books, SonRise Devotionals, Straight Street Books

Iron Stream Fiction: Bling! Romance, Firefly Southern Fiction, Heritage Beacon Historical Romance, IlluminateYA, Smitten Historical Romance, Trailblazer Western Fiction, Candlelight Romance, Guiding Light Women's Fiction, Lamplighter Mysteries & Suspense, Iron Herring Speculative Fiction

Iron Stream Kids: New Hope Kids
Harambee
Brookstone: Brookstone Creative Group, Brookstone Publishing Group
Life Bible Study

IRON STREAM MEDIA

100 Missionary Ridge, Birmingham, AL 35242 | 888-811-9934
submissions@ironstreammedia.com | *www.ironstreammedia.com*
Susan Cornell, senior editor

Submissions: Length: 50,000-90,000 words. Responds in four months.
Bible: NASB.
Royalty: no advance
Types and topics: business, leadership, spiritual growth, Bible studies,
devotionals, fiction
Imprints: Iron Stream (nonfiction, including New Hope books, SonRise
Devotionals, Straight Street Books), Iron Stream Fiction (novels, including
LPC fiction imprints), Iron Stream Kids (board and picture books, Bible
storybooks, including New Hope Kidz), Harambee (multicultural),
Brookstone (indie publishing, design and publicity services), Life Bible
Study (digital Bible study curriculum direct to churches)
Guidelines: *www.ironstreammedia.com/submission-process*
Tip: "All submissions must follow the guidelines. No query letters."

JOURNEYFORTH

1700 Wade Hampton Blvd., Greenville, SC 29614 | 864-546-4600
journeyforth@bju.edu | *www.journeyforth.com*

Parent company: BJU Press/Bob Jones University
Mission statement: We publish youth fiction and biographies as well as
teen and adult nonfiction that reflect a solidly biblical worldview and
encourage Christians to live out their faith.
Submissions: Publishes six to eight titles per year; receives 150-200
submissions annually. First-time authors: 45%. Length: ages 6–8,
8,000 to 10,000 words; ages 9–12, 30,000 to 40,000 words; ages 12
and up, 40,000 to 60,000 words. Responds in three months. Bible:
KJV, NKJV, ESV, NASB.
Royalty: 10-15%, sometimes gives advance
Types and topics: African-American, Asian, Bible study, biography,
Christian living/spirituality, family, Hispanic, marriage, Bible studies,
children, fiction, first-chapter, middle grade, teen/YA
Types of books: ebook, offset paperback
Guidelines: *www.bjupress.com/books/freelance.php*

Tip: "We are looking for writing that has a fresh and engaging voice, but text that is not filled with jargon or idioms that would date the content quickly."

JUDSON PRESS

1075 First Ave., King of Prussia, PA 19406 | 800-458-3766
acquisitions@judsonpress.com | *www.judsonpress.com*
Cheryl Price, acquisitions editor

> **Denomination:** American Baptist
> **Parent company:** American Baptist Home Mission Societies
> **Mission statement:** to produce Christ-centered leadership resources for the transformation of individuals, congregations, communities, and cultures
> **Submissions:** Publishes 12 titles per year; receives 300 submissions annually. First-time authors: 25%. Length: 128-244 pages. Responds in three to six months. Bible: NRSV.
> **Royalty:** 10-15%, sometimes gives advance
> **Average first print run:** 2,500
> **Types and topics:** African-American, Asian, Christian education, Christian living/spirituality, Hispanic, history, ministry, church resources, devotionals, ministry resources
> **Types of books:** ebook, offset paperback, POD
> **Guidelines:** *www.judsonpress.com/Content/Site189/ BasicBlocks/102582018Judson_00000128361.pdf*
> **Tip:** "Most open to practical books that are unique and compelling, for a clearly defined niche audience. Theologically and socially we are a moderate publisher. And we like to see a detailed marketing plan from an author committed to partnering with us."

KREGEL PUBLICATIONS

2450 Oak Industrial Dr. NE, Grand Rapids, MI 49505 | 616-451-4775
KPacquisitions@kregel.com | *www.kregel.com*
Sarah De Mey, editorial coordinator
Janyre Tromp, acquisitions editor, fiction, women's
Robert Hand, academic director

> **Types and topics:** Bible study, biography, Christian living/spirituality, church life, discipleship, family, marriage, ministry, parenting, theology, women, Bible reference/commentaries, Bible studies, children, devotionals, teen/YA; fiction: historical, romance, romantic suspense, teen/YA
> **Guidelines:** *www.kregel.com/contact-us/submissions-policy*

LEAFWOOD PUBLISHERS

ACU, Box 29138, Abilene, TX 79699 | 325-674-2720
manuscriptsubmissions@groupmail.acu.edu | *www.leafwoodpublishers.com*
Jason Fikes, director

Denomination: Church of Christ

Parent company: Abilene Christian University

Mission statement: to explore Scripture, Christian identity, spiritual formation, and our current cultural context

Submissions: Publishes 25 titles per year; receives 110+ submissions annually. First-time authors: 20%. Length: 50,000-75,000 words. Responds in nine months if unsolicited. Bible: NIV, ESV.

Royalty: 14-25%, gives advance

Types and topics: Bible study, Christian education, Christian living/spirituality, history, social issues, spiritual formation, theology

Types of books: audiobook, ebook, offset paperback

Guidelines: *store.acupressbooks.com/pages/author-resources*

Tip: "Our editorial team enjoys working with authors to elevate their teaching voice and message, but every author has to bring their own platform to the table. Authors should be mindful that while we can support their plans, we cannot create platform out of thin air. We can only make a limited number of investments in authors, and platform (or lack thereof) is often a determining factor.

"First-time authors need to build a multi-step and in many cases, multi-year plan to grow their audience so that by the time of their book release they are hitting on all cylinders. While many would like to rush the publishing process, it takes time to do this work correctly. Have patience with yourself and try to be discerning about the right partners that you need in your work."

LEXHAM PRESS

1313 Commercial St., Bellingham, WA 98225
editor@lexampress.com | *www.lexhampress.com*
Jesse Myers, acquisitions

Parent company: FaithLife Corporation, makers of Logos Bible Software

Submissions: Responds in eight weeks or not interested.

Types and topics: Bible study, ministry, theology, academic, Bible reference/commentaries

Types of books: print, ebooks, and innovative resources for Logos Bible Software

Guidelines: *www.lexhampress.com/manuscript-submission*

LIGHTHOUSE CHRISTIAN PUBLISHING

754 Roxholly Walk, Buford, CA 30518 | 770-709-2268
info@lighthousechristianpublishing.com | *www.lighthousechristianpublishing.com*
Andy Overett

> **Parent company:** Lighthouse eMedia and eMusic
> **Mission statement:** to provide high-quality original works at the least possible prices
> **Submissions:** Publishes 30 titles per year; receives 200 submissions annually. First-time authors: 80%. Length: fiction, 300-320 pages. Responds in four to six weeks.
> **Royalty:** 50%, no advance
> **Types and topics:** all topics in fiction and nonfiction
> **Types of books:** audiobook, ebook, POD
> **Guidelines:** *lighthouse ebooks.com/custom.html*
> **Tip:** Looking for unique stories.

LIGHTHOUSE TRAILS PUBLISHING, LLC

PO Box 387, Talent, OR 97540 | 541-897-0341
david@lighthousetrails.com | *www.lighthousetrails.com*
David Dombrowski, acquisitions editor

> **Mission statement:** to bring clarity and light to areas of spiritual darkness or deception
> **Submissions:** Publishes two to four titles per year; receives 50-75 submissions annually. First-time authors: 30%. Length: 160-300 pages. Responds in two months. Bible: KJV.
> **Royalty:** 12-17% of net, 20% of retail
> **Types and topics:** biography, memoir/personal narrative, missionaries, fiction, nonfiction
> **Guidelines:** *www.lighthousetrails.com/content/11-submit-manuscript*
> **Tip:** "Any book we consider will not only challenge the more scholarly reader, but also be able to reach those who may have less experience and comprehension. Our books will include human interest and personal experience scenarios as a means of getting the point across. Read a couple of our books to better understand the style of writing we are looking for. We also have a doctrinal statement on our website that helps to define us."

LION HUDSON

Wilkinson House, Jordan Hill Rd., Oxford OX2 8DR, United Kingdom

colinf@lionhudson.com | *www.lionhudson.com*
Colin Forbes, senior editorial manager

Parent company: SPCK Group

Submissions: Receives 400 submissions annually. If no response in three months, consider it a rejection.

Types and topics: Christian living/spirituality, children, fiction

Imprints: Lion Books (general market), Lion Children's Books, Lion Fiction (Christian worldview to general market), Candle Books (Christian children), Monarch Books (Christian)

Guidelines: *www.lionhudson.com/authors-and-illustrators/prospective-authors*

LITTLE LAMB BOOKS

PO Box 211724, Bedford, TX 76095 | 817-505-8719
subs@littlelambbooks.com | *www.littlelambbooks.com*
Rachel Pellegrino, publisher and managing editor

Parent company: Lamb Publishing, LLC

Mission statement: to shepherd the next generation of faithful readers

Submissions: Publishes three to five titles per year; receives 200-250 submissions annually. First-time authors: 85%. Length: picture books, 500 words; chapter books, 1,500-5,000; middle grade, 30,000-60,000 words; young adult, 50,000-80,000 words. Responds in three to four months. Bible: NIV. Accepts unsolicited submissions only in March and September.

Royalty: varies, no advance

Types and topics: animals, belonging, courage, friendship, holidays, multicultural, nature, prayer, self-confidence, sports, travel, values, devotionals, first-chapter, middle grade, picture books, teen/YA; fiction: adventure, contemporary, mystery, romance, suspense

Types of books: ebook, hardcover, offset paperback, POD

Also does: die-cut stickers, bookmarks, coloring pages, digital printables, educator packets, etc.

Guidelines: *littlelambbooks.com/subs*

Tip: "We're seeking evergreen content that is diverse and original from a biblical worldview. Your story should entertain without being preachy, should inspire without being sappy, and should have original concepts, strong characters, interesting settings, and curious plots. Your pitch should hook us from the beginning, and your query should follow our guidelines."

LITURGICAL PRESS

PO Box 7500, Collegeville, MN 56321-7500

submissions@litpress.org | www.litpress.org
> **Denomination:** Catholic
> **Types and topics:** Bible, liturgy, prayer, theology, nonfiction
> **Guidelines:** *www.litpress.org/Authors/submit_manuscript*

LOVE INSPIRED

195 Broadway, 24th floor, New York, NY 10007 | 212-207-7900
www.LoveInspired.com
Tina James, executive editor
Melissa Endlich, senior editor
Emily Rodmell, editor
Shana Asaro, editor
Dina Davis, associate editor
> **Parent company:** Harlequin/HarperCollins Publishers
> **Mission statement:** to uplift and inspire through stories
> **Submissions:** Publishes 144 titles per year; receives 500-1,000 submissions annually. First-time authors: 15%. Length: 55,000 words. Responds in three months. Bible: KJV preferred.
> **Royalty:** on retail, gives advance
> **Types and topics:** romance, romantic suspense
> **Types of books:** mass-market paperback
> **Imprints:** Love Inspired (contemporary romance), Love Inspired Suspense (contemporary romantic suspense)
> **Guidelines:** *harlequin.submittable.com/submit*
> **Tip:** "We're looking for compelling stories with engaging characters, a sustained conflict and an emotionally satisfying romance."

LOVE2READLOVE2WRITE PUBLISHING, LLC

PO Box 103, Camby, IN 46113 | 317-550-9755
editor@love2readlove2writepublishing.com |
www.love2readlove2writepublishing.com
Michele Israel Harper, acquisitions editor
> **Submissions:** Publishes four to six titles per year; receives 150-200 submissions annually. First-time authors: 20%. Length: 60,000-90,000 words. Responds in two to three months. Bible: NKJV.
> **Royalty:** 50%, advance: $50
> **Types and topics:** fiction: fantasy, speculative, teen/YA
> **Type of books:** POD
> **Guidelines:** *www.love2readlove2writepublishing.com/submissions*
> **Tip:** "Be professional, be succinct, and know your audience."

LOYOLA PRESS

3441 N. Ashland Ave., Chicago, IL 60657 | 773-281-1818
submissions@loyolapress.com | *www.loyolapress.com*
Gary Jansen, executive editor, acquisitions

Denomination: Catholic
Submissions: Publishes 20 titles per year; receives 500 submissions annually. Length: 25,000-75,000 words or 150-300 pages. Responds in four to six weeks. Bible: NRSV (Catholic Edition).
Royalty: advance
Types and topics: Christian living/spirituality
Guidelines: *www.loyolapress.com/general/submissions*
Tip: "Looking for books and authors that help make Catholic faith relevant and offer practical tools for the well-lived spiritual life."

MAURICE WILEY MEDIA

143 Northumberland St., Belfast, Ireland BT13 2JF | 08456439318
author@MauriceWylieMedia.com | *www.MauriceWylieMedia.com*

Mission statement: One goal: to give the best!
Submissions: Publishes 20 titles per year; receives 50 submissions annually. First-time authors: 80%. Length: 70,000 words. Responds in four to six days. Bible: NKJV.
Royalty: 30%, sometimes gives advance
Types and topics: all topics, adults and children
Types of books: audiobook, ebook, hardcover, offset paperback
Also does: author-branded websites
Guidelines: *mauricewyliemedia.com/book-publishing*
Tip: Send a "good cover letter, background/short testimony, book potential."

MOODY PUBLISHERS

820 N. LaSalle Blvd., Chicago, IL 60610 | 800-678-8812
randall.payleitner@moody.edu | *www.moodypublishers.com*
Randall Payleitner, editorial director
Judy Dunagan, acquisitions editor, women and Bible study, judy.dunagan@moody.edu
Drew Dyck, editor, pastors and church leaders, drew.dyck@moody.edu
John Hinkley, acquisitions editor, marriage, family, relationships, John.Hinkley@moody.edu

Parent company: Moody Bible Institute
Mission statement: to resource the church's work of discipling all people

Submissions: Publishes 50-60 titles per year; receives thousands of submissions annually. First-time authors: 20%. Responds in one to two months. Bible: NASB, ESV, NKJV. Books need to fit one of these categories: marriage and family resources—how to be a better mom, dad, grandparent, etc.; church leaders—pastors, community care, leading in a church context; Bible study materials—how to better study God's Word, primarily for women and young people; Christian living—how to help people take that next step in the Christian life; and ministry partners—those who work to make a better world in some way from orphan care to responsible finances.

Royalty: advances begin at $500

Types and topics: Bible study, Christian living/spirituality, church life, family, marriage, parenting, women, Bible reference/commentaries

Guidelines: *www.moodypublishers.com/About/faq/manuscripts*

Tip: "Most open to books that (1) have a great idea at the core, (2) are executed well, and (3) can demonstrate an audience clamoring for the content."

MOUNTAIN BROOK FIRE

mountainbrookink@gmail.com | *fire.mountainbrookink.com*
Miralee Ferrell, lead acquisitions editor

Parent company: Mountain Brook Ink

Mission statement: We're dedicated to quality worldbuilding, spellbinding plots, and high-stakes adventures with a whole lot of heart for middle grade, young adult, and adult audiences.

Submissions: Length: minimum 75,000 words. Responds in two months. Bible: KJV, NKJV, NIV.

Royalty: 30-40%, advance: $25

Types and topics: fiction: middle grade, YA, dystopian, fantasy, science fiction, speculative, supernatural

Types of books: audiobook, ebook, POD

Guidelines: *fire.mountainbrookink.com/submission-guidelines*

Tip: "Manuscripts need not be explicitly 'Christian'; we are equally happy with general market. However, we're looking for fiction that is clean. Books having a Christian worldview without having a faith thread will work as well."

MOUNTAIN BROOK INK

mountainbrookink@gmail.com | *www.mountainbrookink.com*
Miralee Ferrell, lead acquisitions editor

Mission statement: to publish fiction you can believe in that embodies restoration and/or renewal

Submissions: Publishes 12 titles per year; receives 50+ submissions annually. First-time authors: 75%. Length: minimum 75,000 words. Responds in two months. Bible: KJV, NKJV, NIV.

Royalty: 30-40%, advance: $25

Types and topics: fiction: contemporary, historical, mystery, romance, romantic suspense, suspense/thriller, women's

Types of books: audiobook, ebook, POD

Imprint: Mountain Brook Fire (speculative fiction)

Guidelines: *mountainbrookink.com/submission-guidelines-for-inquiries*

Tip: "Send the best work you've done, preferably that's been edited so it shines."

MT. ZION RIDGE PRESS, LLC

295 Gum Springs Rd. NW, Georgetown, TN 37336 | 423-458-4256
mtzionridgepress@gmail.com | *mtzionridgepress.com*
Tamera Lynn Kraft, managing editor
Michelle Levigne, managing editor

Mission statement: to publish Christian books off the beaten path: fiction with a Christian worldview that doesn't fit the mold, nonfiction that goes deeper in Scripture than the bubblegum Christianity you find elsewhere

Submissions: Publishes seven titles per year; receives 30 submissions annually. First-time authors: 50%. Length: 50,000-100,000 words. Responds in two months. Bible: ESV, NIV, NKJV, KJV for historical.

Royalty: 30% books, 20% audiobooks, no advance

Types and topics: African-American, Asian, Bible study, Christian living/spirituality, Hispanic, Bible studies, devotionals; fiction: biblical, contemporary, historical, mystery, romance, suspense/thriller, westerns, women's

Types of books: audiobook, ebook, POD

Guidelines: *mtzionridgepress.com/about*

Tip: "Make sure it has a strong Christian worldview and is a little bit different from the norm."

MY HEALTHY CHURCH

1445 N. Boonville Ave., Springfield, MO 65802 | 417-831-8000
newproducts@myhealthychurch.com | *www.myhealthychurch.com*

Denomination: Assemblies of God

Submissions: Responds in two to three months.

Types and topics: Bible studies, church resources

Guidelines: *myhealthychurch.com/store/startcat.cfm?cat=tWRITGUID*

Tip: "The content of all our books and resources must be compatible with the beliefs and purposes of the Assemblies of God."

NAVPRESS

3820 N. 30th St., Colorado Springs, CO 80904

inquiries@navpress.com | *www.navpress.com*

Caitlyn Carlson, acquisitions editor

Deborah Gonzalez, associate acquisitions and developmental editor

Parent company: The Navigators

Submissions: Publishes 20 titles per year; receives 1,000 submissions annually. First-time authors: 40%. Length: 40,000 words. Responds in two months.

Royalty: 16-22%, gives advance

Types and topics: Christian living/spirituality, counseling, discipleship, family, leadership, marriage, parenting, prayer, relationships, spiritual growth, women, Bible studies

Guidelines: *www.navpress.com/faq*

Tip: "Proposals with strong discipleship elements are preferred. Authors should have a ministry platform that supports their discipleship elements. NavPress does not accept unsolicited manuscripts."

NELSON BOOKS

PO Box 141000, Nashville, TN 37214-1000 | 615-889-9000

www.thomasnelson.com/nelsonbooks

Jenny Baumgartner, senior acquisitions editor

Parent company: Thomas Nelson Publishers/HarperCollins Christian Publishing

Submissions: Publishes fewer than 100 titles per year.

Types and topics: biography, business, Christian living/spirituality, leadership, spiritual growth, devotionals

Types of books: audiobook, ebook, hardcover, offset paperback

Guidelines: none

NEW GROWTH PRESS

PO Box 4485, Greensboro, NC 27404 | 336-378-7775

submissions@newgrowthpress.com | *www.newgrowthpress.com*

Barbara Juliani, editorial director

Rush Witt, acquisitions editor

Mission statement: to reach every church and home with gospel-centered resources that point to Jesus and help every person grow closer to Christ

Submissions: Responds in six weeks or not interested.

Types and topics: Christian living/spirituality, counseling, family, parenting, relationships, Bible studies, children, devotionals, fiction, teen/YA

Guidelines: *newgrowthpress.com/submissions*

NEW HOPE PUBLISHERS

100 Missionary Ridge, Birmingham, AL 35252 | 866-266-8399

submissions@ironstreammedia.com | www.newhopepublishers.com

Susan Cornell, senior editor

Parent company: Iron Stream Media

Submissions: Publishes 20-25 nonfiction, 10-15 fiction titles per year; receives 100+ submissions annually. First-time authors: 20%. Length: 40,000-50,000 words. Responds in four months. Bible: any. Note: This imprint will be discontinued and rolled into Iron Stream books.

Royalty: 12-14%; sometimes gives variable advance, depending on publishing history

Types and topics: Christian living/spirituality, contemporary issues, family, leadership, parenting, Bible studies, children, teen/YA; fiction: romance, romantic suspense, seasonal, speculative, suspense/thriller, women's

Imprint: New Hope Kidz (children)

Guidelines: *www.newhopepublishers.com/proposals*

Tip: "Proposals must be polished and free of errors. Marketing plans in proposal must show author's knowledge of market, platform, and genre. Please include previous sales figures (if any) and author's biography as related to book topic."

NORTHWESTERN PUBLISHING HOUSE

N16W23379 Stone Ridge Dr., Waukesha, WI 53188-1108 | 800-662-6022

braunj@nph.wels.net | online.nph.net

John Braun

Denomination: Wisconsin Evangelical Lutheran Synod

Mission statement: to deliver biblically sound, Christ-centered resources within the Wisconsin Evangelical Lutheran Synod and beyond

Types and topics: family, history, theology, Bible reference/commentaries, devotionals

Guidelines: *online.nph.net/manuscript-submission*

OLIVIA KIMBRELL PRESS

PO Box 470, Fort Knox, KY 40121-0470 | 859-577-1071
admin@oliviakimbrellpress.com | myokpress.com
Heather McCurdy, editor
Gregg Bridgeman, editor-in-chief

Mission statement: We specialize in previously unpublished authors who write about contemporary life and the challenges Christians face in our very secular fallen world.

Submissions: Specializes in true-to-life, meaningful Christian fiction and nonfiction titles intended to uplift the heart and engage the mind. Primary focus on "Roman Road" small-group guides or reader's guides to accompany nonfiction and fiction.

Types and topics: Christian living/spirituality, family, health, social issues, devotionals; fiction: biblical, fantasy, historical romance, romantic suspense, science fiction, speculative

Imprints: CAVE (historical fiction around the time of Christ), Sign of the Whale (biblical and speculative fiction), House of Bread (nutrition)

Guidelines: *www.oliviakimbrellpress.com/submission.html*

Tip: "Must meet our stated editorial standards. Follow our submission guidelines. Fiction series preferred over standalone titles. Complete manuscripts only."

OUR DAILY BREAD PUBLISHING

3000 Kraft Ave. SE, Grand Rapids, MI 49507 | 616-974-2210
dawn.anderson@odb.org | www.ourdailybreadpublishing.org
Dawn Anderson, executive editor
Joyce Dinkins, executive editor, VOICES
Katara Patton, senior editor and acquisitions

Parent company: Our Daily Bread Ministries

Mission statement: to feed the soul with the Word of God

Submissions: Publishes 24-36 titles per year; receives 100 submissions annually. First-time authors: fewer than 10%. Length: approximately 192 pages. Responds in three months. Bible: NIV, NLT, ESV.

Royalty: 12-18%, no advance

Average first print run: 3,000-50,000

Types and topics: African-American, Asian, Bible study, Christian living/spirituality, contemporary issues, Hispanic, men, pop reference, prayer, social issues, women, children, devotionals

Types of books: audiobook, board books, ebook, hardcover, offset paperback
Guidelines: *dhp.org/writers-guidelines*
Tip: "We look for strongly Bible-based content with practical application for everyday living."

OUR SUNDAY VISITOR, INC.

200 Noll Plaza, Huntington, IN 46750-4303 | 260-356-8400
www.osv.com

Denomination: Catholic
Mission statement: to assist Catholics to be more aware and secure in their faith and capable of relating their faith to others
Submissions: Publishes 30-40 titles per year; receives 500 submissions annually. First-time authors: 10%. Responds in six to eight weeks.
Royalty: 10-12%, advance: $1,500
Types and topics: apologetics, biography, Christian living/spirituality, church life, culture, evangelism, family, history, marriage, ministry, parenting, prayer, devotionals, prayer guides
Imprint: OSV Kids (children and teens)
Guidelines: *osv.submittable.com/submit*
Tip: "All books published must relate to the Catholic Church; unique books aimed at our audience. Give as much background information as possible on author qualification, why the topic was chosen, and unique aspects of the project. Follow our guidelines. We are expanding our religious education product line and programs."

P&R PUBLISHING

1102 Marble Hill Rd., Phillipsburg, NJ 08865 | 908-454-0505
dave@prpbooks.com | *www.prpbooks.com*
David Almack, acquisitions director
Amanda Martin, editorial director
Melissa Craig, children's editor

Denomination: Reformed
Mission statement: to publish excellent books that promote biblical understanding and godly living as summarized in the Westminster Confession of Faith and Catechisms
Submissions: Publishes 35 titles per year; receives 150-200 submissions annually. First-time authors: 10%. Length: 40,000-60,000 words. Responds in three months. Bible: ESV.
Royalty: 14-16%, gives advance
Average first print run: 3,500

Types and topics: Christian living/spirituality, counseling, theology, academic, Bible reference/commentaries, children, devotionals, teen/YA

Types of books: audiobook, ebook, hardcover, offset paperback

Guidelines: *www.prpbooks.com/manuscript-submissions*

Tip: "Needs to have a Reformed theological perspective."

PACIFIC PRESS

PO Box 5353, Nampa, ID 83653-5353 | 208-465-2500

booksubmissions@pacificpress.com | www.pacificpress.com

Scott Cady, acquisitions editor

Denomination: Seventh-Day Adventist

Mission statement: to provide readers with a wide variety of books that connect them with God and help them develop a relationship with Him; provide information about God, His character, and His ways; and encourage and uplift them in the struggles of life

Submissions: Publishes 35-40 titles per year; receives 500 submissions annually. First-time authors: 5%. Length: 40,000-90,000 words or 128-320 pages. Responds in one to three weeks.

Royalty: 12-16%, advance: $1,500

Types and topics: Bible study, biography, Christian living/spirituality, contemporary issues, health, history, marriage, memoir/personal narrative, parenting, prayer, theology, children, fiction

Guidelines: *www.pacificpress.com/authors___artists/books*

Tip: "Most open to spirituality, inspirational, and Christian living. Our website has the most up-to-date information, including samples of recent publications. For more information, see *www.adventistbookcenter.com*. Do not send full manuscript unless we request it after reviewing your proposal."

PARACLETE PRESS

PO Box 1568, Orleans, MA 02653-1568 | 508-255-4685

submissions@paracletepress.com | www.paracletepress.com

Jon M. Sweeney, publisher and editor-in-chief

Denomination: Catholic, Protestant

Submissions: Publishes 40 titles per year. Responds in one month.

Types and topics: Advent/Christmas picture books, Christian living/spirituality, grief, Lent/Easter picture books, prayer, children; fiction: contemporary, fantasy, horror, science fiction

Imprint: Raven (fiction)

Guidelines: *www.paracletepress.com/pages/submission-guidelines*

PARAKLESIS PUBLISHING

113 Winn Ct., Waleska, GA 30183 | 404-500-6328
submissions@paraklesispress.com | ParaklesisPress.com
Sally Apokedak, editor

> **Mission statement:** to delight children with fun language; smart, humble, comical, relatable characters; charming illustrations; and exciting plots, all while also giving these young minds plenty of food for thought
>
> **Submissions:** Publishes four titles per year; receives 75 submissions annually. First-time authors: 50%. Length: 32-400 pages. Responds in three months. Bible: ESV.
>
> **Royalty:** 20-30%, sometimes gives advance of $500 maximum
>
> **Types and topics:** Bible study, children, picture books, fiction: contemporary, fantasy, mystery
>
> **Types of books:** POD hardcover and paperback
>
> **Guidelines:** *paraklesispress.com/submit-to-us*
>
> **Tip:** "Write something interesting and entertaining that doesn't need a ton of editing and that is not offensive to Christians and you'll have a good chance of getting published here."

PAULINE BOOKS & MEDIA

50 Saint Paul's Ave., Boston, MA 02130-3491 | 617-522-8911
editorial@paulinemedia.com | www.pauline.org

> **Denomination:** Catholic
>
> **Parent company:** Daughters of St. Paul
>
> **Submissions:** Publishes 20 titles per year; receives 300+ submissions annually. First-time authors: 10%. Length: 10,000-60,000 words. Responds in two months. Bible: NRSV.
>
> **Royalty:** 5-10%, gives advance
>
> **Types and topics:** Christian living/spirituality, evangelism, family, prayer, spiritual formation, theology, activities and puzzles, board books, children, fiction, first-chapter, middle grade, picture books, prayer guides, teen/YA
>
> **Types of books:** ebook, paperback
>
> **Imprints:** Pauline Kids, Pauline TEEN
>
> **Guidelines:** *www.pauline.org/Publishing/Submit-a-Manuscript*

PAULIST PRESS

997 Macarthur Blvd., Mahwah, NJ 07430-9990
submissions@paulistpress.com | www.paulistpress.com
Trace Murphy, editorial director

Denomination: Catholic
Submissions: Responds in six to eight weeks.
Types and topics: academic, children, nonfiction
Guidelines: *www.paulistpress.com/Pages/Center/auth_res_0.aspx*

PELICAN BOOK GROUP

Harbourlight Books, Prism Book Group, Pure Amore, Watershed Books, White Rose Publishing

PRAYERSHOP PUBLISHING

PO Box 10667, Terre Haute, IN 47802 | 812-238-5504
jon@prayershop.org | *prayershop.org*
Jonathan Graf, publisher

> **Parent company:** Harvest Prayer Ministries, Church Prayer Leaders Network
> **Mission statement:** Prayer Shop Publishing is a publishing ministry focused solely on prayer. Every product we produce will take you deeper in your prayer relationship with Jesus Christ. Our primary vision with our products is to help churches become houses of prayer.
> **Submissions:** Publishes six to eight titles per year; receives 15-25 submissions annually. First-time authors: 25%. Length: 80-144 pages. Responds in six to ten weeks. Bible: NIV. "We are looking for prayer topics that would move believers from just praying for their own needs to prayer that is focused on growing God's Kingdom."
> **Royalty:** 10-15%, no advance
> **Average first print run:** 1,000-5,000
> **Types and topics:** prayer, revival, devotionals, prayer guides
> **Types of books:** ebook, offset paperback
> **Guidelines:** none
> **Tip:** "Currently looking for book manuscripts, booklets, and materials that can be formatted via CD and print into training kits. We are mostly interested in products that will in some way enhance the prayer life of a local church."

PRISM BOOK GROUP

PO Box 1738, Aztec, NM 87410
customer@prismbookgroup.com | *www.prismbookgroup.com*
Jacqueline Hopper, acquisitions editor, jhopper@prismbookgroup.com
Paula Mowery, acquisitions editor, pmowery@prismbookgroup.com

> **Parent company:** Pelican Book Group

Mission statement: to publish quality books that reflect the salvation and love offered by Jesus Christ

Submissions: Length: 25,000-80,000 words. Responds in three to four months. Bible: NIV, NAB.

Royalty: 40% download, 7% print, sometimes gives advance

Types and topics: fiction: contemporary, fantasy, historical, mystery, romance, romantic suspense, science fiction, suspense/thriller, teen/YA

Types of books: ebook, POD

Imprints: Prism Lux (Christian), Prism CW (clean and wholesome)

Guidelines: *pelicanbookgroup.com/ec/index.php?main_ page=page&id=76*

Tip: "Our books offer clean and compelling reads for the discerning reader. We will not publish graphic language or content and look for well-written, emotionally charged stories, intense plots, and captivating characters."

PURE AMORE

PO Box 1738, Aztec, NM 87410

customer@pelicanbookgroup.com | pelicanbookgroup.com

Nicola Martinez, editor-in-chief

Parent company: Pelican Book Group

Mission statement: to publish quality books that reflect the salvation and love offered by Jesus Christ

Submissions: Length: 40,000-45,000 words. Responds in one to four months.

Royalty: 40% download, 7% print, sometimes gives advance

Types and topics: Only contemporary Christian romance. Pure Amore romances are sweet in tone and in conflict. These stories are the emotionally driven tales of youthful Christians between the ages of 21 and 33 who are striving to live their faith in a world where Christ-centered choices may not fully be understood.

Types of books: ebook, POD

Guidelines: *pelicanbookgroup.com/ec/index.php?main_page=page&id=69*

Tip: "Pure Amore romances emphasize the beauty in chastity, so physical interactions, such as kissing or hugging, should focus on the characters' emotions, rather than heightened sexual desire; and scenes of physical intimacy should be integral to the plot and/or emotional development of the character or relationship."

RANDALL HOUSE

PO Box 17306, Nashville, TN 37217 | 615-361-1221

books@randallhouse.com | D6family.com

Dr. Danny Conn, senior acquisitions editor

Denomination: Free Will Baptist

Mission statement: to build believers through church and home

Submissions: Publishes 8-12 titles per year; receives 40 submissions annually. First-time authors: 20%. Length: 20,000-100,000 words. Responds in three months. Bible: ESV, NIV, KJV.

Royalty: 15-20%, sometimes gives advance

Types and topics: Christian living/spirituality, discipleship, family, Free Will Baptist history and doctrine, Hispanic, theology

Types of books: ebook, hardcover, offset paperback

Guidelines: *rhpweb.s3.amazonaws.com/Book-Proposal-Guide.pdf*

Tip: "Provide insightful material with practical application on a subject that fits our genres."

RESOURCE PUBLICATIONS

199 W. 8th Ave., Ste. 3, Eugene, OR 97401 | 541-344-1528
proposal@wipfandstock.com | *wipfandstock.com/search-results/ ?imprint=resource-publications*

Parent company: Wipf and Stock

Submissions: Responds in one to two months.

Types and topics: biography, fiction, poetry, sermons

Types of books: ebook, POD

Guidelines: *wipfandstock.com/submitting-a-proposal*

RESURRECTION PRESS

77 West End Rd., Totowa, NJ 07572 | 973-890-2400
info@catholicbookpublishing.com | *www.catholicbookpublishing.com*
Anthony Buono, editor

Denomination: Catholic

Parent company: Catholic Book Publishing Corp.

Submissions: Responds in four to six weeks.

Types and topics: Christian living/spirituality, healing, ministry, prayer

Guidelines: *www.catholicbookpublishing.com/page/faq#manuscript*

REVELL BOOKS

6030 E. Fulton Rd., Ada, MI 49301 | 616-676-9185
bakerpublishinggroup.com/revell
Andrea Doering, editorial director
Kelsey Bowen, acquisitions editor
Rachel McRae, acquisitions editor
Vicki Crumpton, executive editor and acquisitions

Parent company: Baker Publishing Group
Types and topics: apologetics, Bible study, biography, Christian living/
spirituality, church life, culture, family, marriage, memoir/personal
narrative, children, fiction, teen/YA
Guidelines: *bakerpublishinggroup.com/contact/submission-policy*

ROSE PUBLISHING

PO Box 3473, Peabody, MA 01961 | 800-358-3111
lpennings@hendricksonrose.com | www.hendricksonrose.com
Lynette Pennings, managing editor

Parent company: Hendrickson Publishing Group/Tyndale House Ministries
Mission statement: to make the Bible and its teachings easy to understand
Types and topics: Bible, Bible reference/commentaries, charts

ROSEKIDZ

PO Box 3473, Peabody, MA 01961 | 800-358-3111
kmcgraw@hendrickson.com | www.hendricksonrose.com
Karen McGraw, managing editor

Parent company: Hendrickson Publishing Group/Tyndale House Ministries
Mission statement: to help kids grow closer to God in a hands-on way
Types and topics: activities and puzzles, children, crafts, devotionals, fiction
Type of books: offset paperback

SALEM BOOKS

300 New Jersey Ave., NW, Ste. 500, Washington, DC 20001
www.regnery.com/custom/salem-books
Tim Peterson, publisher and acquisitions

Parent company: Regnery Publishing/Salem Media Group
Mission statement: to enrich the lives of Christians and proclaim the
gospel of Jesus to the world through the written word
Types and topics: Christian living/spirituality

SCEPTER PUBLISHERS

PO Box 360694, Strongsville, OH 44136 | 212-354-0670
info@scepterpublishers.org | www.scepterpublishers.org
Nathan Davis, editor

Denomination: Catholic
Mission statement: to help people find God in ordinary life and realize
sanctity in work, family life, and everyday activities; to assist people
in their quest to live an integrated life where every moment, even the

most ordinary is offered up like a prayer; to immerse people in the contemplative life even while living in the midst of the world, so that they might learn the will of God

Submissions: Publishes 8-18 titles per year.

Types and topics: Christian living/spirituality

Guidelines: *scepterpublishers.org/pages/publishing-services*

SCRIVENINGS PRESS

15 Lucky Ln., Morrilton, AR 72110 | 501-548-2736

scriveningspress@gmail.com | *scriveningspress.com*

Linda Fulkerson, owner and acquisitions

Mission statement: to produce great books for our readers and help our authors build their careers

Submissions: Publishes 28 titles per year; receives 100 submissions annually. First-time authors: 80%. Length: 50,000-90,000 words. Responds in four to six weeks. Bible: any.

Royalty: 12% print, 50% ebook, 40% Kindle Unlimited pages read, no advance

Types and topics: fiction: historical, mystery, romance, romantic suspense, speculative, women's

Types of books: ebook, POD

Imprints: Scrivenings Press (general fiction), Expanse Books (speculative fiction)

Guidelines: *scriveningspress.com/submissions*

Tip: "We are a small publishing house, and we try to keep a family feel among our staff and authors. We encourage all our authors to encourage one another and to cross-promote books from other authors within our company."

SHORT AND SWEET BOOK SERIES

See listing in the periodicals section, "Adult Markets."

SMITTEN HISTORICAL ROMANCE

100 Missionary Ridge, Birmingham, AL 35242 | 888-811-9934

editor@smittenromance.com | *shoplpc.com/smitten-historical-romance*

Denise Weimer, managing editor

Parent company: Iron Stream Media

Mission statement: to engage the reader from the first paragraph to the last in a story that touches the mind, heart, and spirit

Submissions: Publishes eight titles per year; receives 50 submissions annually. First-time authors: 30%. Length: 60,000-90,000 words. Responds in 3-12 weeks. Bible: NIV. Note: This imprint will be discontinued and rolled into Iron Stream Fiction.

Royalty: 40%, no advance

Types and topics: historical romance

Types of books: audiobook, ebook, POD

Guidelines: *shoplpc.com/smitten*

Tip: "Submit stories steeped in real history/places populated by fascinating characters and a happily-ever-after ending that satisfies the reader. The history and Christian content should be organic to the time period, never preachy, and not overshadow the story. Implied Christian content without overt evangelism is preferred."

SMYTH & HELWYS BOOKS

6316 Peake Rd., Macon, GA 31210-3960 | 478-757-0564
proposal@helwys.com | *www.helwys.com*
Leslie Andres, editor

>   **Submissions:** Responds in several weeks.
>
>   **Types and topics:** Bible study, Christian living/spirituality, leadership, ministry
>
>   **Guidelines:** *www.helwys.com/submit-a-manuscript*

SONRISE DEVOTIONALS

100 Missionary Ridge, Birmingham, AL 35252 | 866-266-8399
lpcnonfictionsubmissions@gmail.com | *shoplpc.com/sonrise-devotionals*
Cindy Sproles, managing editor

>   **Parent company:** Iron Stream Media
>
>   **Mission statement:** to encourage individuals to develop a stronger relationship with Christ through personal quiet time
>
>   **Submissions:** Publishes four titles per year; receives 50 submissions annually. First-time authors: 50%. Length: 50,000-85,000 words. Responds in six months. Bible: any. Note: This imprint will be discontinued and rolled into Iron Stream books.
>
>   **Royalty:** 50%, no advance
>
>   **Types and topics:** devotionals
>
>   **Types of books:** audiobook, ebook, POD
>
>   **Guidelines:** *shoplpc.com/sonrise*
>
>   **Tip:** "Looking for devotions that move away from niche audiences and return to devotions that address everyone at any season in their lives."

SPRINKLE PUBLISHING

2270 Ferguson Rd., Ste. 116, Ontario, OH 44906-5200 | 419-709-1435
Dr.Sprinkle@wsministries.ws | *www.wsministries.ws/home/sprinkle-publishing*
Dr. Wanda J. Sprinkle, editor

> **Parent company:** Wanda Sprinkle Ministries, LLC
> **Mission statement:** to make publishing affordable through our ministry as we specialize in first-time authors
> **Submissions:** Publishes seven titles per year; receives 20 submissions annually. First-time authors: 95%. Length: maximum 200 pages. Responds in two weeks.
> **Royalty:** 50-60%, no advance
> **Average first print run:** minimum 100
> **Types and topics:** autobiography, biography, Christian living/spirituality, inspirational, spiritual maturity, devotionals, fiction, poetry
> **Types of books:** hardcover, offset paperback, spiral binding
> **Guidelines:** by email or mail
> **Tip:** "Must agree to our doctrinal absolutes of Scripture alone, Christ alone, faith alone, grace alone, and glory to God alone."

STRAIGHT STREET BOOKS

100 Missionary Ridge, Birmingham, AL 35252 | 866-266-8399
lpcnonfictionsubmissions@gmail.com | *shoplpc.com/straight-street-books*
Cindy Sproles, managing editor

> **Parent company:** Iron Stream Media
> **Mission statement:** to provide guides to current topics and issues from a Christian worldview and help readers know God better
> **Submissions:** Publishes four titles per year; receives 50 submissions annually. First-time authors: 85%. Length: 50,000-85,000 words. Responds in six months. Bible: any. Note: This imprint will be discontinued and rolled into Iron Stream books.
> **Royalty:** 40%, no advance
> **Types and topics:** Christian living/spirituality, disabilities, marriage
> **Types of books:** audiobook, ebook, POD
> **Guidelines:** *shoplpc.com/straight-street*
> **Tip:** "Fresh and unique subjects. We do not accept memoirs."

THOMAS NELSON FICTION

PO Box 141000, Nashville, TN 37214-1000 | 615-889-9000
www.thomasnelson.com/fiction
Jocelyn Bailey, acquisitions editor

Laura Wheeler, acquisitions editor
Kimberly Carlton, acquisitions editor

Parent company: Thomas Nelson Publishers/HarperCollins Christian Publishing

Submissions: Agents only.

Types and topics: romance, historical, thriller, suspense, humor, mystery

Types of books: audiobook, ebook, offset paperback

Tip: "As part of a faith-based house, we thrive with authors who are Christians because we understand their worldview—as well as how to help them reach the widest audience possible. And we don't have any artificial requirements for faith content. Our goal is to let the story be the story."

THOMAS NELSON GIFT

PO Box 141000, Nashville, TN 37214-1000 | 615-889-9000

www.thomasnelson.com/gift
Adria Haley, acquisitions editor

Parent company: Thomas Nelson Publishing/HarperCollins Christian Publishing

Submissions: Agents only.

Types of books: hardcover

Tip: "A gift book is designed to be shared. It's a beautiful keepsake that makes an ideal gift, a way to mark a special occasion or holiday, a message of the heart, and it usually satisfies a strong felt need. Featuring two or four-color interiors, sometimes photography or illustrations, and beautiful covers complete with special effects like foil, fabric, gilding, and padding."

THOMAS NELSON PUBLISHERS

www.thomasnelson.com

Nelson Books (spiritual growth and practical living), W Publishing (memoirs, help and hope for doing life better, select practical living), Thomas Nelson Fiction, Thomas Nelson Gift, Grupo Nelson (Spanish), Tommy Nelson (children and teens), Emanate Books (Charismatic)

TOMMY NELSON

PO Box 141000, Nashville, TN 37214-1000 | 615-889-9000

www.tommynelson.com
Mackenzie Howard, associate publisher

Parent company: Thomas Nelson Publishers/HarperCollins Christian Publishing

Mission statement: to expand children's imaginations and nurture their faith while pointing them to a personal relationship with God

Submissions: Agents only.

Types and topics: Bible storybooks, board books, devotionals, first-chapter, middle grade, picture books, teen/YA

Types of books: board books, hardcover, offset paperback, picture books

THE TRINITY FOUNDATION

PO Box 68, Unicoi, TN 37692 | 423-743-0199

tjtrinityfound@aol.com | www.trinityfoundation.org

Thomas W. Juodaitis, president

Mission statement: to promote the Protestant Christian religion

Submissions: Publishes three titles per year; receives ten submissions annually. First-time authors: 1%. Length: 150-200 pages. Responds in three to five days. Bible: KJV, NKJV.

Royalty: none, flat fee up to $2,000, no advance

Average first print run: 1,000-2,000

Types and topics: Christian living/spirituality, philosophy, theology, nonfiction

Types of books: ebook, hardcover, offset paperback

Guidelines: by email

Tip: "Check the content at the website and see if your submission is in line with it."

TULIP PUBLISHING

PO Box 3150, Lansvale, NSW 2166, Australia | +61 2 9055 2195

submissions@tulippublishing.com.au | tulippublishing.com.au

Denomination: Reformed

Mission statement: to provide rich resources for the Kingdom within Australia and abroad, both for the edification of the saints and ultimately, the glorification of God

Submissions: Publishes four to six titles per year; receives 20 submissions annually. First-time authors: 33%. Length: 120-250 pages. Responds in three months. Bible: ESV.

Royalty: 30-60%, no advance

Average first print run: 1,000

Types and topics: Christian living/spirituality, history, theology, academic

Types of books: hardcover, offset paperback

Guidelines: *tulippublishing.com.au/about/submissions*

Tip: "Write your pitch succinctly. Outline what your book hopes to achieve and how it addresses the matter. Ensure the manuscript is articulated and expressed well, and even circulate it among mature friends or family first to get additional feedback prior to submission."

TYNDALE HOUSE PUBLISHERS

351 Executive Dr., Carol Stream, IL 60188 | 630-668-8300
www.tyndale.com
Jon Farrar, acquisitions director, nonfiction
Elizabeth Jackson, acquisitions editor, fiction
Jillian Schlossberg, senior acquisitions editor, nonfiction
Becky Brandvik, senior director, gift and specialty

> **Mission statement:** to help readers discover the life-giving truths of God's Word
>
> **Submissions:** Publishes 100+ titles per year. First-time authors: 5%. Length: fiction, 75,000-100,000 words. Responds in three to six months. Bible: NLT.
>
> **Types and topics:** biography, Christian living/spirituality, counseling, family, finances, leadership, marriage, memoir/personal narrative, parenting, children, devotionals, teen/YA; fiction: biblical, children, contemporary, futuristic, historical, romance, suspense/thriller, teen/YA
>
> **Types of books:** audiobook, ebook, hardcover, offset paperback
>
> **Imprints:** Hendrickson Publishers, Rose Publishing, RoseKidz, Tyndale Kids (children), Wander (YA), Tyndale Español (Spanish), Tyndale Refresh (health and wellness), Tyndale Momentum (nonfiction)
>
> **Guidelines:** none

TYNDALE KIDS

351 Executive Dr., Carol Stream, IL 60188 | 630-668-8300
kidsandwandersubmissions@tyndale.com | *www.tyndale.com*
Linda Howard, associate publisher and acquisitions

> **Parent company:** Tyndale House Publishers
>
> **Mission statement:** to bring kids and families closer to God through publishing books with excellent content, creative formats, and outstanding design
>
> **Submissions:** Publishes 10-15 titles per year; receives 300-400 submissions annually. First-time authors: 5%. Length: varies according to the age group. Responds in two to three months. Bible: NLT.
>
> **Royalty:** 10-24%, advance varies according to platform, previous sales history, and uniqueness of proposal

Types and topics: African-American, Asian, Hispanic, Bible stories, board books, devotionals, fiction, first-chapter, middle grade, nonfiction, picture books, YA
Types of books: audiobook, ebook, hardcover, offset paperback, POD
Imprints: Wander (YA fiction and nonfiction)
Guidelines: none
Tip: "Looking for a solid, well-written proposal; strong platform; excellent writing."

W PUBLISHING

PO Box 141000, Nashville, TN 37214-1000 | 615-889-9000
www.thomasnelson.com/wpublishing
Kyle Olund, senior acquisitions editor
Dawn Hollomon, acquisitions editor

Parent company: Thomas Nelson Publishing/HarperCollins Christian Publishing
Submissions: Agents only.
Types and topics: help and hope for doing life better, select practical living, memoir
Types of books: audiobook, ebook, offset paperback, hardcover
Guidelines: none
Tip: "W prides itself on the ability to provide authors a nurturing, faith-friendly, boutique style publishing experience."

WARNER CHRISTIAN RESOURCES

2902 Enterprise Dr., Anderson, IN 46013 | 765-644-7721
editors@warnerpress.org | *www.warnerpress.org*
Karen Rhodes, kids and family ministry editor

Denomination: Church of God
Mission statement: to equip the church, to advance the Kingdom and to give hope to future generations
Submissions: Publishes three to five titles per year; receives 50+ submissions annually. First-time authors: 50%. Responds in six to eight weeks. Bible: KJV, NIV, ESV, NKJV.
Royalty: sometimes gives advance based on the author and type of book
Types and topics: Bible studies, small group resources, small-group study guides
Types of books: ebook, offset paperback
Guidelines: *www.warnerpress.org/custom.aspx?id=3*
Tip: "Do your research and visit our website to view what we already produce."

WATERBROOK MULTNOMAH

10807 New Allegiance Dr. #500, Colorado Springs, CO 80921 | 719-590-4999
info@waterbrookmultnomah.com | *www.waterbrookmultnomah.com*
Andrew Stoddard, editorial director
Becky Nesbitt, executive editor, fiction acquisitions
Susan Tjaden, executive editor
Paul Pastor, editor, pastoral and spiritual growth
Sara Rubio, children's editor
Bunmi Ishola, children's editor

Parent company: Crown Publishing Group/Penguin Random House
Submissions: Publishes 60 titles per year; receives 300 submissions annually. First-time authors: 15%. Length: 208-400 pages. Responds in one to two months.
Royalty: advance
Types and topics: Christian living/spirituality, home and lifestyle, memoir/personal narrative, relationships, spiritual growth, Bible studies, children, devotionals; fiction: Amish, historical, romantic suspense
Types of books: audiobook, ebook, hardcover, offset paperback, POD
Imprint: Ink & Willow (gifts)
Tip: "We recommend working with an agent whose clientele aligns with your strengths as a writer."

WATERSHED BOOKS

PO Box 1738, Aztec, NM 87410
customer@pelicanbookgroup.com | *www.pelicanbookgroup.com*
Nicola Martinez, editor-in-chief

Parent company: Pelican Book Group
Mission statement: to publish quality books that reflect the salvation and love offered by Jesus Christ
Submissions: Length: 25,000-65,000 words. Responds in three to four months. Bible: NIV, NAB. Interested in series ideas.
Royalty: 40% on download, 7% on print, sometimes offers advances
Types and topics: fiction: teen/YA, adventure, coming-of-age, crime, mystery, romance, science fiction, supernatural, suspense, westerns
Type of books: POD
Guidelines: *pelicanbookgroup.com/ec/index.php?main_page=page&id=60*
Tip: "We want to see something other than dystopian."

WESTMINSTER JOHN KNOX PRESS

100 Witherspoon St., Louisville, KY 40202-1396

submissions@wjkbooks.com | *www.wjkbooks.com*

David Dobson, publisher and acquisitions

Denomination: Presbyterian

Parent company: Presbyterian Publishing Corporation

Submissions: Publishes 60 titles per year. Responds in two to three months.

Types and topics: Bible study, culture, ethics, ministry, theology, worship, academic

Types of books: hardcover, offset paperback

Imprints: Flyaway Books (children), Geneva Press (Presbyterian Church U.S.A.)

Guidelines: *www.wjkbooks.com/Pages/Item/1345/Author-Relations.aspx*

WHITAKER HOUSE

1030 Hunt Valley Cir., New Kensington, PA 15068 | 724-334-7000

publisher@whitakerhouse.com | *www.whitakerhouse.com*

Christine Whitaker, acquisitions editor

Parent company: Whitaker Corporation

Submissions: Publishes 75-100 titles per year; receives 200 submissions annually. First-time authors: 30%. Length: 50,000-80,000 words. Responds in one to two months. Bible: KJV.

Royalty: 15-18%, sometimes offers advance

Types and topics: African-American, Asian, Charismatic, Christian living/spirituality, Hispanic, children, devotionals, fiction

Types of books: audiobook, ebook, hardcover, offset and POD paperback

Imprint: Whitaker Playhouse (parents of young children)

Guidelines: *s3.amazonaws.com/whitaker-house-s3/wp-content/uploads/20190828134818/WhitakerHouse-Book-Submission-Guidelines.pdf*

Tip: "Follow the questions and suggestions on our submission guidelines."

WHITE ROSE PUBLISHING

PO Box 1738, Aztec, NM 87410

customer@pelicanbookgroup.com | *www.pelicanbookgroup.com*

Nicola Martinez, editor-in-chief

Parent company: Pelican Book Group

Mission statement: to publish quality books that reflect the salvation and love offered by Jesus Christ

Submissions: Length: short stories, 10,000-20,000 words; novelettes, 20,000-35,000 words; novellas, 35,000-60,000 words; novels, 60,000-80,000 words. Responds in three to four months. Bible: NIV, NAB.

Royalty: 40% on download, 7% on print, sometimes gives advance

Types and topics: romance fiction

Types of books: ebook, POD

Guidelines: *pelicanbookgroup.com/ec/index.php?main_page=page&id=58*

Tip: "The setting for White Rose books can be contemporary, historical or futuristic. They can be straight romances or include other factors such as mystery, suspense or supernatural elements, etc.; however, an element of faith must be present in all White Rose stories—without becoming overbearing or preachy. Please specify in your proposal if your story includes elements beyond simple romance."

WHITEFIRE PUBLISHING

13607 Bedford Rd. NE, Cumberland, MD 21502 | 866-245-2211
r.white@whitefire-publishing.com | *www.whitefire-publishing.com*
Roseanna White, managing editor

Mission statement: to publish books that shine the Light of God into the darkness and embrace the motto of "Where Spirit Meets the Page"

Submissions: Publishes 24 titles per year; receives 200 submissions annually. First-time authors: 20%. Length: 60,000-100,000 words. Responds in three months. Bible: KJV for historicals.

Royalty: 50% ebooks, 10% print, advance: $1,500-$2,000

Types and topics: all topics nonfiction; fiction: contemporary, general, historical, romance, suspense, women's

Types of books: audiobook, ebook, POD

Imprints: WhiteSpark (young readers), Ashberry Lane (romance), WhiteFire (nonfiction and fiction), Chrism Press (Catholic and Orthodox fiction)

Guidelines: *whitefire-publishing.com/submissions*

Tip: "Familiarize yourself with our titles and mission."

WHITESPARK PUBLISHING

13607 Bedford Rd. NE, Cumberland, MD 21502 | 866-245-2211
r.white@whitefire-publishing.com | *www.whitefire-publishing.com*
Roseanna White, managing editor

Parent company: WhiteFire Publishing

Mission statement: to engender a love of reading in kids with faith-based books

Submissions: Publishes five to ten titles per year; receives 100 submissions annually. First-time authors: 10%. Responds in three months.

Royalty: 50% ebooks, 10% print, advance: $200-$1,000

Types and topics: all topics, middle grade, picture books, YA

Types of books: audiobook, ebook, picture books, POD

Guidelines: *whitespark-publishing.com/submissions*

Tip: "Come with fresh ideas on how to reach the young readership."

WILD HEART BOOKS

14250 Hwy. 55 West, Blacksburg, SC 29702 | 704-363-0360

submissions@wildheartbooks.org | *wildheartbooks.org*

Misty M. Beller, managing editor

Mission statement: to provide the kind of exciting historical stories readers love, complete with heroes to make them swoon, strong heroines, and inspirational messages to encourage their faith

Submissions: Publishes 12 titles per year; receives 50 submissions annually. First-time authors: 10%. Length: minimum 50,000 words, ideally 55,000-75,000 words. Responds in two to three weeks. Bible: KJV.

Royalty: 40-50%, no advance

Types and topics: historical fiction: African-American, Asian, Hispanic, Native American, romance

Types of books: ebook, large print, POD

Guidelines: *www.wildheartbooks.org/submissions.html*

Tip: "Our focus is Christian historical romance, so make sure your book fits the specifics of what we prefer on our submissions page. If you don't hear back from us, within four weeks of submission, please don't hesitate to contact Misty at *misty@wildheartbooks.org.*"

WILLIAM CAREY PUBLISHING

10 W. Dry Creek Cir., Littleton, CO 80120 | 720-372-7036

submissions@WCLBooks.com | *www.missionbooks.org*

Denise Wynn, director of publishing

Parent company: Frontier Ventures

Mission statement: to publish resources that edify, equip, and empower disciples of Jesus to make disciples of Jesus

Submissions: Responds in three to six months.

Types and topics: biography, ethnography, missions, academic

Guidelines: *missionbooks.org/submissions*

Tip: "We want our books to sound like the intelligent conversation you have with friends over dinner. You may site statistics and research (like you might reference an article in a reputable source), but you are sharing it in the context of a story that makes the research matter to real people doing Kingdom work."

WINGED PUBLICATIONS

PO Box 8047, Surprise, AZ 85374 | 623-910-4279
cynthiahickey@outlook.com | www.wingedpublications.com
Cynthia Hickey, CEO, acquisitions editor
Gina Welborn, acquisitions editor
Christina Rich, acquisitions editor
Patty Smith Hall, acquisitions editor

Mission statement: Where Your Stories Take Flight
Submissions: Publishes 50 titles per year. First-time authors: 25%. Length: minimum 20,000 words. Responds in two weeks. Bible: NIV.
Royalty: 60%, no advance
Types and topics: memoir/personal narrative, humor; fiction: fantasy, historical romance, mystery, romance, romantic suspense, science fiction, suspense/thriller, teen/YA, women's
Types of books: ebook, POD
Imprints: Soaring Beyond (stories of hope, devotionals, self-help), Aisling Books (fantasy, science fiction), Jurnee Books (young adult, juvenile fiction), Gordian Books (mystery, suspense, thriller), Forget Me Not Romances (contemporary and historical romances), Take Me Away Books (women's fiction, comedy)
Guidelines: *wingedpublications.com/what-were-looking-for*
Tip: "Send the cleanest proposal you can."

WIPF AND STOCK PUBLISHERS

199 W. 8th Ave., Ste. 3, Eugene, OR 97401-2960 | 541-344-1528
rodney@wipfandstock.com | www.wipfandstock.com
Rodney Clapp, editor

Submissions: Publishes 500+ in all imprints annually. Responds in two months.
Types and topics: Bible, church history, ethics, history, ministry, philosophy, theology, academic
Types of books: ebook, offset paperback
Imprints: Resource Publications (leaders, pastors, educators), Cascade Books (academic)
Guidelines: *wipfandstock.com/submitting-a-proposal*

Tip: "It is your responsibility to submit a manuscript that has been fully copyedited by a professional copy editor."

WORTHY KIDS

6100 Tower Cir., Ste. 210, Franklin, TN 37067 | 615-221-0996
idealsinfo@hbgusa.com | *www.worthykids.com*
Rebekah Moredock, assistant editor
Peggy Schaefer, associate editor
Melinda Rathjen, senior editor

> **Parent company:** Worthy Publishing/Hachette Book Group
>
> **Mission statement:** to create books that are much more than just words and pictures—they're an opportunity for a moment of joy between a child and his or her loved one
>
> **Submissions:** Publishes 30-35 titles per year; receives 200 submissions annually. First-time authors: fewer than 10%. Length: maximum 200 words for board books, 600 words for picture books. Responds in one month. Bible: NLT.
>
> **Royalty:** sometimes offers advances, some products are flat fee
>
> **Average first print run:** 10,000
>
> **Types and topics:** holidays, board books, children, first-chapter, picture books, middle grade fiction and nonfiction
>
> **Types of books:** audiobook, board books, ebook, hardcover, offset paperback, picture books
>
> **Guidelines:** by email
>
> **Tip:** "Carefully study the types of books our house has published and submit proposals that show an understanding of the marketplace, include recent competitive titles, and identify what sets your book apart."

WORTHY PUBLISHING

6100 Tower Cir., Ste. 210, Franklin, TN 37067 | 615-932-7600
www.worthypublishing.com
Karen Longino, acquisitions editor
Beth Adams, acquisitions editor
Sean McGowan, editor and acquisitions
India Hunter, associate editor and acquisitions

> **Parent company:** Hachette Book Group
>
> **Submissions:** Publishes 36 titles per year.
>
> **Types and topics:** biography, Christian living/spirituality, contemporary issues, culture, spiritual growth, devotionals, fiction, gift

Imprints: Worthy Books (broad spectrum of genres), Worthy Kids (children, holiday magazines), Ellie Claire (gifts), Museum of the Bible Books (Bible study)

YWAM PUBLISHING

PO Box 55787, Seattle, WA 98155 | 800-922-2143
books@ywampublishing.com | *www.ywampublishing.com*
Tom Bragg, publisher

Parent company: Youth With A Mission

Types and topics: evangelism, leadership, missions, relationships, Bible studies, devotionals

Guidelines: *www.ywampublishing.com/topic.aspx?name=submission*

ZONDERKIDZ

3900 Sparks Dr. SE, Grand Rapids, MI 49512 | 616-698-6900
ZonderkidzSubmissions@harpercollins.com | *www.zonderkidz.com*
Katherine Easter, acquisitions editor

Parent company: Zondervan/HarperCollins Christian Publishing

Mission statement: to inspire young lives through imagination and innovation

Types and topics: Bibles, children, fiction, nonfiction, teen/YA

Guidelines: none

Tip: "We are seeking fresh fiction and nonfiction for children ages 0-18. Under our Zonderkidz and Zondervan imprints, we look for engaging picture books and board books, timeless storybook Bibles, faith-centric fiction from established authors, and nonfiction from key voices in the Christian sphere."

ZONDERVAN

Grand Rapids, MI and Nashville, TN
www.zondervan.com
Andy Rogers, nonfiction acquisitions editor
Carolyn McCready, executive editor
Kyle Rohane, acquisitions editor

Parent company: HarperCollins Christian Publishing

Submissions: Publishes 120 titles per year. Bible: NIV.

Types and topics: biography, Christian living/spirituality, church life, contemporary issues, family, finances, marriage, ministry, academic, Bible reference/commentaries, gift; fiction: contemporary, fantasy, historical, mystery, romance, science fiction, suspense/thriller

Imprints: Zondervan Books (nonfiction), Zondervan Reflective (leadership, ministry, faith and culture), Zondervan Fiction, Zonderkidz (children, teens), Zondervan Academic (textbooks, Bible reference), Zondervan Gift (gift books)

Guidelines: *www.harpercollinschristian.com/write-for-us*

ZONDERVAN ACADEMIC

3900 Sparks Dr. SE, Grand Rapids, MI 49512 | 616-698-6900

submissions@zondervan.com | *www.zondervanacademic.com*

Katya Covrett, executive acquisitions editor

Parent company: Zondervan/HarperCollins Christian Publishing

Mission statement: to reflect the breadth and diversity—both theological and global—within evangelical scholarship while maintaining our commitment to the heart of orthodox Christianity

Submissions: Responds in six weeks or not interested. Bible: NIV.

Types and topics: academic, Bible reference/commentaries

Types of books: ebook, hardcover, offset paperback

Guidelines: *www.harpercollinschristian.com/authors/manuscript-information*

ZONDERVAN REFLECTIVE

3900 Sparks Dr. SE, Grand Rapids, MI 49512 | 616-698-6900

submissions@zondervan.com | *www.zondervan.com/zondervanreflective*

Parent company: Zondervan/HarperCollins Christian Publishing

Mission statement: to provide guidance and inspiration for effective leadership in business and ministry

Submissions: Responds in six weeks or not interested. Bible: NIV.

Types and topics: contemporary issues, culture, leadership, ministry, nonfiction

Types of books: ebook, hardcover, offset paperback

Guidelines: *www.harpercollinschristian.com/authors/manuscript-information*

Tip: "The authors are expected to have demonstrable expertise on the subject being addressed."

PART 2

INDEPENDENT
BOOK
PUBLISHING

2

INDEPENDENT BOOK PUBLISHERS

PUBLISHING A BOOK YOURSELF NO LONGER CARRIES THE STIGMA self-publishing has had in the past—if you do it right. Even some well-published writers are now hybrid authors, with independently published books alongside their royalty books. Others have built their readerships with traditional publishers, then moved to independent publishing where it is possible to make more money per sale.

Independent book publishers require the author to pay for part of the publishing costs or to buy a certain number of books. They call themselves by a variety of names, such as book packager, cooperative publisher, self-publisher, custom publisher, subsidy publisher, or simply someone who helps authors get their books printed. Services vary from including different levels of editing and proofreading to printing your manuscript as is.

Whenever you pay for any part of the production of your book, you are entering into a nontraditional relationship. Some independent publishers also offer a form of royalty publishing, so be sure you understand the contract they give you before signing it.

Some independent publishers will publish any book, as long as the author is willing to pay for it. Others are as selective about what they publish as a royalty publisher is. Some independent publishers will do as much promotion as a royalty publisher—for a fee. Others do none at all.

If you are unsuccessful in placing your book with a royalty publisher but feel strongly about seeing it published, an independent publisher can make printing your book easier and often less expensive than doing it yourself. POD, as opposed to a print run of 1,000 books or more, could save you upfront money, although the price per copy is higher. Having your manuscript produced only as an ebook is also a less-expensive option.

Entries in this chapter are for information only, not an endorsement of publishers. For every complaint about a publisher, several other authors may sing the praises of it. Before you sign with any company, get more than one bid to determine whether the terms you are offered are competitive.

A legitimate independent publisher will provide a list of former clients as references. Also buy a couple of the publisher's previous books to check the quality of the work: covers, bindings, typesetting, etc. See if the books currently are available through any of the major online retailers.

Get answers before committing yourself. You may also want someone in the book-publishing industry to review your contract before you sign it. Some experts listed in the "Editorial Services" chapter review contracts.

If you decide not to use an independent publisher but do the work yourself, at least hire an editor, proofreader, cover designer, and interior typesetter-designer. The "Editorial Services" and "Design and Production Services" chapters will help you locate professionals with skills in these areas, as well as printing companies. Plus the "Distribution Services" and "Publicity and Marketing Services" chapters can help you solve one of the biggest problems of independent publishing: getting your books to readers.

ACW PRESS

4854 Aster Dr., Nashville, TN 37211 | 615-331-8668
acwriters@aol.com | *www.acwpress.com*
Reg A. Forder, publisher

> **Types:** gift books, hardcover, offset paperback, POD
> **Services:** copyediting, design, packages of services, proofreading, substantive editing
> **Production time:** two to four months
> **Books per year:** 30
> **Tip:** "We offer a high-quality publishing alternative to help Christian authors get their material into print. High standards, high quality. If authors have a built-in audience, they have the best chance to make self-publishing a success."

ALTEN INK

1888 Montara Way, San Jacinto, CA 92583 | 951-327-3698
AltenInk3@gmail.com | *www.AltenInk.blogspot.com*
Deborah L. Alten, publisher

> **Types:** ebooks, offset paperback, picture books
> **Services:** à la carte options, design, online bookstore, packages of services
> **Production time:** six months
> **Tip:** "Email us. You will get a quicker response."

AMPELOS PRESS

951 Anders Rd., Lansdale, PA 19446 | 484-991-8581
mbagnull@aol.com | *writehisanswer.com/ampelospress*
Marlene Bagnull, publisher

> **Types:** ebooks, offset paperback, POD
> **Services:** copyediting, design, manuscript evaluation, proofreading, substantive editing
> **Production time:** six months
> **Books per year:** two
> **Tip:** "Especially interested in issues fiction and nonfiction, as well as books about missions and the needs of children. Author pays a one-time fee, maintains all rights, and receives 100% royalty from Amazon KDP."

BELIEVERS BOOK SERVICES

2329 Farragut Ave., Colorado Springs, CO 80907 | 719-641-7862
dave@believersbookservices.com | *believersbookservices.com*
Dave Sheets, owner

> **Types:** ebooks, gift books, hardcover, paperback, picture books, POD
> **Services:** à la carte options, author websites, copyediting, design, distribution, manuscript evaluation, packages of services, proofreading, substantive editing
> **Production time:** three months
> **Books per year:** 45-50
> **Tip:** "Start thinking about strategy for publishing, marketing, and launching as soon as possible in the process. This strategy process will help produce a stronger book."

BK ROYSTON PUBLISHING

PO Box 4321, Jeffersonville, IN 47131 | 502-802-5385
bkroystonpublishing@gmail.com | *www.bkroystonpublishing.com*
Julia A. Royston, CEO

> **Types:** ebooks, hardcover, offset paperback, picture books
> **Services:** à la carte options, copyediting, design, distribution, manuscript evaluation, online bookstore, packages of services, proofreading
> **Production time:** three months
> **Books per year:** 40-50
> **Tip:** "1. Passion for the message of the book. 2. Actively participate in social media 3. Must be willing to market and promote your book."

BOOKBABY

7905 N. Crescent Blvd., Pennsauken, NJ 08110 | 877-961-6878
info@bookbaby.com | *www.bookbaby.com*

Types: comic book, ebooks, gift books, hardcover, offset paperback, picture books, POD
Services: author websites, copyediting, design, distribution, manuscript evaluation, online bookstore, proofreading, social-media ads, substantive editing
Production time: as quick as five days
Tip: Has ebook and printed-book distribution network for self-published authors around the globe.

BROWN CHRISTIAN PRESS

16250 Knoll Trail Dr., Ste. 205, Dallas, TX 75248 | 972-381-0009
publishing@brownbooks.com | *www.brownchristianpress.com*

Types: audiobooks, ebooks, gift books, hardcover, paperback
Services: author websites, copyediting, design, distribution, ghostwriting, indexing, marketing, proofreading, substantive editing
Production time: six months
Tip: "We are a relationship publisher and work with our authors from beginning to end in the journey of publishing."

CALLED WRITERS CHRISTIAN PUBLISHING

1900 Rice Mine Rd. N. 401, Tuscaloosa, AL 35406 | 205-872-4509
shannon@calledwriters.com | *CalledWriters.com*
Shannon McKinney, relationship builder

Types: offset paperback, POD
Services: à la carte options, copyediting, design, manuscript evaluation, marketing, packages of services, proofreading, substantive editing
Production time: six months
Books per year: two
Also does: royalty contracts
Tip: "God will open the right doors for you at the right time. Don't give up."

CARPENTER'S SON PUBLISHING

307 Verde Meadow Dr., Franklin, TN 37067 | 615-472-1128
larry@christianbookservices.com | *carpenterssonpublishing.com*
Larry Carpenter, president-CEO, editor

Types: audiobooks, ebooks, gift books, hardcover, offset paperback, picture books, POD
Services: à la carte options, author websites, copyediting, design, distribution, indexing, manuscript evaluation, marketing, promotional materials, proofreading, substantive editing
Production time: three to six months
Books per year: 100
Tip: "Make sure someone is selling your book to the bookstores."

CASTLE GATE PRESS

244 E. Glendale Rd., St. Louis, MO 63119 | 314-962-1940
p.wheeler@castlegatepress.com | *castlegatepress.com*
Phyllis Wheeler, owner

Types: audiobooks, ebooks, POD
Services: à la carte options, copyediting, design, manuscript evaluation, proofreading, substantive editing
Production time: depends on manuscript editing needs
Books per year: one or two
Tip: "Castle Gate Press was a traditional publisher from 2013-2018. One of our books is an Amazon genre bestseller, and another won a Selah Award for Christian fiction in the speculative category. Yet another was a finalist for Selah and also for the Realm Award, and another a finalist for the Grace Award. In short, we provide award-winning editing."

CHRISTIAN FAITH PUBLISHING

832 Park Ave., Meadville, PA 16335 | 800-955-3794
Chris@christianfaithpublishing.com | *www.Christianfaithpublishing.com*
Chris Rutherford, president

Types: ebooks, hardcover, offset paperback, POD
Services: à la carte options, copyediting, design, distribution, indexing, manuscript evaluation, marketing, packages of services, promotional materials
Production time: 8-10 months
Books per year: 1,200
Also does: royalty contracts
Tip: "Be mindful of the fact that it is quite challenging to publish a book and have commercial success."

CLM PUBLISHING CO. LTD.

PO Box 1217, Grand Cayman, Cayman Islands KY-11108 | 345-926-2507
production@clmpublishing.com | *www.clmpublishing.com*
Karen E. Chin, managing editor

Types: ebooks, gift books, hardcover, offset paperback, picture books,
POD
Services: à la carte options, author websites, copyediting, design,
distribution, manuscript evaluation, marketing, online bookstore,
packages of services, promotional materials, proofreading,
substantive editing
Production time: three months
Also does: royalty contracts
Tip: "Even after many rejection letters, never stop writing. There is
always a publisher for you."

COLEMAN JONES PRESS

info@colemanjonespress.com
Tracee and Ross Jones, owners

Types: audiobooks, curriculum, ebooks, hardcover, picture books,
POD
Services: author websites, design, distribution, marketing, packages of
services, promotional materials
Production time: three to six months
Tip: "Write for the sake of getting the gospel out, not for the money.
When choosing a cover or illustrator, make sure your design looks
like something that is in major retail stores."

COVENANT BOOKS

11661 Hwy. 707, Murrells Inlet, SC 29576 | 843-507-8373
contact@covenantbooks.com | *www.covenantbooks.com*
Denice Hunter, president

Types: ebooks, hardcover, offset paperback, POD
Services: à la carte options, copyediting, design, distribution,
marketing, online bookstore, packages of services
Production time: six months
Books per year: 1,000
Also does: royalty contracts
Tip: "Publishing a book can be a fun and enlightening process. Take
your time, and choose a publisher you feel comfortable with."

CREATIVE ENTERPRISES STUDIO

1507 Shirley Way, Ste. A, Bedford, TX 76022-6737 | 817-312-7393
AcreativeShop@aol.com | *CreativeEnterprisesStudio.com*
Mary Hollingsworth, publisher

> **Types:** audiobooks, ebooks, gift books, hardcover, offset paperback, picture books, POD
> **Services:** author websites, book trailer, coaching, copyediting, design, ghostwriting, marketing, proofreading, substantive editing, warehousing
> **Production time:** six months
> **Books per year:** ten
> **Tip:** "Contact us by email to set a phone conference to discuss your work before proceeding otherwise."

CREDO HOUSE PUBLISHERS

2200 Boyd Ct. NE, Grand Rapids, MI 49525-6714
publish@credocommunications.net | *www.credohousepublishers.com*
Timothy J. Beals, publisher

> **Types:** offset paperback
> **Services:** à la carte options, author websites, copyediting, design, distribution, indexing, manuscript evaluation, marketing, online bookstore, packages of services, promotional materials, proofreading, substantive editing
> **Production time:** three months
> **Books per year:** 30
> **Tip:** "Come prepared. Be persistent. Get published."

DCTS PUBLISHING

PO Box 40216, Santa Barbara, CA 93140 | 805-570-3168
dennis@dctspub.com | *www.dctspub.com*
Dennis Hamilton, publisher

> **Types:** ebooks, offset paperback, picture books
> **Services:** design, manuscript evaluation, promotional materials, proofreading, substantive editing
> **Production time:** three months
> **Books per year:** five
> **Tip:** "Place as many eyes on your manuscript as possible."

DEEP RIVER BOOKS, LLC

PO Box 310, Sisters, OR 97759 | 541-549-1139
andy@deepriverbooks.com | *www.deepriverbooks.com*
Andy Carmichael, publisher

Types: audiobooks, ebooks, hardcover, offset paperback, POD
Services: copyediting, design, distribution, manuscript evaluation, marketing, online bookstore, packages of services, promotional materials, substantive editing
Production time: 9-14 months
Books per year: 30-35
Also does: royalty contracts
Tip: "Check our website on how we work with authors before you submit."

DEEPER REVELATION BOOKS

PO Box 4260, Cleveland, TN 37320-4260 | 423-478-2843
pastormikeshreve@gmail.com | *www.deeperrevelationbooks.org*
Mike Shreve, founder and president

Types: ebooks, gift books, hardcover, offset paperback, picture books, POD
Services: author websites, copyediting, design, distribution, manuscript evaluation, marketing, online bookstore, promotional materials, proofreading, substantive editing
Production time: four months
Books per year: 15
Imprints: Deeper Revelation Books (nonfiction), Pure Heart Publications (fiction), Children of Promise (children), Pivotal Publications (success and social issues)
Tip: "One book that is well written and published with excellence can change the world."

DESTINY IMAGE PUBLISHERS

167 Walnut Bottom Rd., Shippensburg, PA 17257 | 717-532-3040
manuscripts@norimediagroup.com | *norimediagroup.com/pages/publish-with-us*
Mykela Krieg, executive acquisitions director

Types: ebooks, paperback
Services: copyediting, design, manuscript evaluation, marketing, proofreading, substantive editing
Production time: 12 months
Tip: Requires prepurchase of 500 to 3,000 copies. "Focuses on Spirit-

empowered themes: supernatural God encounters, healing/ deliverance, prophecy and prophetic ministry, gifts of the Holy Spirit, prayer and intercession, the presence and glory of God, and dreams/dream interpretation."

EABOOKS PUBLISHING

1567 Thornhill Cir., Oviedo, FL 32765 | 407-712-3431
Cheri@eabookspublishing.com | *www.eabookspublishing.com*
Cheri Cowell, founder and CEO

> **Types:** audiobook, ebook, gift book, hardcover, picture book, POD
> **Services:** author websites, copyediting, design, distribution, manuscript evaluation, marketing, packages of services, promotional materials, proofreading, substantive editing
> **Production time:** five to six months
> **Books per year:** 50
> **Also does:** royalty contracts
> **Tip:** "Allow us to help you understand your options, and hear our heart for you and your project."

EBOOK LISTING SERVICES

PO Box 57, Glenwood, MD 21738 | 443-280-5077
sales@taegais.com | *ebooklistingservices.com*
Amy Deardon, CEO

> **Types:** audiobooks, ebooks, POD
> **Services:** à la carte options, design, distribution, marketing, packages of services, promotional materials
> **Production time:** one to three months
> **Books per year:** 20
> **Tip:** "We empower independent authors to become successful. Unlike most other independent publishers, we set you up so you are the publisher, rather than publishing through the independent company. You can create your own publishing company name and logo, and we help you with that. You remain fully in charge of all decisions, rights, and profits from start to forever. Once your book is published, you can buy as few or as many books as you want at the lowest printer's price (a 200-page book costs less than $3.50); and books are delivered in a week or two through Amazon. We also have additional packages that can list your book with the Library of Congress and help you rank higher on Amazon's search engines so readers can actually find your book and buy it. We provide you with ownership of your book and work with you to make that succeed."

ELECTRIC MOON PUBLISHING, LLC

PO Box 466, Stromsburg, NE 68666 | 402-366-2033
laree@emoonpublishing.com | www.emoonpublishing.com
Laree Lindburg, owner-manager

> **Types:** audiobooks, ebooks, gift books, hardcover, offset paperback, picture books, POD
> **Services:** à la carte options, author websites, copyediting, design, distribution, manuscript evaluation, packages of services, promotional materials, proofreading, substantive editing
> **Production time:** 9-12 months
> **Books per year:** 10-12
> **Tip:** "Ask questions. We are glad to provide an explanation."

ESSENCE PUBLISHING

20 Hanna Ct., Belleville, ON K8P 5J2, Canada | 800-238-6376, 613-962-2360
s.brunton@essence-publishing.com | www.essence-publishing.com
Sherrill Brunton, publishing manager

> **Types:** ebooks, gift books, offset paperback, picture books, POD
> **Services:** copyediting, design, distribution, indexing, manuscript evaluation, marketing, online bookstore, promotional materials, proofreading, substantive editing
> **Production time:** three months
> **Books per year:** 100-150
> **Tip:** "Submit a copy of your manuscript for your free evaluation."

FAIRWAY PRESS

5450 N. Dixie Hwy., Lima, OH 45807-9559 | 800-241-4056, 419-227-1818
david@csspub.com | www.fairwaypress.com
David Runk, publisher

> **Types:** ebooks, hardcover, offset paperback, POD
> **Services:** copyediting, design, proofreading
> **Production time:** six to nine months
> **Books per year:** 10-15
> **Tip:** "This is the subsidy division of CSS Publishing Company. No longer does color illustrations or four-color books."

FAITH BOOKS & MORE

PO Box 1024, Athens, OH 45701 | 678-232-6156
publishing@faithbooksandmore.com | www.faithbooksandmore.com
Nicole Antoinette Smith, owner

Types: hardcover, offset paperback, POD
Services: copyediting, design, manuscript evaluation, proofreading
Production time: three months
Books per year: five
Tip: "Write, rewrite, write, and rewrite again until you're 100% satisfied with your manuscript."

FIESTA PUBLISHING

1219 E. Colter St. #16, Phoenix, AZ 85014 | 602-795-5868
julie@fiestapublishing.com | *www.fiestapublishing.com*
Julie Castro, owner

Types: ebooks, POD
Services: à la carte options, copyediting, design, distribution, marketing, online bookstore, packages of services, promotional materials, proofreading, substantive editing
Production time: 6-12 weeks
Tip: "It usually takes longer than one thinks to publish a quality book."

FILLED BOOKS

529 County Road 31, Millry, AL 36558 | 251-754-9335
editor@empoweredpublications.com | *www.filledbooks.com*
Bridgett Henson, book coach

Types: ebooks, hardcover, POD
Services: copyediting, design, distribution, manuscript evaluation, marketing, packages of services, promotional materials, proofreading, substantive editing
Production time: four weeks
Tip: Free publishing for Christian ministers with the purchase of 250 paperbacks.

FIRESIDE PRESS

contact@firesidepress.com | *firesidepress.com* ·
Suzanne Parrott, president and lead designer

Types: audiobooks, ebooks, gift books, hardcover, offset paperback, picture books, POD
Services: author websites, copyediting, design, distribution, indexing, manuscript evaluation, marketing, packages of services, promotional materials, proofreading, substantive editing
Production time: six months to two years
Tip: "Fireside Press offers professional, personal, and affordable services every author deserves."

FRUITBEARER PUBLISHING, LLC

PO Box 777, Georgetown, DE 19947 | 302-856-6649
cfa@candyabbott.com | *www.fruitbearer.com*
Elizabeth Boerner, author liaison

> **Types:** ebooks, gift books, hardcover, offset paperback, picture books, POD
>
> **Services:** à la carte options, copyediting, design, distribution, manuscript evaluation, marketing, online bookstore, packages of services, promotional materials, proofreading, substantive editing
>
> **Production time:** four to six months
>
> **Books per year:** 12+
>
> **Also does:** royalty contracts
>
> **Tip:** "We're looking for manuscripts that would receive a nod of approval from God. The book doesn't have to be religious, but it does need to be wholesome. Fruitbearer's chief concern is to keep in step with the Holy Spirit and exemplify the Fruit of the Spirit. If you're looking for a publisher who will walk you through the publishing process and not put you on an assembly line, we might be a good fit."

FUSION HYBRID PUBLISHING

PO Box 206, Nesbit, MS 38651 | 901-590-6584
victoria@endgamepress.com | *www.fusionhybridpublishing.com*
Alice, acquisitions

> **Types:** audiobooks, ebooks, gospel tracts, hardcover, offset paperback, picture books, POD
>
> **Services:** à la carte options, copyediting, design, distribution, indexing, manuscript evaluation, marketing, online bookstore, packages of services, promotional materials, proofreading, substantive editing
>
> **Production time:** 6-12 months
>
> **Books per year:** three to four
>
> **Tip:** "Fusion is a great option for those who are excited to get to market faster than traditional houses and have a great audience already."

HEALTHY LIFE PRESS

12838 Southampton Cir., Bristol, VA 24202 | 877-331-2766
healthylifepress@gmail.com | *www.HealthyLifePress.com*
Dr. David Biebel, publisher

Types: ebooks, gift books, hardcover, picture books, POD
Services: copyediting, design, manuscript evaluation, online bookstore, promotional materials, proofreading, substantive editing
Production time: three to six months
Books per year: 8-12
Tip: "Healthy Life Press is a cooperative (author-subsidized) and collaborative company, sharing costs and net proceeds equitably. We welcome well-written, edited, and ready-for-design manuscripts on topics the author is passionate about and about which he or she is able to provide a new, different, unique, or original perspective. Submit book proposal plus three sample chapters. Inquiries and manuscripts by email only. Do not inquire by phone, except for clarification."

HONEYCOMB HOUSE PUBLISHING, LLC

315 3rd St., New Cumberland, PA 17070 | 215-767-9600
dave@fessendens.net | *www.davefessenden.com/honeycomb-house-publishing-llc*
David E. Fessenden, proprietor and publisher

Types: audiobooks, ebooks, hardcover, offset paperback
Services: à la carte options, author websites, copyediting, design, distribution, manuscript evaluation, marketing, online bookstore, packages of services, promotional materials, proofreading, substantive editing
Production time: 6-12 months
Books per year: one or two
Tip: "A project is more likely to be successful if you have a complete manuscript and a clear idea of what services you need to have done. If you are not clear on these points, I can consult with you to firm up your plan."

IMMORTALISE

PO Box 656, Noarlunga Centre, SA 5168 Australia
toastercide@gmail.com | *www.immortalise.com.au*
Ben Morton, editor

Types: ebooks, hardcover, offset paperback, picture books
Services: à la carte options, copyediting, design, manuscript evaluation, online bookstore, packages of services, promotional materials, proofreading, substantive editing
Production time: varies
Tip: "All our services are optional and there is no cost for enquiries. We will publish any book so long as the content is not likely to get anyone sued."

INSCRIPT BOOKS

PO Box 611, Bladensburg, MD 20710 | 240-342-3293
inscript@dovechristianpublishers.com | inscriptpublishing.com
Raenita Wiggins, acquisitions editor

> **Types:** ebooks, hardcover, offset paperback, picture books, POD
> **Services:** à la carte options, copyediting, design, distribution, indexing, marketing, online bookstore, packages of services, proofreading, substantive editing
> **Production time:** one to two months
> **Books per year:** ten
> **Tip:** "We receive new proposals via our online form only. Carefully review publishing guidelines on website."

MORGAN JAMES FAITH

5 Penn Plaza, 23rd Floor, New York City, NY 10001 | 212-655-5470
terry@morganjamespublishing.com | www.morganjamespublishing.com
W. Terry Whalin, acquisition editor

> **Types:** audiobooks, ebooks, hardcover, offset paperback, picture books, POD
> **Services:** design, distribution, marketing, online bookstore, promotional materials
> **Production time:** three to six months
> **Books per year:** 25-30
> **Also does:** royalty publishing
> **Tip:** "General-market publisher with a Christian division. Our books have been on *The New York Times* bestseller list more than twenty-five times (broad distribution). For nonfiction, requires authors to purchase 2,500 copies at print costs plus $2 over lifetime of agreement. Pays 20-30% royalties on sales; pays small advance. Email proposal with sample chapters or full manuscript. Only 30% of authors have agents."

NORDSKOG PUBLISHING

4562 Westinghouse St., Ste. E, Ventura, CA 93003 | 805-642-2070
jerry@nordskogpublishing.com | nordskogpublishing.com
Michelle Shelfer, editor

> **Types:** hardcover, paperback
> **Services:** copyediting, design, marketing
> **Tip:** "Looking for the best in sound theological and applied Christian faith books, both nonfiction and fiction."

PARSON PLACE PRESS, LLC

PO Box 8277, Mobile, AL 36689-0277 | 251-643-6985

MLWhite@parsonplacepress.com | www.parsonplacepress.com

Michael L. White, founder and managing editor

> **Types:** ebooks, hardcover, offset paperback
>
> **Services:** design, distribution, online bookstore, proofreading, substantive editing
>
> **Production time:** three months
>
> **Books per year:** two to four
>
> **Also does:** royalty contracts
>
> **Tip:** "Read the Author Guidelines and FAQ pages on the publisher's website before contacting anyone or submitting anything at Parson Place Press."

REDEMPTION PRESS

PO Box 427, Enumclaw, WA 98022 | 360-226-3488

Athena@redemption-press.com | www.redemption-press.com

Micah Juntanen, director of acquisitions

> **Types:** audiobooks, devotional journals, ebooks, gift books, hardcover, offset paperback, picture books, POD
>
> **Services:** à la carte options, author websites, coaching, copyediting, design, distribution, indexing, manuscript evaluation, marketing, online bookstore, promotional materials, proofreading, substantive editing
>
> **Production time:** 4-12 months
>
> **Books per year:** 150
>
> **Also does:** She Writes for Him Bootcamps and Conferences to train and equip
>
> **Tip:** "Always have a professional editor review your work and then have the humility to take their advice. Even seasoned writers need developmental editing so the message has the best chance to make an impact. Don't cut this corner if you're serious about glorifying God in your writing. Do your due diligence to find out the best option for you and your manuscript. Pray for wisdom and discernment in your publishing journey."

SALVATION PUBLISHER AND MARKETING GROUP

PO Box 40860, Santa Barbara, CA 93140 | 805-252-9822

opalmaedailey@aol.com

Opal Mae Dailey, editor

Types: ebooks, hardcover, offset paperback
Services: copyediting, design, manuscript evaluation, proofreading, substantive editing
Production time: six to nine months
Books per year: five to seven
Tip: "Turning taped messages into book form for pastors is a specialty of ours. We do not accept any manuscript we would be ashamed to put our name on."

SERMON TO BOOK

424 W. Bakerview Rd., Ste. 105 #215, Bellingham, WA 98226 | 360-223-1877
info@sermontobook.com | *www.sermontobook.com*
Caleb Breakey, lead book director

Types: audiobooks, ebooks, offset paperback, POD
Services: author websites, copyediting, design, distribution, indexing, manuscript evaluation, marketing, online bookstore, packages of services, promotional materials, proofreading, substantive editing
Production time: seven to nine months
Books per year: 60
Tip: "Check out our materials at *SermonToBook.com.*"

STONE OAK PUBLISHING

PO Box 2011, Friendswood, TX 77549 | 832-569-4282
stoneoakpublishing@gmail.com | *stoneoakpublishing.com*
Karen Porter, acquisitions

Types: ebooks, hardcover, offset paperback, POD
Services: à la carte options, copyediting, design, distribution, indexing, manuscript evaluation, marketing, packages of services, promotional materials, proofreading, substantive editing
Production time: six to eight months
Books per year: ten
Also does: royalty contracts
Tip: "Send us a well-thought-out email detailing the information about your book."

STRONG TOWER PUBLISHING

PO Box 973, Milesburg, PA 16863 | 814-206-6778
strongtowerpubs@aol.com | *www.strongtowerpublishing.com*
Heidi L. Nigro, publisher

Types: ebooks, POD

Services: copyediting, design, manuscript evaluation, online bookstore, proofreading, substantive editing

Production time: three to four months

Books per year: one or two

Tip: Specializes in books on end-times topics from the prewrath rapture perspective. Pays 25% royalty on sales.

TEACH SERVICES, INC.

11 Quartermaster Cir., Fort Oglethorpe, GA 30742-3886 | 800-367-1844
T.Hullquist@TEACHServices.com | www.teachservices.com
Timothy Hullquist, author advisor

Types: ebooks, gift books, hardcover, offset paperback, picture books, POD

Services: à la carte options, author websites, copyediting, design, distribution, indexing, manuscript evaluation, marketing, online bookstore, packages of services, promotional materials, proofreading, substantive editing

Production time: one to four months

Also does: royalty contracts

Tip: "We specialize in marketing our titles to Seventh-day Adventists."

TMP BOOKS

3 Central Plaza, Ste. 307, Rome, GA 30161
info@tmpbooks.com | www.TMPbooks.com
Tracy Ruckman, publisher

Types: audiobooks, ebooks, hardcover, picture books, POD

Services: à la carte options, author websites, copyediting, design, distribution, manuscript evaluation, marketing, packages of services, promotional materials, proofreading, substantive editing

Production time: six months

Books per year: 12-24

Tip: "Study published books aimed at your target market; know your market."

TRACT PLANET

990 Berry Leaf Ct., Apopka, FL 32703 | 877-778-7228
support@tractplanet.com | www.tractplanet.com
Andy Lawniczak, owner and designer

Type: gospel tracts

Services: design, promotional materials

Production time: varies

Tip: "We focus on Gospel tracts that follow the Way of the Master method of evangelism."

TRAIL MEDIA

PO Box 1285, Orange, CA 92856

admin@ChisholmTrailMedia.com | *www.chisholmtrailmedia.com*
Christine "CJ" Simpson, director of publishing

Types: ebooks, gift books, picture books, POD

Services: à la carte options, copyediting, manuscript evaluation, marketing, packages of services, promotional materials, proofreading, substantive editing

Production time: negotiable

Tip: "Our goal is to help new authors publish their work by coordinating the services needed with experts in the field and publishing in a co-op fashion under the Trail Media imprint, so 100% of the revenue generated goes to ministry of the authors. In many cases, we find scholarships and grants to help missionaries and those in the persecuted church. Trail Media is a ministry of modified tentmaking models."

TRILOGY CHRISTIAN PUBLISHING

PO Box A, Santa Ana, CA 92711 | 855-214-2665
www.trilogy.tv

Types: ebooks, hardcover, POD

Services: copyediting, design, illustrations, marketing, online bookstore

Also does: royalty contracts

Tip: "The Trinity Broadcasting Family of Networks is blazing a trail worldwide, with fresh, innovative programs that entertain, inspire, and change lives. In addition to the 8,000 cable and satellite affiliates that reach over 100 million homes across America and every inhabited continent, the TBN Family of Networks will continue to aggressively expand their reach as they deliver content across all social media and digital platforms. As part of your book release TBN will use its social media platforms such as Facebook (1.2 million Likes), Twitter (80,000 Followers) and Instagram (133,000 Followers) to promote it. From there, all of the social media strength of Trilogy Christian Publishing will be deployed."

TULPEN PUBLISHING
11043 Depew St., Westminster, CO 80020 | 303-438-7276
tulpenpublishing@gmail.com | *TulpenPublishing.com*
Sandi Rog, acquisitions editor
>**Types:** ebooks, POD
>**Services:** copyediting, design, distribution, manuscript evaluation, marketing, online bookstore, proofreading, substantive editing
>**Production time:** 12-20 months
>**Tip:** Only accepts submissions via email. See the website for submission guidelines.

VIDE PRESS
videpress.com
Tom Frieling, publisher
>**Types:** ebooks, paperback
>**Services:** copyediting, design, distribution, marketing, proofreading
>**Tip:** "We are always searching for new voices, articulate Christian writers who have the courage to confront the issues challenging today's culture and our faith."

WESTBOW PRESS
1663 Liberty Dr., Bloomington, IN 47403 | 866-928-1240
www.westbowpress.com
>**Types:** audiobooks, ebooks, gift books, hardcover, offset paperback, POD
>**Services:** book trailer, copyediting, design, distribution, illustrations, indexing, manuscript evaluation, marketing, Spanish translation, substantive editing
>**Tip:** Independent publishing division of Thomas Nelson and Zondervan, HarperCollins Christian Publishing.

WORD ALIVE PRESS
119 De Boets St., Winnipeg, MB R2J 3R9, Canada | 866-967-3782
jen@wordalivepress.ca | *www.wordalivepress.ca*
Jen Jandavs-Hedlin
>**Types:** ebooks, gift books, hardcover, offset paperback, POD
>**Services:** copyediting, design, distribution, marketing, online bookstore, packages of services
>**Production time:** four to five months
>**Tip:** "We understand the Canadian Christian market, and our authors

benefit from that expertise. When working with Word Alive Press, you will have access to the same supply-chain distribution that traditional publishers use to help you reach the widest audience possible with your message."

XULON PRESS

2301 Lucien Way, Ste. 415, Maitland, FL 32751 | 407-339-4217, 866-381-2665
www.xulonpress.com
Donald Newman, executive director of publishing

> **Types:** ebooks, hardcover, offset paperback, POD
> **Services:** à la carte options, book trailer, copyediting, design, ghostwriting, illustrations, manuscript evaluation, marketing, online bookstore, packages of services, promotional materials, substantive editing
> **Production time:** three to six months

ZOË LIFE CHRISTIAN COMMUNICATIONS

PO Box 871066, Canton, MI 48187 | 734-578-6703
sabrina.adams@zoelifepub.com | *www.zoelifebooks.org*
Sabrina Adams, publisher

> **Types:** ebooks, hardcover, offset paperback, picture books
> **Services:** à la carte options, author websites, copyediting, design, distribution, manuscript evaluation, marketing, online bookstore, packages of services, proofreading, substantive editing
> **Production time:** three to six months
> **Books per year:** 12-24
> **Tip:** "Plan Plan Plan then write."

Note: See "Editorial Services" and "Publicity and Marketing Services" for help with these needs.

DESIGN AND PRODUCTION SERVICES

829 DESIGN | LINNÉ GARRETT
8749 Cortina Cir., Roseville, CA 95678-2940 | 916-581-1777
linne@829design.com | *www.829design.com*

> **Contact:** email, phone, website contact form
> **Services:** book-cover design, book-interior design, ebook conversion, typesetting, website design
> **Charges:** custom, flat fee
> **Credentials/experience:** "For over 20 years we have been successfully delivering creative design agency services for niche brands, ambitious startups, small businesses and private clients worldwide. 829 was founded in 2000 by Linné Garrett, whose passion for print and publication design naturally led 829 into the realm of digital design. Today, we offer carefully considered bespoke marketing and design solutions tailor-made to your needs. We strive to be strategic, smart and special. Exceptional quality of thought goes into everything we do. Our in-house boutique design agency services include brand positioning, visual brand identity, print design, book + book cover design, bespoke web design, packaging design and more. If you wish to discuss a new project, please email a brief outline of your requirements to hello@829design.com, and we'll arrange a mutually convenient time for a call. We are a Christian based, woman-owned small business utilizing our unique expertise and creative talents to further the Kingdom of Christ. We would be honored to work with you!"

AUTHOR SUPPORT SERVICES | RUSSELL SHERRARD
Carmichael, CA | 916-967-7251
russellsherrard@reagan.com | *www.sherrardsebookresellers.com/WordPress/author-support-services-the-authors-place-to-get-help*

> **Contact:** email

Services: book-cover design, ebook conversion, pdf creation

Charges: flat fee

Credentials/experience: "Writing and editing since 2009; currently providing freelance services for multiple clients."

BACK•DOOR DESIGN

backdoordesign99@gmail.com | backdoordesign99.wixsite.com/info

Contact: email, website contact form

Services: book-cover design, book-interior design, ebook conversion, illustrations, typesetting

Charges: custom, flat fee

Credentials/experience: "At back • door DESIGN, our mission is to create high-quality book designs at DIY prices. We are all about book design, from front cover to back cover and everything in between. Adobe Certified Associate in Print & Digital Publication Using Adobe InDesign."

BELIEVERS BOOK SERVICES | DAVE SHEETS

2329 Farragut Ave., Colorado Springs, CO 80907 | 719-641-7862

dave@believersbookservices.com | www.believersbookservices.com

Contact: email

Services: book-cover design, book-interior design, ebook conversion, illustrations, printing, typesetting, website design

Charges: custom

Credentials/experience: "Our team has decades of experience in traditional publishing (Tyndale, Multnomah, Harvest House, NavPress), book wholesaling (STL Distribution), book distribution (Advocate Distribution Solutions), book printing (Bethany Press, Snowfall Press), book retailing (Glen Eyrie Bookstore), and independent publishing (Believers Press, BelieversBookServices). We know how to help our clients achieve their goals, while maintaining control over their own book project. We have helped hundreds of authors successfully publish, both in the United States, and around the world."

BETHANY PRESS INTERNATIONAL

6820 W. 115th St., Bloomington, MN 55438 | 888-717-7400

info@bethanypress.com | www.bethanypress.com

Contact: email, phone, website contact form

Service: printing

Charges: flat fee

Credentials/experience: Printer for the majority of Christian publishing houses since 1997. "We partner with publishers and ministries to create, produce, and distribute millions of life-changing Christian books each year. We invest our proceeds in training and sending missionaries through Bethany International."

BLUE LEAF BOOK SCANNING

618 Crowsnest Dr., Ballwin, MN 63021 | 314-606-9322
blue.leaf.it@gmail.com | *www.blueleaf-book-scanning.com*

Contact: email, phone, website contact form
Services: audiobook, document scanning, ebook conversion
Charges: flat fee
Credentials/experience: The first book-scanning service for consumers. Accurate optical character recognition (more than 99.6% accurate on ideal conditions) with excellent format retention. Can scan nearly 200 languages.

BOOK WHISPERS

Capalaba, QLD 4157, Australia | 07 3167 6513
info@bookwhispers.com.au | *bookwhispers.com.au/page/home*

Contact: phone, website contact form
Services: book-cover design, book-interior design, promotional materials, typesetting

BREADBOX CREATIVE | ERYN LYNUM

1437 N. Denver Ave. #167, Loveland, CO 80538 | 970-308-3654
eryn@breadboxcreative.com | *www.breadboxcreative.com/creators*

Contact: website contact form
Service: website design
Charges: flat fee
Credentials/experience: "At Breadbox Creative, we have more than twenty years of experience in web design. The owner, Eryn Lynum, is an author herself and marries her passion for writing with her passion for web design to come alongside writers and speakers and help them further spread the messages God has laid on their hearts. Breadbox Creative works with businesses, writers, and speakers by creating professional WordPress websites, as well as assisting with SEO and social-media platforms. We also offer assistance with preparing book proposals and writing consulting."

BROOKSTONE CREATIVE GROUP | SUZANNE KUHN

100 Missionary Ridge, Birmingham, AL 35242 | 302-514-7899
www.brookstonecreativegroup.com

Contact: website contact form
Services: book-cover design, book-interior design, printing, promotional
materials, website design
Charges: flat fee
Credentials/experience: Suzanne has more than thirty years of book
specific experience. Brookstone is an expansion of her business,
SuzyQ, with a team of almost two dozen professionals who bring a
wide range of knowledge and experience to help you get published.

BUTTERFIELD EDITORIAL SERVICES | DEBRA L. BUTTERFIELD

4810 Gene Field Rd., Saint Joseph, MO 64506 | 816-752-2171
deb@debralbutterfield.com | *themotivationaleditor.com*

Contact: email
Services: book-cover design, book-interior design
Charges: flat fee
Credentials/experience: "Former copywriter for Focus on the Family.
Eleven years' experience as freelance editor. Seven years' editorial
experience with traditional publisher with book layout and cover
design experience as well. Author of eight books, nonfiction and
fiction. I have been blogging on the craft of writing since 2012."

CASTELANE, INC. | KIM MCDOUGALL

Whitehall, PA | 647-281-1554
kimm@castelane.com | *www.castelane.com*

Contact: email
Services: book trailer, book-cover design, ebook conversion
Charges: flat fee
Credentials/experience: "I have made more than five hundred book
video trailers and three hundred book covers since 2009. Samples
and references are available on the website."

CELEBRATION WEB DESIGN | BRUCE SHANK

PO Box 471068, Kissimmee, FL 34747 | 610-989-0402
bruce@celebrationwebdesign.com | *CelebrationWebDesign.com*

Contact: email, phone, website contact form
Service: website design
Charges: custom

Credentials/experience: "Celebration Web Design develops handcrafted websites, branding packages and marketing solutions. Since 2002, our expert staff has been helping individuals and organizations enhance their online presence. Celebration Web Design's team is enthusiastic with focused analysts, developers, and designers who have a passion for technology and online marketing solutions. We consider it a privilege to serve God, by helping individuals and organizations with their website and online marketing needs."

CHRISTIANPRINT.COM
6820 W. 115th St., Bloomington, MN 55438 | 888-201-1322
info@bethanypress.com | www.christianprint.com

Contact: phone, website contact form
Service: printing
Charges: flat fee
Credentials/experience: A division of Bethany Press, founded in 1997. Prints ancillary products, such as business cards, brochures, booklets, banners, postcards, posters, and signs.

DESIGN BY INSIGHT | ERIN ULRICH
PO Box 80282, Simpsonville, SC 29680
erin@designbyinsight.net | designbyinsight.net

Contact: website contact form
Service: website design
Charges: flat fee
Credentials/experience: "In today's world, your website matters more than ever. You need an online space designed to help you reach your goals. Sometimes that's easier said than done. We're here to listen to what you hope to achieve and develop a website strategy that gets results. We have been designing and building WordPress sites for over 10 years. Our clients include writers, small-business owners, nonprofits, and more. Whether you're starting from scratch or ready to take your web presence to the next level, we want to partner with you to see your vision become a reality."

DESIGN CORPS | JOHN WOLLINKA
1370 Carlson Dr., Colorado Springs, CO 80910 | 719-260-0500
john@designcorps.us | designcorps.us

Contact: email
Services: book-cover design, book-interior design, ebook conversion,

illustrations, typesetting

Charges: flat fee

Credentials/experience: "Design Corps has been serving the Christian community for over 20 years. Our publishing clients have ranged from big publishers (such as Zondervan and Moody Publishers) to self-publishers. We have a love for the Word that we bring with extensive experience in design to covers, interiors, page composition, illustration, and production (printed books and ebooks)."

THE DESIGN IN YOUR MIND | MARY C. FINDLEY

Tulsa, OK | 918-805-0669

mjmcfindley@gmail.com | *findleyfamilyvideopublications.com/the-design-in-your-mind*

Contact: email, website contact form

Services: book-cover design, book-interior design, ebook conversion, illustrations

Charges: flat fee

Credentials/experience: "More than 10 years video and graphic design experience, book covers, formatting, and trailers."

DIGGYPOD | KEVIN OSWORTH

301 Industrial Dr., Tecumseh, MI 49286 | 877-944-7844

kosworth@diggypod.com | *www.diggypod.com*

Contact: email, phone, website contact form

Services: book-cover design, printing

Charges: custom

Credentials/experience: "DiggyPOD has been printing books since 2001. All facets of the book printing take place in our facility."

EAH CREATIVE | EMILIE HANEY

emilie@eahcreative.com | *www.eahcreative.com*

Contact: email

Services: book-cover design, book-interior design, ebook conversion, promotional graphics (digital and print)

Charges: custom, flat fee, hourly rate

Credentials/experience: "Emilie has worked in the design field for over six years in addition to her promotional work for authors of various genres. She believes in keeping creativity and marketability at the core of her designs and works with independent authors as well as publishing houses to create eye-catching covers and promotional items to help authors sell their books. A writer herself,

Emilie is familiar with the Christian-market industry and works with both fiction and nonfiction authors."

EDENBROOKE PRODUCTIONS | MARTY KEITH

615-415-1942

johnmartinkeith@gmail.com | *www.edenbrookemusic.com/booktrailers*

Contact: email
Service: book trailer
Charges: flat fee
Credentials/experience: Produced music for everyone from CBS Television to Discovery Channel.

FISTBUMP MEDIA, LLC | DAN KING

5761 Old Summerwood Blvd., Sarasota, FL 34232 | 941-681-8015

sales@fistbumpmedia.com | *fistbumpmedia.com*

Contact: email, phone
Services: book-cover design, book-interior design, ebook conversion, website design
Charges: flat fee, hourly rate
Credentials/experience: "Our experience in online publishing and digital media goes back over 13 years, and we've been helping writers at all levels for over 8 years. We work with start-up writers trying to publish their first work, and we work with best-sellers who need some extra technical support."

THE FORWORD COLLECTIVE | MOLLY HODGIN

1726 Charity Dr., Brentwood, TN 37027 | 615-497-4322

info@theforwordcollective.com | *www.theforewordcollective.com*

Contact: email, website contact form
Service: book-cover design
Charges: flat fee, hourly rate
Credentials/experience: "The Foreword Collective was founded by Molly Hodgin, a publishing professional with two decades of experience. Most recently, she served as the Associate Publisher for the Specialty Division of HarperCollins Christian Publishing working to acquire and create gift books, children's books, and new media products with authors and brands."

HANNAH LINDER DESIGNS | HANNAH LINDER

hannah@hannahlinderdesigns.com | *www.hannahlinderdesigns.com*

Contact: email, website contact form
Services: book-cover design, book-interior design
Charges: custom, flat fee
Credentials/experience: "Hannah Linder Designs specializes in professional book-cover design with affordable prices. Having designed for both traditional publishing houses and bestselling authors, Hannah understands the importance of an attractive book cover and the trends of today's industry. Also, Hannah is a magna cum laude Graphic Design Associates Degree graduate and an award-winning book cover designer."

HEADSHOTS OF CHICAGO | JIM MUELLER

66 Grove Ct. #1155, Elgin, IL 60120 | 847-220-4239
jim@headshotsofchicago.com | *headshotsofchicago.com*

Contact: email, phone, website contact form
Service: PR photo
Charges: flat fee
Credentials/experience: "I am an award-winning photographer with 20+ years of experience with a concentration on people. Over the years I've photographed a diverse range of faces—a wide array of backgrounds, emotions, and aspirations—with the goal of delighting my clients with best-in-class service and excellent images."

INKSMITH EDITORIAL SERVICES | LIZ SMITH

Mebane, NC | 336-514-2331
liz@inksmithediting.com | *inksmithediting.com*

Contact: email
Services: book-interior design, ebook conversion, typesetting
Charges: hourly rate
Credentials/experience: "In addition to editing and indexing services, Liz Smith offers interior book design (formatting, typesetting) and ebook conversion. She has helped dozens of self-publishing authors go from raw manuscript to polished and published book. Her portfolio and client testimonials can be found on her website."

KELLIE BOOK DESIGN | KELLIE PARSONS

1/23 Apara Way, Nollamara, WA 6061, Australia | 0412 591 687
hello@kelliemaree.com | *www.kelliemaree.com*

Contact: website contact form
Services: book-cover design, book-interior design, ebook conversion, print liaison, typesetting

Charges: flat fee

Credentials/experience: "I hold a BA Creative Industries majoring in Graphic Design & Interactive Media and have 10 years' experience working in the field of Graphic Design. For the past 5 years, I have specialised in Book Design (typesetting and cover design)."

LAURA PACE GRAPHIC DESIGN | LAURA PACE

127 Gambel Oaks Pl., Elizabeth, CO 80107 | 303-906-8850

pacelauradesign@gmail.com | *laurapacedesign.com*

Contact: email, phone

Services: book-cover design, promotional materials

Charges: flat fee

Credentials/experience: "Freelance designer specializing in book-cover and full-cover layouts, as well as a large variety of print material for promotional and advertising purposes. I enjoy working directly with both authors and publishing companies."

MADISON DESIGNS | RUTH DERBY

220 W. Elm St., Hanford, CA 93230 | 559-772-2489

rmadison_1@hotmail.com | *www.ruthiemadison.com*

Contact: email, website contact form

Service: book-cover design

Charges: flat fee

Credentials/experience: More than four years of experience and has had mentors in this field.

MARTIN PUBLISHING SERVICES | MELINDA MARTIN

Palestine, TX | 903-948-4893

martinpublishingservices@gmail.com | *melindamartin.me*

Contact: email, phone, website contact form

Services: book-cover design, book-interior design, ebook conversion, typesetting

Charges: flat fee

Credentials/experience: "More than five years of working with clients' manuscripts to achieve a design that is best for their platforms."

MCLENNAN CREATIVE | ALISON MCLENNAN

1933 Geraldson Dr., Lancaster, PA 17601 | 717-572-2585

alison@mclennancreative.com | *www.mclennancreative.com*

Contact: website contact form
Service: website design
Charges: custom
Credentials/experience: "More than twenty years' experience in the publishing industry."

MEADE AGENCY | KRIS MEADE

460 King St. #200, Charleston, SC 29403 | 843-714-0090
hello@meadeagency.cc | *www.meadeagency.cc*

Contact: email, phone
Service: video production
Charges: custom
Credentials/experience: "Meade Agency is a professional video production company specializing in book trailers, branding videos, and online course creation. We have mastered the production of web-based, on-demand video education. Online courses are a powerful way to monetize a platform, and we've got you covered from filming lessons to the web development of your course. We have worked with a variety of leaders in the industry, such as Proverbs 31 Ministries, HarperCollins, Thomas Nelson, and David C. Cook Publishing."

MISSION AND MEDIA | MICHELLE RAYBURN

11510 County Highway M, New Auburn, WI 54757
info@missionandmedia.com | *missionandmedia.com*

Contact: email, website contact form
Services: book-cover design, book-interior design, ebook conversion, typesetting
Charges: flat fee, free consultation, hourly rate
Credentials/experience: "Michelle works with indie and self-published authors to design a quality book cover and interior. She also coaches those who want to create their own imprint with full control of their own publishing process. Her area of specialty is with Amazon KDP. Michelle has more than 20 years of experience on the writing and editing side of publishing. Portfolio and additional information are available on the website."

PAGE & PIXEL PUBLICATIONS | SUSAN MOORE

La Crosse, WI | 608-780-3400
pageandpixelpublications@gmail.com | *pageandpixelpublications.com*

Contact: email

Services: book-cover design, book-interior design, ebook conversion, typesetting

Charges: hourly rate

Credentials/experience: "Over twenty-five years' experience with Christian publishers and independent authors. Offering individual attention, taking into consideration the client's preferences and matching the design with the theme of the material. Attention to detail. Satisfaction guaranteed. Also offers editorial services. Your one-stop shop for the independent author."

PROFESSIONAL PUBLISHING SERVICES | CHRISTY CALLAHAN

PO Box 461, Waycross, GA 31502 | 912-809-9062

professionalpublishingservices@gmail.com | *professionalpublishingservices.us*

Contact: website contact form

Services: book-cover design, book-interior design, ebook conversion, typesetting

Charges: custom, flat fee

Credentials/experience: "Christy graduated Phi Beta Kappa from Carnegie Mellon University, where she first learned how to use Adobe software. While she earned her MA in Intercultural Studies from Fuller Seminary, she edited sound files for distance-learning classes for the Media Center and designed ads as Women's Concerns Committee chairperson. Christy is an Adobe Certified Associate in Print & Digital Publication Using Adobe InDesign, leveraging her expertise as an editor and proofreader and extensive knowledge of *Chicago* style to create professional-looking book covers and interior layouts."

RANEY DAY CREATIVE | KEN RANEY

1848 Georgia St., Cape Girardeau, MO 63701 | 316-737-9724

kenraney@mac.com | *kenraney-design.blogspot.com*

Contact: email, phone

Services: book-cover design, book-interior design, ebook conversion, illustrations, typesetting

Charges: flat fee, hourly rate

Credentials/experience: "Over 40 years' experience as an illustrator and graphic designer."

RICK STEELE EDITORIAL SERVICES | RICK STEELE

26 Dean Rd., Ringgold, GA 30736 | 706-937-8121

rsteelecam@gmail.com | *steeleeditorialservices.myportfolio.com*

Contact: website contact form

Services: book-cover design, book-interior design, ebook conversion, printing, typesetting
Charges: flat fee
Credentials/experience: "Rick Steele has the skills and years of experience to take your edited manuscript to printed-page format with a professional, attractive page layout. Can help with cover design, page layout, and file submission to Amazon Kindle Direct Publishing (KDP) and Ingram Spark."

ROSEANNA WHITE DESIGNS | ROSEANNA WHITE
roseannamwhite@gmail.com | *www.RoseannaWhiteDesigns.com*

Contact: email, website contact form
Services: book-cover design, book-interior design, ebook conversion, illustrations, typesetting
Charges: custom, flat fee, hourly rate
Credentials/experience: "Roseanna has been designing and typesetting books for nearly ten years, combining her keen eye and artistic skills with her insider knowledge of the industry. As an author herself, she knows how important it is for the appearance of a book to match the words and strives to bring your story to life at a single glance. She has worked for publishing houses and independently for some of Christian fiction's top authors."

SCOTT LA COUNTE
Anaheim, CA | 714-404-7182
Roboscott@gmail.com | *scottdouglas.org/coaching*

Contact: email, website contact form
Services: audiobook, book-cover design, book-interior design, ebook conversion, printing, self-publishing coach, typesetting, website design
Charges: custom, flat fee, hourly rate
Credentials/experience: "20 years in the publishing industry; 2,000,000+ books sold."

SCREE, LLC | LANDON OTIS
Sandpoint, ID | 208-290-4624
landon@scree.it | *scree.it*

Contact: website contact form
Service: website design
Charges: hourly rate
Credentials/experience: "Professional, full-time web developer at a local design and marketing firm. Websites include

veritasincorporated.com and *mineralchurch.org.*"

STARCHER DESIGNS | KARA STARCHER

Chloe, WV

info@starcherdesigns.com | *www.starcherdesigns.com*

Contact: email

Services: book-cover design, book-interior design, typesetting

Charges: custom

Credentials/experience: "I have a BA in Publishing, and I've won multiple design awards from the WV Press Association and from CSPA."

SUZANNE FYHRIE PARROTT

PO Box 571, Gleneden Beach, OR 97388

author@suzannefyhrieparrott.com | *www.SuzanneFyhrieParrott.com*

Contact: website contact form

Services: book-cover design, book-interior design, ebook conversion, illustrations

Charges: custom, flat fee, hourly rate

Credentials/experience: "Suzanne graduated from the University of Washington in 1981 and has earned several Montana Addy Awards for design excellence, working with such clients as Yellowstone Park, Old West Trail, Columbia Paint, Winston Fly Rod Company, and Montana Power Company. She is currently the lead designer for First Steps Publishing, Fireside Press, Penman Productions, and several other publishing companies. Her primary design focus is book design and publication, producing original layouts/designs in print and digital (ebook/audio), as well as creating a complete marketing plan for your publication success."

TLC BOOK DESIGN | TAMARA DEVER

Austin, TX

tamara@tlcgraphics.com | *www.TLCBookDesign.com*

Contact: email

Services: book-cover design, book-interior design, ebook conversion, printing, typesetting, website design

Charges: custom

Credentials/Experience: "TLC provides award-winning book design, editorial, printing, and guidance with a personal touch that takes the stress out of book creation and gives serious authors and publishers high-quality books they are proud to represent. The recipients of over

200 industry awards, we've been joyfully serving the publishing industry for twenty-five years."

TRILION STUDIOS | BRIAN WHITE

Lawrence, KS | 785-841-5500

hello@TriLionStudios.com | www.TriLionStudios.com

Contact: email, phone

Services: book-cover design, illustrations, logo design, video production, website design

Charges: flat fee, hourly rate

Credentials/experience: Twenty years in the design/web design/ branding industry. Has worked with nonprofits and churches for more than fifteen years.

VIVID GRAPHICS | LARRY VAN HOOSE

2273 Snow Hill Rd., Galax, VA 24333 | 276-233-0276

larry@vivid-graphics.com | www.vivid-graphics.com

Contact: email, phone, website contact form

Services: book-cover design, book-interior design, ebook conversion, printing

Charges: custom, flat fee, hourly rate

Credentials/experience: "Publish and design magazines, literature, ads, websites, billboards; client consultant developing effective marketing and advertising programs; write and edit copy for literature, videos, ads, and training materials."

WRITER'S TABLET AGENCY | TERRI WHITEMORE

4371 Roswell Rd. #315, Marietta, GA 30062 | 770-648-4101

WritersTablet@gmail.com | www.Writerstablet.org

Contact: email

Services: book-cover design, book-interior design, ebook conversion, typesetting

Charges: flat fee

Credentials/experience: "Becoming a published author requires a lot more than a knack for writing and a great story. Partnering with the Writer's Tablet Agency will put you on the fast-track to seeing your name in print. Learn how to navigate the complex world of publishing alongside passionate published authors with years of experience. From polishing your final manuscript to launching your book, Writer's Tablet simplifies the Road to Publication."

YO PRODUCTIONS, LLC | YOLANDA SANDERS

PO Box 1543, Reynoldsburg, OH 43068 | 614-452-4920

info_4u@yoproductions.net | www.yoproductions.net

Contact: email

Services: book-cover design, book-interior design, typesetting

Charges: custom

Credentials/experience: "We work side-by-side with our clients to understand your needs and then to produce a quality product that meets them, using the most up-to-date software versions available. Don't have a solid design idea? Don't worry! We will help you brainstorm as well, if needed. We treat every project as if it were our own, and give the time and attention needed to make it a masterpiece."

Note: See "Editorial Services" and "Publicity and Marketing Services" for help with these needs.

4

DISTRIBUTION SERVICES

AMAZON ADVANTAGE
advantage.amazon.com

Advantage is a simple way to sell your books on one of the world's leading online retail websites even if you don't publish your books through Amazon or another company that will list them on this site. Advantage provides marketing and vendor support to maximize your sales. Titles enrolled in Advantage are eligible for Search Inside, customer service, order fulfillment services, and more. Annual fee for unlimited titles is $99, plus 55% commission. New enrollment is paused for improvements, but you may register your email for reopening notification.

AMAZON MARKETPLACE (SELLER CENTRAL)
sell.amazon.com

Marketplace has two selling plans: individual for 99¢ per book and professional for $39.99 per month. Both plans have other selling fees as well. You can manage inventory, update pricing, communicate with buyers, contact support, and add new products all from the Seller Central website.

CHRISTIANBOOK
PO Box 7000, Peabody, MA 01961-7000 | 800-247-4784
email through the website | www.christianbook.com

Sometimes distributes independently published books.

NOVELLA DISTRIBUTION
Unit 3, 5 Currumbin Ct., Capalaba, QLD 4157 Australia | +61 07 3167 6519
sales@novelladistribution.com.au | bookstores.novelladistribution.com.au

Provides warehousing and distribution to trade bookstores (Christian and general market), as well as library and educational suppliers and major online retailers. Also operates a specialist division that is the supplier of choice for many Christian schools in Australia.

PATHWAY BOOK SERVICE

34 Production Ave., Keene, NH 03431 | 800-345-6665

pbs@pathwaybook.com | *www.pathwaybook.com*

Provides warehousing, order fulfillment, and trade distribution. It is a longtime distributor to Ingram and Baker & Taylor, the vendors of choice for most bookstores. Pathway uploads new-title spreadsheets to Ingram and Baker & Taylor, as well as to *Amazon.com*, Barnes & Noble, and Books-A-Million on a weekly basis. Distribution outside of North America is available through Gazelle Book Services in the United Kingdom. Also provides the option of having Pathway add titles to its Amazon Advantage account, which is at a lower discount and often a lower shipping cost per book than individual accounts.

STONEWATER BOOKS

info@stonewaterbooks.com | *www.stonewaterbooks.com*

Stonewater Books is a go-between service for indie authors. Each year Stonewater puts writers together in two sales cycles of books and sells those books through Anchor Book distributor, where bookstores and online retailers can order them.

PART 3

PERIODICAL PUBLISHERS

TOPICS AND TYPES

This chapter is not an exhaustive list of types of manuscripts and topics editors are looking for, but it is a starting place for some of the more popular ones. For instance, almost all periodicals take manuscripts in categories like Christian living, so they are not listed here. Plus writers guidelines tend to outline general areas, not every specific type and topic an editor will buy.

CONTEMPORARY ISSUES
Brio
Catholic Sentinel
Christian Herald
Christianity Today
The Covenant Companion
Faith Today
Focus on the Family
Holiness Today
Influence
Light + Life Magazine
Light Magazine
Ministry
New Frontier Chronicle
Now What?
Our Sunday Visitor Newsweekly
Presbyterians Today
St. Anthony Messenger
The War Cry

DEVOTIONS
Eternal Ink
Focus on the Family

Gems of Truth
Mature Living
ParentLife

ESSAY
America
The Canadian Lutheran
The Christian Century
The Christian Librarian
Commonweal
Faith Today
Image
Love Is Moving
The Lutheran Witness
Our Sunday Visitor Newsweekly
Poets & Writers
Relief
Sharing
U.S. Catholic
The Writer
The Writer's Chronicle
Writer's Digest

EVANGELISM

Blue Ridge Christian News
Christian Research Journal
CommonCall
Evangelical Missions Quarterly
Faith on Every Corner
Just Between Us
Mature Living
Net Results
New Identity Magazine
Outreach
The War Cry

FAMILY

Boundless
Celebrate Life Magazine
Columbia
CommonCall
Creative Inspirations
Faith & Friends
Faith on Every Corner
Focus on the Family
HomeLife
Influence
Joyful Living Magazine
Light Magazine
Ministry
The Mother's Heart
ParentLife
St. Anthony Messenger
Vibrant Life

FICTION

See Short Story.

FILLERS

Angels on Earth
Bible Advocate
Blue Ridge Christian News
Christian Herald
Creation Illustrated
Eternal Ink
FellowScript
Focus on the Family Clubhouse
Focus on the Family Clubhouse Jr.
Freelance Writer's Report
Guideposts
LIVE
The Mother's Heart
Words for the Way

FINANCES/MONEY

Boundless
Columbia
Joyful Living Magazine
Just Between Us
Net Results

HOW-TO

Blue Ridge Christian News
Canada Lutheran
Canadian Mennonite
Celebrate Life Magazine
Charisma Leader
Christian Herald
Christian Standard
CommonCall
Creation Illustrated
Evangelical Missions Quarterly
Faith Today
Focus on the Family
HomeLife

Homeschooling Today
InSite
The Journal of Adventist Education
Joyful Living Magazine
Just Between Us
Leading Hearts
Light Magazine
LIVE
The Lutheran Witness
Mature Living
Ministry
The Mother's Heart
Mutuality
Net Results
New Identity Magazine
Outreach
ParentLife
Parish Liturgy
Poets & Writers
Prayer Connect
SAConnects
Story Embers
Teachers of Vision
Vibrant Life
Words for the Way
The Writer
Writer's Digest
WritersWeekly.com
Writing Corner

INTERVIEW/PROFILE

The Arlington Catholic Herald
Brio
byFaith
Cadet Quest
Canada Lutheran
Catholic Sentinel
Celebrate Life Magazine

Charisma
Charisma Leader
Christ Is Our Hope
The Christian Century
Christian Herald
The Christian Journal
Christianity Today
Columbia
CommonCall
The Covenant Companion
Creation
Creation Illustrated
DTS Magazine
Evangelical Missions Quarterly
Faith & Friends
Faith Today
Focus on the Family Clubhouse
Focus on the Family Clubhouse Jr.
Friends Journal
Guide
Homeschooling Today
Image
InSite
International Journal of Frontier
    Missiology
Joyful Living Magazine
Leading Hearts
Leben
Light + Life Magazine
The Lutheran Witness
Nature Friend
Our Sunday Visitor Newsweekly
Outreach
Peer
Poets & Writers
Point
Power for Living
St. Anthony Messenger

testimony/ENRICH
Today's Christian Living
U.S. Catholic
Vibrant Life
The War Cry
The Writer
The Writer's Chronicle
Writer's Digest

LEADERSHIP/MINISTRY

Charisma Leader
CommonCall
Evangelical Missions Quarterly
Holiness Today
InSite
Just Between Us
Love Is Moving
Ministry
Net Results
Outreach

MARRIAGE

Boundless
Faith & Friends
Focus on the Family
HomeLife
Joyful Living Magazine
Mature Living
The Mother's Heart
St. Anthony Messenger

NEWSPAPER

Anglican Journal
The Arlington Catholic Herald
Blue Ridge Christian News
Catholic New York
Catholic Sentinel
Christian Courier

Christian Herald
Christian News Northwest
The Good News (Florida)
The Good News (New York)
The Good News Journal
The Messianic Times
New Frontier Chronicle
Our Sunday Visitor Newsweekly
The Southeast Outlook

PARENTING

Columbia
Faith on Every Corner
Focus on the Family
HomeLife
Just Between Us
Light Magazine
Mature Living
The Mother's Heart
Parenting Teens
ParentLife

PERSONAL EXPERIENCE

Angels on Earth
Anglican Journal
Bible Advocate
Blue Ridge Christian News
The Breakthrough Intercessor
Canada Lutheran
Catholic New York
Catholic Sentinel
Celebrate Life Magazine
Chicken Soup for the Soul Book
  Series
Christ Is Our Hope
Christian Herald
The Covenant Companion
Creation Illustrated

Divine Moments Book Series
DTS Magazine
Eternal Ink
Faith & Friends
Faith on Every Corner
Friends Journal
Guide
Guideposts
Highway News
Holiness Today
The Journal of Adventist Education
Joyful Living Magazine
Just Between Us
Leading Hearts
LEAVES
LIVE
Love Is Moving
The Lutheran Witness
Mature Living
The Mother's Heart
Mutuality
Mysterious Ways
New Identity Magazine
Now What?
Point
Power for Living
SAConnects
Sharing
Short and Sweet Book Series
Standard
Teachers of Vision
testimony/ENRICH
Today's Christian Living
Vibrant Life
The War Cry
Words for the Way

POETRY

America
Bible Advocate
Chicken Soup for the Soul Book
    Series
The Christian Century
Christian Courier
Commonweal
Creation Illustrated
Creative Inspirations
Eternal Ink
Faith on Every Corner
Focus on the Family Clubhouse Jr.
Friends Journal
Gems of Truth
Image
LEAVES
LIVE
Love Is Moving
The Lutheran Witness
Mutuality
Power for Living
Relief
Sharing
Sojourners
St. Anthony Messenger
Story Embers
Teachers of Vision
Time Of Singing
U.S. Catholic
Words for the Way

PROFILE

See Interview.

REVIEWS

Anglican Journal
byFaith
Canadian Mennonite
Celebrate Life Magazine
Charisma
The Christian Century
Christian Courier
Christian Herald
The Christian Journal
Christian Librarian
Christian Research Journal
Christian Retailing
Christianity Today
Evangelical Missions Quarterly
Faith & Friends
Faith on Every Corner
Faith Today
FellowScript
The Good News (New York)
The Journal of Adventist Education
Leading Hearts
LEAVES
Light Magazine
Love Is Moving
The Messianic Times
Ministry
The Mother's Heart
Mutuality
New Frontier Chronicle
Sojourners
Time Of Singing
Words for the Way
The Writer

SEASONAL

The Anglican Journal
Blue Ridge Christian News

Brio
Canada Lutheran
Canadian Mennonite
Catholic New York
Celebrate Life Magazine
Charisma
The Christian Century
Christian Courier
Christian Herald
The Christian Journal
Christian Standard
Columbia
Creation
Divine Moments Book Series
DTS Magazine
Eternal Ink
Faith on Every Corner
Faith Today
FellowScript
Focus on the Family Clubhouse
Focus on the Family Clubhouse Jr.
Freelance Writers Report
Gems of Truth
Guide
Highway News
HomeLife
InSite
The Journal of Adventist Education
LIVE
Love Is Moving
The Messenger
The Mother's Heart
Nature Friend
Our Little Friend
Outreach
Poets & Writers
Power for Living
Presbyterians Today

Primary Treasure
Short and Sweet Book Series
The Southeast Outlook
Sports Spectrum
Standard
Teachers of Vision
testimony/ENRICH
Time Of Singing
U.S. Catholic
The War Cry
Words for the Way
Writer's Digest

SHORT STORY/ FICTION

Blue Ridge Christian News
Brio
Cadet Quest
Creation Illustrated
Focus on the Family Clubhouse
Focus on the Family Clubhouse Jr.
Gems of Truth
Image
LIVE
Love Is Moving

Mature Living
Nature Friend
Relief
St. Anthony Messenger
Story Embers

TAKE-HOME PAPER

Gems of Truth
Guide
LIVE
Our Little Friend
Power for Living
Primary Treasure
Standard

THEOLOGY

byFaith
The Canadian Lutheran
Christianity Today
Faith & Friends
Mature Living
Ministry
Presbyterians Today

6

ADULT MARKETS

AMERICA

106 W. 56th St., New York, NY 10019-3803 | 212-581-4640
articles@americamedia.org | *www.americamagazine.org*
Matt Malone, S.J., editor in chief

Denomination: Catholic
Parent company: America Media, Jesuit Conference of the United States and Canada
Type: monthly digital and print magazine, circulation 46,000
Audience: primarily Catholic, two-thirds are laypeople, college educated
Purpose: to provide a smart Catholic take on faith and culture
Submissions: Submit complete manuscript through the website. Unsolicited freelance: 100%. Responds in two weeks.
Length: 800-2,500 words; poetry, 30 lines maximum
Topics: Christian living, culture, trends
Rights: electronic, first
Payment: competitive rates, on acceptance
Guidelines: *americamedia.submittable.com/submit*
Tip: "We are known across the Catholic world for our unique brand of excellent, relevant, and accessible coverage. From theology and spirituality to politics, international relations, arts and letters, and the economy and social justice, our coverage spans the globe."

ANGELS ON EARTH

110 William St., Ste. 901, New York, NY 10038 | 212-251-8100
www.guideposts.org/our-magazines/angels-on-earth-magazine
Colleen Hughes, editor-in-chief

Parent company: Guideposts
Type: bimonthly digital and print magazine, circulation 550,000
Audience: general
Purpose: to tell true stories of heavenly angels and earthly ones who

find themselves on a mission of comfort, kindness, or reassurance

Submissions: Submit complete manuscript through the website at *guideposts.org/tell-us-your-story*. Unsolicited freelance: 90%. Responds in two months or isn't interested.

Length: 1,500 words maximum

Manuscripts accepted per year: 40-60

Topic: angels

Rights: all

Payment: $25-$500, on publication

Kill fee: 20%

Sample: 7 x 10" SASE with four stamps

Tip: "We are not limited to stories about heavenly angels. We also accept stories about human beings doing heavenly duties."

ANGLICAN JOURNAL

80 Hayden St., Toronto, ON M4Y 3G2, Canada | 416-924-9199

editor@anglicanjournal.com | *www.anglicanjournal.com*

Denomination: Anglican

Parent company: Anglican Church of Canada

Type: monthly digital and print newsletter, circulation 123,000, advertising accepted

Audience: denomination

Purpose: to share compelling news and features about the Anglican Church of Canada and the Anglican Communion and religion in general

Submissions: Only accepts email as attachment. Unsolicited freelance: none, query first. Responds in two weeks.

Length: 500-1,000 words

Seasonal submissions: two months in advance

Preferred Bible version: NRSV

Topics: Christian living, denomination, events, issues

Rights: first

Payment: $75-$100, on acceptance

Guidelines: *www.anglicanjournal.com/about-us/writers-guidelines*

Sample: on the website

Tip: Looking for "local church/parish news stories, book reviews, spiritual reflection."

THE ARLINGTON CATHOLIC HERALD

200 N. Glebe Rd., Ste. 600, Arlington, VA 22203 | 703-841-2590

editorial@catholicherald.com | *www.catholicherald.com*

Ann Augherton, managing editor

Denomination: Catholic

Parent company: Arlington, Virginia, Diocese

Type: weekly digital and print newspaper, circulation 70,000, advertising accepted

Audience: denomination

Purpose: to support the Church's mission to evangelize by providing news from a Catholic perspective

Submissions: Email query letter.

Sample: on the website

BIBLE ADVOCATE

PO Box 33677, Denver, CO 80233

bibleadvocate@cog7.org | baonline.org

Sherri Langton, associate editor

Denomination: Church of God (Seventh Day)

Type: bimonthly digital and print magazine, circulation 13,000

Audience: denomination, general

Purpose: to advocate the Bible and represent the Church of God (Seventh Day)

Submissions: Send complete manuscript by email. Unsolicited freelance: 25-30%. Responds in four to ten weeks.

Length: 600-1,300 words

Topics: Christian living, theme-related

Rights: electronic, first, onetime, reprint (with info on where/when previously published)

Payment: articles, $25-$65; poems and fillers, $20; on publication

Manuscripts accepted per year: 10-20

Preferred Bible version: NIV, NKJV

Theme list: on the website

Guidelines: *baonline.org/write-for-us*

Sample: 9 x 12" envelope with three stamps

Tip: "Please read past issues of the magazine before you submit and become familiar with our style. No snail-mail submissions or PDFs. No Christmas or Easter manuscripts."

BLUE RIDGE CHRISTIAN NEWS

261 Oak Ave., Spruce Pine, NC 28777 | 828-413-0050

cathy@brcnews.com | blueridgechristiannews.com

Cathy Pritchard, editor

Parent company: The Ninevah Productions, Inc.

Type: monthly digital and print newspaper; circulation 16,000 print,

3,000 digital; advertising accepted

Audience: people seeking to know more about God

Purpose: to share the good news of Jesus and other positive, uplifting, and good news from around the world

Submissions: Only accepts email. Unsolicited freelance: 10%. Responds in one week.

Length: 1,000 words

Topics: Christian living, evangelism

Rights: all, electronic, first, reprint (with info on where/when previously published)

Payment: none

Manuscripts accepted per year: 100

Seasonal submissions: one month in advance

Preferred Bible version: KJV, NKJV, NASB

Guidelines: not available

Sample: $3, email request

Tip: "Looking for positive, uplifting, good news."

THE BREAKTHROUGH INTERCESSOR

PO Box 121, Lincoln, VA 20160-0121 | 540-338-4131
breakthrough@intercessors.org | *www.intercessors.org*
Claudette Ammons, managing editor

Parent company: Breakthrough

Type: quarterly digital and print magazine, circulation 4,000

Audience: adults interested in growing their prayer lives

Purpose: to encourage people to pray and to equip them to do so more effectively

Submissions: Only accepts complete manuscript by email.

Length: 600-1,000 words

Topics: prayer

Rights: electronic, first, onetime

Payment: none

Guidelines: *www.intercessors.org/media/downloads/Guidelines%20 &%20PermissionForm.pdf*

Sample: on the website

byFAITH

1700 N. Brown Rd., Ste. 105, Lawrenceville, GA 30043 | 678-825-1005
ddoster@byfaithonline.com | *byfaithonline.com*
Dick Doster, editor

Denomination: Presbyterian

Type: quarterly digital and print magazine, advertising accepted

Audience: denomination

Purpose: to provide news of the Presbyterian Church in America, to equip readers to become a more active part of God's redemptive plan for the world, and to help them respond biblically and intelligently to the questions our culture is asking

Submissions: Only accepts complete manuscript by email.

Length: 500-3,000 words

Topics: Christian living, culture, denomination, theology

Guidelines: *byfaithonline.com/about*

Tip: "Theologically, the writers are Reformed and believe the faith is practical and applicable to every part of life. Most of our writers (though not all) come from the PCA."

CANADA LUTHERAN

600–177 Lombard Ave., Winnipeg, MB R3B 0W5, Canada | 888-786-6707

editor@elcic.ca | canadalutheran.ca

Kenn Ward, editor

Rachel Genge, British Columbia Synod, csynodeditor@gmail.com

Richard Janzen, Synod of Alberta and the Territories, cleditor.richard@gmail.com

Anno Bell, Saskatchewan Synod, clsaskeditor@gmail.com

Rev. R. David Lowe, Manitoba/Northwestern Ontario Synod, mnoeditor@gmail.com

Liz Zehr, Eastern Synod, ezehr@elcic.ca

Denomination: Evangelical Lutheran Church in Canada

Type: monthly print magazine, circulation 14,000

Audience: denomination

Purpose: to engage the Evangelical Lutheran Church in Canada in a dynamic dialogue in which information, inspiration, and ideas are shared in a thoughtful and stimulating way

Submissions: Only accepts email.

Length: 700-1,200 words

Topics: Christian living, denomination, seasonal

Rights: onetime

Guidelines: *www.elcic.ca/clweb/contributing.html*

Tip: "As much as is possible, the content of the magazine is chosen from the work of Canadian writers. The content strives to reflect the Evangelical Lutheran Church in Canada in the context of our Canadian society."

THE CANADIAN LUTHERAN

3074 Portage Ave., Winnipeg, MB R3K 0Y2, Canada | 800-588-4226

editor@lutheranchurch.ca | www.canadianlutheran.ca

Matthew Block, editor
Michelle Heumann, regional news

Denomination: Lutheran
Type: bimonthly digital and print magazine, circulation 20,000
Audience: denomination
Purpose: to inspire, motivate, and inform
Submissions: Only accepts complete manuscript by email.
Topics: culture, denomination, theology
Rights: first
Payment: none
Guidelines: *www.canadianlutheran.ca/editors-and-submissions*
Sample: *issuu.com/thecanadianlutheran*
Tip: "All feature articles with doctrinal content must go through doctrinal review to ensure fidelity to the Scriptures. As a result, authors may occasionally be asked to rewrite some sections of their article before publication."

CANADIAN MENNONITE

490 Dutton Dr., Unit C5, Waterloo, ON N2L 6H7, Canada | 519-884-3810
submit@canadianmennonite.org | *www.canadianmennonite.org*
Virginia A. Hostetler, executive editor

Denomination: Mennonite
Parent company: Canadian Mennonite Publishing Service
Type: biweekly digital and print magazine, circulation 8,500, advertising accepted
Audience: denomination
Purpose: to report news and viewpoints of the people and churches of the Mennonite Church Canada
Submissions: Publishes primarily the writing of correspondents and related organizations. Email query letter first. To get an assignment, be acquainted with the magazine and its readership. Responds in one week.
Length: 500-800 words
Topics: theme-related
Rights: first, onetime, reprint (with info on where/when previously published)
Payment: 10¢/word, on publication
Kill fee: none
Manuscripts accepted per year: few
Seasonal submissions: three months
Theme list: available on website

Guidelines: not available

Sample: on the website

Tip: "Writers for our magazine need to know and understand the interests and concerns of Mennonites in Canada."

CATHOLIC NEW YORK

1011 First Ave., Ste. 1721, New York, NY 10022 | 212-688-2399

cny@cny.org | www.cny.org

John Woods, editor-in-chief

Denomination: Catholic

Parent company: Ecclesiastical Communications Corp.

Type: biweekly digital and print newspaper, circulation 127,000, advertising accepted

Audience: denomination

Purpose: to publish news and information of interest to Catholics in the Archdiocese of New York

Submissions: Email query or complete manuscript as attachment. Unsolicited freelance: 2%. Responds in one month.

Length: 600 words

Topics: Christian living, moral issues

Rights: onetime

Payment: $125, on publication

Manuscripts accepted per year: five to ten

Seasonal submissions: two weeks in advance

Preferred Bible version: NAB

Guidelines: not available

Sample: on the website

Tip: "We use freelancers from New York to cover evening and weekend events."

CATHOLIC SENTINEL

2838 E. Burnside, Portland, OR 97214 | 503-281-1191

edl@CatholicSentinel.org | www.CatholicSentinel.org

Ed Langlois, managing editor

Denomination: Catholic

Parent company: Archdiocese of Portland

Type: bimonthly print newspaper, advertising accepted

Audience: Catholics who live in Oregon

Purpose: to feature Oregon people and Oregon issues that relate to Catholics

Submissions: Email query letter.

Length: 600-1,500 words
Topics: Christian living, issues
Payment: variable rates
Guidelines: *catholicsentinel.org/Content/About-Us/About-Us/Article/
Article-Submission/15/60/11770*

CELEBRATE LIFE MAGAZINE

PO Box 1350, Stafford, VA 22555 | 540-659-4171
clmag@all.org | www.clmagazine.org
Susan Ciancio, editor

Denomination: Catholic
Parent company: American Life League
Type: quarterly digital and print magazine, circulation 7,500,
advertising accepted
Audience: pro-life
Purpose: to inspire, encourage, and educate pro-life activists
Submissions: Only accepts complete manuscript; email as attachment.
Unsolicited freelance: 25%. Responds in one to two months.
Length: 800-1,800 words
Topics: ethics, issues; see list of possible topics in the guidelines
Rights: first
Payment: 10-25¢/word, on publication
Kill fee: sometimes
Manuscripts accepted per year: six
Seasonal submissions: six months ahead
Preferred Bible version: NJB
Guidelines: *www.clmagazine.org/submission-guidelines*
Sample: email for copy
Tip: "Most in need of timely investigative reports and personal
experiences."

CHARISMA

600 Rinehart Rd., Lake Mary, FL 32746 | 407-333-0600
jeff.struss@charismamedia.com | www.charismamag.com
Jeff Struss, director of content development

Denomination: Charismatic
Parent company: Charisma Media
Type: monthly digital and print magazine, circulation 207,000,
advertising accepted
Audience: passionate, Spirit-filled Christians
Purpose: to empower believers for life in the Spirit

Submissions: Email query letter. Unsolicited freelance: 20%. Responds in two to three months.

Length: 700-2,600 words

Topics: Christian living, Christmas, Easter, prayer, prophecy, seasonal, spiritual warfare

Rights: all

Payment: on publication

Seasonal submissions: five months ahead

Preferred Bible version: MEV

Guidelines: *charismamag.com/about/write-for-us*

Sample: on the website

Tip: "Please take time to read—even study—at least one or two of our recent issues before submitting a query. Sometimes people submit their writing without ever having read or understood our magazine or its readers, and sometimes people will have read our magazine years ago and think it's the same as it has always been, but magazines undergo many changes through the years."

CHARISMA LEADER

600 Rinehart Rd., Lake Mary, FL 32746 | 407-333-0600
jeff.struss@charismamedia.com | *www.ministrytodaymag.com*
Jeff Struss, director of content development

Denomination: Charismatic

Parent company: Charisma Media

Type: quarterly digital and print magazine, circulation 30,000

Audience: pastors, ministry leaders, business leaders

Purpose: to inspire and assist ministry leaders

Submissions: Email query letter. Unsolicited freelance: 20%. Responds in two to three months.

Length: 700-2,600 words

Topics: leadership, ministry

Rights: all

Payment: on publication

Preferred Bible version: MEV

Guidelines: *charismamag.com/about/write-for-us*

Sample: on the website

Tip: "Departments: For the most part, this is the type of article that will be accepted from outside writers. These are the 'nuts and bolts' of our magazine and run no longer than 700 words. These departments are categorized under the areas of Ministry Life, Leadership, Outreach and Facilities."

CHICKEN SOUP FOR THE SOUL BOOK SERIES

PO Box 700, Cos Cob, CT 06807

www.chickensoup.com

Amy Newmark, publisher and editor-in-chief

Parent company: Chicken Soup for the Soul Publishing, LLC
Type: book
Purpose: to share happiness, inspiration, and hope
Submissions: Only accepts complete manuscript through the website. Unsolicited freelance: 98%. Also takes submissions from children and teens for some books.
Topics: upcoming books: *www.chickensoup.com/story-submissions/possible-book-topics*
Length: 1,200 words maximum
Payment: $200 plus ten copies of the book, on publication
Theme list: available on website
Guidelines: *www.chickensoup.com/story-submissions/story-guidelines*
Tip: "A Chicken Soup for the Soul story is an inspirational, true story about ordinary people having extraordinary experiences. . . . These stories are personal and often filled with emotion and drama. . . . Poems tell a story; no rhyming. . . . The most powerful stories are about people extending themselves, or performing an act of love, service, or courage for another person."

CHRIST IS OUR HOPE

16555 Weber Rd., Crest Hill, IL 60403 | 815-221-6100

magazine@dioceseofjoliet.org | *www.dioceseofjoliet.org/magazine/sectioncontent.php?secid=1*

Carlos Briceño, editor

Denomination: Catholic
Parent company: Diocese of Joliet, Illinois
Type: monthly print magazine
Audience: denomination
Purpose: to tell inspiring stories of faith and share information with the goal of educating and evangelizing others
Submissions: Email query letter.
Topics: Catholic life, local news
Payment: none
Guidelines: *www.dioceseofjoliet.org/magazine/sectioncontent.php?secid=5*
Sample: on the website

THE CHRISTIAN CENTURY

104 S. Michigan Ave., Ste. 1100, Chicago, IL 60603-5901 | 312-263-7510
submissions@christiancentury.org | *www.christiancentury.org*
Steve Thorngate, managing editor
Jill Peláez Baumgaertner, poetry, poetry@christiancentury.org

Type: biweekly print magazine, advertising accepted
Audience: ecumenical, mainline ministers, educators, and church leaders
Purpose: to explore what it means to believe and live out the Christian faith in our time
Submissions: Only accepts email, query letter. Unsolicited freelance: 90%. Responds in four to six weeks.
Length: articles, 1,500-3,000 words; poetry, to 20 lines
Topics: culture, issues, justice
Rights: all, reprint (with info on where/when previously published)
Payment: articles, $100-$300; poems, $50; reviews, to $75; on publication
Manuscripts accepted per year: 150
Seasonal submissions: four months in advance
Preferred Bible version: NRSV
Guidelines: *www.christiancentury.org/submission-guidelines*
Sample: *www.christiancentury.org/magazine*
Tip: "Keep in mind our audience of sophisticated readers, eager for analysis and critical perspective that goes beyond the obvious. We are open to all topics if written with appropriate style for our readers."

CHRISTIAN COURIER

2 Aiken St., St. Catherines, ON L2N 1V8, Canada | 800-969-4838
editor@christiancourier.ca | *www.christiancourier.ca*
Angela Reitsma Bick, editor-in-chief
Amy MacLachlan, features, features@christiancourier.ca
Brian Bork, reviews, reviews@christiancourier.ca

Denomination: Christian Reformed
Type: biweekly digital and print newspaper, circulation 2,500, advertising accepted
Purpose: to connect Christians with a network of culturally savvy partners in faith for the purpose of inspiring all to participate in God's renewing work with his creation
Submissions: Email query or complete manuscript. Accepts

simultaneous submissions. Responds in one to two weeks, only if accepted.

Length: articles, 700-1,200 words; reviews, 750 words

Rights: onetime, reprint (with info on where/when previously published)

Payment: articles, $50-$70; reviews, $30-$70; poetry, $45; reprints, none; on publication

Seasonal submissions: three months in advance

Preferred Bible version: NIV

Guidelines: *www.christiancourier.ca/write-for-us*

Sample: *www.christiancourier.ca/past-issues*

Tip: "Suggest an aspect of the theme which you believe you could cover well, have insight into, could treat humorously, etc. Show that you think clearly, write clearly, and have something to say that we should want to read. Have a strong biblical worldview and avoid moralism and sentimentality."

CHRISTIAN HERALD

PO Box 68526, Brampton, ON L6R 0J8, Canada | 905-874-1731
info@christianherald.ca | *christianherald.ca*
Fazal Karim, Jr., publisher and editor-in-chief

Type: monthly digital and print newspaper, circulation 27,000, advertising accepted

Audience: Southern Ontario's Christian community

Purpose: to keep Southern Ontario's Christian community informed of news and events

Submissions: Email query letter. Unsolicited freelance: 10%. Responds in two weeks.

Length: 300-900 words

Topics: wide variety

Rights: all, electronic, first, onetime, reprint (with info on where/when previously published)

Payment: 10¢-30¢/word, on acceptance or publication

Kill fee: sometimes

Sample: on the website

Manuscripts accepted per year: six

Seasonal submissions: two months

Guidelines: by email

Tip: "Book/music/movie reviews are a great place to start and build a relationship."

THE CHRISTIAN JOURNAL

1032 W. Main, Medford, OR 97501 | 541-773-4004
info@thechristianjournal.org | thechristianjournal.org
Chad McComas, senior editor

Parent company: Set Free Christian Fellowship
Type: monthly digital and print magazine, circulation 1,200
Audience: both Christians and non-Christians
Purpose: to provide inspiration and encouragement with the body of Christ in the Rogue Valley, Oregon
Submissions: Email complete manuscript or query letter. Responds in two weeks.
Length: 300–500 words, average around 400
Topics: Christian living, theme-related
Rights: onetime
Payment: none
Seasonal submissions: one month
Preferred Bible version: NIV
Theme list: available on website
Guidelines: *thechristianjournal.org/writers-information/guidelines-for-writers*
Sample: on the website
Tip: "Call or email with your idea."

CHRISTIAN LIBRARIAN

PO Box 4, Cedarville, OH 45314 | 937-766-2255
tcl@acl.org | www.acl.org/index.cfm/publications/the-christian-librarian
Garrett Trott, editor-in-chief
Craig Kubic, book reviews, ckubic@swbts.edu

Parent company: Association of Christian Librarians
Type: biannual print journal
Audience: primarily Christian librarians in institutions of higher learning
Purpose: to publish articles, provide a membership forum, and encourage writing
Submissions: Email complete manuscript as attachment.
Length: 1,000-5,000 words + 100-word abstract
Topics: library science
Rights: first
Payment: none
Guidelines: *www.acl.org/index.cfm/publications/the-christian-librarian/guidelines-for-authors*

CHRISTIAN NEWS NORTHWEST

710 E. Foothills Dr., Ste. 103C, Newberg, OR 97132 | 503-537-9220
cnnw@cnnw.com | *cnnw.com*
Tim Hirsch, editor

Parent company: Salt Media, LLC
Type: monthly digital and print newspaper, circulation 26,000, advertising accepted
Audience: evangelical Christian community in western and central Oregon and southwest Washington
Purpose: to encourage and inform the evangelical Christian community in our part of the Pacific Northwest
Submissions: Email complete manuscript as attachment or in body of message. Gives assignments.
Preferred Bible version: NIV
Sample: on the website
Tip: Note: A management change was scheduled for after the book went to press, and the current editor expected submission details to change. Check the website for updates.

CHRISTIAN RESEARCH JOURNAL

PO Box 8500, Charlotte, NC 28271-8500 | 704-887-8200
response@equip.org | *www.equip.org*
Melanie Cogdill, managing editor

Parent company: Christian Research Institute
Type: quarterly print journal
Audience: thoughtful laypeople, academics, scholars
Purpose: to equip Christians to discern errors in doctrine, biblical interpretation, and reasoning; to evangelize people of other faiths and belief systems; and to present a strong defense of Christian beliefs and ethics
Submissions: Email complete manuscript or query letter. Responds in four months.
Length: 1,700-3,500 words
Topics: apologetics, cults and new religions, evangelism
Rights: first, reprint
Payment: $175-$325
Kill fee: 50%
Guidelines: *www.equip.org/wp-content/uploads/2021/08/Writers-Guidelines.AUGUST-2021.pdf*
Tip: "Almost nothing can better prepare you to write for the *Christian Research Journal* than familiarity with the *Journal* itself. If you are

not a regular reader of the *Journal*, you should read all the articles in recent issues that correspond to the type of article you wish to write."

CHRISTIAN RETAILING

600 Rinehart Rd., Lake Mary, FL 32746 | 407-333-0600
jeff.struss@charismamedia.com | *www.christianretailing.com*
Jeff Struss, director of content development

Parent company: Charisma Media
Type: bimonthly digital and print journal, advertising accepted
Audience: retailers, church bookstores, publishers, music labels, distributors, and others working and volunteering in the Christian products industry
Purpose: to champion the world of Christian resources and to provide critical information and insight to advance business and ministry
Submissions: Assignments only; email query letter for assignment.
Topics: bookstores, trends
Payment: varies by assignment
Preferred Bible version: MEV
Guidelines: *www.christianretailing.com/index.php/general/28335-writersguidelines-christian-retailing*
Sample: on the website

CHRISTIAN STANDARD

16965 Pine Ln., Ste. 202, Parker, CO 80134 | 800-543-1353
cs@christianstandardmedia.com | *www.christianstandard.com*
Michael C. Mack, editor

Denomination: Christian Churches, Churches of Christ
Parent company: Christian Standard Media
Type: bimonthly digital and print magazine
Audience: paid and volunteer leaders
Purpose: to leverage the power of our unity and to resource Christian churches to fulfill Christ's commission
Submissions: Email query letter as attachment. Unsolicited freelance: 5%, 95% assigned. Responds in one to three months.
Length: maximum 1,800 words, prefers 500-1,200 words
Topics: theme-related
Rights: first, reprint (with info on where/when previously published)
Payment: $50-$250, on acceptance
Kill fee: sometimes
Manuscripts accepted per year: 15
Seasonal submissions: six to eight months

Preferred Bible version: NIV
Theme list: available on website
Guidelines: *christianstandard.com/writersguidelines*
Sample: on the website

CHRISTIANITY TODAY

465 Gundersen Dr., Carol Stream, IL 60188-2498 | 630-260-6200
editor@christianitytoday.com | *www.christianitytoday.com*
Ted Olsen, editorial director
Andy Olsen, managing editor
Matt Reynolds, books editor, mreynolds@christianitytoday.com

Type: monthly digital and print magazine, 4.3 million page views/
month, advertising accepted
Audience: Christian leaders throughout North America
Purpose: to provide evangelical thought leaders a sense of community,
coherence, and direction through thoughtful, biblical commentary
on issues and through careful, caring reporting of the news
Submissions: Only accepts query letter through the website.
Unsolicited freelance: small percentage.
Length: 300-1,800 words
Topics: Christian living, culture, issues
Rights: first
Payment: varies, on acceptance
Preferred Bible version: NIV
Guidelines: *help.christianitytoday.com/hc/en-us/
articles/360047411253-How-do-I-write-for-CT-*
Sample: articles are on the website
Tip: "We are most interested in stories of Christians living out their
faith in unique ways that impact the world for the better and
communicate truth in a way that is deep, nuanced, and challenging."

COLUMBIA

1 Columbus Plaza, New Haven, CT 06510-3326 | 203-752-4398
columbia@kofc.org | *www.kofc.org/en/news-room/columbia/index.html*
Alton J. Pelowski, editor

Denomination: Catholic
Parent company: Knights of Columbus
Type: monthly digital and print magazine, circulation 1.7 million
Audience: general Catholic family
Submissions: Email query letter.
Seasonal submissions: six months in advance

Length: 700-1,500 words
Topics: current events, family, finances, health, issues, parenting, trends
Rights: electronic, first
Payment: varies, on acceptance
Guidelines: *www.kofc.org/en/news-room/columbia/guidelines.html*
Sample: *www.kofc.org/en/columbia/cover/201610.html*

COMMONCALL: THE BAPTIST STANDARD MAGAZINE

PO Box 259019, Plano, TX 75025 | 214-630-4571
kencamp@baptiststandard.com | *www.baptiststandard.com*
Ken Camp, managing editor

Denomination: Baptist
Parent company: Baptist Standard Publishing
Type: quarterly print magazine
Audience: denomination
Purpose: to inform, inspire, and challenge people to live like Jesus
Topics: evangelism, family, leadership, ministry, missions, Texas Baptist history
Tip: "Looking for stories about everyday Christians who are putting their faith into action."

COMMONWEAL

475 Riverside Dr., Rm. 405, New York, NY 10115 | 212-662-4200
editors@commonwealmagazine.org | *www.commonwealmagazine.org*
Dominic Preziosi, editor

Denomination: Catholic
Type: monthly digital and print magazine
Audience: educated, committed Catholics, as well as readers from other faith traditions
Purpose: to provide a forum for civil, reasoned debate on the interaction of faith with contemporary politics and culture
Submissions: Send complete manuscript or query letter through the website. Responds in six to eight weeks.
Length: 750-3,000 words
Topics: issues, literature and the arts
Manuscripts accepted per year: poems, 30
Rights: all
Payment: on publication
Guidelines: *www.commonwealmagazine.org/contact-us*
Sample: request by email
Tip: Articles fall into three categories: (1) "'Upfronts,' running from

1,500 to 2,500 words, are brief, 'newsy' and reportorial, giving facts, information, and some interpretation behind the 'headlines of the day.' (2) Longer articles, running from 2,500 to 5,000 words, are more reflective and detailed, bringing new information or a different point of view to a subject, raising questions, and/or proposing solutions to the dilemmas facing the world, nation, church, or individual. (3) The 'Last Word' column, running from 750 to 1,300 words, is a more personal reflection, on some aspect of the human condition: spiritual, individual, political, or social."

THE COVENANT COMPANION (COV)

8303 W. Higgins Rd., Chicago, IL 60631 | 773-907-3328
editor@covchurch.org | *covenantcompanion.com*
Cathy Norman Peterson, managing editor

Denomination: Evangelical Covenant Church
Type: biannual print magazine
Audience: denomination
Purpose: to inform, stimulate thought, and encourage dialogue on issues that impact the church and its members
Submissions: Email or mail.
Length: 1,200-1,800 words
Topics: Christian living, church, church outreach, denomination, issues, justice
Rights: onetime
Payment: $35-$100 two months after publication
Guidelines: *covenantcompanion.com/submit-story*
Tip: "We are interested in what is happening in local churches, conferences, and other Covenant institutions and associations, as well as reports from missionaries and other staff serving around the world. Human interest stories are also welcome."

CREATION

PO Box 4545, Eight Mile Plains, QLD 4113, Australia | 073 340 9888
m.wieland@creation.info | *creation.com/creation-magazine*
Dr. Don Batten, Dr. Tas Walker, Dr. Jonathan Sarfati, editors

Parent company: Creation Ministries International
Type: quarterly digital and print magazine, circulation 40,000
Audience: families, homeschoolers, age 9 to adulthood
Purpose: to support the effective proclamation of the Gospel by providing credible answers that affirm the reliability of the Bible, in particular its Genesis history

Submissions: Only accepts complete manuscript, cover letter required; email as attachment. Unsolicited freelance: 20%. Responds in one week. Accepts submissions from teens.

Length: maximum 1,500 words

Topics: creation science, evolution's errors

Rights: will be requested

Payment: none

Manuscripts accepted per year: more than 100

Seasonal submissions: six months in advance

Preferred Bible version: ESV

Guidelines: *creation.com/creation-magazine-writing-guidelines*

Sample: on the website

Tip: "Looking for articles on creation/evolution debate."

CREATIVE INSPIRATIONS

PO Box 19051, Kalamazoo, MI 49009 | 269-348-5712

creativeinspirations01@gmail.com | *authormjreynolds.com*

MJ Reynolds, publisher, editor

Type: bimonthly digital magazine

Audience: poets and people who appreciate poetry

Purpose: to publish inspirational poetry

Submissions: Email as attachment or in body of message, or mail submission. Unsolicited freelance: 100%. Responds in one to two weeks. Also takes submissions from teens.

Topics: Christian living, family, nature

Rights: onetime

Payment: none

Manuscripts accepted per year: varies

Preferred Bible version: NIV

Guidelines: by email

Sample: request by email

Tip: "Follow the submission guidelines."

DIVINE MOMENTS BOOK SERIES

Grace Publishing, PO Box 1233, Broken Arrow, OK 74013-1233 | 918-346-7960

terri@grace-publishing.com | *www.grace-publishing.com*

Terri Kalfas, compiler and editor

Parent company: Grace Publishing

Type: two or three books per year

Audience: general and Christian

Purpose: to show how faith works in everyday life experiences

Submissions: Only accepts complete manuscript; email as attachment. Unsolicited freelance: 100%. Responds in two weeks.
Length: 500-2,000 words
Topics: brokenness, Christmas, questioning, romance, theme-related
Rights: onetime
Payment: none, royalties donated to Samaritan's Purse
Manuscripts accepted per year: maximum 50
Seasonal submissions: six months
Preferred Bible version: any
Theme list: available on website
Guidelines: *grace-publishing.com*
Tip: "We need stories for these books: *Lost Moments, Questionable Moments, Favorite Moments, Christmas Moments, Patriotic Moments.*"

DTS MAGAZINE

3909 Swiss Ave., Dallas, TX 75204
magazine@dts.edu | *www.dts.edu/magazine*
Rebecca Walton, editor

Parent company: Dallas Theological Seminary (DTS)
Type: quarterly digital and print magazine, circulation 35,000
Audience: evangelical laypeople, students, alumni, donors, and friends
Purpose: to apply biblical truth to life as a ministry to friends of Dallas Theological Seminary
Submissions: Email query letter. Responds in six to eight weeks.
Length: 1,500-2,000 words
Topics: Christian living
Rights: first, reprint
Payment: $300, $100 for reprints
Seasonal submissions: six months in advance
Guidelines: *voice.dts.edu/magazine/editorial-policies*
Sample: *voice.dts.edu/magazine*
Tip: "DTS Magazine is a ministry of Dallas Theological Seminary. We prefer articles written by our alumni, faculty, students, staff, board members, donors and their families."

ETERNAL INK

4706 Fantasy Ln., Alton, IL 62002 | 618-466-7860
sonsong@charter.net
Mary-Ellen Grisham, editor

Type: biweekly e-zine, circulation 450
Audience: general

Purpose: to inspire, edify, and enlighten

Submissions: Only accepts email in body of message. Unsolicited freelance: 5-10%. Responds in two weeks.

Length: 400-600 words

Topics: Christian living, seasonal

Rights: onetime, reprint

Payment: none

Sample: email request

Manuscripts accepted per year: 200

Seasonal submissions: two months

Preferred Bible version: NIV

Guidelines: by email

Tip: Looking for "scriptural studies, verses or passages, clearly focused and easy to understand."

EVANGELICAL MISSIONS QUARTERLY

PO Box 398, Wheaton, IL 60187 | 678-392-4577

emq@wheaton.edu | *missionexus.org/emq*

Marv Newell, editorial director

Parent company: Missio Nexus

Type: quarterly digital journal

Audience: missionaries, mission agency executives, mission professors, missionary candidates, students, mission pastors, mission-minded church leaders, mission supporters, and agency board members

Purpose: to increase the effectiveness of the evangelical missionary enterprise

Submissions: Email complete manuscript as attachment.

Length: 2,000-3,000 words

Topics: church planting, culture, discipleship, evangelism, leadership, missions, trends

Rights: first

Guidelines: *missionexus.org/emq/submit-an-article-to-emq*

Tip: "We are not a scholarly journal written for academics, but desire material that is academically respectable, reflecting careful thought and practical application to missions professionals, and especially working missionaries. We like to see problems not only diagnosed, but solved either by way of illustration or suggestion."

FAITH & FRIENDS

The Salvation Army, 2 Overlea Blvd., Toronto, ON M4H 1P4, Canada | 416-422-6226

faithandfriends@can.salvationarmy.org | *salvationist.ca/editorial/faith-and-friends*
Giselle Randall, features editor

Denomination: The Salvation Army
Type: monthly digital and print magazine, circulation 50,000+
Audience: general
Purpose: to show Jesus Christ at work in the lives of real people and to
provide spiritual resources for those who are new to the Christian faith
Submissions: Email query letter as attachment. Looking for stories
about people whose lives have been changed through an encounter
with Jesus: conversion, miracles, healing, faith in the midst of crisis,
forgiveness, reconciliation, answered prayers, and more. Profiles of
people who have found hope and healing through their ministries,
including prisoners, hospital patients, nursing-home residents, single
parents in distress, addicts, the unemployed, or homeless.
Length: 750-1,200 words
Topics: Christian living, family, marriage, theology
Rights: first, reprint
Payment: none
Preferred Bible version: TNIV
Guidelines: *salvationist.ca/files/salvationarmy/Magazines/FAITH-
FRIENDS.pdf*
Sample: on the website

FAITH ON EVERY CORNER

159 Hudson Cajah Mountain Rd., Hudson, NC 28638 | 828-305-8571
team@faithoneverycorner.com | *www.faithoneverycorner.com/magazine.html*
Craig Ruhl, managing editor
Karen Ruhl, publisher and editor in chief

Parent company: Faith On Every Corner, LLC
Type: monthly digital magazine, circulation 2,500
Audience: families, seekers
Purpose: to inspire, educate, and show how everyday people are making
a difference in their communities through acts of faith and service
Submissions: Only accepts email as attachment. Unsolicited freelance:
75%. Responds in two to five days. Accepts submissions from teens.
Faith On Every Corner is now being read in more than 85 countries,
so use universal illustrations and language.
Length: 350-1,200 words
Topics: Christian living, encouragement, evangelism, family, parenting,
service
Rights: onetime

Payment: none
Manuscripts accepted per year: 250
Seasonal submissions: one to two months
Preferred Bible version: NIV, NLT, CSB, KJV, NKJV, ESB
Theme list: available on website, also by email
Guidelines: *www.faithoneverycorner.com/submission-guidelines.html;*
   also by email
Sample: on the website
Tip: "Feel free to pitch ideas for articles, stories or other content by
   email."

FAITH TODAY

9821 Leslie St., Ste. 103, Richmond Hill, ON L4B 3Y4 Canada
editor@faithtoday.ca | www.faithtoday.ca
Bill Fledderus, senior editor
Karen Stiller, senior editor

Parent company: The Evangelical Fellowship of Canada
Type: bimonthly digital and print magazine; circulation: print, 12,000,
   online, 5,000; advertising accepted
Audience: Canadian evangelicals
Purpose: to connect, equip, and inform Canada's four million
   evangelical Christians from Anglican and Baptist to Pentecostal
   and Salvation Army
Submissions: Email query letter with clips. Unsolicited freelance:
   10%. Responds in one week.
Length: 350-1,800 words
Topics: church, issues, trends
Rights: electronic, first, onetime, reprint (with info on where/when
   previously published)
Payment: on acceptance
Payment: 15¢-25¢ CAD/word
Kill fee: sometimes
Manuscripts accepted per year: 100
Seasonal submissions: four months
Guidelines: *www.faithtoday.ca/writers*
Sample: *www.faithtoday.ca/digital*
Tip: "What is the Canadian angle? How does your approach include
   diverse Canadian voices from different churches, regions,
   generations, etc.?"

FOCUS ON THE FAMILY

8605 Explorer Dr., Colorado Springs, CO 80920
FocusMagsSubmissions@family.com | *www.focusonthefamily.com/magazine*
Sheila Seifert, editorial director

Parent company: Focus on the Family
Type: bimonthly print magazine
Audience: parents, primarily of ages 4-12
Purpose: to encourage, teach, and celebrate God's design for the family
Submissions: Email complete manuscript or query letter. Responds in eight weeks or not interested.
Length: 50-1,500 words
Topics: family, marriage, parenting
Rights: first
Payment: on acceptance
Payment: 25¢/word; $50 for short pieces
Guidelines: *www.focusonthefamily.com/magazine/call-for-submissions*
Sample: articles are on the website
Tip: "Looking for stories about how parents have dealt with challenges and come up with active, practical ways (beyond explaining or talking) of solving those problems."

FRIENDS JOURNAL

1216 Arch St., Ste. 2A, Philadelphia, PA 19107 | 215-563-8629
martink@friendsjournal.org | *www.friendsjournal.org*
Martin Kelly, senior editor

Denomination: Religious Society of Friends
Type: monthly digital and print magazine
Audience: denomination
Purpose: to communicate Quaker experience in order to connect and deepen spiritual lives
Submissions: Email through the website. Departments, around 1,500 words or fewer: "Celebration," "Earthcare," "Faith and Practice," "First-day School," "Friends in Business," "History," "Humor," "Life in the Meeting," "Lives of Friends," "Pastoral Care," "Q&A," "Reflection," "Religious Education," "Remembrance," "Service," "Witness."
Length: 1,200-2,500 words
Topics: theme-related
Rights: first
Payment: none
Theme list: available on website

Guidelines: *www.friendsjournal.org/submissions*
Sample: articles are on the website

GEMS OF TRUTH

7407-7415 Metcalf Ave., Overland Park, KS 66204 | 913-432-0331
www.heraldandbanner.com
Gordon L. Snider, editor of publications

Denomination: Church of God
Parent company: Herald and Banner Press
Type: weekly take-home paper
Audience: denomination
Submissions: Only accepts manuscripts through the website.
Length: fiction, 1,000-2,000 words
Topics: Christian living
Seasonal submissions: six to eight months in advance
Preferred Bible version: KJV
Sample: download from website

THE GOOD NEWS (FLORIDA)

PO Box 670368, Coral Springs, FL 33067 | 954-564-5378
ShellyP@goodnewsfl.org | *www.goodnewsfl.org*
Shelly Pond, editor

Parent company: Good News Media Group, LLC
Type: monthly digital and print newspaper; circulation 80,000 print,
    30,000 digital; advertising accepted
Audience: Dade, Broward and Palm Beach, Florida areas
Submissions: Email query letter with clips.
Length: 500-800 words
Payment: 10¢/word
Sample: on the website

THE GOOD NEWS (NEW YORK)

PO Box 18204, Rochester, NY 14618 | 585-271-4464
info@TheGoodNewsNY.org | *www.thegoodnewswny.com*
Alexandre V. Boutakov, editor

Type: bimonthly print newspaper, circulation 4,400, advertising
    accepted
Audience: New York state
Submissions: Email query letter.
Sample: on the website

THE GOOD NEWS JOURNAL

9701 Copper Creek, Austin, TX 78729 | 512-260-1800
goodnewsjournal10@gmail.com | *www.thegoodnewsjournal.net*
Bill Myers, editor

> **Type:** bimonthly digital and print newspaper, advertising accepted
> **Audience:** Capital MetroPlex and Central Texas areas
> **Purpose:** to provide leadership to individuals and corporations with a positive, patriotic, godly perspective
> **Submissions:** Email query letter.
> **Length:** 350 words
> **Payment:** none
> **Sample:** on the website

GRACECONNECT

PO Box 544, Winona Lake, IN 46590 | 574-268-1122
lcgates@bmhbooks.com | *www.graceconnect.us*
Liz Cutler Gates, executive director

> **Denomination:** Grace Brethren
> **Parent company:** Brethren Missionary Herald Company
> **Type:** quarterly print magazine
> **Audience:** pastors, elders, and other leaders
> **Purpose:** to build bridges of communication between the people and churches of the denomination
> **Submissions:** Only accepts through the website.
> **Length:** 1,000-1,500 words, sometimes 600-800 words or up to 2,000 words
> **Guidelines:** *graceconnect.us/grace-stories/submit-a-story-idea*
> **Tip:** "Feature stories should have a Grace Brethren connection."

GUIDEPOSTS

110 William St., Ste. 901, New York, NY 10038 | 212-251-8100
submissions@guideposts.com | *www.guideposts.org/brand/guideposts-magazine*
Rick Hamlin and Amy Wong, executive editors

> **Type:** bimonthly digital and print magazine
> **Audience:** general
> **Purpose:** to help readers find peace of mind, solve tough personal problems, and build satisfying relationships
> **Submissions:** Submit queries and manuscripts through the online form at *guideposts.org/tell-us-your-story*. Unsolicited freelance: 40%. Responds in two months or not interested. Publishes true, first-

person stories about people who have attained a goal, surmounted an obstacle, or learned a helpful lesson through their faith. A typical story is a first-person narrative with a spiritual point the reader can apply to his or her own life. Short anecdotes similar to full-length articles, 50-250 words, for departments: "Someone Cares," stories of kindness and caring, *sc@guideposts.com*; "Mysterious Ways," "Family Room," "What Prayer Can Do." Also takes inspiring quotes for "The Up Side," *upside@guideposts.com*.

Length: articles, 1,500 words; department anecdotes, 50-250 words
Rights: all
Payment: $100-$500, on acceptance
Kill fee: 20% but not to first-time freelancers
Manuscripts accepted per year: 40-60
Guidelines: *www.guideposts.org/writers-guidelines*
Tip: "Be able to tell a good story, with drama, suspense, description, and dialog. The point of the story should be some practical spiritual help that the subject learns through his or her experience. Use unique spiritual insights, strong and unusual dramatic details."

HEARTBEAT

PO Box 9, Hatfield, AR 71945 | 870-389-6196
heartbeat@cmausa.org | *www.cmausa.org/cma_national/heartbeat.asp*
Misty Bradley, editor

Parent company: Christian Motorcyclists Association
Type: monthly digital and print magazine
Audience: motorcyclists
Purpose: to inspire leaders and members to be the most organized, advanced, equipped, financially stable organization, full of integrity in the motorcycling industry and the Kingdom of God
Submissions: Email complete manuscript.
Topic: motorcycling

HIGHWAY NEWS

1525 River Rd., Marietta, PA 17547 | 717-426-9977
editor@transportforchrist.org | *tfcglobal.org/highway-news/current-issue*
Joanna Maart, managing editor

Parent company: Transport for Christ, International
Type: monthly digital magazine, circulation 18,000-20,000
Audience: truck drivers and their families
Purpose: to lead truck drivers, as well as the trucking community, to Jesus Christ and help them grow in their faith

Submissions: Email complete manuscript. Unsolicited freelance: 10-20%.

Length: 800-1,000 words

Topics: trucking life

Rights: first, reprint

Payment: none

Seasonal submissions: six months in advance

Preferred Bible version: ESV

Guidelines: by email

Sample: download from the website

Tip: "Articles submitted for publication do not have to be religious in nature; however, they should not conflict with or oppose guidelines and principles presented in the Bible."

HOLINESS TODAY

17001 Prairie Star Pkwy., Lenexa, KS 66220 | 913-577-0500

holinesstoday@nazarene.org | *www.holinesstoday.org*

Nate Gilmore, content editor

Denomination: Nazarene

Type: bimonthly digital and print magazine, circulation 11,000, advertising accepted

Audience: denomination

Purpose: to keep readers connected with the Nazarene experience and provide tools for everyday faith

Submissions: Email complete manuscript as attachment. Unsolicited freelance: 30%. Responds in one day. Also accepts submissions from children and teens.

Length: 700-1,100 words

Topics: denomination, ministry, teaching

Rights: first, reprint (with info on where/when previously published)

Payment: $135, on publication

Kill fee: yes

Manuscripts accepted per year: six to eight

Preferred Bible version: NIV

Theme list: available by email

Guidelines: by email

Tip: "We are always interested in hearing from Nazarene pastors, lay leaders, and experts in their fields. We are a Nazarene publication that wants our articles to be relevant and applicable to real-life scenarios and the world we live in."

HOMELIFE

1 Lifeway Plaza, Nashville, TN 37234-0172 | 615-251-2196
homelife@lifeway.com | *www.lifeway.com/en/product-family/homelife-magazine*
David Bennett, managing editor

Denomination: Southern Baptist
Parent company: LifeWay Christian Resources
Type: monthly print magazine, circulation 250,000
Audience: parents
Purpose: to address all things faith, family, and life
Submissions: Email complete manuscript as attachment. Gives assignments. Unsolicited freelance: 10%. Responds in several weeks.
Length: 1,500-7,500 words
Topics: faith, living on mission, marriage, parenting
Rights: first
Payment: $100-$400, on publication
Manuscripts accepted per year: 20
Seasonal submissions: four months in advance
Preferred Bible version: CSB
Guidelines: by email
Sample: on the website
Tip: "Include full bio, church name, and denomination with submission."

HOMESCHOOLING TODAY

PO Box 1092, Somerset, KY 42502 | 606-485-4105
editor@homeschoolingtoday.com | *homeschoolingtoday.com*
Ashley Wiggers, co-executive editor
Kay Chance, co-executive editor

Parent company: Paradigm Press
Type: triannual digital and print magazine, circulation 5,000-6,000, advertising accepted
Audience: homeschooling parents
Purpose: to encourage the hearts of homeschoolers and give them tools to instill a love of learning in their children
Submissions: Email complete manuscript as attachment. Responds in six months or not interested. Feature articles include information about a topic, unit study, encouragement, challenge, or an interview, 900-1,200 words. Departments: "Faces of Homeschooling," true stories about real homeschooling families, 600-900 words; "The Home Team," physical education, 600-900 words; "Homeschooling around the

World," 600-900 words; "Language Learning," foreign languages, 600-900 words; "Thinking," logic, critical thinking, 600-900 words; "Unit Study," 800-1500 words; "Family Math," 600-900 words.

Length: 600-1,500 words
Topics: education, homeschooling
Rights: electronic, first, reprint
Payment: 10¢/published word
Guidelines: *homeschoolingtoday.com/write-for-us*

IMAGE

3307 Third Ave. W, Seattle, WA 98119 | 206-281-2988
mkenagy@imagejournal.org | *imagejournal.org*
Mary Kenagy Mitchell, executive editor
Shane McCrae, poetry editor, shanemccrae@imagejournal.com
Melissa Pritchard, fiction editor, mpritchard@imagejournal.org
Nick Ripatrazone, culture editor, nripatrazoe@imagejournal.org
Lauren F. Winner, creative nonfiction editor, lwinner@imagejournal.org

Type: quarterly print journal
Audience: people interested in art and literature
Purpose: to demonstrate the continued vitality and diversity of contemporary art and literature that engage with the religious traditions of Western culture
Submissions: Submit complete manuscript or query letter through the website. Accepts simultaneous submissions. Responds in five months.
Length: 3,000-6,000 words
Topics: literature and the arts
Rights: first
Payment: $25/published page; $3/line for poetry; minimum $100, maximum $400
Guidelines: on website
Tip: "All the work we publish reflects what we see as a sustained engagement with one of the western faiths—Judaism, Christianity, or Islam. That engagement can include unease, grappling, or ambivalence as well as orthodoxy; the approach can be indirect or allusive, but for a piece to be a fit for *Image*, some connection to faith must be there."

INFLUENCE

1445 N. Boonville Ave., Springfield, MO 65802 | 417-862-2781
editor@influencemagazine.com | *influencemagazine.com*
John Davidson, senior editor

152

Denomination: Assemblies of God
Type: bimonthly digital and print magazine
Audience: pastors and other leaders
Purpose: to provide a Christ-centered, Spirit-empowered perspective that propels people to engage their faith—as individuals, in community, and with the global Church
Submissions: Email complete manuscript or query letter.
Length: 700-1,000 words
Topics: career, community, current events, family
Rights: first
Guidelines: *influencemagazine.com/submission-guidelines*
Sample: *influencemagazine.com/en/issues*
Tip: "Both online and in print, we aim to unite and edify the Church through content marked by integrity and creativity. Our approach to the Christian life is holistic, offering a faith-based context for cultural and current events, as well as providing practical insight for your family, daily life, career and community."

INSITE

PO Box 62189, Colorado Springs, CO 80962-2189 | 719-260-9400
editor@ccca.org | www.ccca.org
Leah Gooderl, editor

Parent company: Christian Camp and Conference Association
Type: bimonthly digital and print magazine, circulation 8,500
Audience: camp and conference-center leaders
Purpose: to maximize ministry for member camps and conference centers
Submissions: Email, query letter. Unsolicited freelance: 1-2%. Responds in one week.
Length: 1,000-1,500 words
Topics: business, camping ministry, discipleship, facilities, leadership, legal, relationships
Rights: all
Payment: $300, on publication
Kill fee: sometimes
Seasonal submissions: six months ahead
Preferred Bible version: NIV
Theme list: available on website
Guidelines: *www.ccca.org/ccca/Publications.asp*
Sample: via email
Tip: "All articles must be applicable to camps and conference centers."

INTERNATIONAL JOURNAL OF FRONTIER MISSIOLOGY

1605 E. Elizabeth St., Pasadena, CA 91104 | 734-765-0368
editors@ijfm.org | www.ijfm.org
Brad Gill, editor

Parent company: International Society for Frontier Missiology
Type: quarterly print journal
Audience: mission professors, executives, and researchers; missionaries, young-adult mission mobilizers
Purpose: to cultivate an international fraternity of thought in the development of frontier missiology
Submissions: Only accepts query letter.
Length: 2,000-6,000 words
Topics: missions
Payment: none
Guidelines: *www.ijfm.org/author_info.htm*
Sample: on the website

THE JOURNAL OF ADVENTIST EDUCATION

12501 Old Columbia Pike, Silver Spring, MD 20904-6600 | 301-680-5069
mcgarrellf@gc.adventist.org | jae.adventist.org
Faith-Ann McGarrell, editor

Denomination: Seventh-day Adventist
Parent company: General Conference of Seventh-day Adventists
Type: quarterly digital journal, circulation 10,000-16,000, advertising accepted
Audience: educators and administrators
Purpose: to aid professional teachers and educational administrators worldwide, kindergarten to higher education
Submissions: Submit complete manuscript through the website. Unsolicited freelance: 10%. Responds in four to six weeks.
Length: 1,500-2,500 words
Topics: Christian education
Rights: first, reprint (with info on where/when previously published)
Payment: varies, on publication
Manuscripts accepted per year: 32
Seasonal submissions: six months in advance
Preferred Bible version: NIV
Guidelines: *jae.adventist.org/calls-for-manuscripts*
Sample: download from the website
Tip: Wants "articles on best practices for teaching and pedagogy that can be applied in education settings both nationally and internationally."

JOYFUL LIVING MAGAZINE

PO Box 311, Palo Cedro, CA 97073 | 530-247-7500
joyfullivingmagazineredding@gmail.com | *joyfullivingmagazine.com*
Cathy Jansen, editor in chief

Type: quarterly digital magazine, advertising accepted
Audience: general
Purpose: to share encouragement and hope, to help readers grow
spiritually and emotionally, and to help them in their everyday lives
with practical issues
Submissions: Email complete manuscript as attachment.
Length: 200-700 words
Topics: aging, Christian living, depression, family, finances, health,
marriage, singleness, work
Payment: none
Guidelines: *joyfullivingmagazine.com/writers-info.html*
Sample: *www.joyfullivingmagazine.com/issues*
Tip: "*Joyful Living* is dedicated to sharing encouragement and hope
to people of all ages. That encouragement finds its way through
articles of hope, love, caring, sharing. Also we have articles on
health, finance and other subjects that help us grow in maturity
and in our daily living."

JUST BETWEEN US

777 S. Barker Rd., Brookfield, WI 53045 | 262-786-6478
submissions@justbetweenus.org | *www.justbetweenus.org*
Shelly Esser, executive editor

Parent company: Elmbrook Church
Type: quarterly print magazine, circulation 8,000
Audience: women
Purpose: to encourage and equip women for a life of faith and service
Submissions: Email complete manuscript as attachment. Responds in
six to eight weeks or not interested.
Length: articles, 1,000-1,200 words; testimonies, 450 words
Topics: Christian living, evangelism, faith, finances, friendship,
ministry, parenting, prayer, relationships, spiritual warfare
Payment: none
Preferred Bible version: NIV
Guidelines: *justbetweenus.org/magazine/writers-guidelines-for-just-
between-us*
Sample: *justbetweenus.org/magazine-sample-issue*
Tip: "Articles should be personal in tone, full of real-life anecdotes as

well as quotes/advice from noted Christian professionals, and be biblically based. Articles need to be practical and have a distinct Christian and serving perspective throughout."

LEADING HEARTS

PO Box 6421, Longmont, CO 80501 | 303-835-8473
amber@leadinghearts.com | *leadinghearts.com*
Amber Weigland-Buckley, editor

> **Parent company:** Right to the Heart Ministries
> **Type:** bimonthly digital magazine, circulation 60,000, advertising accepted
> **Audience:** women who lead hearts at home, church, work, and community; ages 35-50
> **Submissions:** Assignment only. To audition for an assignment, email an article of 1,200 words maximum and a short résumé. Gives preferred consideration to members of AWSA.
> **Length:** 800 words maximum; columns, 250-500 words
> **Topics:** theme-related
> **Rights:** first, reprint
> **Payment:** none
> **Preferred Bible version:** NIV
> **Theme list:** not available
> **Guidelines:** *leadinghearts.com/wp-content/uploads/2014/06/ WritersGuidelines.pdf*
> **Sample:** download from the website

LEAVES

PO Box 87, Dearborn, MI 48121-0087 | 313-561-2330
editor.leaves@mariannhill.us | *www.mariannhill.us/leaves.html*
Rev. Thomas Heier , editor-in-chief

> **Denomination:** Catholic
> **Parent company:** Marianhill Mission Society
> **Type:** bimonthly print magazine, circulation 10,000
> **Audience:** Catholics, primarily in the Detroit, Michigan, area
> **Purpose:** to promote devotion to God and testimony of His blessings
> **Submissions:** Submit complete manuscript by email or mail.
> **Length:** 250 words
> **Topics:** Christian living, prayer
> **Rights:** first, reprint
> **Payment:** none
> **Manuscripts accepted per year:** 40

Preferred Bible version: RSV Catholic edition
Sample: articles are on the website
Tip: Greatest need is for personal testimonies.

LEBEN

2150 River Plaza Dr., Ste. 150, Sacramento, CA 95833 | 916-473-8866
editor@leben.us | www.leben.us
Wayne C. Johnson, editor

Parent company: City Seminary of Sacramento, California
Type: quarterly print journal
Audience: general
Purpose: to tell the stories of the people and events that make up the Reformation tradition
Submissions: Popular history publication that aims at a general readership. Only accepts query letter through the website.
Length: 500-2,500 words
Topics: Reformers
Guidelines: *www.leben.us/writers*
Tip: "Focus on lesser-known events and people. We have no shortage of submissions about Luther, Calvin, Zwingli, etc."

LIGHT + LIFE MAGAZINE

770 N. High School Rd., Indianapolis, IN 46214 | 317-244-3660
jeff.finley@fmcusa.org | lightandlifemagazine.com
Jeff Finley, executive editor

Denomination: Free Methodist
Parent company: Free Methodist Church - USA
Type: monthly print magazine, circulation 14,000
Audience: general
Purpose: to offer encouragement, provide resources, deal with contemporary issues, share denominational news, and offer faith to unbelievers
Submissions: Submit complete manuscript or query letter by email as attachment. Unsolicited freelance: 50%. Responds in two months.
Length: 800-2,100 words
Topics: theme-related
Rights: first, onetime, reprint (with info on where/when previously published)
Payment: $50-$100, on publication
Preferred Bible version: NIV
Theme list: available via email

Guidelines: *fmcusa.org/lightandlifemag/writers*
Sample: download from the website
Tip: "We search for authors who write competently, provide clear information, and employ contemporary style and illustrations."

LIGHT MAGAZINE

901 Commerce St., Ste. 550, Nashville, TN 37203 | 615-244-2495
nicolet@erlc.com | *erlc.com/light*
Lindsay Nicolet, managing editor

Denomination: Southern Baptist
Parent company: The Ethics and Religious Liberty Commission
Type: biannual digital and print journal, circulation 10,000, advertising accepted
Audience: church and ministry leaders
Purpose: to bear witness to the gospel by speaking to congregations and consciences with a thoroughly Christian moral witness
Submissions: Email complete manuscript as attachment. Unsolicited freelance: 10%. Responds in one week.
Length: 1,500 words
Topics: culture, ethics, family, justice, parenting, politics
Rights: all
Payment: depends on article and writer
Manuscripts accepted per year: ten
Preferred Bible version: CSB
Guidelines: not available
Sample: email request
Tip: "Looking for articles tied to current events and focus on local church ministry."

LIVE

1445 N. Boonville Ave., Springfield, MO 65802-1894 | 417-862-2781
WQuick@ag.org | *myhealthychurch.com*
Wade Quick, editor

Denomination: Assemblies of God
Parent company: Gospel Publishing House
Type: weekly take-home paper, circulation 12,000
Audience: denomination
Purpose: to encourage Christians in living for God through stories that apply biblical principles to everyday problems
Submissions: Only accepts email as attachment. Unsolicited freelance: 100%.

Length: 200-1,200 words; poetry, 12-25 lines
Topics: Christian living
Rights: first, reprint
Payment: 10¢/word for first rights, 7¢/word for reprint, $42-$60 for poetry, on acceptance
Seasonal submissions: 18 months
Preferred Bible version: NLT
Guidelines: *myhealthychurch.com/store/startcat.cfm?cat=tWRITGUID*
Tip: "Stories should be encouraging, challenging, and/or humorous. Even problem-centered stories should be upbeat. Stories should not be preachy, critical, or moralizing. They should not present pat, trite, or simplistic answers to problems. No Bible fiction or sci-fi. Make sure the stories have a strong Christian element, are written well, have strong takeaways, but do not preach."

LUTHERAN FORUM

PO Box 327, Delhi, NY 13753-0327 | 607-746-7511
lutheranforum.org
R. David Nelson, editor

Denomination: Lutheran
Parent company: American Lutheran Publicity Bureau
Type: quarterly print journal
Audience: denomination
Purpose: to offer insightful, confessional commentary and scholarship to the Lutheran churches in America
Submissions: Email complete manuscript or query letter. Responds in three months.
Length: 2,000-3,000 words
Topics: wide variety
Rights: first
Payment: none
Guidelines: *alpb.org/writers-guidelines*
Tip: "Prospective writers are encouraged to reflect on what moves them most, intellectually and spiritually, and then, armed with adequate research and forethought, put their ideas to paper."

THE LUTHERAN WITNESS

1333 S. Kirkwood Rd., St. Louis, MO 63122-7226 | 800-248-1930
lutheran.witness@lcms.org | *witness.lcms.org*
Roy S. Askins, managing editor

Denomination: Lutheran Church Missouri Synod

Type: monthly print magazine, circulation 120,000
Audience: denomination
Purpose: to interpret the contemporary world from a Lutheran perspective
Submissions: Email or mail complete manuscript.
Length: 500, 1,000, or 1,500 words
Topics: theme-related
Rights: electronic, first
Payment: based on both article length and complexity and author's credentials, on acceptance
Preferred Bible version: ESV
Theme list: available on website
Guidelines: *witness.lcms.org/contribute*
Tip: "Because of the magazine's long lead time, and because many features are planned at least six months in advance of the publication date, your story should have a long-term perspective that keeps it relevant several months from the time you submit it."

MATURE LIVING

1 Lifeway Plaza, MSN 136, Nashville, TN 37234-0175 | 615-251-2000
matureliving@lifeway.com | *www.lifeway.com/en/product-family/mature-living-magazine*
Debbie Dickerson, managing editor

Denomination: Southern Baptist
Parent company: LifeWay Christian Resources
Type: monthly print magazine
Audience: ages 55 and older
Purpose: to equip mature adults as they live a legacy of leadership, stewardship, and discipleship
Submissions: Assignment only; email for possible assignment. Open for "Kicks and Grins," fun stories of your grandkids, 25-125 words; challenging biblical word search puzzles; and crossword puzzles.
Topics: caregiving, evangelism, marriage, parenting, relationships, theology
Preferred Bible version: CSB
Sample: on the website

THE MESSENGER

440 Main St., Steinbach, MB R5G 1Z5, Canada | 204-326-6401
messenger@emconference.ca | *emcmessenger.ca*
Rebecca Roman, interim editor

Denomination: Mennonite

Type: bimonthly digital and print magazine, circulation 2,700

Audience: members and adherents of churches within the Evangelical Mennonite Conference

Purpose: to inform concerning events and activities of the denomination, instruct in godliness and victorious living, and inspire to earnestly contend for the faith

Submissions: Only accepts query letter. Unsolicited freelance: 50%. Responds in two weeks.

Length: 1,200-1,500 words

Topics: wide variety

Rights: first, reprint (with info on where/when previously published)

Payment: $150, on publication

Kill fee: always

Manuscripts accepted per year: few, mostly assigned

Seasonal submissions: minimum three months in advance

Preferred Bible version: NIV

Guidelines: *emcmessenger.ca/submission-guidelines*

Sample: *issuu.com/emcmessenger*

Tip: "Always query first. A lead article involves a mixture of teaching, interpretation, and opinion. Effective writers 'inform, instruct, and inspire.' They display an informed opinion, a balance in approach, a Christ-centered focus, and concern for the well-being of the Church. The writer is expected to observe and comment on conference trends and issues as deemed fit. The purpose of a lead article is not to create controversy, but to motivate thought and action."

THE MESSIANIC TIMES

50 Alberta Dr., Amhurst, NY 14226 | 866-612-7770

editor@messianictimes.com | *www.messianictimes.com*

Sheila Fisher, editorial coordinator

Denomination: Messianic

Parent company: Times of the Messiah Ministries

Type: bimonthly digital and print newspaper, advertising accepted

Audience: Messianic community

Purpose: to provide accurate, authoritative, and current information to unite the international Messianic Jewish community, teach Christians the Jewish roots of their faith, and proclaim that Yeshua is the Jewish Messiah

Submissions: Query by email.

METHODIST HISTORY JOURNAL

36 Madison Ave., Madison, NJ 07940 | 973-408-3189
atday@gcah.org | *www.gcah.org*
Alfred T. Day, III, general secretary

Denomination: United Methodist
Parent company: General Commission on Archives and History, United Methodist Church
Type: biannual print journal
Audience: denomination
Submissions: Email complete manuscript as attachment.
Length: 5,000 words maximum
Topics: United Methodist history
Payment: none
Guidelines: *www.gcah.org/research/methodist-history-journal*
Tip: "Articles on the history of other denominations and subjects will be considered when there are strong ties to events and persons significant to the history of the United Methodist tradition. Manuscripts pertaining to strictly local, as opposed to national or international interest, are not accepted."

MINISTRY

12501 Old Columbia Pike, Silver Spring, MD 20904 | 301-680-6518
ministrymagazine@gc.adventist.org | *www.ministrymagazine.org*
Pavel Goia, editor

Denomination: Seventh-day Adventist
Type: monthly digital and print magazine, circulation 18,000+
Audience: pastors, professors, administrators, chaplains, pastoral students, lay leaders
Purpose: to deepen spiritual life, develop intellectual strength, and increase pastoral and evangelistic effectiveness of all ministers in the context of the three angels' messages of Revelation 14:6-12
Submissions: Email complete manuscript as attachment.
Length: 1,500-2,000 words; reviews, 600 words maximum
Topics: family, issues, ministry, pastoral/preaching, relationships, theology
Rights: all
Payment: determined on amount of research done and other work needed to prepare manuscript, on acceptance
Guidelines: *www.ministrymagazine.org/about/article-submission*
Sample: articles are on the website

Tip: "Because Ministry's readership includes individuals from all over the world, you will want to use words, illustrations, and concepts that will be understood by readers in various parts of the world. Avoid illustrations that are understood in one country but may be confusing in others."

THE MOTHER'S HEART

PO Box 275, Tobaccoville, NC 27050 | 336-775-8519
marilla@alwrightpublishing.com | *www.the-mothers-heart.com*
Marilla, submissions editor

> **Parent company:** alWright! Publishing
> **Type:** bimonthly digital magazine, circulation 100,000
> **Audience:** moms at home, homeschoolers, large families, homesteaders, DIYers
> **Purpose:** to serve and encourage mothers in the many facets of staying at home and raising a family
> **Submissions:** Email query letter as attachment or in body of message. Gives assignments. To get an assignment, email *KymAWright@gmail.com*. Simultaneous OK. Unsolicited freelance: 20%. Responds in two months.
> **Length:** 1,000-2,000 words
> **Topics:** adoption story, Christian living, DYI, family, fostering, gardening, homeschooling, hospitality, organization, parenting, special needs, time management
> **Rights:** electronic, first, reprint (with info on where/when previously published)
> **Payment:** on publication
> **Payment:** $10-$100
> **Manuscripts accepted per year:** 30
> **Seasonal submissions:** six months in advance
> **Preferred Bible version:** any
> **Guidelines:** *tmhmag.com/Writers%20Guidelines%202016-2019.pdf;* also by email
> **Sample:** *tmhmag.com/subscribe.htm*
> **Tip:** "Break in with an adoption story, homeschool, gardening, parenting, DIY."

MUTUALITY

122 W. Franklin Ave., Ste. 218, Minneapolis, MN 55404 | 612-872-6898
mutuality@cbeinternational.org | *www.cbeinternational.org/publication/mutuality-blog-magazine*

Sarabeth Marcello, editor

Parent company: Christians for Biblical Equality
Type: quarterly digital and print magazine, circulation 1,200
Audience: Christian leaders, women in ministry, seminary and
university students, and laity interested in gender, the Bible, and
issues of justice
Purpose: to provide inspiration, encouragement, and information
on topics related to a biblical view of mutuality between men and
women in the home, church, and world
Submissions: Email complete manuscript as attachment. Responds in
one month or more.
Length: articles, 800-1,800 words; reviews, 500-800 words
Topics: theme-related
Rights: electronic, first
Payment: one-year CBE membership ($49–$59 value) or up to three
CBE recordings (up to $30 value)
Preferred Bible version: NIV
Theme list: available on website
Guidelines: *www.cbeinternational.org/content/write-mutuality*
Sample: *www.cbeinternational.org/content/mutuality-sample-issue*

MYSTERIOUS WAYS

110 William St., Ste. 901, New York, NY 10038 | 212-251-8100
www.guideposts.org/brand/mysterious-ways-magazine
Diana Aydin, editor

Parent company: Guideposts
Type: bimonthly digital and print magazine
Audience: general
Purpose: to encourage through true stories of extraordinary moments
and everyday miracles that reveal a spiritual force at work in our lives
Submissions: Submit complete manuscript through the website.
Length: 750-1,500 words; departments, 50-350 words
Rights: all
Payment: varies
Guidelines: *www.guideposts.org/tell-us-your-story*
Tip: "Looking for true stories of unexpected and wondrous experiences
that reveal a hidden hand at work in our lives. The best stories are
those that present a credible, well-detailed account that can even
leave skeptics in awe and wonder. A typical *Mysterious Ways* story
is written in dramatic style, with an unforeseen twist that inspires
the reader to look for miracles in his or her own life. It may be told

from a 1st-person or 3rd-person perspective, and can be your own experience or someone else's story. We are also on the lookout for recent experiences."

NET RESULTS

308 West Blvd. N, Columbia, MO 65203 | 888-470-2456

bill@netresults.org | *netresults.org*

Bill Tenny-Brittian, managing editor

Parent company: The Effective Church Group

Type: bimonthly digital magazine

Audience: pastors, church volunteers, and Christian organizations

Purpose: to help church leaders do effective ministry, taking their churches deeper in Christ and further in Christ's mission

Submissions: Email query letter. Responds in four to six weeks.

Length: 1,750 words

Topics: Christian education, evangelism, finances, hospitality, leadership, ministry, pastoral/preaching

Rights: all, electronic, reprint

Payment: on publication

Preferred Bible version: TNIV

Theme list: available on website

Guidelines: *netresults.org/writers/writers-guidelines*

Sample: *netresults.org/preview-past-issues*

Tip: "We look for practical, hands-on ministry ideas that an individual can put into practice. The best ideas are those the author has actually used successfully."

NEW FRONTIER CHRONICLE

30840 Hawthorne Blvd., Rancho Palos Verde, CA 90275 | 562-491-8343

new.frontier@usw.salvationarmy.org | *www.newfrontierchronicle.org*

Christin Davis Thieme, editor-in-chief

Denomination: The Salvation Army

Parent company: The Salvation Army Western Territory

Type: monthly print newspaper

Audience: denomination in the territory

Purpose: to empower Salvationists to communicate and engage with the Army's mission

Submissions: Only accepts query letter. Shares information from across The Salvation Army world, reports that analyze effective programs to identify the unique features and trends for what works, tips to help local congregations better engage in the issues of today, and influential voices on relevant (and sometimes controversial) matters.

Topics: denomination

NEW IDENTITY MAGAZINE

PO Box 1002, Mount Shasta, CA 96067 | 310-947-8707

submissions@newidentitymagazine.com | *www.newidentitymagazine.com*

Cailin Briody Henson, editor-in-chief

Type: quarterly digital and print magazine

Audience: new believers

Purpose: to provide diverse, Bible-centered content to help lead new believers and seekers to a fuller understanding of the Christian faith

Submissions: Submit complete manuscript through the website. Responds in two to three weeks. Departments: "Grow," teaching new believers and seekers about different Christian perspectives on topics, understanding Christian concepts, jargon, disciplines, practical application of Scripture, etc.; "Connect," encouraging new believers and seekers with testimonies, articles about relationships, fellowship, church, community, discussions and expressions of faith; "Live," engaging new believers and seekers to live out their faith in the real world, with stories of people actively pursuing God and their passions, organizations and resources to apply one's gifts, talents and desires to serve God and others, sharing the love of Christ in everyday arenas.

Length: 500-2,500 words

Topics: Christian living, church, evangelism, relationships, salvation, service

Rights: electronic, first

Payment: none

Guidelines: *www.newidentitymagazine.com/write/writers-guidelines*

Sample: on the website

Tip: "Articles need creative, well thought-out ideas that offer new insight. We value well researched, factually and biblically supported content."

NOW WHAT?

PO Box 33677, Denver, CO 80233

nowwhat@cog7.org | *nowwhat.cog7.org*

Sherri Langton, associate editor

Denomination: Church of God (Seventh Day)

Type: monthly digital magazine

Audience: seekers

Purpose: to address the felt needs of the unchurched

Submissions: Email complete manuscript or query letter. Unsolicited freelance: 100%. Responds in four to ten weeks. Avoid unnecessary jargon or technical terms. No Christmas or Easter pieces or fiction.

Length: 1,000-1,500 words

Topics: issues, salvation

Rights: electronic, first, reprint (with info on where/when previously published)

Payment: $25-$65, on publication

Manuscripts accepted per year: 10-12

Preferred Bible version: NIV

Guidelines: *nowwhat.cog7.org/send_us_your_story*

Sample: on the website

Tip: "Think how you can explain your faith, or how you overcame a problem, to a non-Christian. Use storytelling techniques, like dialogue, scenes, etc., with the conflict clearly stated."

OUR SUNDAY VISITOR NEWSWEEKLY

200 Noll Plaza, Huntington, IN 46750 | 260-356-8400

oursunvis@osv.com | *www.osvnews.com*

Gretchen R. Crowe, editorial director

Denomination: Catholic

Type: weekly digital and print newspaper

Audience: denomination

Purpose: to provide timely coverage of important national and international religious events reported from a Catholic perspective

Submissions: Submit complete manuscript or query letter only through the website. Responds in four to six weeks.

Length: 500-2,000 words

Topics: denomination, issues

Payment: on acceptance

Preferred Bible version: RSV

Guidelines: *osv.submittable.com/submit*

Tip: "Our mission is to examine the news, culture, and trends of the day from a faithful and sound Catholic perspective—to see the world through the eyes of faith. Especially interested in writers able to do news analysis (with a minimum of 3 sources) or news features."

OUTREACH

5550 Tech Center, Colorado Springs, CO 80919
theeditors@outreachmagazine.com | www.outreachmagazine.com
James P. Long, editor

> **Type:** bimonthly print magazine
> **Audience:** pastors and church leadership, as well as laypeople who are passionate about outreach
> **Purpose:** to further the Kingdom of God by empowering Christian churches to reach their communities for Jesus Christ
> **Submissions:** Email or mail query letter with clips. Responds in two months.
> **Length:** 200-2,500 words
> **Topics:** church outreach, evangelism, ministry, small groups
> **Rights:** first, reprint (with info on where/when previously published)
> **Payment:** $700-$1,000 for feature articles
> **Seasonal submissions:** six months ahead
> **Guidelines:** *www.outreachmagazine.com/magazine/3160-writers-guidelines.html*
> **Tip:** "While most articles are assigned, we do accept queries and manuscripts on speculation. Please don't query us until you've studied at least one issue of *Outreach*. If you're interested in writing on assignment, submit a cover letter, published writing samples, résumé, and a list of topics you specialize in or are interested in covering. We keep these on file and do not respond to all writing queries or return writing samples."

PARENTING TEENS

1 Lifeway Plaza, Nashville, TN 37234-0172 | 615-251-2196
lwt@lifeway.com | www.lifeway.com/en/product-family/parenting-teens
Scott Latta, editor

> **Denomination:** Southern Baptist
> **Parent company:** LifeWay Christian Resources
> **Type:** monthly print magazine
> **Audience:** parents of teens
> **Purpose:** to give parents encouragement and challenge them in their relationship with Christ so that they, in turn, can guide their teens
> **Submissions:** Manuscripts by assignment only. Email résumé, bio, and clips to get assignments.
> **Topics:** parenting
> **Preferred Bible version:** CSB
> **Sample:** on the website

PARENTLIFE

1 Lifeway Plaza, Nashville, TN 37234-0172 | 615-251-2196

parentlife@lifeway.com | *www.lifeway.com/en/product-family/*
parentlife-magazine

Nancy Cornwell, content editor

Denomination: Southern Baptist
Parent company: LifeWay Christian Resources
Type: monthly print magazine
Audience: parents of children from birth to preteen
Purpose: to encourage and equip parents with biblical solutions that will transform families
Submissions: Email query letter. Responds in six to twelve months.
Length: 500-1,500 words
Topics: discipline, education, parenting, spiritual growth
Preferred Bible version: CSB
Guidelines: by email
Sample: order from the website
Tip: "Serves as a springboard for parents who may feel exasperated or overwhelmed with information by offering a biblical approach to raising healthy, productive children. Offers practical ideas and information for individual parents and couples."

PARISH LITURGY

16565 S. State St., South Holland, IL 60473 | 708-331-5485

acp@acpress.org | *www.americancatholicpress.org*

Rev. Michael Gilligan, executive director

Denomination: Catholic
Parent company: American Catholic Press
Type: quarterly print magazine, circulation 1,500
Audience: parish priests, music directors, liturgy planners
Purpose: to provide material for each Sunday: themes, comments, petitions, and music suggestions
Submissions: Mail complete manuscript. Unsolicited freelance: 50%. Responds in two months.
Length: 300 words
Topics: liturgy, music
Rights: all
Payment: variable, on publication
Kill fee: yes
Preferred Bible version: CR
Guidelines: none

Sample: 9 x 12" envelope with $2 postage

Tip: "We use articles on the liturgy only—period. Send us well-informed articles on the liturgy."

POINT

11002 Lake Hart Dr., Orlando, FL 32832 | 407-563-6083

mickey.seward@converge.org | *www.converge.org/point-magazine*

Mickey Seward, editor

Denomination: Baptist

Parent company: Converge

Type: triannual digital magazine

Audience: church planters

Purpose: to share captivating stories of God's work through His church and best practices for church planting, strengthening churches and missions

Submissions: Only accepts query letter with clips.

Length: 300-1,400 words

Rights: electronic, first, reprint

Payment: $60-$80, on publication

Sample: on the website

POWER FOR LIVING

4050 Lee Vance Dr., Colorado Springs, CO 80918 | 719-536-0100

Powerforliving@davidccook.com | *www.cookministries.org*

Karen Bouchard, managing editor

Parent company: David C. Cook

Type: weekly take-home paper

Audience: general, ages 50 and older

Purpose: to connect God's truth to real life

Submissions: Looking for inspiring stories and articles about famous and ordinary people whose experiences and insights show the power of Christ at work in their lives.

Length: 1,200-1,500 words; poetry, 20 lines

Topics: wide variety, including holidays

Rights: first, onetime, reprint

Payment: articles, $375; poems, $50; columns, $150; devotions, $100; on acceptance

Manuscripts accepted per year: feature articles, 20; poems, 6-12; columns, 5-8; devotions, rare

Preferred Bible version: NIV, KJV

Guidelines: *davidccook.org/power-for-living*

PRAYER CONNECT

PO Box 10667, Terre Haute, IN 47801 | 812-238-5504
editor@prayerconnect.net | *prayerleader.com/magazine*
Carol Madison, editor

Parent company: Church Prayer Leaders Network

Type: quarterly digital and print magazine, circulation 3,000, advertising accepted

Audience: pastors and local church prayer leaders

Purpose: to encourage and equip you in all aspects of prayer, but with the ultimate goal of developing our readers to be intercessors who pray for their friends and families, churches, communities, and the world effectively and with passion

Submissions: Email complete manuscript or query letter as attachment, or mail it. Unsolicited freelance: 15%. Responds in two to three weeks.

Length: 250-1,500 words

Topics: prayer, revival

Rights: first, reprint (with info on where/when previously published)

Payment: 10¢/word, 5¢/word for reprints; on publication

Kill fee: sometimes

Manuscripts accepted per year: 30-40

Preferred Bible version: NIV

Theme list: available via email

Guidelines: *www.prayerleader.com/about-us/write-for-us*

Sample: *www.prayerleader.com/free-issue-pdfs*

Tip: "Short ideas, prayer tips, are the easiest way to break in at *Prayer Connect.*"

PRESBYTERIANS TODAY

100 Witherspoon St., Louisville, KY 40202-1396 | 800-728-7228
editor@pcusa.org | *www.presbyterianmission.org/ministries/today*
Donna Frischknecht Jackson, editor

Denomination: Presbyterian Church (USA)

Type: bimonthly digital and print magazine

Audience: denomination

Purpose: to explore practical issues of faith and life, tell stories of Presbyterians who are living their faith, and cover a wide range of church news and activities

Submissions: Only accepts query letter. Unsolicited freelance: 25%. Responds in two weeks.

Length: 1,500 words

Topics: Bible study, church, denomination, Presbyterians, theology
Payment: on acceptance
Payment: $75-$300
Seasonal submissions: three months in advance
Preferred Bible version: NRSV
Guidelines: click on Writer's Guidelines
Sample: click on Digital Edition

RELEVANT

55 W. Church St., Ste. 211, Orlando, FL 32801 | 407-660-1411
submissions@relevantmediagroup.com | relevantmagazine.com
Emily Brown, associate editor

Type: bimonthly digital magazine + annual print
Audience: Christians in their 20s and 30s
Purpose: to challenge people to go further in their spiritual journey; live selflessly and intentionally; care about positively impacting the world around them; and find the unexpected places God is speaking in life, music, and culture
Submissions: Email complete manuscript or query letter as attachment. Responds in one to two weeks or not interested.
Length: 750-1,000 words
Topics: Christian living, culture, faith, justice
Payment: none
Guidelines: *www.relevantmagazine.com/how-write-relevant*
Sample: on the website

RELIEF: A JOURNAL OF ART & FAITH

8933 Forestview, Evanston, IL 60203
editor@reliefjournal.com | www.reliefjournal.com
Daniel Bowman, Jr., editor in chief
Katie Karnehm-Esh, creative nonfiction, katie@reliefjournal.com
Aaron Housholder, fiction, aaron@reliefjournal.com
Julie L. Moore, poetry, julie@reliefjournal.com

Type: biannual print journal
Audience: general
Purpose: to promote full human flourishing in faith and art
Submissions: Submit manuscript through the website only during October 1 to March 31. Costs $2.50 to submit a manuscript. Simultaneous OK.
Length: stories, 8,000 words maximum; poetry, 1,000 words

maximum; creative nonfiction essays, 5,000 words maximum

Rights: first

Payment: none

Guidelines: *www.reliefjournal.com/print-submit*

SACONNECTS

440 W. Nyack Rd., West Nyack, NY 10994-1739 | 845-620-7200

saconnects.org

Robert Mitchell, managing editor

 Denomination: The Salvation Army

 Type: monthly digital magazine

 Audience: denomination in the Eastern territory

 Submissions: Accepts manuscripts only through the website.

 Topics: denomination

 Guidelines: *saconnects.org/submission-guidelines-magazine*

SHARING

PO Box 780909, San Antonio, TX 78278-0909 | 877-992-5222

sharing@OSLToday.org | *osltoday.org/sharing-magazine*

Jamie Henry, editor

 Parent company: International Order of St. Luke the Physician

 Type: bimonthly print magazine

 Audience: general

 Purpose: to inspire, educate, and inform about Christian healing of body, soul, and spirit

 Submissions: Email manuscript as attachment.

 Length: articles, 200-1,500 words; poetry, 30-50 words

 Topics: healing

 Rights: onetime

 Payment: none

 Tip: "Share your stories, experiences, thoughts, insights, inspirational poems, and testimonies of God's amazing power to heal."

SHORT AND SWEET BOOK SERIES

Grace Publishing, PO Box 1233, Broken Arrow, OK 74013-1233 | 918-346-7960

shortandsweettoo@gmail.com | *www.grace-publishing.com*

Susan King, compiler and editor

 Parent company: Grace Publishing

 Type: two or three books per year

 Audience: general

Purpose: to show, using words of one syllable or multi-syllables of five letters or less—with certain specific exceptions—how faith works in everyday life experiences

Submissions: Email complete manuscript as attachment. Unsolicited freelance: 100%. Responds in one week after deadline.

Length: varies

Topics: theme-related

Rights: onetime

Payment: none, royalties donated to World Christian Broadcasting

Manuscripts accepted per year: maximum 50 articles per book

Seasonal submissions: six months

Preferred Bible version: any

Theme list: available via email

Guidelines: *grace-publishing.com*

Tip: "Follow guidelines and exceptions exactly."

SOJOURNERS

3333 14th St. NW, Ste. 200, Washington, DC 20010 | 202-328-8842

queries@sojo.net | *www.sojo.net*

Jim Rice, editor

reviews, reviews@sojo.net

Type: monthly digital and print magazine

Audience: community influencers

Purpose: to explore the intersections of faith, politics, and culture; uncover in depth the hidden injustices in the world around us; and tell the stories of hope that keep us grounded, inspired, and moving forward

Submissions: Submit query letter by email in body of message. Responds in six to eight weeks.

Length: articles, 1800-2000 words; poetry, 25-40 lines

Topics: Christian living, culture, faith, justice, politics

Rights: all

Payment: unspecified, $25 per poem; on publication

Guidelines: *sojo.net/magazine/write*

Sample: buy from the website

THE SOUTHEAST OUTLOOK

920 Blankenbaker Pkwy., Louisville, KY 40243 | 502-253-8600

jglassner@secc.org | *www.southeastoutlook.org*

Jacob Glassner, editor

Parent company: Southeast Christian Church

Type: weekly digital and print newspaper, circulation 25,000, advertising accepted
Audience: Louisville, Kentucky, and surrounding communities
Purpose: to connect people to Jesus and one another
Submissions: Assignment only. Responds in one week.
Length: 600-800 words
Topics: Christian living
Rights: onetime
Payment: none
Seasonal submissions: one month in advance
Guidelines: none
Sample: on the website

SPORTS SPECTRUM

640 Plaza Dr., Ste. 110, Highlands Ranch, CO 80129 | 866-821-2971
jon@sportsspectrum.com | *sportsspectrum.com*
Jon Ackerman, managing editor

Parent company: Pro Athletes Outreach
Type: quarterly digital and print magazine and digital newsletter, circulation 4,000, advertising accepted
Audience: sports fans
Purpose: to share stories of sports persons displaying an athletic lifestyle pleasing to God
Submissions: Email query letter with clips as attachment. Gives assignments. Simultaneous okay. Unsolicited freelance: 10%. Responds in one week.
Length: 1,500-2,000 words
Topics: sports
Rights: all
Payment: 15¢/word, on acceptance
Manuscripts accepted per year: two or three
Seasonal submissions: two to three months
Preferred Bible version: NIV
Guidelines: not available
Sample: call the office
Tip: "Come with a story idea and plan for executing it."

ST. ANTHONY MESSENGER

28 W. Liberty St., Cincinnati, OH 45202-6498 | 513-241-5615
MagazineEditors@Franciscanmedia.org | *www.FranciscanMedia.org/ st-anthony-messenger*

Christopher Heffron, editorial director

Denomination: Catholic

Type: monthly print magazine

Audience: family-oriented, majority are women ages 40-70

Purpose: to offer readers inspiration from the heart of Catholicism—the Gospels and the experience of God's people

Submissions: Email query letter. Responds in eight weeks.

Length: feature articles, 2,000-2,500 words; fiction, 2,000-2,500 words

Topics: church, education, family, issues, marriage, sacraments, spiritual growth

Rights: first

Payment: 20¢/word, on acceptance

Manuscripts accepted per year: short stories, 12

Preferred Bible version: NAB

Guidelines: *www.franciscanmedia.org/writers-guide*

Sample: articles are on website

STANDARD

PO Box 843336, Kansas City, MO 4184-3336 | 816-931-1900

standard.foundry@gmail.com | *www.thefoundrypublishing.com/curriculum/adult.html?use_program=54*

Jeanette Gardner Littleton, editor

Denomination: Nazarene

Parent company: The Foundry Publishing

Type: weekly take-home paper, circulation 40,000

Audience: denomination

Purpose: to encourage and inspire our audience and to reinforce curriculum

Submissions: Only accepts email. Primarily assignment only. To get an assignment, send clips of personal-experience articles. Response time varies.

Length: 400 and 800-900 words

Topics: theme-related

Rights: all, first, reprint

Payment: $35 and $50, on acceptance

Manuscripts accepted per year: 104

Seasonal submissions: one year

Preferred Bible version: NIV

Theme list: available by email

Guidelines: by email

Sample: email request

Tip: "Writers should know basics of Wesleyan-Arminian theological perspective. Write to the theme list; please indicate which theme you're proposing it for. Nonfiction cannot be preachy. Put full contact information in the body of the manuscript, not only in the email. It helps to know if you're Nazarene or another Wesleyan/holiness denomination."

TEACHERS OF VISION

PO Box 45610, Westlake, OH 44145 | 888-798-1124

tov@ceai.org | *ceai.org/teachers-of-vision-magazine*

Dawn Molnar, managing editor

Parent company: Christian Educators Association International

Type: triannual digital and print magazine; circulation 4,000 print, 11,750 digital; advertising accepted

Audience: Christian educators in public schools

Purpose: to provide biblically principled resources that encourage, equip, and empower Christian educators

Submissions: Email complete manuscript or query letter with clips as attachment. At times gives regularly published authors assignments; does not give assignments based on queries. Simultaneous accepted. Unsolicited freelance: 8%. Responds in two weeks during school year.

Length: features, 600-1,400 words; personal experience, 600-1,200 words; methodology, 600-800 words; inspirational, 600-1200 words

Topics: teaching, theme-related

Rights: electronic, first, reprint

Payment: $50-$100, on publication

Kill fee: yes

Manuscripts accepted per year: 40+

Seasonal submissions: nine months

Preferred Bible version: NIV

Theme list: available on website

Guidelines: *www.ceai.org/wp-content/uploads/2021/10/2022-tov-writers-guidelines.pdf*

Sample: *ceai.org/teachers-of-vision-magazine*

Tip: "Our published writers are: able to integrate secular and spiritual insights; faithful to the teachings of Scripture; mindful of our audience (Christian educators); up-to-date on trends in contemporary education, positive, encouraging, and inspiring; focused on education in general or how the issue's theme relates to education; clear, concise, and creative."

TESTIMONY/ENRICH

2450 Milltower Ct., Mississauga, ON L5N 5Z6, Canada | 905-542-7400

testimony@paoc.org | *testimony.paoc.org*

Stacey McKenzie, editor

Denomination: Pentecostal Assemblies of Canada

Parent company: Pentecostal Assemblies of Canada

Type: quarterly digital and print magazine

Audience: general and leaders

Purpose: to celebrate what God is doing in and through the Fellowship, while offering encouragement to believers by providing a window into the struggles that everyday Christians often encounter

Submissions: Email query letter. Responds in six to eight weeks.

Length: 800-1,000 words

Topics: Christian living, denomination

Rights: first

Seasonal submissions: four months in advance

Preferred Bible version: NIV

Guidelines: *testimony.paoc.org/submit*

Tip: "Our readership is 98% Canadian. We prefer Canadian writers or at least writers who understand that Canadians are not Americans in long underwear. We also give preference to members of this denomination, since this is related to issues concerning our fellowship."

TIME OF SINGING: A JOURNAL OF CHRISTIAN POETRY

PO Box 5276, Conneaut Lake, PA 16316

timesing@zoominternet.net | *www.timeofsinging.com*

Lora Zill, editor

Parent company: Wind & Water Press

Type: quarterly print journal, circulation 200

Audience: adults who study, write, and/or read poetry

Purpose: to provide a market for poets and readers passionate about exploring the great themes of God, His work in creation, and our response, through the art and craft of poetry

Submissions: Email complete manuscript as attachment or in body of message, or mail it. Simultaneous accepted. Unsolicited freelance: 95%. Responds in three to four months. Also accepts submissions from teens. Assigns book reviews of *Time of Singing* poets; inquire for an assignment.

Length: 40 lines

Topics: Christian worldview

Rights: first, onetime, reprint (with info on where/when previously published)

Payment: none

Manuscripts accepted per year: 150

Seasonal submissions: six months in advance

Preferred Bible version: any

Guidelines: *www.timeofsinging.com*; also by email and mail with SASE

Sample: $4 each or 2/$7, no envelope needed (checks, money orders payable to Wind & Water Press)

Tip: "I look for poems that challenge assumptions and explore ideas. Show me insights. Don't be afraid to wrestle with God in your work. (Greeting card type poetry and sermons are not accepted.) TOS poetry doesn't toe a denominational line, but reflects a broadly defined Christian worldview. I am looking for free verse, forms, and fresh rhyme. Invite your reader into your poem. You don't have to provide answers; in fact, the best poetry doesn't. Think outside the theological box. Read widely and study poetry. It's worth your time and devotion. I cannot critique submissions but will comment on work that is close to publication."

TODAY'S CHRISTIAN LIVING

PO Box 5000, Iola, WI 54945 | 715-445-5000

danb@jpmediallc.com | *www.todayschristianliving.org*

Dan Brownell, editor

Type: bimonthly digital and print magazine, advertising accepted

Audience: general

Purpose: to challenge Christians in their faith so they may be strengthened to fulfill the call of God in their lives

Submissions: Email complete manuscript. Simultaneous accepted.

Length: feature testimony, 1,200-1,400 words; "Turning Point," 750-800 words; "Grace Notes," 750-800 words; humor, 35-50 words

Topics: Christian living

Rights: all

Payment: Less than 750 words: $25; 750-800 words, $75; 801-1,199 words, $100; 1,200-1,800 words, $150; within 60 days of publication

Guidelines: *todayschristianliving.org/writers-guidelines*

Sample: *todayschristianliving.org/free-digital-issue-with-newsletter-signup*

Tip: "Potential articles will be placed in a holding file for possible future use and will be reviewed each time an issue is being planned and prepared. An article may be used relatively soon, or after a year or two, or it may never be used at all. But remember, you're free to submit an article to other publications unless we purchase and contract it."

U.S. CATHOLIC

205 W. Monroe St., Chicago, IL 60606 | 312-544-8169
submissions@uscatholic.org | *www.uscatholic.org*
Emily Sanna, managing editor

Denomination: Catholic
Type: monthly digital and print magazine
Audience: denomination
Submissions: Email complete manuscript. Responds in six to eight weeks.
Length: articles, 800-3,500 words; reviews, 315 words; fiction, 1,500 words
Topics: denomination
Payment: $75-$500
Guidelines: *www.uscatholic.org/writers-guide*
Seasonal submissions: six months in advance
Guidelines: on website
Tip: "U.S. Catholic does not consider submissions that have simultaneously been sent to any other publication or that have appeared elsewhere in any form, either in print or online. This includes articles published on personal blogs or excerpts from books, published or unpublished."

VIBRANT LIFE

PO Box 5353, Nampa, ID 83653-5353 | 208-465-2584
heather.quintana@pacificpress.com | *www.vibrantlife.com*
Heather Quintana, editor

Denomination: Seventh-day Adventist
Parent company: Pacific Press Publishing Association
Type: bimonthly digital and print magazine
Audience: general
Purpose: to promote physical health, mental clarity, and spiritual balance from a practical, Christian perspective
Submissions: Email complete manuscript as attachment, or mail it.
Length: 450-1,000 words plus sidebar if informational
Topics: exercise, family, health, medicine, nutrition, spiritual balance
Rights: first, reprint
Payment: $100-$300, on acceptance

Guidelines: *www.vibrantlife.com/writers-guidelines-2*

Tip: "Information must be reliable—no faddism. Articles should represent the latest findings on the subject, and if scientific in nature, should be properly documented. (References to other lay journals are generally not acceptable.)"

THE WAR CRY

615 Slaters Ln., Alexandria, VA 22314 | 703-684-5500

war_cry@usn.salvationarmy.org | *www.thewarcry.org*

Major Jamie Satterlee, director of publications

Jeff McDonald, editorial director

Denomination: The Salvation Army

Type: monthly digital and print magazine, circulation 160,000, advertising accepted

Audience: Salvation Army members and associates and general public

Purpose: to represent the mission of The Salvation Army to proclaim the Gospel of Jesus Christ and serve human need in His name without discrimination

Submissions: Submit only through the website. Simultaneous accepted. Unsolicited freelance: 50%. Responds in four to six weeks. Query to get an assignment.

Length: 800-1,250 words

Topics: Christian living, culture, discipleship, evangelism, issues, Salvation Army, trends

Rights: first

Payment: 35¢/word, on acceptance

Kill fee: sometimes

Manuscripts accepted per year: 40

Seasonal submissions: six months in advance

Preferred Bible version: NLT

Theme list: available on website

Guidelines: *www.thewarcry.org/submission-guidelines*

Sample: on the website or send 9 x 12" self-addressed envelope

Tip: "Some association/connection/explication of The Salvation Army is helpful when possible."

7

TEEN/YOUNG ADULT MARKETS

BOUNDLESS.ORG

8605 Explorer Dr., Colorado Springs, CO 80920 | 719-531-3400
editor@boundless.org | www.boundless.org
Lisa Anderson, director

Parent company: Focus on the Family

Type: website, 300,000 visitors per month

Audience: single young adults in 20s and 30s

Purpose: to help Christian young adults grow up, own their faith, date with purpose, and prepare for marriage and family

Submissions: Only accepts query letter with clips.

Preferred Bible version: ESV

Types of manuscripts: articles, blog posts

Length: articles, 1,200-1,800 words; blog posts, 500-800 words

Topics: adulthood, Christian living/spirituality, relationships

Rights: all

Guidelines: *www.boundless.org/about/write-for-us*

Sample: on the website

Tip: "Aim to engage our readers' hearts, as we're primarily in the business of affecting lives, not changing society. Use personal stories as illustrations and to spark our readers' imaginations." Topics must fit in these three categories: (1) adulthood: being single, career, family, money; (2) faith: spiritual growth, ministry; (3) relationships: dating, marriage, sexuality, community.

THE BRINK

See entry in "Daily Devotional Booklets and Websites."

BRIO

8605 Explorer Dr., Colorado Springs, CO 80920 | 719-531-3400
submissions@briomagazine.com | *focusonthefamily.com/parenting/brio-magazine*
Pam Woody, editorial director

Parent company: Focus on the Family
Type: bimonthly print magazine, circulation 60,000
Audience: teen girls
Purpose: to provide inspiring stories, fashion insights, fun profiles, and practical tips, all from a biblical worldview
Submissions: Only accepts complete manuscript. Email as attachment or mail.
Types of manuscripts: articles, profiles, short stories
Length: 200-1,400 words
Topics: entertainment, prayer, relationships, seasonal, social media
Rights: first
Payment: on acceptance, minimum 30¢ per word
Guidelines: *media.focusonthefamily.com/brio/pdf/brio-writers-guidelines-2019.pdf*
Sample: on the website
Tip: "We are looking for unique and interesting nonfiction articles, especially stories about real-life teen girls. Every article should have a Christian emphasis, though it shouldn't be preachy or overbearing. The topics, concepts, and vocabulary should be appropriate for our teen audience."

LOVE IS MOVING

9821 Leslie St., Ste. 103, Richmond Hill, ON L4B 3Y4, Canada | 905-479-5885
ilana@loveismoving.ca | *www.loveismoving.ca*
Ilana Reimer, editor

Parent company: The Evangelical Fellowship of Canada
Type: triannual digital and print magazine, circulation 10,100, advertising accepted
Audience: Canadian young adults
Purpose: to reflect a biblical concept of love and challenge readers to live out their faith with passion for Jesus and compassion for others
Submissions: Only accepts email as attachment. Send query letter with clips. Unsolicited freelance: 20%. Response in two to four days.
Seasonal submissions: three months in advance
Preferred Bible version: NIV
Types of manuscripts: essays, opinion, personal experience, poetry,

short stories, reviews, also artwork and photography

Length: 600-1,200 words

Topics: Christian living/spirituality, church, culture, ministry

Rights: first, reprint (with info on where/when previously published)

Payment: none, drawing for Amazon gift cards

Manuscripts accepted per year: 100

Guidelines: *loveismoving.ca/about/contribute*

Theme List: available on website and via email

Sample: *www.faithtoday.ca/Subscribe-LIM*

Tip: "We're looking for smart, thoughtful writers who are wrestling with timely topics in the Canadian Church and broader culture through the lens of their faith. Demonstrate your knowledge on the topic you're pitching and don't be afraid to show your enthusiasm!"

PEER

615 Sisters Ln., Alexandria, VA 22314 | 703-684-5500

peer@usn.salvationarmy.org | *peermag.org*

Captain Jamie Satterlee, editor

Denomination: The Salvation Army

Type: monthly digital and print magazine; circulation: print 30,000, digital 1,400

Audience: 16-22 years old

Purpose: to ignite a faith conversation that will deepen biblical perspective, faith, and holy living by addressing topics related to faith, community, and culture

Submissions: Only accepts complete manuscript through the website. Response in one week. Accepts submissions from teens.

Preferred Bible version: NLT

Types of manuscripts: articles, profiles

Length: 800 words

Topics: Christian living/spirituality, culture, current events

Rights: first, onetime

Payment: 35¢/word, 15¢/word for reprints

Guidelines: *peermag.org/contribute*

TAKE FIVE PLUS

See entry in "Daily Devotional Booklets and Websites."

UNLOCKED

See entry in "Daily Devotional Booklets and Websites."

8

CHILDREN'S MARKETS

CADET QUEST

1333 Alger St. SE, Grand Rapids, MI 49507 | 616-241-5616
submissions@CalvinistCadets.org | *www.calvinistcadets.org/cadet-quest-magazine*
Steve Bootsma, editor

Parent company: Calvinist Cadet Corps
Type: bimonthly print magazine, circulation 6,000
Audience: boys ages 9-14
Purpose: to help boys grow more Christlike in all areas of life
Submissions: Email complete manuscript in body of message, or mail it. Unsolicited freelance: 5-10%. Response in four months before publication. Accepts submissions from children and teens.
Preferred Bible version: NIV
Types of manuscripts: profiles, projects, puzzles, short stories
Length: 1,000-1,500 words
Topics: camping, Christian athletes, nature, sports, theme-related
Rights: all, first, reprint
Payment: at least 5¢ per word
Manuscripts accepted per year: 20
Theme list: available on website
Guidelines: *calvinistcadets.org/wp-content/uploads/Quest-Guidelines.pdf*
Sample: download from website
Tip: "Looking for fun fiction, without being preachy, for preteen boys. It needs to have some action, and don't be cliché with a Jesus-always-wins type of ending."

FOCUS ON THE FAMILY CLUBHOUSE

8605 Explorer Dr., Colorado Springs, CO 80920 | 719-531-3400
Rachel.Pfeiffer@fotf.org | *focusonthefamily.com/clubhouse-magazine*
Rachel Pfeiffer, associate editor

Parent company: Focus on the Family
Type: monthly print magazine, circulation 90,000

Audience: ages 8-12

Purpose: to inspire, entertain, and teach Christian values to children

Submissions: Accepts complete manuscripts only by mail. Unsolicited freelance: 15%. Response in three months. Accepts submissions from children and teens.

Seasonal submissions: eight months in advance

Preferred Bible version: HCSB

Types of manuscripts: articles, crafts, interviews, quizzes, recipes, short stories

Length: 500-2,000 words

Topics: apologetics, Christian living

Rights: first

Payment: on acceptance, 15-25¢ per word, kill fee sometimes

Manuscripts accepted per year: 80

Guidelines: *focusonthefamily.com/clubhouse-magazine/about/ submission-guidelines*

Sample: $3.99 at *focusonthefamily.com/kidmags*

Tip: "Study the magazine to learn the voice and style. Best way to break in is through nonfiction, especially 'Truth Pursuer' and kid-profile articles. Once an author publishes with us three or more times, we often begin to give assignments. We also give assignments to writers whom we meet at Christian writers conferences."

FOCUS ON THE FAMILY CLUBHOUSE JR.

8605 Explorer Dr., Colorado Springs, CO 80920 | 719-531-3400

Kate.Jameson@fotf.org | *focusonthefamily.com/clubhouse-jr-magazine*

Kate Jameson, associate editor

Parent company: Focus on the Family

Type: monthly print magazine, circulation 60,000

Audience: ages 3-7

Purpose: to inspire, entertain, and teach Christian values to children

Submissions: Accepts complete manuscript only by mail. Unsolicited freelance: 15%. Response in three months. Accepts submissions from children and teens.

Seasonal submissions: eight months in advance

Preferred Bible version: NIrV

Types of manuscripts: activities, Bible stories retold, biography, crafts, interviews, poetry, profiles, rebus stories, recipes, short stories

Length: 400-1,000 words

Topics: animals, Bible stories, Christian living, nature, science

Rights: first

Payment: on acceptance, 15-25¢ per word

Manuscripts accepted per year: 50

Guidelines: *focusonthefamily.com/clubhouse-jr-magazine/about/submission-guidelines*

Sample: $3.99 at *focusonthefamily.com/kidmags*

Tip: "Read the magazine to learn our style and reading level. Aim at early and beginning readers. Rebus and Bible stories are a great way to break in. Once an author publishes with us three or more times, we often begin to give assignments. We also give assignments to writers whom we meet at Christian writers conferences."

GUIDE

PO Box 5353, Nampa, ID 83653-5353

guide.magazine@pacificpress.com | *www.guidemagazine.org*

Lori Futcher, editor

Denomination: Seventh-day Adventist

Parent company: Pacific Press Publishing Association

Type: weekly Sunday school take-home paper, circulation 26,000

Audience: ages 10-14

Purpose: to show readers, through stories that illustrate Bible truth, how to walk with God now and forever

Submissions: Mail complete manuscript, or submit it through the website. Query via email. Unsolicited freelance: 75%; 20% assigned. Response in four to six weeks. Accepts submissions from teens.

Seasonal submissions: eight months in advance

Preferred Bible version: NKJV

Types of manuscripts: biography, humor, personal experience, profiles, quizzes

Length: 450-1,200 words

Topics: adventure, Christian living, missions, nature

Rights: first, reprint (with info on where/when previously published)

Payment: on acceptance; 7-10¢ per word, $25-40 for games and puzzles

Guidelines: *www.guidemagazine.org/writers-guidelines*

Sample: download from guidelines page

Tip: "Use your best short-story techniques (dialogue, scenes, a sense of plot) to tell a true story starring a kid ages 10-14. Bring out a clear spiritual/biblical message. We publish multipart true stories regularly, two to twelve parts, 1,200 words each. All topics indicated need to be addressed within the context of a true story."

NATURE FRIEND

4253 Woodcock Ln., Dayton, VA 22821 | 540-867-0764
editor@naturefriendmagazine.com | *www.naturefriendmagazine.com*
Kevin Shank, editor

Parent company: Dogwood Ridge Outdoors
Type: monthly print magazine, circulation 10,000
Audience: ages 6-14, 80% are ages 8-12
Purpose: to increase awareness of God and appreciation for God's works and gifts, to teach accountability toward God's works, and to teach natural truths and facts
Submissions: Email complete manuscript as attachment. Simultaneous OK. Unsolicited freelance: 55%. Accepts submissions from children and teens.
Seasonal submissions: four months in advance
Preferred Bible version: KJV only
Types of manuscripts: crafts, experiments, photo features, profiles, projects, short stories
Length: 500-800 words
Topics: animals, astronomy, first aid, flowers, gardening, marine life, nature, photography, science, weather
Rights: first, reprint
Payment: on publication, 5¢ per edited word, 3¢ per word for reprints
Manuscripts accepted per year: 40-50
Guidelines: *naturefriendmagazine.com/contributors/tips-for-getting-published*
Sample: *naturefriendmagazine.com/sample-issues*
Tip: "While talking animals can be interesting and teach worthwhile lessons, we have chosen to not use them in *Nature Friend*. Excluded are puzzle-type submissions such as 'Who Am I?'"

OUR LITTLE FRIEND

PO Box 5353, Nampa, ID 83653
anita.seymour@pacificpress.com | *primarytreasure.com*
Anita Seymour, managing editor

Denomination: Seventh-day Adventist

Parent company: Pacific Press Publishing Association
Type: weekly Sunday school take-home paper, circulation 16,000
Audience: ages 1-5
Purpose: to teach about Jesus and the Christian life
Submissions: Email complete manuscript as attachment. Response in one month.
Seasonal submissions: eight to nine months in advance
Preferred Bible version: ICB, NIrV
Type of manuscripts: true stories
Length: one to two double-spaced pages
Topics: Christian living, God's love, holidays, nature
Rights: electronic, onetime
Payment: on acceptance, $25-50
Manuscripts accepted per year: 52
Theme list: available via mail with SASE
Guidelines: *www.primarytreasure.com/for-writers*
Tip: "We need true, age-appropriate stories that teach about the Christian life." See extensive topic list in the guidelines.

PRIMARY TREASURE

PO Box 5353, Nampa, ID 83653
anita.seymour@pacificpress.com | *www.primarytreasure.com*
Anita Seymour, managing editor

Denomination: Seventh-day Adventist
Parent company: Pacific Press Publishing Association
Type: weekly Sunday school take-home paper, circulation 14,000
Audience: ages 6-9
Purpose: to teach children about the love of God and the Christian life through true stories
Submissions: Email complete manuscript as attachment. Unsolicited freelance: 80%. Response in one month.
Seasonal submissions: eight months in advance
Type of manuscripts: true stories
Length: three to five double-spaced pages
Topics: Christian living, holidays, nature
Rights: electronic, onetime
Payment: on acceptance, $25-50
Manuscripts accepted per year: 104
Theme list: available via mail with SASE
Guidelines: *www.primarytreasure.com/for-writers*
Tip: "We need age-appropriate stories that teach about Jesus and the Christian life." See topics list in the guidelines.

191

9

WRITERS MARKETS

FELLOWSCRIPT

PO Box 99509, Edmonton, AB T5B 0E1, Canada

fseditor@gmail.com | *www.inscribe.org/fellowscript*

Nina Morey, editor-in-chief

Parent company: InScribe Christian Writers' Fellowship

Type: quarterly digital and print magazine, circulation 200, advertising accepted

Audience: members of InScribe Christian Writers' Fellowship

Purpose: to provide support, inspiration, and instruction and provide members with an opportunity to submit work

Submissions: Only accepts complete manuscript via email. Response in four weeks. Submission deadlines are February 1, May 1, August 1, and November 1. Plans six months ahead.

Types: feature articles, 750-1,000 words; columns, 500-750 words; reviews, 150-300 words; fillers/tips, 25-500 words; general articles, 700 words

Topic: writing

Rights: electronic, onetime, reprint

Payment: on publication; 2.5¢ CAD per word for onetime rights, 1.5¢ per word for reprint rights, extra .5¢ for electronic rights for no more than three months

Seasonal submissions: six months in advance

Guidelines: *www.inscribe.org/fellowscript/submission-guidelines*

Tip: "We always prefer material specifically slanted toward the needs and interests of Canadian Christian writers. We do not publish poetry except as part of an instructional article, nor do we publish testimonials. We give preference to members and to Canadian writers."

FREELANCE WRITER'S REPORT

PO Box A, North Stratford, NH 03590 | 603-922-8338

submission@writers-editors.com | *www.writers-editors.com*

Dana K. Cassell, editor

Parent company: Writers-Editors Network
Type: monthly digital and print newsletter
Audience: established writers
Purpose: to help serious, professional freelance writers—whether full-time or part-time—improve their earnings and profits from their editorial businesses
Submissions: Only accepts complete manuscript; email as attachment or in body of message. Unsolicited freelance: 25%. Response in one week.
Types of manuscripts: The bulk of the content is market news and marketing information—how to build a writing/editing business, how to maximize income.
Length: articles to 900 words, prose fillers to 400 words, likes bulleted lists
Topic: writing
Rights: onetime, reprint (with info on where/when previously published)
Payment: on publication, 10¢ per edited word
Manuscripts accepted per year: 50
Seasonal submissions: two months ahead
Guidelines: *www.writers-editors.com/Writers/Membership/Writer_Guidelines/writer_guidelines.htm*
Sample: *freelancekeys.com/samplecopy*
Tip: "No articles on the basics of freelancing since readers are established freelancers. Looking for marketing and business-building for freelance writers, editors, and book authors."

POETS & WRITERS MAGAZINE

90 Broad St., Ste. 2100, New York, NY 10004-2272 | 212-226-3586
editor@pw.org | *www.pw.org*
Melissa Faliveno, senior editor

Parent company: Poets & Writers, Inc.
Type: bimonthly print magazine, circulation 100,000, advertising accepted
Audience: writers of poetry, fiction, and creative nonfiction
Purpose: to provide practical guidance for getting published and pursuing writing careers
Submissions: Query letter with clips via email or mail. Response in four to six weeks.
Types of manuscripts: "News & Trends," 500-1,200 words; "The Literary Life," essays, 1,500-2,500 words; "The Practical Writer,"

how-to and advice, 1,500-2,500 words; profiles and interviews,
2,000-3,000 words

Topic: writing

Rights: all, reprint

Payment: when scheduled for production, $150-500

Seasonal submissions: four months in advance

Guidelines: *www.pw.org/about-us/submission_guidelines*

Sample: sold at large bookstores and online

Tip: Most open to "News & Trends," "The Literary Life," and "The
Practical Writer."

STORY EMBERS

140 Churchill Ln., Mount Airy, NC 27030

submissions@storyembers.org | *storyembers.org*

Brianna Storm Hilverty, managing editor

Type: biweekly website, 30,000 hits per month

Audience: Christian writers

Purpose: to help Christian writers enthrall readers through honest
storytelling that fearlessly grapples with hard issues

Submissions: Only accepts email as attachment. Unsolicited
freelance: 40%. Response in three weeks.

Types of manuscripts: how-to on writing, especially fiction; also
takes fiction and poetry

Length: 750-3,000

Topic: writing

Rights: first

Payment: none

Manuscripts accepted per year: 100

Guidelines: *storyembers.org/submissions*

Sample: see the website

Tip: "In our fiction, we're looking for stories that honestly depict the
human experience as it is and that grapple with Christian themes
without being simplistic or heavy-handed. In our nonfiction, we're
looking for articles that delve into specific writing subjects in-depth
in a practical way."

WORDS FOR THE WAY

5042 E. Cherry Hills Blvd., Springfield, MO 65809 | 417-812-5232

ozarksACW@yahoo.com | *www.ozarksacw.org*

Renee Vajko-Srch, managing editor

Jeanetta Chrystie, acquisitions editor

Parent company: Ozarks Chapter of American Christian Writers

Type: bimonthly digital and print newsletter; circulation 55 print, 150 digital; advertising accepted

Audience: writers at all levels

Purpose: to encourage and educate Christians to follow their call to write and learn to write well

Submissions: Complete manuscript or query letter only by email. Unsolicited freelance: 95%. Response in three weeks. Accepts submissions from teens.

Types of manuscripts: All submissions must speak to writing, the writing life, how to write better, etc., including any poetry or fillers. Personal experience: writing stories that teach something about the writing life. Encouragement to follow God's call to write. Poetry, sidebars, columns, fillers.

Length: features, 600-900 words; general writing how-to, 400-600 words; sidebars, 200-400 words; reviews, 200-400 words; devotions, 250-500 words; poetry, 12-40 lines

Topic: writing

Rights: electronic, first, onetime, reprint (with info on where/when previously published)

Payment: none

Manuscripts accepted per year: 45

Seasonal submissions: two months in advance

Bible version: any translation, no paraphrases

Guidelines: *www.OzarksACW.org/guidelines.php*

Sample: request by email

Tip: "We want content that speaks to our Christian writers by teaching and encouraging them. Specific current needs: how to write in a specific genre (your choice), how to grow spiritually through writing, how to organize a book, how to handle taxes as a freelancer. Also, we need devotions for the website that encourage, inspire, and teach (not preach) Christians to follow their calling to write."

THE WRITER

Editorial, Madavor Media, 25 Braintree Hill Office Park, Ste. 404, Braintree, MA 02184

tweditorial@madavor.com | *www.writermag.com*

Nicki Porter, senior editor

Type: monthly print and digital magazine, circulation 30,000, advertising accepted

Audience: writers at all levels

Purpose: to expand and support the work of professional and aspiring writers with a straightforward presentation of industry information, writing instruction, and professional and personal motivation

Submissions: Only accepts query letters. Unsolicited freelance: 80%. If no response in two weeks, probably not interested.

Types of manuscripts: Primarily looking for how-to articles on the craft of writing. Also has a variety of columns and departments: "Breakthrough," first-person articles about a writer's experience in breaking through to publication, 1,000 words; "Writing Essentials," basics of the craft of writing, 1,000-1,400 words; "Market Focus," reports on specific market areas, 1,000-1,400 words; "Off the Cuff," essays on a particular aspect of writing or the writing life, 1,000-1,400 words; "Freelance Success," any topic helpful for freelance writers; "Poet to Poet," how-to on writing poetry, 500-750 words; "Take Note," topical items of literary interest, 200-500 words; "Writer at Work," specific writing problem and how it was successfully overcome on the way to publication, 1,000-1,400 words. Uses some sidebars.

Topic: writing

Rights: first

Payment: on acceptance, varies by type and department

Guidelines: *www.writermag.com/the-magazine/submission-guidelines;* theme list on website

Sample: sold at large bookstores

Tip: "Personal essays must provide takeaway advice and benefits for writers. Include plenty of how-to, advice, and tips on techniques. Be specific. All topics must relate to writing."

THE WRITER'S CHRONICLE

5700 Rivertech Ct., Ste. 225, Riverdale Park, MD 20737-1250 | 240-696-7700
chronicle@awpwriter.org | *www.awpwriter.org/magazine_media/writers_ chronicle_overview*
Supriya Bhatnagar, editor

Parent company: The Association of Writers & Writing Programs

Type: bimonthly print and digital magazine, circulation 35,000, advertising accepted

Audience: serious writers, writing students and teachers

Purpose: to provide diverse insights into the art of writing that are accessible, pragmatic, and idealistic for serious writers; articles are used as teaching tools

Submissions: Only accepts query via email or through the website.

The magazine is published during the academic year. Submit only from February 1 through September 30. Unsolicited freelance: 90%. Response in three months.

Types of manuscripts: Interviews, 3,000-5,000 words; profiles and appreciations of contemporary writers, 2,000-5,000 words; essays on the craft of writing, 2,500-5,000 words. Uses some sidebars. Also buys blog posts year round for The Writer's Notebook, 500-1,500 words, $100 per post.

Topic: writing

Rights: electronic, first

Payment: on publication, $18 per 100 words

Guidelines: *www.awpwriter.org/magazine_media/submission_guidelines*

Tip: "Keep in mind that 18,000 of our 35,000 readers are students or just-emerging writers."

WRITER'S DIGEST

4665 Malsbary Rd., Blue Ash, OH 45242

wdsubmissions@aimmedia.com | *www.writersdigest.com*

Amy Jones, editor-in-chief

Parent company: Active Interest Media

Type: bimonthly print and digital magazine, circulation 60,000, advertising accepted

Audience: aspiring and professional writers

Purpose: to celebrate the writing life and what it means to be a writer in today's publishing environment

Submissions: Only accepts email in body of message. Query first. Unsolicited freelance: 20% unsolicited; 60% assigned. Response in two to four months.

Types of manuscripts: "Inkwell," opinion pieces, 800-900 words and short how-to pieces, trends, humor, 300-600 words; "5-Minute Memoir," 600-word essay reflections on the writing life; author profiles, 800-1,200 words; articles on writing techniques, 1,000-2,400 words; market reports

Topic: writing

Rights: electronic, first

Payment: on acceptance, 30-50¢ per word, kill fee 25%

Seasonal submissions: eight months in advance

Guidelines: *www.writersdigest.com/resources/submission-guidelines;* theme list on website

Sample: available at newsstands and through *www.writersdigestshop.com*

Tip: "Although we welcome the work of new writers, we believe the established writer can better instruct our readers. Please include your publishing credentials related to your topic with your submission."

WRITERSWEEKLY.COM

12441 N. Main St. #38, Trenton, GA 30752 | 305-768-0261
brian@booklocker.com | *writersweekly.com*
Brian Whiddon, managing editor

Parent company: BookLocker.com
Type: weekly digital newsletter, circulation 100,000
Audience: freelance writers
Purpose: to help freelance writers find writing opportunities and improve their businesses
Submissions: Only accepts query letter. Unsolicited freelance: 30%. Response in one to two weeks.
Types of manuscripts: feature articles on how to make more money writing, articles on paying Christian markets for writers, features that teach book-marketing techniques, book and author backstories
Length: 600 words
Topics: marketing, writing
Rights: first, reprint
Payment: on acceptance, $60
Manuscripts accepted per year: 100-200
Guidelines: *writersweekly.com/writersweekly-com-writers-guidelines;* theme list on website
Sample: on the website
Tip: "Understand that we are not a publication about writing but earning income through writing. Proofread your query letter— spelling, capitalization, and punctuation errors leap out at us and tell us what we can expect from you as a writer. SELL us your idea— don't just say "I want to write about . . . ."

WRITING CORNER

contests@writingcorner.com | *writingcorner.com*

Type: website
Audience: writers at all levels
Purpose: to provide concrete, useful advice from those who have been in the trenches and made a successful journey with their writing
Submissions: Only accepts complete manuscript or query letter by email. Response in two days.
Types of manuscripts: how-to articles on writing fiction and nonfiction, writing life, tips and tricks, basic and advance writing

techniques

Length: 600-900 words

Topic: writing

Rights: onetime, reprint

Payment: none

Guidelines: *writingcorner.com/main-pages/submission-guidelines*

Sample: on the website

Tip: "Our site visitors are from all areas of writing, so keep that audience in mind when writing for us."

PART 4

SPECIALTY MARKETS

10

DAILY DEVOTIONAL BOOKLETS AND WEBSITES

Note that many of these markets assign all manuscripts. If there is no information listed on getting an assignment, request a sample copy and writers guidelines if they are not on the website. Then write two or three sample devotions to fit that particular format, and send them to the editor with a request for an assignment.

THE BRINK

114 Bush Rd., Nashville, TN 37217 | 800-877-7030
thebrink@randallhouse.com | *www.thebrinkonline.com*
David Jones, senior editor

Denomination: Free Will Baptist
Parent company: Randall House
Audience: young adults
Type: quarterly print
Submissions: Devotions are by assignment only to coordinate with the curriculum. For feature articles, such as interviews, stories, and opinion pieces, email query with 100-200-word excerpt if available. Does not respond unless interested. Rights: first, reprint, onetime. Bible: ESV.
Guidelines: *thebrinkonline.com/contact*
Payment: varies
Tip: "Be very specific in your pitch. Seek to address an important biblical or cultural issue from a biblical worldview, rather than just providing verses or biblical commentary about a theme or topic."

CHRIST IN OUR HOME

PO Box 1209, Minneapolis, MN 55440-1209 | 800-328-4648
afsubmissions@1517.media | *www.augsburgfortress.org*

> **Denomination:** Evangelical Lutheran Church in America
> **Parent company:** Augsburg Fortress/1517 Media
> **Audience:** adults
> **Type:** quarterly print, email, audio
> **Submissions:** Assignments only. Submit sample devotions as explained in the guidelines. Length: 1190 characters, including spaces, maximum. Rights: all. Bible: NRSV.
> **Guidelines:** download from *ms.augsburgfortress.org/downloads/ Submission%20Guidelines.pdf?redirected=true*
> **Tip:** "*Christ in Our Home* is read by people in many nations, so avoid thinking only in terms of those who live in the U.S."

CHRISTIANDEVOTIONS.US

PO Box 6494, Kingsport, TN 37663 | 423-384-4821
christiandevotionsministries@gmail.com | *www.ChristianDevotions.us*
Martin Wiles, managing editor

> **Parent company:** Christian Devotions Ministries
> **Audience:** adults, teens
> **Type:** daily website
> **Submissions:** Accepts freelance submissions. Length: 300-400 words. Email as attached Word document. Payment: none. Rights: onetime, reprint. Bible: author's choice, must be referenced.
> **Guidelines:** *www.christiandevotions.us/writeforus*
> **Payment:** none
> **Tip:** "Follow our guidelines."

DEVOKIDS

PO Box 6494, Kingsport, TN 37663 | 423-384-4821
sandramillerhart@gmail.com | *devokids.com*
Sandra Miller Hart, executive editor

> **Parent company:** Christian Devotions Ministries
> **Audience:** children
> **Type:** website
> **Submissions:** Takes freelance submissions. Length: 75-250 words. Email as an attached Word document. Rights: onetime.
> **Also accepts:** submissions from kids
> **Guidelines:** *devokids.com/write-for-us*
> **Payment:** none

Tip: "We need kid-friendly posts related to crafts, puzzles, coloring pages, games, fun activities, art, and photography. Share an easy and fun recipe for children."

FORWARD DAY BY DAY

412 Sycamore St., Cincinnati, OH 45202-4110 | 800-543-1813
editorial@forwardmovement.org | *www.forwardmovement.org*
Richelle Thompson, managing editor

Denomination: Episcopal
Parent company: Foreward Movement
Audience: adults
Type: quarterly print, website, daily podcast and email
Submissions: Devotions are written on assignment. To get an assignment, send three sample meditations based on three of the following Bible verses: Psalm 139:21; Mark 8:31; Acts 4:12; Revelation 1:10. Likes author to complete an entire month's worth of devotions. Length: 210 words, including Scripture.
Guidelines: *www.forwardmovement.org/Pages/About/Writers-Guidelines.aspx*
Payment: $300 for a month of devotions
Tip: "*Forward Day by Day* is not the place to score points on controversial topics. Occasionally, when the Scripture passage pertains to it, an author chooses to say something about such a topic. If you write about a hot-button issue, do so with humility and make certain your comment shows respect for persons who hold a different view."

FRUIT OF THE VINE

211 N. Meridian St., Ste. 101, Newberg, OR 97132 | 503-538-9775
fv@barclaypress.com | *www.barclaypress.com*
Cleta Crisman, editor

Denomination: Quaker
Parent company: Barclay Press
Audience: adults
Type: quarterly print
Submissions: Accepts freelance submissions, one week at a time. Length: 250-290 words. Rights: onetime. Bible: NIV.
Guidelines: *tinyurl.com/y8vwx5gj*
Payment: subscription
Tip: "We ask writers to submit devotional readings for seven days, starting with Sunday. Writers have the freedom to choose their

own themes and Bible readings. It helps to follow a general theme throughout the week. Indicate references for Bible quotations in parentheses in the body of the devotional. If you use a translation other than the New International Version, please indicate the translation for each quotation."

GOD'S WORD FOR TODAY

1445 N. Boonville Ave., Springfield, MO 65802 | 417-862-2781
DDawson@ag.org | *ag.org/Resources/Devotionals/Gods-Word-for-Today*
Dilla Dawson, editor

Denomination: Assemblies of God
Parent company: Gospel Publishing House
Audience: adults
Type: quarterly print, website
Submissions: Request writers guidelines and sample assignment (unpaid). After samples are approved, writers will be added to the list for assignments. Length: 210 words. Rights: all. Bible: NIV.
Payment: $25/devotion
Tip: "Writers will receive detailed guidelines upon inquiry."

INKSPIRATIONS ONLINE

PO Box 3847, Mooresville, NC 28117 | 813-505-7676
humbleauthor@yahoo.com | *inkspirationsonline.com*
Tina Yeager, publisher

Parent company: Divine Encouragement, LLC
Audience: writers
Type: weekly website
Submissions: Accepts freelance submissions. Length: 400 words. Rights: reprint, onetime, electronic. Bible: any.
Guidelines: *inkspirationsonline.com/submission-guidelines*
Payment: none
Tip: "Submissions must target writers and maintain a devotional style. Please refrain from submitting how-to articles or preachy, didactic posts."

KEYS FOR KIDS DEVOTIONAL

2060 43rd St. SE, Grand Rapids, MI 49508 | 616-647-4500
editorial@keysforkids.org | *www.keysforkids.org*
Courtney Lasater, editor

Parent company: Keys for Kids Ministries

Audience: children
Type: quarterly print, website, phone app
Submissions: Takes only freelance submissions. Rights: all. Length: 375 words, including short fiction story. Buys 30-40 per year. Seasonal four to five months ahead. Bible version: NKJV.
Guidelines: *keysforkids.org/writersguidelines*
Payment: $30 on acceptance
Tip: "Include illustration in devotional story that uses a real-world object/situation to help kids understand a spiritual truth."

LIGHT FROM THE WORD

PO Box 50434, Indianapolis, IN 46250-0434 | 317-774-7900
submissions@wesleyan.org | www.wesleyan.org/communication/dailydevo
Susan LeBaron, project communications manager

Denomination: Wesleyan
Parent company: Wesleyan Publishing House
Audience: adults
Type: quarterly print, website
Submissions: Must be affiliated with The Wesleyan Church. Email three sample devotions to fit the format and request an assignment. Write "Devotion Samples" in the subject line. Length: 200-240 words. Rights: all. Bible: NIV.
Guidelines: *www.wesleyan.org/wph/writers-guidelines*
Payment: $200 for seven devotions
Tip: "Writing must lead readers to discover a biblical truth and apply that truth to their lives."

LIVING FAITH

PO Box 292824, Kettering, OH 45429 | 800-246-7390
info@livingfaith.com | livingfaith.com
Terence Hegarty, editor

Denomination: Catholic
Audience: adults
Type: quarterly print
Submissions: Assignments only; email one or two samples and credentials to request an assignment. Bible: NAB.
Guidelines: click FAQ
Tip: "*Living Faith* provides daily reflections based on a Scripture passage from the daily Mass. With readings for daily Mass listed at the bottom of each devotion, this booklet helps Catholics pray and meditate in spirit with the seasons of the Church Year."

LIVING FAITH FOR KIDS

PO Box 292824, Kettering, OH 45429 | 800-246-7390
editor@livingfaithkids.com | *www.livingfaith.com/kids*
Connie Clark, editor

> **Denomination:** Catholic
> **Audience:** children
> **Type:** quarterly print
> **Submissions:** Assignments only; email samples and credentials to request an assignment.
> **Tip:** "*Living Faith for Kids* features daily devotions based on the daily Scripture readings from the Catholic Mass. Each quarterly issue helps children 8-12 develop the habit of daily prayer and build their relationship with Jesus and the Church."

LOVE LINES FROM GOD

128 Leyland Ct., Greenwood, SC 29649 | 864-554-3204
mandmwiles@gmail.com | *lovelinesfromgod.blogspot.com*
Martin Wiles, managing editor

> **Audience:** adults
> **Type:** daily website
> **Submissions:** Accepts freelance submissions. Length: 400 words. Rights: first. Bible version: NIV.
> **Guidelines:** *lovelinesfromgod.blogspot.com/p/write-for-us_3.html*
> **Payment:** none
> **Tip:** "We are looking for devotions that encourage, not preach. Following the submission guidelines will result in a better chance of having the submission accepted."

PATHWAYS—MOMENTS WITH GOD

2902 Enterprise Dr., Anderson, IN 46013 | 800-741-7721
editors@warnerpress.org | *www.warnerpress.org/curriculum/adult-curriculum/pathways.html*
Kevin Stiffler, editor

> **Denomination:** Church of God
> **Parent company:** Warner Christian Resources
> **Audience:** adults
> **Type:** quarterly print
> **Submissions:** Written on assignment only. To be considered as a writer, submit a sample devotional. Length: 140-150 words. Should give readers living examples of what the Bible passage is about and how it

can apply to life.

Guidelines: *www.warnerpress.org/submission-guidelines*

THE QUIET HOUR AND DEVOTIONS

4050 Lee Vance Dr., Colorado Springs, CO 80919

thequiethour@davidccook.com | *www.davidccook.org, www.standardlesson.com/ standard-lesson-resources*

Scott Stewart, editor

> **Parent company:** David C Cook
> **Audience:** adults
> **Type:** quarterly print
> **Submissions:** *Devotions* and *The Quiet Hour* jointly publish new devotionals. By assignment only. Must have North American postal address for contract and payment. Length: 200 words. Rights: all. Bible versions: NIV, KJV.
> **Guidelines:** *dcc-knowledge-base.s3-us-west-2.amazonaws.com/Devotions-and-Quiet-Hour-Writers-Guidelines.pdf*
> **Payment:** $140 for seven
> **Tip:** "Submit spec devotional on a key verse you select in a Scripture passage of your choice. Begin with anecdotal opening then transition to relevant biblical insight and encouragement for a life of faith rooted in the key verse."

REFLECTING GOD

PO Box 419427, Kansas City, MO 64141 | 816-931-1900

dcbrush@wordaction.com | *reflectinggod.com*

Duane Brush, editor

> **Denomination:** Nazarene
> **Parent company:** The Foundry Publishing
> **Audience:** adults
> **Type:** daily website
> **Submissions:** Send a couple of sample devotions to fit the format and request an assignment. Length: 180-200 words.
> **Payment:** $115 for seven
> **Tip:** "Our purpose is the pursuit to embrace holy living. We want to foster discussion about what it means to live a holy life in the 21st century."

REJOICE!

35094 Laburnum Ave., Abbotsford, BC V2S 8K3, Canada | 540-434-6701

DorothyH@mennomedia.org | *www.faithandliferesources.org/periodicals/rejoice*

Dorothy Hartman, editor

Denomination: Mennonite
Parent company: MennoMedia
Audience: adults
Type: quarterly print
Submissions: Prefers that you send a couple of sample devotions and inquire about assignment procedures. Length: 250-300 words. Rights: first. Bible version: prefers NRSV.
Also accepts: Testimonies: 500-600 words, eight per year. Poems: free verse, light verse, 60 characters, eight per year; submit maximum of three poems.
Payment: devotionals, $100-125 for seven; poems, $25; on publication
Tip: "Don't apply for assignment unless you are familiar with the publication and Anabaptist theology."

THE SECRET PLACE

1075 First Ave., King of Prussia, PA 19406 | 610-768-2434
thesecretplace@judsonpress.com | *www.judsonpress.com*
Ingrid Dvirnak, editor

Denomination: American Baptist
Parent company: Judson Press
Audience: adults
Type: quarterly print
Submissions: Accepts freelance submissions; does not give assignments. Length: 200 words. Rights: first, reprint, onetime, electronic. Bible: NRSV.
Guidelines: *www.judsonpress.com/Content/Site189/ BasicBlocks/10258GUIDELINES_00000128358.pdf*
Payment: $20 each
Tip: "Bible verses should be less familiar verses."

TAKE FIVE PLUS

1445 N. Boonville Ave., Springfield, MO 65802 | 417-862-2781
WQuick@ag.org | *myhealthychurch.com*
Wade Quick, team leader

Denomination: Assemblies of God
Parent company: Gospel Publishing House
Audience: teens
Type: quarterly print
Submissions: Assignment only. Request writers guidelines and sample assignment (unpaid) via email. After samples are approved, writers will be added to the list for assignments. Length: 210-235 words.

Rights: all. Bible version: NIV.

Payment: $25 each, on acceptance

Tip: "Study the publication before attempting the sample assignment."

THESE DAYS: DAILY DEVOTIONS FOR LIVING BY FAITH

100 Witherspoon St., Louisville, KY 40202 | 800-624-2412

mlindberg@presbypub.com | *www.thethoughtfulchristian.com/Pages/Item/ 59264/These-Days.aspx*

Laura M. Cheifetz, editor

Denomination: Presbyterian

Parent company: Presbyterian Publishing Corporation

Audience: adults

Type: quarterly print

Submissions: Accepts freelance submissions. Length: 190 words. Rights: first. Bible version: NRSV.

Payment: $100 or $150 worth of books for seven devotions

Tip: "Write thoughtful entries based on a Scripture passage, use gender-inclusive language for God and humanity, and include a brief closing prayer."

UNLOCKED

2060 43rd St. SE, Grand Rapids, MI 49508 | 616-647-4500

editorial@unlocked.org | *unlocked.org*

Hannah Howe, editor

Parent company: Keys for Kids Ministries

Audience: teens

Type: quarterly print, website

Submissions: Accepts only freelance submissions. Rights: all. Length: devotion, 200-315 words; fiction, 200-350 words; poetry, 16-23 lines. Takes teen writers. Bible version: CSB, NIV, NLT, WEB.

Guidelines: *unlocked.org/writers-guidelines*

Payment: $30 on acceptance

Tip: "We are open to styles and genres not typically seen in teen devotionals as long as they fit the overall purpose outlined in our guidelines. We want our devotional pieces to challenge teens and help them wrestle with things they're dealing with, not talk down to them or shy away from deep topics."

THE UPPER ROOM

1908 Grand Ave., Nashville, TN 37212 | 615-340-7252

ureditorial@upperroom.org | *upperroom.org*

Andrew Garland Breeden, acquisitions editor

Denomination: United Methodist
Parent company: The Upper Room
Audience: adults
Type: bimonthly print, website
Submissions: Accepts freelance submissions. Length: 300 words, which include everything on the printed page. Rights: first, exclusive for one year. Bible versions: NIV, NRSV, CEB, KJV. Prefers submissions through the website.
Guidelines: *submissions.upperroom.org/en/guidelines*
Payment: $30, on publication
Tip: "A strong devotional will include three main elements: 1. A personal story or experience. 2. A connection to Scripture. 3. A way for the reader to apply the message to his or her own life."

THE WORD IN SEASON

PO Box 1209, Minneapolis, MN 55440 | 414-963-1222
rochelle@writenowcoach.com | *www.augsburgfortress.org*
Rochelle Melander, managing editor

Denomination: Evangelical Lutheran Church in America
Parent company: Augsburg Fortress/1517 Media
Audience: adults
Type: quarterly print
Submissions: Gives assignments based on samples. Request guidelines, and write trial devotions. Length: 200 words. Rights: all. Bible: NRSV. Also available as an Amazon ebook.
Guidelines: download from *ms.augsburgfortress.org/downloads/ Submission%20Guidelines.pdf?redirected=true*
Payment: $40
Tip: "We prefer writers with a background in Lutheran theology and who have used the historical critical method to study the Bible."

11

DRAMA

CHRISTIAN PUBLISHERS, LLC

PO Box 248, Cedar Rapids, IA 52406 | 319-368-8009
editor@christianpub.com | www.christianpub.com
Rhonda Wray, editor

Parent company: Brooklyn Publishers
Audiences: adults, children, teens
Types: children, full-length musicals, full-length plays, one-act musicals, one-act plays, readers theater, skit compilations, teens
Submissions: Submit complete script, preferably through the website form or as an email attachment. Simultaneous submission is OK. Replies in at least three months. Publishes 15-30 scripts per year; receives 250 submissions. Length: prefers 10-30 minutes, occasionally up to an hour.
Also publishes: banners
Payment: 10% royalty, often to a fixed amount, no advance
Guidelines: *www.christianpub.com/default.aspx?pg=ag*
Tip: "We like drama that is so enthralling it doesn't need elaborate productions with complicated sets and hard-to-obtain costumes and props. Scripts that meet a need in the life of a church are also welcome, such as mother-daughter event scripts. We embrace all styles, from humorous to solemn and worshipful. It would be most helpful to go to our website and familiarize yourself with the types of works we carry. Please include a cast list and production notes that share with would-be directors anything they need to know in order to stage your drama effectively."

CSS PUBLISHING GROUP, INC.

See entry in "Traditional Book Publishers."

DRAMA MINISTRY

2814 Azalea Pl., Nashville, TN 37204 | 866-859-7622
service@dramaministry.com | *www.dramaministry.com*
Vince Wilcox, general manager and editor

> **Audiences:** adults, children, teens
>
> **Types:** monologues, readers theater, short skits
>
> **Submissions:** Open to all topics, including seasonal/holidays, for children, youth, and adults. Email or mail script. Buys all rights.
>
> **Guidelines:** *www.dramaministry.com/faq*

ELDRIDGE CHRISTIAN PLAYS AND MUSICALS

PO Box 4904, Lancaster, PA 17804 | 850-385-2463
newworks@histage.com | *www.95church.com*
Susan Shore, editor

> **Audiences:** adults, children, teens
>
> **Types:** children, full-length musicals, full-length plays, one-act plays, readers theater, skit compilations, teens
>
> **Submissions:** Publishes 15-20 scripts per year; receives 300 submissions annually. Length: plays and musicals, minimum 30 minutes. Submit complete script via email. Simultaneous is OK. Responds in three months.
>
> **Payment:** 50% royalty plus 10% copy sales, no advance
>
> **Guidelines:** *95church.com/submission-guidelines*
>
> **Tip:** "We like all kinds of plays and are always open to new ideas. Generally speaking, our customers like plays with more female than male roles or flexible casting in which roles can be played by either men or women. This is not a hard-and-fast rule, however. We like easy costuming and scenery, if possible, as many church budgets are limited."

12

GREETING CARDS
AND GIFTS

BLUE MOUNTAIN ARTS
PO Box 1007, Boulder, CO 80306 | 303-449-0536
editorial@sps.com | *www.sps.com*
> **Audiences:** adults, teens
> **Products:** gifts, greeting cards
> **Submissions:** General card publisher with some inspirational cards. Looking for contemporary prose or poetry written from personal experience that reflects the thoughts and feelings people today want to communicate to one another but don't always know how to put into words. Have a loved one in mind as you write. Considers writings on special occasions (birthday, anniversary, congratulations, etc.), as well as the challenges and aspirations of life. Not looking for rhymed poetry, religious verse, humor, or one-liners. Length: 50 to 300 words. Buys all rights. Accepts freelance submissions by email, website form, or mail. Responds in two months or not interested. Holiday deadlines: Christmas and general holidays, July 15; Valentine's Day, September 12; Easter, November 8; Mother's Day and graduation, December 13; Father's Day, February 7.
> **Guidelines:** *www.sps.com/greeting-card-guidelines-submissions*
> **Payment:** $300 per poem for worldwide, exclusive rights to publish it on a greeting card and other products; $50 per poem for one-time use in a book

DICKSONS, INC.
709 B Ave. E, Seymour, IN 47274 | 812-522-1308
submissions@dicksonsgifts.com | *www.dicksonsgifts.com*
> **Audience:** adults
> **Products:** figurines, crosses, wall decor, mugs, flags
> **Submissions:** Two to eight lines, maximum sixteen, suitable for

plaques, bookmarks, etc. Email submission. Responds in three months. Subjects can cover any gift-giving occasion and Christian, inspirational, and everyday social-expression topics. Phrases or acrostics of one or two lines for bumper stickers are also considered.

Payment: royalty, negotiable

Tip: Looking for religious verses.

ELLIE CLAIRE

6100 Tower Cir., Ste. 210, Franklin, TN 37013 | 615-932-7600

ellieclaire.com

Jeana Ledbetter, acquisitions editor

Parent company: Worthy Publishing/Hachette Book Group

Audience: adults

Products: journals, devotionals, gift books

Submissions: Submit through agents only. Buys all rights.

Payment: flat fee, royalty

Tip: "We operate in the gift market, and the writing will need to reflect that. We are not interested in Bible studies but in inspirational and encouraging devotions, funny stories with a spiritual component, and compilations from a Christian worldview."

INK & WILLOW

10807 New Allegiance Dr., Ste. 500, Colorado Springs, CO 80921 | 719-590-4999

info@waterbrookmultnomah.com | *waterbrookmultnomah.com/ink-and-willow*

Jamie Lapeyrolerie, senior marketing manager and acquisitions

Parent company: WaterBrook Multnomah

Audience: adults

Products: journals, adult coloring books

Submissions: Submit through agents only.

Tip: "Ink & Willow encompasses a line of interactive products that infuse contemplation and inspiration into the regular spiritual practice of creative-minded Christians, wherever they are in their faith journey. Each thoughtfully curated gift product is based in biblical truth and sparks a reminder of how God reveals beauty in the midst of our ordinary."

WARNER CHRISTIAN RESOURCES

2902 Enterprise Dr., Anderson, IN 46013 | 800-741-7721

editors@warnerpress.org | *www.warnerpress.org*

Robin Fogle, editor

Audiences: adults, children

Product: greeting cards

Submissions: Themes include birthday, anniversary, baby congratulations, sympathy, get well, kid's birthday and get well, thinking of you, friendship, Christmas, praying for you, encouragement. Use a conversational tone with no lofty poetic language, such as *thee, thou, art*. Don't preach or use a negative tone. Strive to share God's love and provide a Christian witness. Length: average of four lines. Responds in six to eight weeks. Email or mail with SASE. Buys all rights. Deadlines: everyday, July 31; Christmas, October 1.

Guidelines: *www.warnerpress.org/submission-guidelines*

Tip: "We only produce boxed greeting cards—no personal, counter-line style cards."

13

TRACTS

The following companies publish gospel tracts but do not have writers guidelines. If you are interested in writing for them, email or phone to find out if they currently are looking for submissions. Also check your denominational publishing house to see if it publishes tracts.

FELLOWSHIP TRACT LEAGUE

PO Box 164, Lebanon, OH 45036 | 513-494-1075
mail@fellowshiptractleague.org | *www.fellowshiptractleague.org*

GOOD NEWS PUBLISHERS

1300 Crescent St., Wheaton, IL 60187 | 630-682-4300
info@crossway.org | *www.crossway.org/tracts*

GOSPEL TRACT SOCIETY

PO Box 1118, Independence, MO 64051 | 816-461-6086
gospeltractsociety@gmail.com | *gospeltractsociety.org*

GRACE VISION PUBLISHERS

321-745-9966 (text only)
www.gracevision.com

MOMENTS WITH THE BOOK

PO Box 322, Bedford, PA 15522 | 814-623-8737
email through the website | *mwtb.org*

TRACT ASSOCIATION OF FRIENDS

1501 Cherry St., Philadelphia, PA 19102
info@tractassociation.org | *www.tractassociation.org*

14

BIBLE CURRICULUM

This list includes only the major, nondenominational curriculum publishers. If you are in a denominational church, also check its publishing house for curriculum products. Plus some organizations, like Awana and Pioneer Clubs, produce curriculum for their programs.

Since Bible curriculum is written on assignment only, you'll need to get samples for age groups you want to write for (from the company's website, large Christian bookstores, or your church) and study the formats and pieces. Look for editors' names on the copyright pages of teachers manuals, or call the publishing house for this information.

Then write query letters to specific editors. Tell why you're qualified to write curriculum for them, include a sample of curriculum you've written or other sample of your writing, and ask for a trial assignment. Since the need for writers varies widely, you may not get an assignment for a year or more.

Some of these companies also publish undated, elective curriculum books that are used in a variety of ministries. Plus some book publishers publish lines of Bible-study guides. (See "Traditional Book Publishers.") These are contracted like other books with a proposal and sample chapters.

DAVID C. COOK
4050 Lee Vance Dr., Colorado Springs, CO 80918 | 800-323-7543
shop.davidccook.org
Type: Sunday school
Imprints: The Action Bible, Bible-in-Life, Echoes, Gospel Light, HeartShaper, SEEN Youth, Standard Lesson, Tru Ministry

GROUP PUBLISHING
1515 Cascade Ave., Loveland, CO 80538 | 800-447-1070
submissions@group.com | *www.group.com*
Types: Sunday school, vacation Bible school, children's worship

Imprints: Be Bold, Dig In, FaithWeaver NOW, Fearless Conversation, Hands-On Bible, LIVE, Simply Loved, KidsOwn Worship
Guidelines: *grouppublishingps.zendesk.com/hc/en-us/ articles/211878258-Submissions*

PENSACOLA CHRISTIAN COLLEGE

PO Box 17900, Pensacola, FL 32522-7900 | 877-356-9385
www.joyfullifesundayschool.com

Type: Sunday school
Imprint: Joyful Life

UNION GOSPEL PRESS

PO Box 301055, Cleveland, OH 44130 | 800-638-9988
editorial@uniongospelpress.com | *uniongospelpress.com*

Type: Sunday school

URBAN MINISTRIES, INC.

1551 Regency Ct., Calumet City, IL 60409-5448 | 800-860-8642
urbanministries.com

Types: Sunday school, vacation Bible school

15

MISCELLANEOUS

These companies publish a variety of books and other products that fall into the specialty-markets category, such as puzzle books, game books, children's activity books, craft books, charts, church bulletins, and coloring books.

BARBOUR PUBLISHING
See entry in "Traditional Book Publishers."

BEAMING BOOKS
See entry in "Traditional Book Publishers."

BROADSTREET PUBLISHING
See entry in "Traditional Book Publishers."

CHRISTIAN FOCUS PUBLICATIONS
See entry in "Traditional Book Publishers."

CSS PUBLISHING GROUP, INC.
See entry in "Traditional Book Publishers."

DAVID C. COOK
See entry in "Traditional Book Publishers."

GROUP PUBLISHING
See entry in "Traditional Book Publishers."

PAULINE BOOKS AND MEDIA
See entry in "Traditional Book Publishers."

ROSE PUBLISHING
See entry in "Traditional Book Publishers."

ROSEKIDZ
See entry in "Traditional Book Publishers."

WARNER CHRISTIAN RESOURCES
2902 Enterprise Dr., Anderson, IN 46013 | 800-741-7721
editors@warnerpress.org | *www.warnerpress.org*

Church bulletins: Short devotions that tie into a visual image and incorporate a Bible verse. Especially interested in material for holidays and special Sundays, such as Christmas, New Year's Day, Palm Sunday, Easter, Pentecost, and Communion. General themes are also welcome. Length: 250 words maximum. Deadline: April 30 annually. Buys all rights. Payment varies.

Children's coloring and activity books: Most activity books focus on a Bible story or biblical theme, such as love and forgiveness. Ages range from preschool (ages 2-5) to upper elementary (ages 8-10). Include activities and puzzles in every upper-elementary book. Coloring-book manuscripts should present a picture idea and a portion of the story for each page. Deadlines: May 1 and October 1. Payment varies.

Guidelines: *www.warnerpress.org/submission-guidelines*

PART 5

SUPPORT
FOR
WRITERS

16

LITERARY AGENTS

Asking editors and other writers is a great way to find a reliable agent. You may also want to visit *www.sfwa.org/other-resources/for-authors/writer-beware/agents* for tips on avoiding questionable agents and choosing reputable ones.

The general market has an Association of American Literary Agents (*www.aalitagents.org*), also known as AALA. To be a member, the agent must agree to a code of ethics. The website has a searchable list of agents. Some listings below indicate at least one agent belongs to the AALA. Lack of such a designation, however, does not indicate the agent is unethical; most Christian agents are not members.

A DROP OF INK LITERARY AGENCY

8587 Green Valley Rd. SE, Caledonia, MI 49316 | 616-443-1993
tomdean@adropofink.pub | *www.adropofink.pub*

Agent: Tom Dean
Agency: Established in 2020. Represents 20 clients. Also does publishing consulting and marketing consulting.
Types of books: adult nonfiction
New clients: Open to well-established book authors and writers met at conferences. First contact: website form, referral from current client. Responds in five to seven business days.
Commission: 15%
Tip: "Be as thorough as possible in your initial proposal draft."

ALIVE LITERARY AGENCY

5001 Centennial Blvd. #50742, Colorado Springs, CO 80908
www.aliveliterary.com

Agents: Bryan Norman, Lisa Jackson, Rachel Jacobson
Agency: Established in 1989. Represents more than 125 clients. Member of Association of American Literary Agents.

Types of books: adult fiction, adult nonfiction, crossover, middle grade
New clients: Only taking proposals by referral or request. Contact through the website. Responds in six to eight weeks to referrals only.
Commission: 15%

AMBASSADOR LITERARY AGENCY

PO Box 50358, Nashville, TN 37205 | 615-370-4700
info@AmbassadorAgency.com | *www.AmbassadorAgency.com*

Agent: Wes Yoder
Agency: Established in 1997. Represents 25-30 clients.
Types of books: adult fiction, adult nonfiction, crossover
New clients: Open to unpublished book authors. Contact by email with a short description of the manuscript and a request to submit for review. Responds in four to six weeks.
Commission: 15%

APOKEDAK LITERARY AGENCY

113 Winn Ct., Waleska, GA 30183 | 404-500-6328
submissions@sally-apokedak.com | *sally-apokedak.com*

Agent: Sally Apokedak
Agency: Established in 2017. Represents almost 20 clients. Specialty: children's fiction.
Types of books: adult nonfiction, children's fiction, children's nonfiction
New clients: Willing to take on anyone—new or experienced—if she falls in love with the book. Initial contact: email with synopsis, list of comp books, and the full manuscript; or referral from current client. Accepts simultaneous submissions. Responds in three months.
Commission: 15%
Tip: "Study the markets so you can be sure your book fits in—has the right word count, for instance—but also so you can be sure your book is offering a fresh perspective. The books that will sell are the ones that are the same shape and size and genre as others on the shelves, but that have a fresh take on an old message. And, of course, they have to be really well written. Voice is vital."

AUTHORIZEME LITERARY AGENCY

PO Box 1816, South Gate, CA 90280 | 310-508-9860
AuthorizeMeNow@gmail.com | *www.AuthorizeMe.net*

Agent: Sharon Norris Elliott

Agency: Established in 2019. Represents 35 clients. The AuthorizeMe company also offers consulting, coaching, editing, book development, and the AuthorizeMe Academy's 12 masterclass series. These services are offered apart from the literary agency and are at a cost when used. Some of these services may be recommended but are not required for representation. (See the website for details.)

Types of books: adult fiction, Bible study, Christian living, devotionals, early readers, memoir, parenting, picture books, women's issues, women's nonfiction

New clients: Represents clients of all ethnicities. Is welcoming and sensitive to POC (People of Color), African American pastors, and all authors new or seasoned who are teachable and excited about sharing God's truth that will change lives by ushering readers into God's presence. Contact: email, website form, referral from current client. Query first and include a one-sheet. Simultaneous OK. Responds in one to two months.

Commission: 15%

Tip: "Love Jesus, be teachable, desire excellence, remain humble, smile a lot."

BANNER LITERARY

PO Box 1828, Winter Park, CO 80482
mike@mikeloomis.co | *www.mikeloomis.co*

Agent: Mike Loomis

Agency: Established in 2004. Represents 48 clients. Other services: See listing in "Publicity and Marketing Services."

Types of books: adult nonfiction, business, inspiration, politics, self-help

New clients: Open to writers who have not published a book and self-published writers. Contact through email or website form. Responds in two weeks.

Commission: 15%

Tip: "Send your web address with query."

BBH LITERARY

david@bbhliterary.com | *www.bbhliterary.com*

Agents: David Bratt; Laura Bardolph Hubers, *laura@bbhliterary.com*

Agency: Established in 2021. Represents five clients. Also does publicity and developmental editing. See listings in "Editorial

Services" and "Publicity and Marketing Services."

Types of books: adult nonfiction

New clients: Open to all book writers. Contact: email, website form, referral from current client. Accepts simultaneous submissions. Responds in one week.

Commission: 15%

Tip: "Please tell us why your book has some urgency to its message. We are most interested in books that speak to real life in a complicated world with nuance and wisdom."

THE BINDERY AGENCY

2727 N. Cascade Ave., Ste. 170, Colorado Springs, CO 80207

info@thebinderyagency.com | www.thebinderyagency.com

Agents: Alexander Field, *afield@thebinderyagency.com*; Estee Zandee, *ezandee@thebinderyagency.com*; Ingrid Beck, *ibeck@thebinderyagency.com*; Andrea Heinecke, *aheinecke@thebinderyagency.com*; Trinity McFadden, *tmcfadden@thebinderyagency.com*; John Blase, *jblase@thebinderyagency.com*

Agency: Established in 2017. Represents more than 150 clients.

Types of books: adult fiction, adult nonfiction, biography, business, Christian living, culture, leadership, memoir, parenting, personal development, relationships, spirituality

New clients: Represents well-established book writers, first-time book authors, self-published writers, and writers met at conferences. Initial contact: email, referral from current client, mail. Query first or send full proposal. Accepts simultaneous submissions. Responds in eight to ten weeks.

Commission: 15%

Tip: "The Bindery represents a wide variety of writers, including established authors who have published dozens of books, as well as first-time authors. Feel free to query our team at this email address: *info@thebinderyagency.com*, and allow time for a response before emailing a specific agent. We will read every query. If we're interested in following up, we will do our best to respond in a timely manner. If you've been referred to one of our literary agents by an author we know or represent, feel free to reach out to that agent directly."

THE BLYTHE DANIEL AGENCY, INC.

PO Box 64197, Colorado Springs, CO 80962-4197 | 719-213-3427

blythe@theblythedanielagency.com | www.theblythedanielagency.com

Agents: Blythe Daniel; Stephanie Alton, *stephanie@ theblythedanielagency.com*

Agency: Established in 2005. Represents 100 clients. Sells to general market too. Other services: traditional publicity (media-driven), blog campaigns, launch teams, podcast interviews, writing, branding, social media, and email coaching. See listing in "Publicity and Marketing Services."

Types of books: adult nonfiction, Bible studies, business, Christian living, church resources, current events, devotionals, general market nonfiction, gift books, leadership, marriage, men's issues, parenting, social issues, spiritual growth, teen/YA nonfiction, women's issues

New clients: Open to writers who have not published a book, well-established book writers, writers met at conferences. Initial contact: email with full proposal or referral from current client. Accepts simultaneous submissions. Responds in eight weeks.

Commission: 15% of standard book royalties, other formats vary

Tip: "Visit our website to see the types of projects we represent and services we offer. We are happy to consider your project, coaching needs, or marketing you want to pursue. We have a projects manager who assists us with these (*rebecca@theblythedanielagency.com*)."

BOOKS & SUCH LITERARY MANAGEMENT

52 Mission Cir., Ste. 122, PMB 170, Santa Rosa, CA 95409-5370
representation@booksandsuch.com | *www.booksandsuch.com*

Agents: Janet Kobobel Grant, Wendy Lawton, Rachel Kent, Cynthia Ruchti, Barb Roose, Mary DeMuth

Agency: Established in 1996. Represents 250 clients.

Types of books: adult fiction, adult nonfiction, children's fiction, children's nonfiction, teen/YA fiction, teen/YA nonfiction

New clients: Open to writers who have not published a book, well-established book writers, and self-published writers. Contact by email with query first. Accepts simultaneous submissions. Responds in six to eight weeks if interested.

Commission: 15%

Tip: "Provide clear and compelling details about your project in your query. We read each query we receive and forward it to the agent most likely to be interested in your project if it seems to be a good fit for our agency."

CHRISTIAN LITERARY AGENT

PO Box 428, Newburg, PA 17257 | 717-423-6621
keith@christianliteraryagent.com | *www.christianliteraryagent.com*

Agent: Keith Carroll

Agency: Established in 2010. Represents 10-15 new clients annually. Other service: writer coach.

Types of books: adult nonfiction

New clients: Open to first-time book authors and self-published writers. Initial contact: email, website form. Responds in two to four weeks.

Commission: 10%

Fee: $90 application fee

Tip: "I try to help you make your material more of an effective read."

THE CHRISTOPHER FEREBEE AGENCY

submissions@christopherferebee.com | *christopherferebee.com*

Agents: Christopher Ferebee, Angela Scheff, Jana Burson

Agency: Established in 2011.

Types of books: adult fiction, adult nonfiction

New clients: Submit query letter and proposal as email attachment. Responds in four weeks.

Tip: "As a small agency, we focus our efforts on a very select group of authors. Our primary focus and attention is always on existing client relationships. But we are looking for the right authors with important ideas."

CREATIVE MEDIA AGENCY, INC.

query@cmalit.com | *cmalit.com*

Agent: Paige Wheeler, *paige@cmalit.com*

Agency: Established in 1997. Represents more than 30 clients. Member of Association of American Literary Agents.

Types of books: adult fiction, adult nonfiction, business, lifestyle, parenting, relationships, women's issues

New clients: Open to writers at all levels, including self-published and those who have not published a book. Query by email. Simultaneous queries OK. Responds in six to eight weeks.

Commission: 15%

Tip: "Please check out our website."

CURTIS BROWN, LTD.

10 Astor Pl., New York, NY 10003-6935 | 212-473-5400
lbp@cbltd.com | www.curtisbrown.com

Agent: Laura Blake Peterson
Agency: Member of Association of American Literary Agents. General agency that handles some religious/inspirational books.
Types of books: adult fiction, adult nonfiction, children's fiction, children's nonfiction
New clients: Email query, and attach the first 50 pages of your manuscript. Include "lbpquery" in the subject line of your email. Responds in three to four weeks only if interested in your book.
Commission: 15%

CYLE YOUNG LITERARY ELITE, LLC

PO Box 1, Clarklake, MI 49230 | 330-651-1604
submissions@cyleyoung.com | cyleyoung.com

Agents: Cyle Young, Tessa Emily Hall, Del Duduit, Megan Burkhart
Agency: Established in 2018. Represents 80 clients. Specialty: children's and nonfiction.
Types of books: adult fiction, adult nonfiction, children's fiction, children's nonfiction, middle grade, teen/YA fiction, teen/YA nonfiction
New clients: Currently closed to queries and proposals except when meeting one of the agents at a writers conference or an online writing event. Check the website for changes in this policy. Simultaneous submissions OK. Responds in three months or longer.
Commission: 15%
Tip: "We look for projects with great writing, big ideas, and great platform."

DUNAMIS WORDS

www.cherylricker.com/dunamis-words

Agent: Cheryl Ricker
Agency: Established in 2015. Represents 15 clients.
Types of books: adult fiction, business, charismatic, Christian living, current events, devotionals, gift books, leadership, marriage, memoir, ministry, parenting, social issues, women's issues
New clients: Accepts queries—maximum of six pages—only through the website. If interested, will ask for more information and sample chapters.

Tip: "One's heart matters as much as one's calling and ability to write. These authors work diligently at growing their craft and tuning their antennae to the Creator and wellspring of life. From a deep abiding relationship with Christ flows the richest substance and wisdom."

EMBOLDEN MEDIA GROUP

PO Box 953607, Lake Mary, FL 32795

submissions@emboldenmediagroup.com | *emboldenmediagroup.com*

Agents: Jevon Bolden, Quantrilla Ard, Cynthia Crawford

Agency: Established in 2017. Represents 28 clients. Also offers content development, editorial, writing coaching.

Types of books: fiction, devotionals, health/wellness, leadership, memoir, picture books, self-help, social justice, spiritual growth, YA

New clients: Open to writers at every level. Email a query, use the website form, or current client referral. Accepts simultaneous submissions. Responds in 8-12 weeks.

Commission: 15%

Tip: "As you consider a potential publishing partnership with us, read through our submission guidelines at *emboldenmediagroup.com/ literary-representation*. Then, scroll through and see the beautiful array of authors we represent. We hope you see yourself there."

FINE PRINT LITERARY MANAGEMENT

115 W. 29th St., 3rd Fl., New York, NY 10001 | 212-279-1282

peter@fineprintlit.com | *www.fineprintlit.com*

Agent: Peter Rubie

Agency: General agency that handles some spirituality books.

Types of books: adult fiction, adult nonfiction, middle grade, teen/YA fiction

New clients: Open to unpublished authors and new clients. Email query.

Commission: 15%

GARDNER LITERARY, LLC

PO Box 1089, Monument, CO 80132 | 719-440-0069

rachelle@gardner-literary.com | *rachellegardner.com*

Agent: Rachelle Gardner

Agency: Established in 2021. Represents 35 clients. Specialties: next generation voices in the faith community, books about the intersection of faith and culture, deconstructing and reconstructing faith, asking hard questions about faith. Also offers coaching to unagented authors. See website for details.

Types of books: adult nonfiction

New clients: Open to all authors with established platforms with social media and/or a podcast. First contact by email query. Simultaneous OK. See detailed submission guidelines on the website. Responds in about a week.

Commission: 15%

Tip: "I'm known for representing writers who are Christian but not on the conservative side. My authors are typically inclusive and affirming, and many are advocates for various justice issues."

GARY D. FOSTER CONSULTING

733 Virginia Ave., Van Wert, OH 45891 | 419-238-4082

gary@garydfoster.com | *www.garydfoster.com*

Agent: Gary Foster

Agency: Established in 1989. Represents more than 50 clients.

Types of books: adult nonfiction

New clients: Open to unpublished book and well-established authors. Initial contact: email or mail full proposal or referral from current client. Accepts simultaneous submissions. Responds in one to three weeks.

Commission: 15%

Fee: nominal fee on signing representation agreement

Tip: "Think about how you will build your market-exposure platform."

THE GATES GROUP

sarah@the-gates-group.com | *www.the-gates-group.com*

Agents: Don Gates, Sarah Coverstone

Agency: Established in 2013. Represents more than 50 authors. Member of Association of American Literary Agents.

Types of books: adult nonfiction, Bible studies, children's fiction, children's nonfiction, curriculum, devotionals, gift books, leadership

New clients: Open to writers who have not published a book and well-established book writers. Initial contact: email, referral from current client. Responds quickly.

Commission: 15%

Tip: "Have a good attitude."

GOLDEN WHEAT LITERARY

goldenwheatliterary.com

Agents: Jessica Schmeidler, *jessica@goldenwheatliterary.com*; Nicole Payne, *submissions@goldenwheatliterary.com*

Agency: Established in 2015. Also sells to the general market.

Types of books: adult fiction, devotionals, general-market fiction, memoir, middle grade, picture books, teen/YA nonfiction

New clients: Email query letter and first three chapters, all in body of message; no attachments. If no response in six months, assume the agent is not interested.

HARTLINE LITERARY AGENCY

123 Queenston Dr., Pittsburgh, PA 15235 | 412-829-2483
www.hartlineagency.com

Agents: Jim Hart, *jim@hartlineliterary.com*; Joyce A. Hart, *joyce@ hartlineliterary.com*; Cyle Young, *cyle@hartlineliterary.com*; Linda Glaz, *linda@hartlineliterary.com*; Patricia Riddle-Gaddis, *patricia@ hartlineliterary.com*

Agency: Established in 1992. Represents 200 clients. Responds in three months; but due to a high volume of submissions, they are not always able to respond to projects that are not a good fit for the agency. See website for individual agents' interests.

Types of books: adult fiction, Bible reference, Bible study, biography, business, Christian living, church and ministry, early readers, leadership, middle grade, parenting, picture books, self-help, social issues, teen/YA fiction, teen/YA nonfiction

New clients: Open to all writers except self-published. Initial contact: email with full proposal, website form. Accepts simultaneous submissions. Responds in six to eight weeks.

Commission: 15%

Tip: "In most cases we need to see a full book proposal to make an informed decision on representation. Be patient, do your homework and know which agent is best suited for your work. Please only submit to one agent at Hartline. Attending writers conferences is very important."

HIDDEN VALUE GROUP

27758 Santa Margarita Pkwy. #361, Mission Viejo, CA 92691 | 949-573-5207
njernigan@hiddenvaluegroup.com | *www.HiddenValueGroup.com*

Agent: Nancy Jernigan

Agency: Established in 2001. Clients: 17. Member of Association of American Literary Agents.

Types of books: family, leadership, marriage, mental health, women's nonfiction

New clients: Open to well-established book writers only. Email full proposal. Responds in two weeks.

Commission: 15%

Tip: "No poetry. Be familiar with the publishing process."

ILLUMINATE LITERARY AGENCY

support@illuminateliterary.com | illuminateliterary.com

Agents: Jenni Burke, Tawny Johnson

Agency: Established in 2006. Represents almost 60 clients. Specialty: adult nonfiction.

Types of books: adult nonfiction, Bible studies, business, children's fiction, children's nonfiction, church and ministry, culture, devotionals, family, gift books, leadership, lifestyle, memoir, personal development, relationships, spiritual growth, women's issues

New clients: Open to writers who are well-established or have not published a book and have a significant platform. Initial contact: website form, referral from current client, full proposal. Responds in four weeks if proposal catches their interest.

Commission: 15%

Tip: "Please thoroughly review our website before submitting."

K J LITERARY SERVICES, LLC

1540 Margaret Ave., Grand Rapids, MI 49507 | 616-551-9797

kim@kjliteraryservices.com | www.kjliteraryservices.com

Agent: Kim Zeilstra

Agency: Established in 2006.

New clients: Only taking new authors by referral at this time. Initial contact by email or phone. Also does: editing, proofreading, project management, permissions.

Commission: 15%

KIRKLAND MEDIA MANAGEMENT

PO Box 1539, Liberty, TX 77575 | 936-581-3944

jessica@kirklandmediamanagement.com | jessiekirkland.com

Agent: Jessica Kirkland

Agency: Established in 2015. Sells to general market too.

Types of books: adult fiction, adult nonfiction, TV/movie scripts

New clients: For fiction: Email a one-sheet first. If she likes the story, she will request a proposal and sample chapters at that time. For nonfiction: Email a full proposal plus three sample chapters. If no response in three months, not interested.

Commission: 15%

Tip: "She is searching for powerful stories that encourage, equip, challenge, and change, but is most enthusiastic about inspirational true stories."

THE KNIGHT AGENCY

232 W. Washington St., Madison, GA 30650 | 706 473-0994

pamela.harty@knightagency.net | *knightagency.net*

Agents: Pamela Harty

Agency: General agency established in 1996. Member of Association of American Literary Agents.

Types of books: adult fiction, children's fiction, children's nonfiction, Christian living

New clients: Open to writers who have not published a book, well-established book writers, and self-published writers. Initial contact by query via Query Manager on the website. All other queries will not be reviewed or returned. Responds in six weeks.

Commission: 15%

Tip: "Please visit our website for submission guidelines."

LITERARY MANAGEMENT GROUP, LLC

8530 Calistoga Way, Brentwood, TN 37027 | 615-812-4445

brucebarbour@literarymanagementgroup.com

www.literarymanagementgroup.com

Agent: Bruce R. Barbour

Agency: Established in 1996. Represents more than 100 clients. Also does: book packaging and publishing consulting.

Types of books: adult nonfiction

New clients: No unpublished authors or self-published books. Email proposal. Accepts simultaneous submissions. Responds in three to four weeks.

Commission: 15%

MACGREGOR AND LEUDEKE

PO Box 1316, Manzanita, OR 97124

amanda@macgregorliterary.com | *www.MacGregorLiterary.com*

Agents: Amanda Luedeke, *amanda@macgregorliterary.com*; Chip MacGregor, *chip@macgregorliterary.com*; Alina Mitchell, *alina@macgregorliterary.com*

Agency: Established in 2006. Member of Association of American

Literary Agents. Represents 50-70 clients. Specialty: memoir, Christian living.

Types of books: adult fiction, adult nonfiction, biography, business, Christian living, culture, current events, health/wellness, history, leadership, mental health, self-help

New clients: Open to all writers except self-published. The ideal client is someone who is established as an expert in their field or area of influence. Initial contact: email, website form; send full proposal. Accepts simultaneous submissions. Currently, full on submissions. If interested, will be in touch.

Commission: 15%

Tip: "Get to know the projects and people we work with."

MARK SWEENEY & ASSOCIATES

302 Sherwood Dr., Carol Stream, IL 60188 | 615-403-1937
sweeney2@comcast.net

Agents: Mark Sweeney, Janet Sweeney

Agency: Established in 2003. Represents more than 75 clients. Specialty: popular apologetics.

Types of books: adult nonfiction, apologetics, Bible study, Christian living, memoir

New clients: Looking for authors with a great book idea who have both the skill to communicate in writing and a platform from which to write. Open to well-established book writers, as well as those who have not published a book. Initial contact: email, referral from current client. Query first. Responds in one week.

Commission: 15%

Tip: "Check with the agency's current author clients for a referral."

MARTIN LITERARY & MEDIA MANAGEMENT

914 164th St. SE, Ste. B12, #307, Mill Creek, WA 98102 | 206-466-1773
adria@martinliterarymanagment.com | *martinlit.com*

Agent: Adria Goetz

Agency: General agency established in 2003. Adria has more than 25 clients. Specialty: "I look for books that delight readers, that help inspire wonder and imagination, that foster deep empathy and compassion for our fellow human beings, that provide rich character representation of marginalized people groups, that take the reader on an adventure, that uncover fascinating stories from history's footnotes, that explore issues of faith and how to apply Christ's teachings to our own life, that celebrate women and the female experience, that ask nitty gritty questions and don't settle for easy answers, that make people disappointed when they have to close the book and go to bed, and books that add a touch of magic to readers' lives." Other services: film and TV adaptation.

Types of books: adult fiction, adult nonfiction, Christian living, devotionals, middle grade, picture books, teen/YA fiction, teen/YA nonfiction

New clients: Open to writers who have not published a book, self-published writers, writers met at conferences. Contact by email. Accepts simultaneous submissions. Responds in two weeks. Be sure to read *www.martinlit.com/submission-policy.*

Commission: 15%; foreign, 25%

Tip: "Check out my full wish list, which is updated frequently, at *adriagoetz.com.*"

METAMORPHOSIS LITERARY AGENCY

12410 S. Acuff Ct., Olathe, KS 66062 | 646-397-1640

info@metamorphosisliteraryagency.com | *www.metamorphosisliteraryagency.com*

Agent: Stephanie Hansen

Agency: General agency established in 2016. Represents 50+ Christian clients. Specialty: elevating voices that often go unheard.

Types of books: adult fiction, adult nonfiction, middle grade, picture books, teen/YA fiction

New clients: Open to writers who have not published a book. Initial contact: website form, *querymanager.com/query/Query_Metamorphosis/New_Manuscripts.* Responds in six months or earlier.

Commission: 15%

Tip: "Please be sure your manuscript or proposal is in tiptop shape before querying."

NATASHA KERN LITERARY AGENCY, INC.

PO Box 1069, White Salmon, WA 98672

agent@natashakern.com | *natashakernliterary.com*

Agent: Natasha Kern

Agency: Established in 1987. Represents 36 religious clients.

Types of books: adult fiction

New clients: Closed to queries from unpublished writers. Open to meeting with writers at conferences and accepting referrals from current clients and editors. Cannot read unsolicited queries or proposals.

PAPE COMMONS

11327 Rill Pt., Colorado Springs, CO 80921 | 719-648-4019

don@papecommons.com | *papecommons.com*

Agent: Don Pape

Agency: Established in 2020. Clients: 45. Typically responds in two days. Also consults on publishing-industry concerns.

Types of books: adult fiction, adult nonfiction, general-market fiction, general-market nonfiction

New clients: Open to unpublished book authors and self-published writers. Contact: email, referral from a current client; query first.

Commission: 15%

Tip: "A one-page pitch sheet is preferable for considering the project. Social-media presence should be developing and/or robust."

THE SEYMOUR AGENCY

475 Miner Street Rd., Canton, NY 13617 | 239-398-8209

nicole@theseymouragency.com | *www.theseymouragency.com*

Agents: Nichole Resciniti; Julie Gwinn, *julie@theseymouragency.com*; Tina Wainscott, *QueryMe.Online/TinaWainscottTSA*

Agency: Established in 1992. Member of Association of American Literary Agents.

Types of books: adult fiction, adult nonfiction, middle grade, picture books, teen/YA fiction, teen/YA nonfiction

New clients: Open to writers who have not published a book, well-established book writers, self-published writers, and writers met at conferences. Contact by email with one-page query first or referral from current client. Responds in two weeks to queries, three months to proposals.

Commission: 15%

Fees: none

Tip: "Hone your craft. Take advantage of writers groups, critique partners, etc., to polish your manuscript into the best shape it can be."

SPENCERHILL ASSOCIATES

1767 Lakewood Ranch Blvd. #268, Bradenton, FL 34211 | 941-201-6587

submissions@spencerhillassociates.com | *www.spencerhillassociates.com*

Agent: Ali Herring

Agency: General agency established in 2001. Represents 24 clients with Christian books.

Types of books: adult fiction, middle grade, teen/YA fiction

New clients: Open to all book writers. Query first. Accepts simultaneous queries. Responds in 6-12 weeks.

Commission: 15%; foreign, 20%

Tip: "Follow the guidelines listed on the Spencerhill website."

THE STEVE LAUBE AGENCY

24 W. Camelback Rd. A-635, Phoenix, AZ 85013 | 602-336-8910
info@stevelaube.com | *www.stevelaube.com*

> **Agents:** Steve Laube, *krichards@stevelaube.com*; Tamela Hancock Murray, *ewilson@stevelaube.com*; Bob Hostetler, *rgwright@ stevelaube.com*; Dan Balow, *vseem@stevelaube.com*
>
> **Agency:** Established in 2004. Represents more than 300 clients. See website blog post by each agent for what he or she is looking for.
>
> **Types of books:** adult fiction, adult nonfiction
>
> **New clients:** Open to unpublished and published authors. Email proposal as attachment according to the guidelines on the website. Steve Laube also will take proposals by mail. Accepts simultaneous submissions. Responds in 8-12 weeks.
>
> **Commission:** 15%
>
> **Tip:** "Please follow the guidelines! Since your book proposal is like a job application, you want to present yourself in the most professional manner possible. Your proposal will be a simple vehicle to convey your idea to us and, ultimately, to a publisher."

WILLIAM K. JENSEN LITERARY AGENCY

119 Bampton Ct., Eugene, OR 97404 | 541-688-1612
queries@wkjagency.com | *www.wkjagency.com*

> **Agents:** William K. Jensen, Rachel McMillan, Teresa Evenson
>
> **Agency:** Established in 2005. Represents more than 50 clients.
>
> **Types of books:** adult fiction, adult nonfiction, apologetics, biography, cookbook, devotionals, family, gift books, health/ wellness, humor, marriage, men's issues, politics, prophecy, social issues, women's issues
>
> **New clients:** Open to unpublished authors. Contact by email only; no attachments. See the website for complete query details. Accepts simultaneous submissions. Responds in one month or not interested.
>
> **Commission:** 15%

WINTERS & KING, INC.

2448 E. 81st St., Ste. 5900, Tulsa, OK 74137-4259 | 918-494-6868
dboyd@wintersking.com | *wintersking.com/practice-areas/publishing-agent-services*

> **Agent:** Thomas J. Winters
>
> **Agency:** Established in 1983. Represents 150 clients. Part of a law firm. Other services: legal review of publishing contracts, drafting

of work-for-hire agreements to contract writer/editor services, copyright/trademark filing

Types of books: adult fiction, adult nonfiction

New clients: Open to writers with a story to tell. Contact by email. Responds in two weeks.

Commission: 15%

Tip: "Submissions should be carefully edited and free of typos. Accompanying manuscripts or sample chapters for presentation to publishers should be edited, typo-free, and basically print-ready."

WOLGEMUTH & ASSOCIATES

info@wolgemuthandassociates.com | *www.wolgemuthandassociates.com*

Agents: Robert Wolgemuth, Andrew Wolgemuth, Erik Wolgemuth, Austin Wilson

Agency: Established in 1992. Clients: 150. Responds in two weeks if interested.

Types of books: adult nonfiction, Bible studies, children's fiction, children's nonfiction

New clients: Works with well-established book writers only with references from a current client. Contact: email.

Commission: 15%

Tip: "Please include a reference from an existing client."

WORDSERVE LITERARY GROUP

7500 E. Arapahoe Rd., Ste. 285, Centennial, CO 80112 | 303-471-6675

admin@wordserveliterary.com | *www.wordserveliterary.com*

Agents: Greg Johnson, *greg@wordserveliterary.com*; Sarah Freese, *sarah@wordserveliterary.com*; Nick Harrison, *nick@wordserveliterary.com*; Keely Boeving, *keely@wordserveliterary.com*

Agency: Established in 2003. Represents more than 180 clients.

Types of books: adult fiction, adult nonfiction, children's fiction, children's nonfiction, general-market fiction, general-market nonfiction

New clients: Open to well-established book writers, writers who have not published a book yet, self-published writers, and writers met at conferences. Email query or full proposal. Accepts simultaneous submissions. Responds in two to four weeks.

Commission: 15%

Tip: "Follow instructions on our website on how to query our agency."

WORDWISE MEDIA SERVICES

4083 Avenue L, Ste. 255, Lancaster, CA 93536

get.wisewords@gmail.com | *www.wordwisemedia.com/agency*

> **Agents:** Steven Hutson, David Fessenden, Michelle S. Lazurek
>
> **Agency:** Established in 2011. Member of Association of American Literary Agents. Represents 70 clients.
>
> **Types of books:** adult fiction, adult nonfiction, apologetics, children's fiction, children's nonfiction, Christian living, devotionals, picture books
>
> **New clients:** Open to unpublished book authors and writers met at conferences. Contact: website form; query first. Accepts simultaneous submissions. Responds in one month; OK to nudge after then.
>
> **Commission:** 15%
>
> **Tip:** "Follow instructions carefully. Meet us as at a conference. Specify the agent's name in the email subject line if you have a preference."

WTA MEDIA

321 Billingsly Ct., Ste. 7, Franklin, TN 37067

info@wta.media | *thewtagroup.com*

> **Agent:** David Schroeder
>
> **Agency:** Focuses on helping clients develop and market products to go with books and/or films.
>
> **New clients:** Contact by email.

YATES & YATES

1551 N. Tustin Ave., Ste. 710, Santa Ana, CA 92705 | 714-480-4000

email@yates2.com | *www.yates2.com*

> **Agents:** Sealy Yates, Matt Yates, Curtis Yates, Mike Salisbury, Karen Yates
>
> **Agency:** Established in 1989. Represents fewer than 50 clients.
>
> **Types of books:** adult nonfiction
>
> **New clients:** No unpublished authors. Contact by email with full proposal. Responds in one to two months. Other services: author coaching and ecourses available at *authorcoaching.com*.
>
> **Commission:** negotiable
>
> **Tip:** "We serve passionate, articulate, gifted Christian communicators, using our strengths to guide, counsel, and protect them, fiercely advocate for them, and help them advance life- and culture-transforming messages for the sake of the Kingdom."

17

WRITERS CONFERENCES AND **SEMINARS**

Due to the still-fluid situation with COVID-19, many conference directors had not set dates yet or decided if they will host an in-person conference when this book went to print. Also, a few directors already decided to hold their conferences online in 2022; they are listed in the Online section at the end of this chapter.

ALABAMA

SOUTHERN CHRISTIAN WRITERS CONFERENCE

Tuscaloosa, AL | June | *www.southernchristianwriters.com*

Director: Cheryl Wray, 4195 Waldort Dr., Northport, AL 35473; 205-534-0595; *scwritersconference@gmail.com*

Description: The SCWC is a two-day conference for beginners or experienced writers that focuses on several genres: nonfiction books, magazines, fiction, grammar, business aspects, legal aspects, etc.

Faculty: agents, editors, publishers

Attendance: 160-200

CALIFORNIA

CHRISTIAN WRITERS RETREAT AT MOUNT HERMON

Felton, CA (near Santa Cruz) | fall | *www.ChristianWritersRetreat.com*

Director: Kathy Ide, *KathyIde@ChristianWritersRetreat.com*

Description: Get away for a weekend at the prayer-soaked, Spirit-infused Mount Hermon Christian Conference Center, surrounded by stunning coastal redwoods, streams, and waterfalls. Make a special and powerful connection with God there. Get refreshed, rejuvenated, and recharged. Fill your tank, so you can pour out in all the other things you do. Build relationships with people who understand you and want to encourage you, support you, and pray for you. Listen for the Holy Spirit's guidance and direction on your writing and your life. Make some divine connections. And carve out some uninterrupted writing time in this beautiful, inspiring setting.

Attendance: 75

INSPIRE CHRISTIAN WRITERS CONFERENCE AT MOUNT HERMON

Felton, CA (near Santa Cruz) | March 25-29 | *inspirewriters.com/conference*

Director: Robynne Elizabeth Miller, 2850 S.W. Cedar Hills Blvd., Box 138, Beaverton, OR 97005; 530-217-8233; *robynne@robynnemiller.com*

Description: A well-rounded Christian writers conference with tracks and options for new writers through career authors. Top faculty and speakers from across the US offer standard, unique, and innovative workshops and tracks over four days in one of the most beautiful conference locations in the US.

Faculty: agents, editors, publishers

Speakers: Tricia Goyer, Kim Bangs, Bob Hostetler, Robynne E. Miller

Scholarships: full, partial

Attendance: 175

Contest: Two prizes for the best professional and best new writer.

WEST COAST CHRISTIAN WRITERS CONFERENCE

Brentwood, CA (San Francisco area) | February 17-19 | *www.westcoastchristianwriters.com*

Director: Sharon Norris Elliott, *westcoastchristianwriters@gmail.com*

Description: West Coast Christian Writers aims to equip and encourage writers of all levels in the craft and business of writing for publication through an annual conference that offers quality instruction, industry updates, community, and personal inspiration. We're known for our relaxed, warm atmosphere and sense of community.

Faculty: agents, editors, publishers

Scholarships: full, partial

Attendance: 275

Contest: We host an annual writing contest for fiction and nonfiction with cash and prizes for first, second, and third place. Check our website for the theme and guidelines.

COLORADO

COLORADO CHRISTIAN WRITERS CONFERENCE

Estes Park, CO | May 11-14 | *colorado.writehisanswer.com*

Director: Marlene Bagnull, 951 Anders Rd., Lansdale, PA 19446; 484-991-8581; *mbagnull@aol.com*

Description: Sharpen your writing and marketing skills from your choice of eight continuing sessions and more than fifty workshops. Seven keynotes, four or more one-on-one fifteen-minute appointments.

Special track: teens

Faculty: agents, editors, publishers

Scholarships: partial

Attendance: 200

Contest: Entries based on the conference theme of "Write His Answer" from Habakkuk 2:2. Prose (maximum 500 words) or poetry by published and not-yet-published authors. The winner in each of the four categories receives 50% off the registration fee the following year. Entry fee $10.

EVANGELICAL PRESS ASSOCIATION ANNUAL CONVENTION

Colorado Springs, CO | April 10-12 | *www.epaconvention.com*

Director: Lamar Keener, PO Box 1787, Queen Creek, AZ 85142; 888-311-1731; *director@evangelicalpress.com*

Description: The annual EPA Christian media convention is your chance to step away from daily activities to engage and interact with the EPA community. Join together to explore new ideas and learn from one another through powerful seminars, workshops, discussions, and presentations. Focused for periodical editors, but writers are welcome and can meet the editors. Note: This conference changes locations every year.

Faculty: editors

Speakers: John Stonestreet, Trillia Newbell, Lou Ann Sabatier

Attendance: 200

Contest: Freelance writers may submit articles and/or blog entries into contest, which requires EPA membership.

WRITE IN THE SPRINGS

Colorado Springs, CO | April 8-9 | *www.acfwcosprings.com/events*

Director: Jean Alfieri, 3820 N. 30th St., Colorado Springs, CO 80904; *Jean@blessedtobeme.com*

Description: Join us in beautiful Colorado Springs for a day of inspiration, support, and networking while we receive training to hone our craft.

Special tracks: advanced editors, teens

Scholarships: full, partial

Attendance: 50

WRITING FOR YOUR LIFE COLORADO

Highlands Ranch, CO | June 7-8 | *writingforyourlife.com/conferences*

Director: Brian Allain, PO Box 72, Adelphia, NJ 07710; *brian@writingforyourlife.com*

Description: Our conferences feature leading spiritual writers and publishing industry experts, who discuss and teach about various aspects of spiritual writing, how to get published, and how to market. Our conferences have a reputation for high-quality speakers and strong collegiality, and have been consistently rated 4.6 or higher on a scale of 1 to 5.

Faculty: agents

Speakers: Barbara Brown Taylor, Philip Yancey

Scholarships: full

Attendance: 80

CONNECTICUT

reNEW RETREAT FOR NEW ENGLAND WRITING & SPEAKING

West Hartford, CT | November | *www.reNEWwriting.com*

Director: Lucinda Secrest McDowell, PO Box 290707, Wethersfield, CT 06129; 860-402-9551; *info@reNEWwriting.com*

Description: reNEW is a spiritual retreat open to all beginning and seasoned writers and speakers who desire to communicate the good news of Jesus through their written or spoken words. At reNEW, we believe the core of our calling as writers and speakers is faithfulness to Christ. And so, our emphasis is on the need to grow deep inwardly, so we can be effective in our outward reach.

Special track: speaking

Faculty: agents, editors, publishers
Scholarships: partial
Attendance: 50-70

DELAWARE

DELMARVA CHRISTIAN WRITERS CONFERENCE

Georgetown, DE | September 17 | *delmarvawriters.com/conference*

Director: Candy Abbott, 107 Elizabeth St., Georgetown, DE 19947; 302-542-8510; *info@delmarvawriters.com*

Description: The Delmarva Christian Writers Conference is for writers who want to be obedient to God's call to write. It is your opportunity to be encouraged, equipped, and inspired.

Faculty: editors, publishers
Scholarships: partial
Attendance: 60

FLORIDA

FLORIDA CHRISTIAN WRITERS CONFERENCE

Leesburg, FL | October | *Word-Weavers.com/FloridaEvents*

Director: Eva Marie Everson, PO Box 520224, Longwood, FL 32752; 407-414-8188; *FloridaCWC@aol.com*

Description: We offer 10 continuing classes, dozens of one-hour workshops, meetings with professionals and mentors, keynote speaker, and one-day genre intensive. Writers of all levels welcome!

Special tracks: advanced writers, speaking
Faculty: agents, editors, publishers
Speaker: Steven James
Scholarships: full, partial
Attendance: 175
Contest: Go to *word-weavers.com/conferencecontest.*

GEORGIA

PUBLISHING IN COLOR ATLANTA

Atlanta, Ga. | March 10-11 | *publishingincolor.com*

Director: Brian Allain, PO Box 72, Adelphia, NJ 07710;

brian@publishingincolor.com

Description: Publishing in Color has only one objective: increase the number of books published by spiritual writers of color. This includes groups such as African Americans, Asian Americans, Latinx Americans, and Native Americans, who have been under-represented in terms of the number of published books. These conferences foster relationships between spiritual writers of color and representatives of spiritual book-publishing companies, literary agents, and spiritual magazines.

Faculty: agents, editors
Scholarships: full
Attendance: 70

WRITING FOR YOUR LIFE ATLANTA

Atlanta, GA | March 7-8 | *writingforyourlife.com/conferences*

Director: Brian Allain, PO Box 72, Adelphia, NJ 07710; *brian@writingforyourlife.com*

Description: Our conferences feature leading spiritual writers and publishing industry experts, who discuss and teach about various aspects of spiritual writing, how to get published, and how to market. Our conferences have a reputation for high-quality speakers and strong collegiality, and have been consistently rated 4.6 or higher on a scale of 1 to 5.

Faculty: agents
Speaker: Barbara Brown Taylor
Scholarships: full
Attendance: 80

ILLINOIS

WRITE-TO-PUBLISH CONFERENCE

Wheaton, IL (Chicago area) | June 15-18 | *www.writetopublish.com*

Director: Lin Johnson, 9118 W. Elmwood Dr., Ste. 1G, Niles, IL 60714-5820; 847-296-3964; *lin@writetopublish.com*

Description: For more than 50 years, Write-to-Publish has been training writers and connecting them with editors who want to publish their work and with literary agents who want to represent them. You will hear what editors, publishers, and agents in the Christian market are looking for and meet with them one-on-one to discuss your ideas and manuscripts. You also will learn how to write a variety of publishable manuscripts, improve your writing skills, find appropriate markets for your ideas, and deal with the business side of writing. Plus you will have multiple opportunities to get feedback on your manuscripts.

Special track: advanced writers
Faculty: agents, editors, publishers
Speakers: Allie Pleiter, Jane Rubietta
Scholarships: full, partial
Attendance: 175
Contest: Best New Writer and Writer of the Year awards, both for alumni who attend this year. Serious Writer contests in multiple genres for unpublished and published writers.

INDIANA

TAYLOR UNIVERSITY'S PROFESSIONAL WRITERS' CONFERENCE

Upland, IN | July 29-30 | *taylorprofessionalwritersconference.weebly.com*

Director: Linda K. Taylor, 236 W. Reade Ave., Upland, IN 46989; 765-998-5591; *taylorPRWConference@gmail.com*
Description: Hear from agents, editors, and authors who will inspire and encourage you.
Special track: teens
Faculty: agents, editors, publishers
Attendance: 150

KENTUCKY

KENTUCKY CHRISTIAN WRITERS CONFERENCE

Elizabethtown, KY | June | *www.kychristianwriters.com*

Director: Jean Matthew Hall, 704-578-0858, *jean@jeanmatthewhall.com*
Description: Our purpose is to provide an annual, interdenominational event to equip and encourage writers in their quest for publication. The conference provides a safe environment where writers can discover their gifts and share their work.
Faculty: agents, editors, publishers
Attendance: 75

MICHIGAN

MARANATHA CHRISTIAN WRITERS' CONFERENCE

Muskegon, MI | September | *www.maranathachristianwriters.com*

Director: Sherry Hoppen, 4759 Lake Harbor Rd., Norton Shores, MI 49441; 231-798-2161; *info@maranathachristianwriters.com*

Description: A broad variety of publishers, agents, and editors. Up to five one-to-one appointments with the experts at no additional charge.

Faculty: agents, editors, publishers

Scholarships: partial

Attendance: 80

Contest: Leona Hertel Awards Contests; details on the website.

SPEAK UP CONFERENCE

Grand Rapids, MI | July 7-9 | *www.speakupconference.com*

Director: Bonnie Emmorey, 1320 N. Topeka, Wichita, KS 67214; 316-882-9400; *bonnie@speakupconference.com*

Description: This is the premier conference for Christian writers and speakers to advance their personal or professional ministry. We are known for our exclusive opportunities to meet with up to four publishers and industry experts; many books have been published as a result.

Special tracks: advanced writers, speaking

Faculty: agents, editors, publishers

Speaker: Carol Kent

Scholarships: partial

Attendance: 250

MINNESOTA

NORTHWESTERN CHRISTIAN WRITERS CONFERENCE

St. Paul, MN | July 22-23 | *northwesternchristianwritersconference.com*

Director: Melissa Cutter, 3003 Snelling Ave. N, St. Paul, MN 55113; 651-631-5315; *ncwc@unwsp.edu*

Description: Northwestern Christian Writers Conference engages the hearts and minds of writers who are Christians. We celebrate and cultivate Christian writers whose work is inspirational and accessible, artful and nuanced.

Faculty: agents, editors, publishers
Speaker: Susie Larson
Scholarships: full, partial
Attendance: 500
Contest: Scholarships (2+) and awards (5) available.

MISSOURI

AMERICAN CHRISTIAN FICTION WRITERS (ACFW) CONFERENCE

St. Louis, MO | September 8-11 | *www.ACFW.com/conference*

Director: Robin Miller, PO Box 101066, Palm Bay, FL 32910-1066; *director@ACFW.com*

Description: Continuing education sessions and workshop electives specifically geared for five levels of fiction-writing experience from beginner to advanced. New: Track for readers, ACFW Storyfest. Note: This conference changes locations every year.

Special track: advanced writers
Faculty: editors and agents
Scholarships: full
Attendance: 400

Contest: The Genesis Contest is for unpublished writers whose Christian fiction manuscript is completed. The Carol Awards honor the best of Christian fiction from the previous calendar year.

HEART OF AMERICA CHRISTIAN WRITERS NETWORK FALL CONFERENCE

Kansas City, MO | October | *www.hacwn.org*

Director: Jeanette Littleton, 3706 N.E. Shady Lane Dr., Gladstone, MO 64119; 816-459-8016; *hacwnkc@gmail.com*

Description: We specialize in having faculty who are looking for new writers.

Faculty: agents, editors, publishers
Attendance: 100

Contest: In eight categories. Prizes include critiques and consultations.

REALM MAKERS

St. Louis, MO | July | *realmmakers.com*

Director: Scott Minor, *scott@realmmakers.com*

Description: Realm Makers is the premier conference serving speculative fiction writers. This event offers multilevel education in writing craft, the business of being an author, and the spiritual journey writers face. Faculty members are from both CBA and general markets. Note: This conference changes location every year.

Special tracks: advanced writers, teens

Faculty: agents, editors, publishers

Scholarships: full, partial

Attendance: 350

Contest: The Realm Awards are open to new speculative fiction books written by Christian authors, judged by hand-selected industry professionals. Books may win awards in genre-specific categories and contend for the honor of being named Book of the Year.

NORTH CAROLINA

ASHEVILLE CHRISTIAN WRITERS CONFERENCE

Asheville, NC | February 18-20 | *www.ashevillechristianwritersconference.com*

Director: Cindy Sproles, 377 Woodcrest Dr., Kingsport, TN 37663; 423-384-4821; *cindybootcamp@gmail.com*

Description: Training writers one writer at a time to follow their call from God to write.

Special track: advanced editors

Faculty: agents, editors, publishers

Speakers: Bob Hostetler, Eva Marie Everson

Scholarships: partial

Attendance: 130

Contest: Sparrow Award Book Contest judged according to appeal, content, flow, and writing.

BLUE RIIDGE MOUNTAINS CHRISTIAN WRITERS CONFERENCE

Black Mountain, NC | May 29–June 3 | *www.BlueRidgeConference.com*

Director: Edie Melson, 604 S. Almond Dr., Simponsville, SC 29681; 864-373-4232; *Edie@ediemelson.com*

Description: The Blue Ridge Mountains Christian Writers Conference began nearly four decades ago as a Spirit-filled environment where writers could move forward in their writing journey and publishing dreams. The legacy event is focused on God's path for each writer, and the conference is dedicated to meeting professional and spiritual needs.

Special tracks: advanced writers, speaking, teens
Faculty: agents, editors, publishers
Scholarships: partial
Attendance: 500
Contests: The Selah Awards (books published in 2021), The Director's Choice Awards (books published in 2021), The Foundation Awards (for unpublished, registered attendees).

MOUNTAINSIDE MARKETING CONFERENCE

Black Mountain, NC | January | *www.blueridgeconference.com/ mountainside-marketing-retreat*

Director: Edie Melson, 604 S. Almond Dr., Simpsonville, SC 29681; 864-373-4232; *edie@ediemelson.com*
Description: A blogging, branding, and social-media conference.
Speakers: Edie Melson, DiAnn Mills
Attendance: 50

MOUNTAINSIDE NONFICTION RETREAT

Black Mountain, NC | *www.blueridgeconference.com/mountainside- nonfiction-retreat*

Director: Edie Melson, *edie@ediemelson.com*
Description: Nonfiction writing is one of the foundational skill sets every professional writer must have. Even a novelist's career will be enhanced by knowing how to write compelling articles, devotions, and essays.
Attendance: 30-50

MOUNTAINSIDE NOVELIST RETREAT

Black Mountain, NC | September | *www.blueridgeconference.com/ mountainside-novelist-retreat*

Director: Edie Melson, *edie@ediemelson.com*
Description: Writing craft and creativity. Professional faculty. Small, intimate group, critiques, contests, workshops, private appointments, writing time, and fun.
Special track: advanced writers
Faculty: agents, editors, publishers
Attendance: 25-35
Contest: For unpublished writers: Best Title, First Sentence, First Paragraph, First Page, Proposal, Golden Leaf Award.

MOUNTAINSIDE SPEAKING RETREAT

Black Mountain, NC | *www.blueridgeconference.com/mountainside-speaking-retreat*

Director: Edie Melson, *edie@ediemelson.com*

Description: Speaking is an art, but it's also a skill that can be learned. It's a gift to pair with writing or as a singular means of sharing God's Word as we teach and motivate others. Come expecting to learn the techniques that separate the professionals from the amateurs. Included will be techniques on enunciation, hooking the listener, voice inflection, content, poise, and dress.

Special track: speaking

Speakers: DiAnn Mills, Edie Melson, Karen Porter

Attendance: 30-50

SHE SPEAKS CONFERENCE

Concord, NC | July | *shespeaksconference.com*

Director: Lisa Allen, 630 Team Rd. #100, Matthews, NC 28105; 704-849-2270; *shespeaks@Proverbs31.org*

Description: Speaking and writing tracks.

Special track: speaking

Faculty: agents, editors

Attendance: 700

SHE WRITES AND SPEAKS PRESENTS AMPLIFY

Concord, NC | February 11-13 | *www.shewritesandspeaks.com*

Director: Carol Tetzlaff, PO Box 427, Enumclaw, WA 98022; 360-226-3488; *info@redemption-press.com*

Description: Clarify your message. Deepen your impact. Extend your reach. An equipping and empowering conference for Christian communicators. Held in conjunction with the Christian Product Expo Winter Show.

Special tracks: advanced writers, speaking

Faculty: agents, editors, publishers

Speakers: Debbie Alsdorf, Erica Wiggenhorn, Tammy Whitehurst

Scholarships: partial

Attendance: 200

OREGON

CASCADE CHRISTIAN WRITERS CONFERENCE HOSTED BY OREGON CHRISTIAN WRITERS

Canby, OR | June 23-26 | *oregonchristianwriters.org*

Director: Christina Suzann Nelson, PO Box 20214, Keizer, OR 97307; *summerconf@oregonchristianwriters.org*

Description: A conference for all levels of writers with publishers, editors, agents, and published authors on the faculty. Outstanding classes and workshops on all facets of writing and publishing, mentoring opportunities, and time to network in a lovely and relaxed setting.

Faculty: agents, editors, publishers

Speaker: Tricia Goyer

Attendance: 190

OREGON CHRISTIAN WRITERS ONE-DAY CONFERENCES

Portland, Salem, OR | *www.oregonchristianwriters.org*

Director: Traci Heskett, PO Box 20214, Keizer, OR 97307; *contact@oregonchristianwriters.org*

Description: Two or three conferences, each with two morning keynote addresses and two workshops with four choices each. See the website for locations and dates.

Attendance: 100-125

PENNSYLVANIA

MONTROSE CHRISTIAN WRITERS CONFERENCE

Montrose, PA | July 17-22 | *www.montrosebible.org/OurEvents.aspx*

Director: Marsha Hubler, 1833 Dock Hill Rd., Middleburg, PA 17842; 570-837-0002; *marshahubler@outlook.com*

Description: We offer an average of 50 classes presenting fiction, nonfiction, songwriting, poetry, marketing, beginners' classes, and editing. Throughout the week, conferees have the opportunity to discuss their projects one-on-one with any faculty member they choose.

Special tracks: advanced writers, speaking, teens

Faculty: agents, editors, publishers

Scholarships: partial

Attendance: 70-80

Contest: The Shirley Brinkerhoff Memorial Scholarship, $200 grant for tuition, is awarded to a writer actively striving to hone the craft of writing who's not yet secured a publishing contract. Applications are available at *montrosebible.org/writers.htm.*

ST. DAVIDS CHRISTIAN WRITERS' CONFERENCE

Grove City, PA | June 22-26 | *www.stdavidswriters.com/conference*

Director: Sue Boltz, *treasurer@stdavidswriters.com*

Faculty: agents, editors

Scholarships: full, partial

Attendance: 45

Contest: See detailed list on the website.

SUPER SATURDAY

Lancaster, PA | April | *lancasterchristianwriters.com*

Director: JP Robinson, *lancasterwrites@gmail.com*

Description: One-day conference with fiction and nonfiction tracks, keynote, bookstore, and individual consultations with faculty.

Attendance: 80

SOUTH CAROLINA

CAROLINA CHRISTIAN WRITERS CONFERENCE

Spartansburg, SC | March 10-12; 10th is for pastors and ministry leaders only | *www.fbs.org/christian-writers-conference*

Director: Linda Gilden, 250 East Main St., Spartanburg, SC 29306; 864-706-5250; *linda@lindagilden.com*

Description: Carolina Christian Writers Conference exists to help writers grow and move to the next step in their Christian writing careers.

Special track: pastors

Faculty: agents, editors, publishers

Speaker: Karissa McCall Culbreath

Scholarships: full

Attendance: 125

Contest: Kudos contest for book and article writers, published and unpublished.

WRITE2IGNITE MASTER CLASSES FOR CHRISTIAN WRITERS OF CHILDREN AND YOUNG ADULT LITERATURE

Tigerville, SC | September | *write2ignite.com*

Director: Jean Matthew Hall, *info.write2ignite@gmail.com*

Description: Write2Ignite seeks to: (1) inspire and challenge novice to experienced writers, middle school through adult, to serve God and young readers through their writing; (2) facilitate Christian writers' development by providing instruction on writing craft and professional publishing, especially of children's and young-adult literature; and (3) connect authors with one another and with published authors, editors and literary agents, illustrators, and other writing and publishing professionals.

Special tracks: advanced writers, teens

Faculty: agents, editors, publishers

Scholarships: full, partial

Attendance: 90

Contest: Unpublished Picture Book manuscript.

TENNESSEE

MID-SOUTH CHRISTIAN WRITERS CONFERENCE

Memphis, TN | March 18-19 | *MidSouthChristianWriters.com*

Director: Beth Gooch, PO Box 823, Byhalia, MS 38611; 901-277-5525; *midsouthchristianwriters@gmail.com*

Description: We strive to keep this an affordable conference with a balanced presentation to appeal to writers of fiction and nonfiction, from beginners to multipublished professionals.

Faculty: agents, editors, publishers

Speaker: Bob Hostetler

Attendance: 100

TEXAS

TEXAS CHRISTIAN WRITERS CONFERENCE

Houston, TX | August | *www.centralhoustoniwa.com*

Director: Martha Rogers, 6038 Greenmont, Houston, TX 77092; 713-686-7209; *marthalrogers@sbcglobal.net*

Faculty: editors

Attendance: 60
Contest: Inspirational Writers Alive! Open Writing Competition

WASHINGTON

NORTHWEST CHRISTIAN WRITERS RENEWAL

Bellevue, WA | May | *nwchristianwriters.org*

Director: Charles & Perry Harris, PO Box 2706, Woodinville, WA 98072; 206-250-6885; *renewal@nwchristianwriters.org*
Description: This conference is where writers, editors, and publishers can connect, network, and collaborate. Conferees will sharpen their skills, learn strategies, and form connections to boost their success on the writing journey.
Faculty: agents, editors, publishers
Speaker: James L. Rubart
Scholarships: full
Attendance: 130

SHE WRITES FOR HIM WRITING RETREAT

Enumclaw, WA | *www.shewritesforhimconference.com*

Director: Carol Tetzlaff, PO Box 427, Enumclaw, WA 98022; 360-226-3488; *info@redemption-press.com*
Description: An intimate and intensive five-day writing retreat where you will gain all the insight you need to write and publish your story.
Faculty: publishers
Scholarships: partial
Attendance: 12

AUSTRALIA

OMEGA WRITERS CONFERENCE

Kingscliff, NSW, Australia | October 7-9 | *www.omegawriters.org/conference*

Director: Penny Reeve, *conference@aomegawriters.org*
Description: Held every second year to encourage Christian writers towards excellence, impacting society with grace and truth. We want our words to change the world.
Faculty: editors, publishers
Scholarships: partial
Attendance: 100

CANADA

InSCRIBE CHRISTIAN WRITERS' FELLOWSHIP FALL CONFERENCE

Edmonton, AB, Canada | September 30–October 2 | *inscribe.org/fall-conference*

Contact: *president@inscribe.org*

Description: InScribe's Fall Conference features a seasoned author, publisher, or other expert as the keynote speaker; plus we offer a variety of workshop topics and presenters. It's a weekend where writers—whether they are seasoned or beginning—can connect for fellowship, encouragement, and support.

Scholarships: partial

Contest: See *www.inscribe.org/contests.*

WRITE! CANADA

Canada | *writecanada.org*

Contact: Box 77001, Markham, ON L3P 0C8; *info@thewordguild.com*

Description: Write! Canada is an annual writers conference hosted by The Word Guild. Seasoned writers host workshops where writers of all experience levels and genres can meet and hone their skills.

NEW ZEALAND

NZ CHRISTIAN WRITERS RETREAT

Whitianga, New Zealand | April 22-30, 2023 | *www.nzchristianwriters.org*

Director: Justin St. Vincent, 179B St. Johns Rd., St. Johns, Auckland, North Island, New Zealand 1072; *editor@xtrememusic.org*

Description: Our seminar speakers will inspire, refresh, and upskill each of us on our writing journey.

Faculty: editors, publishers

Attendance: 40

ONLINE

ART OF WRITING
November | *thechristyaward.com*

> **Director:** Cindy Carter, ECPA, 5801 S. McClintock Dr., Ste. 104, Mesa, AZ 85283; 480-966-3998; *TheChristyAward@ecpa.org*
>
> **Description:** The Art of Writing program is an online conference for writers, storytellers, and publishing curators, featuring a keynote presentation and three tangible sessions for authors and publishing professionals to enjoy. The networking is also a vibrant part of this event, along with The Christy Award® Gala, honoring the year's best in Christian fiction, that follows in Nashville, Tenn.
>
> **Faculty:** agents, editors, publishers
>
> **Attendance:** 200

GREATER PHILADELPHIA CHRISTIAN WRITERS CONFERENCE
August | *philadelphia.writehisanswer.com*

> **Director:** Marlene Bagnull, 951 Anders Rd., Lansdale, PA 19446; 484-991-8581; *mbagnuill@aol.com*
>
> **Description:** To encourage and equip you to write about a God who is real, who is reachable, and who changes lives. Six continuing sessions, thirty-six workshops, five keynotes, three or four early-bird learning labs.
>
> **Special track:** teens
>
> **Faculty:** agents, editors, publishers
>
> **Scholarships:** partial
>
> **Attendance:** 220
>
> **Contest:** Entries based on the conference theme of "Write His Answer" from Habakkuk 2:2. Prose (maximum 500 words) or poetry by published and not-yet-published authors. The winner in each of the four categories receives 50% off the registration fee for the following year. Entry fee $10.

MT. ZION RIDGE PRESS CHRISTIAN WRITER'S CONFERENCE
May 12-14 | *www.mtzionridgepress.com/writing-off-the-beaten-path-confere*

> **Director:** Tamera Lynn Kraft, *mtzionridgepress@gmail.com*
>
> **Description:** Christian writer's conference online.
>
> **Faculty:** editors, publishers
>
> **Attendance:** 100

PENCON

May 4-6 | *penconeditors.com*

> **Director:** Denise Loock, 699 Golf Course Rd., Waynesville, NC
> 28786; 908-868-5854; *director@penconeditors.com*
> **Description:** PENCON is the only conference for editors in the
> Christian market. Note: This conference is now run virtually every
> May, with in-person regional meetings in various parts of the
> country throughout the year.
> **Faculty:** editors, publishers
> **Speaker:** Jim Watkins
> **Scholarships:** full, partial
> **Attendance:** 75

SHE WRITES FOR HIM BOOTCAMP

Various dates | *www.shewritesforhimbootcamp.com*

> **Director:** Carol Tetzlaff, PO Box 427, Enumclaw, WA 98022; 360-
> 226-3488; *info@redemption-press.com*
> **Description:** In a private online group, you'll enjoy rich teaching,
> small-group coaching, daily encouragements, and the training you
> need to map out your table of contents and the tools you need to
> follow through to book completion.
> **Faculty:** publishers
> **Speakers:** Debbie Alsdorf, Dori Harrell, Cynthia Cavanaugh, and
> Athena Dean Holtz
> **Attendance:** 50 maximum

SHE WRITES FOR HIM: ROAR

October 14-15 | *www.shewritesforhimroar.com*

> **Director:** Carol Tetzlaff, PO Box 427, Enumclaw, WA 98022; 360-
> 226-3488; *info@redemption-press.com*
> **Description:** Equipping you with priceless tips, tricks and tools
> to build your platform and expand your reach. Join us for an
> interactive, hands-on, "apply what you learned" experience!
> **Special track:** advanced writers, speaking
> **Attendance:** 150

SHE WRITES FOR HIM VIRTUAL CONFERENCE

March 31–April 2 | *www.shewritesforhimconference.com*

> **Director:** Carol Tetzlaff, PO Box 427, Enumclaw, WA 98022; 360-
> 226-3488; *info@redemption-press.com*

Description: Three days of a power-packed, live, online event with 30+ publishing-industry professionals to help you strengthen, sharpen, write, and market your message.
Special tracks: advanced writers, speaking
Faculty: agents, editors, publishers
Speakers: Lynn Austin, Laura Story
Attendance: 300+

WRITE YOUR HARD STORY 5-DAY CHALLENGE

various dates | *www.shewritesforhimchallenge.com*

Director: Carol Tetzlaff, PO Box 427, Enumclaw, WA 98022; 360-226-3488; *info@redemption-press.com*
Description: During this action-packed, 5-day challenge you will learn the exact strategies that successfully published writers and authors use to get unstuck and complete the hard story they are called to write.
Speakers: Athena Dean Holtz, Debbie Alsdorf
Attendance: 50

CONFERENCES THAT CHANGE LOCATIONS

The following conferences change locations every year but are listed with their 2022 locations:

AMERICAN CHRISTIAN FICTION WRITERS CONFERENCE

EVANGELICAL PRESS ASSOCIATION ANNUAL CONVENTION

REALM MAKERS

18

WRITERS GROUPS

In addition to the groups listed here, check the national organizations for new groups in your area.

NATIONAL AND ONLINE

ACFW BEYOND THE BORDERS
www.facebook.com/groups/ACFWBeyondtheBorders
> **Contact:** Iola Goulton, *iola@iolagoulton.com*
> **Members:** 100
> **Affiliation:** American Christian Fiction Writers

AMERICAN CHRISTIAN FICTION WRITERS
acfw.com
> **Contact:** Robin Miller, PO Box 101066, Palm Bay, FL; *director@acfw.com*
> **Services:** Email loop, genre Facebook pages, online courses, critique groups, and local and regional chapters. Sponsors contests for published and unpublished writers and conducts the largest fiction writers conference annually.
> **Members:** 2600+
> **Membership fee:** $75 to join, $49/year to renew

CHRISTIAN AUTHORS NETWORK
ChristianAuthorsNetwork.com
> **Contact:** Angela Breidenbach, *can_inc@yahoo.com*
> **Services:** "CAN is a group of traditionally published Christian authors who have joined together in a supportive association to spread the news about books to book lovers everywhere. We operate as a cooperative, Christ-centered marketing organization, to encourage

and teach one another, and get the word out about CAN authors' books to readers, retailers, and librarians."
Members: 140
Membership fee: $50 one-time registration fee, $50/year

CHRISTIAN INDIE AUTHOR NETWORK
www.christianindieauthors.com

Meetings: online, 24/7 Facebook and website
Contact: Mary C. Findley, 918-805-0669, *mjmcfindley@gmail.com*
Members: 400+

THE CHRISTIAN PEN: PROOFREADERS AND EDITORS NETWORK
www.TheChristianPEN.com

Contact: Kathy Ide, *KathyIde@ChristianEditor.com*
Services: "The Christian PEN: Proofreaders and Editors Network provides aspiring, beginning, established, and professional editors and proofreaders with networking, community, and industry discounts. If you are an editor or proofreader, or are thinking about becoming one, join this community of like-minded professionals who share our knowledge and experience with one another."
Members: 731
Membership fee: $25-$90/year

CHRISTIAN WOMEN WRITER'S GROUP
cwwriters.com

Meetings: online, weekly and monthly communications
Contact: Jen Gentry, 918-724-3996, *jennyokiern37@gmail.com*
Members: 100+
Affiliation: Christian Indie Author Network

INSPIRE CHRISTIAN WRITERS
www.inspirewriters.com

Contact: Robynne Miller, 530-217-8233, *inspiredirectors@gmail.com*
Services: "Through Inspire you'll find a community of writers working together to achieve writing and publication goals. By taking advantage of our online and in-person critique groups, you'll give and receive feedback and grow in your craft. We offer web-based and local training through workshops and conferences to help you navigate publishing decisions, create your online presence and polish your writing until it shines. You'll have opportunities to

network with other writers—multi-published as well as those just
starting out."
Members: 150
Membership fee: $50/year
Affiliation: West Coast Christian Writers

PEN-SOULS

Meetings: online and email; monthly reminders are emailed to
members to pray for one another and share urgent, personal
prayer requests and publishing announcements
Contact: Janet Ann Collins, 530-272-4905, *jan@janetanncollins.com*
Members: 10-12

REALM MAKERS

www.realmmakers.com

Meetings: quarterly online
Contact: Scott Minor, *members@realmmakers.com*
Members: 100
Membership fee: ranges from $4.99 to $24.99/month

WORD WEAVERS INTERNATIONAL, INC.

www.Word-Weavers.com

Contact: Eva Marie Everson, president, PO Box 520224, Longwood,
FL; 407-615-4112; *WordWeaversInternational@aol.com*
Services: Local traditional chapters and Zoom online pages for
manuscript critiquing. Sponsors Florida Christian Writers
Conference.
Members: 1,000+ worldwide
Membership fee: $45/year, adults; $35/year, students

WORD WEAVERS ONLINE GROUPS

www.Word-Weavers.com

Meetings: online via Zoom, times vary, two hours
Contact: Eva Marie Everson, 407-615-4112,
WordWeaversInternational@aol.com
Membership fee: $45/year
Affiliation: Word Weavers

ALABAMA

WORD WEAVERS NORTH ALABAMA
www.facebook.com/groups/936711453176211

> **Meetings:** 105 Village Dr. NE, Hartselle; third Thursday of each month, 10:00 a.m.–noon
> **Contact:** Lisa Worthey Smith, 256-612-7404, *lisawsmith57@gmail.com*
> **Members:** 8
> **Membership fee:** $45/year
> **Affiliation:** Word Weavers

WORD WEAVERS SAND MOUNTAIN
www.facebook.com/groups/wordweaverssand

> **Meetings:** Shades of Pemberley Bookstore, 126 S. Broad St., Albertville; fourth Saturday of the month, 10 a.m.–noon
> **Contact:** Dave Warner, 928 821-6469, *dave@warner.house*
> **Members:** 5
> **Membership fee:** $45/year
> **Affiliation:** Word Weavers

ARIZONA

ACFW ARIZONA
www.christianwritersofthewest.com

> **Meetings:** Denny's, 4400 N. Scottsdale Rd., Scottsdale; third Saturday of the month, 1:00-3:00 p.m.
> **Contact:** Ruth Douthitt, *arizona@acfwchapter.com*
> **Members:** 30
> **Membership fee:** $10/year plus national fee
> **Affiliation:** American Christian Fiction Writers

CHANDLER WRITERS' GROUP
chandlerwriters.wordpress.com

> **Meetings:** Ocotillo Rd., Chandler; first Friday of the month, 9:00-11:30 a.m.
> **Contact:** Jenne Acevedo, 480-510-0419, *jenneacevedo@gmail.com*
> **Members:** 12
> **Membership fee:** none

FOUNTAIN HILLS CHRISTIAN WRITERS' GROUP

Meetings: Fountain Hills Presbyterian Church, 13001 N. Fountain Hills Blvd., Fountain Hills; second Friday of the month, 9:00 a.m.–noon

Contact: Jewell Johnson, 480-836-8968, *tykeJ@juno.com*

Members: 12

Membership fee: $10/year

Affiliation: American Christian Writers

WORD WEAVERS NORTHERN ARIZONA

Meetings: Verde Community Church, 102 S. Willard, Cottonwood; second Saturday of the month, 9:30-11:30 a.m.

Contact: Alice Klies, *Alice.Klies@gmail.com*

Membership fee: $45/year

Affiliation: Word Weavers

ARKANSAS

ACFW ARKANSAS

www.facebook.com/groups/127662834752320

Meetings: Springdale; first Monday of every month, 5:30 p.m.

Contact: Robyn Hook, *arkansas@acfwchapter.com*

Members: 15

Membership fee: national fee

Affiliation: American Christian Fiction Writers

ACFW NW ARKANSAS

www.facebook.com/groups/127662834752320

Meetings: Springdale, last Saturday of the month

Contact: Robyn Hook

Members: 20

Membership fee: national fee

Affiliation: American Christian Fiction Writers

CALIFORNIA

ACFW ORANGE COUNTY

www.acfwoc.com

Meetings: place varies; second Thursday of each month, 7:00 p.m.

Contact: Susan K. Beatty, *orangecounty@acfwchapter.com*
Members: 21
Membership fee: $10/year plus national fee
Affiliation: American Christian Fiction Writers

ACFW SAN FRANCISCO BAY AREA
www.acfwsfba.wordpress.com

> **Meetings:** Sunnyvale; third Saturday of odd months, 10 a.m.–noon
> **Contact:** Katie Vorreiter, *acfwsfbayarea@gmail.com*
> **Members:** 15
> **Membership fee:** national fee
> **Affiliation:** American Christian Fiction Writers

WORD WARRIORS
www.facebook.com/wordwarriorswriters

> **Meetings:** 3 Crosses Church, 20600 John Dr., Castro Valley; first
> Monday of the month September–June, 7:00 p.m.
> **Contact:** Debbie Jones Warren, 510-329-4141, *debbiencj@aim.com*
> **Members:** 15
> **Membership fee:** none

COLORADO

ACFW COLORADO SPRINGS
acfwcosprings.com

> **Meetings:** Living Hope Church, 640 Manitou Blvd., Colorado Springs;
> first Saturday of the month, 10:00 a.m.–noon
> **Contact:** Tammie Fickas, *acfwcs.president@acfwcolorado.com*
> **Members:** 45
> **Membership fee:** $25/year plus national fee
> **Affiliation:** American Christian Fiction Writers

SPRINGS WRITERS
springswriters.wordpress.com

> **Meetings:** Woodmen Valley Chapel, 250 E. Woodmen Rd., Colorado
> Springs; second Tuesday of each month, 6:00-8:00 p.m.
> **Contact:** Scoti Springfield Domeij, 719-209-9066, *springswriters@
> gmail.com*
> **Members:** 350

WOLF CREEK CHRISTIAN WRITERS NETWORK

wolfcreekwriters.com

Meetings: CrossRoad Christian Fellowship, 1044 Park Ave., Pagosa Springs and online via Zoom; every Monday 9:00-11:00 a.m.
Contact: Betty J. Slade, 970-264-2824, *bettyslade@centurytel.net*
Members: 35
Membership fee: $30

WORD WEAVERS PIKES PEAK

Meetings: 2650 Leoti Dr., Colorado Springs; third Saturday of each month, 9:30-11:30 a.m.
Contact: Tez Brooks, 407-797-4408, *tezwrites@gmail.com*
Members: 10
Membership fee: $45/year
Affiliation: Word Weavers

WORD WEAVERS WESTERN SLOPE

www.facebook.com/groups/568085077249557

Meetings: The Rock Church, 2170 Broadway Ave., Grand Junction; fourth Saturday of each month, 9:30 a.m.–noon
Contact: Templa Melnick, 970-261-7230, *templa.melnick@gmail.com*
Members: 8
Membership fee: $45/year
Affiliation: Word Weavers

WRITERS ON THE ROCK

www.writersontherock.com

Meetings: various places around Denver and Colorado Springs; monthly
Contact: David Rupert, 720-237-7487, *info@writersontherock.com*
Members: 170

CONNECTICUT

WORD WEAVERS BERKSHIRES

wordweaversberkshires.org

Meetings: Sherman Church, 6 Church Rd., Sherman; third Saturday of the month, 9 a.m.–noon
Contact: Tara Alemany, 860-946-0544, *info@wordweaversberkshires.org*
Members: 15
Affiliation: Word Weavers

DELAWARE

DELMARVA CHRISTIAN WRITERS' ASSOCIATION
www.delmarvawriters.com
> **Meetings:** Abundant Life Church, 20488 Donovan's Rd., Georgetown; third Saturday of the month, 9:00 a.m.–noon
> **Contact:** Candy Abbott, 302-856-6649, *cfa@candyabbott.com*
> **Members:** 20

KINGDOM WRITERS FELLOWSHIP
www.delmarvawriters.com/meetings/kingdom-writers-fellowship
> **Meetings:** Atlanta Road Alliance Church, 22625 Atlanta Rd., Seaford; second Tuesday of the month, 6:00-9:00 p.m.
> **Contact:** Teresa Marine, 302-841-2432, *tdm4Him@yahoo.com*
> **Members:** 10
> **Affiliation:** Delmarva Christian Writers' Fellowship

FLORIDA

ACFW CENTRAL FLORIDA
www.cfacfw.org
> **Meetings:** Grace Covenant Presbyterian Church, 1655 Peel Ave., Orlando; third Saturday of the month, noon–2:00 p.m.
> **Contact:** Dorothy Mays
> **Membership fee:** $15/year plus national fee
> **Affiliation:** American Christian Fiction Writers

SUNCOAST CHRISTIAN WRITERS GROUP
> **Meetings:** The Haus Coffee Shop, 12199 Indian Rocks Rd., Largo; third Thursday of the month, 10:30 a.m.
> **Contact:** Elaine Creasman, 727-251-3756, *emcreasman@aol.com*
> **Members:** 10
> **Membership fee:** none

WORD WEAVERS CLAY COUNTY
www.facebook.com/groups/WordWeaversClayCounty
> **Meetings:** Panera Bread, 1510 County Rd. 220, Fleming Island; second Saturday of every month, 9:00 a.m.
> **Contact:** Victoria Roberts, 904-505-5693, *carpediem4christ@gmail.com*
> **Members:** 12

Membership fee: $45/year
Affiliation: Word Weavers

WORD WEAVERS DESTIN

Meetings: Destin; second Saturday of the month, 9:30 a.m.
Contact: Felicia Ferguson, *fergufl@yahoo.com*
Membership fee: $45/year
Affiliation: Word Weavers

WORD WEAVERS GAINESVILLE

Meetings: 5003 N.W. 13th Ave., Gainesville; second Sunday of the month, 2:00-4:30 p.m.
Contact: June F. Carlson, 352-548-4846, *jfcarlson@bellsouth.net*
Members: 6
Membership fee: $45/year
Affiliation: Word Weavers

WORD WEAVERS JENSEN BEACH

Meetings: First Baptist Jensen Beach, 1400 N.E. Jensen Beach Blvd., Jensen Beach; fourth Saturday of the month, 10:00 a.m.–noon
Contact: Penny Cooke, *LifeCoachPenny@yahoo.com*
Membership fee: $45/year
Affiliation: Word Weavers

WORD WEAVERS LAKE COUNTY

www.facebook.com/groups/1790245144535020

Meetings: Leesburg Library, 100 E. Main, Leesburg; third Saturday of the month, 9:30 a.m.
Contact: M.L. Anderson, 678-477-3649, *andersonwriter@gmail.com*
Members: 15
Membership fee: $45/year
Affiliation: Word Weavers

WORD WEAVERS MERRITT ISLAND

www.facebook.com/groups/1187819688313104

Meetings: Lighthouse Church, 1250 N. Banana River Dr., Merritt Island; fourth Saturday of the month, 10:00 a.m.
Contact: Irene Wintermyer, 248-962-5528, *iwintermyer@yahoo.com*
Members: 5
Membership fee: $45
Affiliation: Word Weavers

WORD WEAVERS OCALA CHAPTER

Meetings: Belleview Public Library, 13145 S.E. County Highway 484, Belleview; second Friday of the month, 10:00 a.m.-12:30 p.m.
Contact: Jennifer Odom, *odomj@live.com*
Members: 10+
Membership fee: $45/year
Affiliation: Word Weavers

WORD WEAVERS ORLANDO

www.facebook.com/groups/216603998394619

Meetings: Calvary Chapel, 5015 Goddard Ave., Orlando; second Saturday of the month, 9:30 a.m.
Contact: Julie Payne Miller, 407-376-6581, *Wordweaversorlando@gmail.com*
Members: 60
Membership fee: $45/year
Affiliation: Word Weavers

WORD WEAVERS PENSACOLA

Meetings: Hillcrest Baptist Church, 800 E. Nine Mile Rd., Pensacola; second Tuesday of the month, 5:30-8:00 p.m.
Contact: Ginny Cruz, 850-748-8895, *ginnycruzwriting@gmail.com*
Members: 5
Membership fee: $45/year
Affiliation: Word Weavers

WORD WEAVERS SARASOTA

Meetings: First United Methodist Church, 104 S. Pineapple Ave., Sarasota, and Zoom; fourth Sunday of the month, 4:00 p.m.
Contact: Sam Wright, 941-900-8231, *drsamwright@comcast.net*
Members: 10
Membership fee: $45/year
Affiliation: Word Weavers

WORD WEAVERS SOUTH FLORIDA

Meetings: 1729 N.W. 36th Ct., Oakland Park; second Saturday of the month, 9:00 a.m.–noon
Contact: Patricia Hartman, *Patricia@PatriciaHartman.net*
Membership fee: $45/year
Affiliation: Word Weavers

WORD WEAVERS TAMPA

Meetings: 1901 S. Village Ave., Tampa; first Saturday of the month, 9:30 a.m.–12:30 p.m.
Contact: Donna Mumma, 813-690-3021, *writemore30@gmail.com*
Members: 25
Membership fee: $45; teens, $35
Affiliation: Word Weavers

WORD WEAVERS TREASURE COAST

www.facebook.com/groups/480150568723000

Meetings: Kings Baptist Church, 3235 58th Ave., Vero Beach; second Saturday of each month, 9:30–noon
Contact: Dr. Laurie Boulden, 321-543-4538, *laurie.boulden@warner.edu*
Members: 10
Membership fee: $45/year
Affiliation: Word Weavers

WORD WEAVERS VOLUSIA

www.facebook.com/groups/227447203952675

Meetings: Faith Church United Brethren, 4700 S. Clyde Morris Blvd., Port Orange; first Monday of each month, except if a holiday then second Monday
Contact: Renee Hanson, 386-341-7576, *rlhhh2@gmail.com*
Members: 18
Membership fee: $45/year
Affiliation: Word Weavers

GEORGIA

ACFW NORTH GEORGIA

www.acfwnga.wix.com/home

Meetings: Buford First United Methodist, 285 E. Main St. NE, Buford; fourth Tuesday of each month, 7:00-9:00 p.m.
Contact: Hope Welborn, *acfwnga@gmail.com*
Members: 20
Membership fee: national fee
Affiliation: American Christian Fiction Writers

ACFW NORTHWEST GEORGIA
acfwnorthwestga.blogspot.com

> **Meetings:** Marietta; second Tuesday of the month, 6:30-8:30 p.m.
> **Contact:** Cindy K. Stewart, *nwgeorgia@acfwchapter.com*
> **Members:** 15
> **Membership Fee:** $15/year plus national fee
> **Affiliation:** American Christian Fiction Writers

CHRISTIAN AUTHORS GUILD
www.christianauthorsguild.org

> **Meetings:** Provino's Italian Restaurant, 440 Ernest W. Barrett Pkwy.
> NW 1, Kennesaw; first Monday of the month, 7:00 p.m.
> **Contact:** *info@christianauthorsguild.org*
> **Members:** 50
> **Membership fee:** $30/year

WORD WEAVERS BROOKHAVEN
www.facebook.com/groups/200656040663612

> **Meetings:** Capital City Club, Brookhaven, call for directions; second
> Saturday each month, 9:30 a.m.–noon
> **Contact:** Debra Bryant, 404-406-2473, *underapalmtree@att.net*
> **Members:** 8
> **Membership fee:** $45/year
> **Affiliation:** Word Weavers

WORD WEAVERS COLUMBUS, GA
www.facebook.com/groups/541016626433688

> **Meetings:** Cornerstone Church of God, 7701 Lloyd Rd., Columbus;
> third Monday of every month, 6:30 p.m.
> **Contact:** Terri Miller, *wordweaverscolumbus@gmail.com*
> **Members:** 10
> **Membership fee:** $45/year
> **Affiliation:** Word Weavers

WORD WEAVERS CONYERS
www.facebook.com/groups/638509006538934

> **Meetings:** Bethel Christian Church, 1930 Bethel Rd. NE, Conyers;
> second Saturday of each month, 10:00 a.m.
> **Contact:** Leigh DeLozier, *leigh@authorleighdelozier.com*
> **Members:** 6

Membership fee: $45/year
Affiliation: Word Weavers

WORD WEAVERS GREATER ATLANTA
Meetings: 4541 Vendome Pl. NE, Roswell; first Saturday of the
  month, 9:30 a.m.–noon
Contact: Barbara Fox, *barb@barbjfox.com*
Membership fee: $45/year
Affiliation: Word Weavers

WORD WEAVERS MACON-BIBB
www.facebook.com/groups/173188826644758
Meetings: Central City Church, 621 Foster Rd., Macon; monthly on
  Sunday, 3:30-5:30 p.m.
Contact: Robin Dance, 423-718-7714, *RobinDance.me@gmail.com*
Members: 45
Membership fee: $45/year
Affiliation: Word Weavers

WORD WEAVERS VALDOSTA
Meetings: Corinth Baptist Church, 4089 Corinth Church Rd., Lake
  Park; third Saturday of the month, 2:00-4:00 p.m.
Contact: Christy Adams, *ChristyAdams008@gmail.com*
Membership fee: $45/year
Affiliation: Word Weavers

WORD WEAVERS WOODSTOCK
Meetings: Prayer & Praise Christian Fellowship, 6409 Bells Ferry
  Rd., Woodstock; third Monday of the month, 6:30-9:00 p.m.
Contact: Frieda Dixon, *friedas@bellsouth.net*
Members: 15
Membership fee: $45/year
Affiliation: Word Weavers

ILLINOIS

ACFW CHICAGO
www.acfwchicago.com
Meetings: Schaumburg Public Library, 130 S. Roselle Rd.,
  Schaumburg; second Friday of every month, 6:30-8:30 p.m.

Contact: Susan Miura, *chicago@acfwchapter.com*
Members: 20
Membership fee: national fee
Affiliation: American Christian Fiction Writers

WORD WEAVERS AURORA

Meetings: Java Plus, 1677 Montgomery Rd., Ste. 106-108, Aurora;
second Saturday of the month, 1:00-3:00 p.m.
Contact: JoDee Starrick, 708-351-4243, *jodee.starrick@gmail.com*
Members: 10
Membership fee: $45/year; teens, $35
Affiliation: Word Weavers

WORD WEAVERS LAND OF LINCOLN

Meetings: The Warehouse at Lincoln Christian University, 100
Campus View Dr., Lincoln; second Saturday of every month,
10:00 a.m.–noon
Contact: Rita Klundt, *ritaklundt@ymail.com*
Members: 10
Membership fee: $45/year
Affiliation: Word Weavers

WORD WEAVERS ON THE BORDER

Meetings: fourth Wednesday of the month, 7:00-8:30 p.m.
Contact: Jim Pas, *drallih@gmail.com*
Members: 10
Membership fee: $45/year
Affiliation: Word Weavers

INDIANA

ACFW INDIANA

www.hoosierink.blogspot.com
Meetings: various places in Indiana, quarterly
Contact: Linda Samaritoni, *acfwindianachapter@gmail.com*
Members: 50
Membership fee: $15/year plus national fee
Affiliation: American Christian Fiction Writers

BLUFFTON CHRISTIAN WRITING CLUB
www.facebook.com/groups/137239503139200
> **Meetings:** River Terrace Retirement Community, 400 Caylor Blvd., Bluffton
> **Contact:** Kayleen Reusser, *kjreusser@adamswell.com*
> **Members:** 10

FORT WAYNE CHRISTIAN WRITING CLUB
> **Meetings:** Waynedale Public Library, 2200 Lower Huntington Rd., Fort
> Wayne; fourth Tuesday of the month, 6:00-8:00 p.m.
> **Contact:** Kayleen Reusser, *kjreusser@adamswells.com*
> **Members:** 10

HEARTLAND CHRISTIAN WRITERS
www.heartlandchristianwriters.com
> **Meetings:** Mount Pleasant Christian Church's Community Life Center,
> 381 N. Bluff Rd., Greenwood; third Monday of every month, 9:30
> a.m. and 6:30 p.m.
> **Contact:** Michele Israel Harper, 317-550-9755,
> *MicheleIsraelHarper@gmail.com*
> **Members:** 45+

WORD WEAVERS FORT WAYNE
www.facebook.com/groups/217400832792519
> **Meetings:** The Chapel, Community Room, 2505 W. Hamilton Rd. S,
> Fort Wayne; second Saturday of each month, 10:00 a.m.
> **Contact:** Jo Massaro, 260-609-5049, *jomassaroministries@gmail.com*
> **Members:** 2
> **Membership fee:** $45
> **Affiliation:** Word Weavers

IOWA

WORD WEAVERS DES MOINES
www.facebook.com/groups/495808943830132
> **Meetings:** The Church at Union Park, 821 Arthur Ave., Des Moines;
> last Monday of the month, 6:30 p.m.
> **Contact:** Susan Lawrence, 515-238-6675, *srlauthor@mchsi.com*
> **Members:** 7
> **Membership fee:** $45/year
> **Affiliation:** Word Weavers

KANSAS

ACFW SOUTHCENTRAL KANSAS
www.facebook.com/pages/American-Christian-Fiction-Writers-ACFW-South-Central-Kansas/114196658701066

> **Meetings:** second Thursday of the month
> **Contact:** Karissa Fisher, *southcentralkansas@acfwchapter.com*
> **Membership Fee:** national fee
> **Affiliation:** American Christian Fiction Writers

KENTUCKY

ACFW LOUISVILLE
www.facebook.com/groups/1876813595891979

> **Contact:** Karen Richardson
> **Members:** 30
> **Membership Fee:** national fee
> **Affiliation:** American Christian Fiction Writers

WORD WEAVERS BOONE COUNTY
www.facebook.com/groups/349709925923088

> **Meetings:** Union, call for details; first Saturday of every month, 10:30 a.m.-12:30 p.m.
> **Contact:** Karisa Moore, 859-380-3449, *karisam660@gmail.com*
> **Members:** 10
> **Membership fee:** $45/year; teens, $35
> **Affiliation:** Word Weavers

LOUISIANA

ACFW LOUISIANA
www.facebook.com/pages/ACFW-Louisiana/1525862364304046

> **Meetings:** Bossier City; last Saturday of the month
> **Contact:** Carole Lehr Johnson, *louisiana@acfwchapter.com*
> **Membership Fee:** national fee
> **Affiliation:** American Christian Fiction Writers

SOUTHERN CHRISTIAN WRITERS GUILD

scwguild.com

Meetings: Gospel Bookstore, Westside Shopping center, 91
Westbank Expressway, Gretna; third Saturday of the month,
10:30 a.m.

Contact: Teena Myers, *scwg@cox.net*

Members: 30

Membership Fee: $50/year (optional, other benefits)

MARYLAND

MOUNTAIN CHRISTIAN WRITER'S GROUP

Meetings: New Life Center, room 26, 1824 Mountain Rd., Bel Air;
Sundays, 2:30-4:30 p.m.

Contact: Christy Struben, 410-259-3673, *cstruben711@gmail.com*

Members: 20-30

Membership fee: none

MICHIGAN

ACFW GREAT LAKES

greatlakeschapter.blogspot.com

Meetings: first Saturday of various months

Contact: Greta Picklesimer, *greatlakes@acfwchapter.com*

Membership Fee: $10/year plus national fee

Affiliation: American Christian Fiction Writers

WORD WEAVERS WEST MICHIGAN–GRANDVILLE

Meetings: Russ' Restaurant, 4440 Chicago Dr. SW, Grandville; first
and third Tuesdays, 6:30-8:30 p.m.

Contact: Kathy Bruins, 616-403-4894, *author@kathybruins.com*

Members: 5

Membership fee: $45/year

Affiliation: Word Weavers

WORD WEAVERS WEST MICHIGAN–HOLLAND

Meetings: City on a Hill, 100 Pine St., Zeeland; first and third
Tuesdays of the month, 12:30-2:00 p.m.

Contact: Kathy Bruins, 616-403-4894, *author@kathybruins.com*

Members: 10
Membership fee: $45/year
Affiliation: Word Weavers

WORD WEAVERS WEST MICHIGAN–MUSKEGON/ NORTON SHORES

Meetings: Norton Shores Public Library, 705 Seminole Rd., Norton
Shores; first and third Tuesdays, 5:45-7:45 p.m.
Contact: Kathy Bruins, 616-403-4894, *author@kathybruins.com*
Members: 10
Membership fee: $45/year
Affiliation: Word Weavers

WORD WEAVERS WEST MICHIGAN–NORTH GRAND RAPIDS

Meetings: Russ' Restaurant, 3531 Alpine Ave. NW, Walker; first and
third Tuesdays of the month, 6:00-8:00 p.m.
Contact: Kathy Bruins, 616-403-4894, *author@kathybruins.com*
Members: 12
Membership fee: $45/year
Affiliation: Word Weavers

MINNESOTA

ACFW MINNESOTA N.I.C.E.

www.acfwmnnice.com

Meetings: Life Point Church, 2220 Edgerton St., Maplewood; fourth
Sunday of the month, 6:00-8:00 p.m.
Contact: Michelle Aleckson, *acfw.mn_nice@yahoo.com*
Members: 25
Membership fee: $25/year plus national fee
Affiliation: American Christian Fiction Writers

MINNESOTA CHRISTIAN WRITERS GUILD

www.mnchristianwriters.com

Meetings: Oak Knoll Lutheran Church, 600 Hopkins Crossroad,
Minnetonka; second Monday of the month, September–May,
7:00-8:30 p.m.
Contact: Jason Sisam, *info@mnchristianwriters.com*
Members: 50
Membership fee: $70/year

MISSISSIPPI

BYHALIA CHRISTIAN WRITERS
www.facebook.com/groups/129990696510
> **Meetings:** First United Methodist Church, 2511 Church St., Byhalia;
> first Saturday of the month, 9:00-11:00 a.m.
> **Contact:** Beth Gooch, 901-277-5525, *gooch.beth@gmail.com*
> **Members:** 20
> **Membership fee:** none
> **Affiliation:** American Christian Writers

MISSOURI

ACFW MOZARKS
www.facebook.com/MozArksACFW
> **Meetings:** Springfield; 3rd Saturday of the month
> **Contact:** Erin Miffin, *mozarks@acfwchapter.com*
> **Membership fee:** national fee
> **Affiliation:** American Christian Fiction Writers

HEART OF AMERICA CHRISTIAN WRITERS NETWORK
www.hacwn.org
> **Meetings:** Colonial Presbyterian Church (Quivira Campus), 12501 W.
> 137th St., Overland Park; second Thursday of every month, 7:00 p.m.
> **Contact:** Jeanette Littleton, 816-459-8016, *HACWN@earthlink.net*
> **Members:** 150
> **Membership fee:** $3/meeting, members; $5/meeting, nonmembers

HEARTLAND CHRISTIAN COLLEGE WRITERS GUILD
> **Meetings:** Heartland Community Church, 6434 Shelby Co. Rd. 150,
> Bethel; first Thursday of the month, 6:30 p.m.
> **Contact:** Josh Smith, *josh@hlcommunity.org*
> **Members:** 25
> **Membership fee:** none

OZARKS CHAPTER OF AMERICAN CHRISTIAN WRITERS
www.OzarksACW.org
> **Meetings:** University Heights Baptist Church, 1010 S. National,
> Springfield; second Saturday, September–May, 10:00 a.m.-2:00 p.m.

Contact: Dr. Jeanetta Chrystie, 417-832-8409, *OzarksACW@yahoo.com*
Members: 50
Membership fee: $20/year; family, $30; newsletter only, $10
Affiliation: American Christian Writers

NEBRASKA

MY THOUGHTS EXACTLY WRITERS
mythoughtsexactlywriters.wordpress.com
    Meetings: Keene Memorial Library, Fremont; third Monday of the
        month, 6:30-8:00 p.m.
    Contact: Cheryl, *mythoughtse@gmail.com*

NEW JERSEY

ACFW NY/NJ
www.facebook.com/groups/955365637934907
    Contact: Olivia Ciotta
    Members: 50
    Membership fee: $20/year plus national fee
    Affiliation: American Christian Fiction Writers

NORTH JERSEY CHRISTIAN WRITERS GROUP
www.njcwg.blogspot.com
    Meetings: Cornerstone Christian Church, 495 Wyckoff Ave., Wyckoff;
        first Saturday of the month, 10:00 a.m.–noon
    Contact: Barbara Higby, 551-804-1014, *bhigby9323@gmail.com*
    Members: 12
    Membership fee: none

NEW YORK

SOUTHERN TIER CHRISTIAN WRITERS
    Meetings: Olean First Baptist Church, 133 S. Union St., Olean; monthly
    Contact: Deb Wuethrich, 716-379-8702, *deborahmarcein@gmail.com*
    Members: 8
    Membership fee: none
    Affiliation: American Christian Writers

WORD WEAVERS NIAGARA

Meetings: Forestview Church of God, 1250 Saunders Settlement Rd., Niagara Falls; third Saturday of the month, 10:00 a.m.–noon
Contact: Renè Diane Aube, 716-534-2910, *renedaube@gmail.com*
Members: 3
Membership fee: $45/year
Affiliation: Word Weavers

WORD WEAVERS WESTERN NEW YORK

Meetings: 2458 Rush-Mendon Rd., Honeoye Falls; third Monday of the month, 6:30-9:00 p.m.
Contact: Karen Rode, 585-571-7124, *karen.a.rode@gmail.com*
Members: 5
Membership fee: $45/year
Affiliation: Word Weavers

NORTH AND SOUTH DAKOTA

ACFW DAKOTAS

www.facebook.com/groups/ACFWDakotas

Meetings: varies by region
Contact: Jan Drexler, *sdmcnear@gmail.com*
Members: 25
Affiliation: American Christian Fiction Writers

NORTH CAROLINA

ACFW NORTH CAROLINA

Meetings: Raleigh
Contact: Kyle Beale, *northcarolina@acfwchapter.com*
Membership fee: national fee
Affiliation: American Christian Fiction Writers

WORD WEAVERS CHAPEL HILL

Meetings: Abundant Joy CWM, 3700 Lyckan Pkwy., Ste. B, Durham; second Monday of the month, 10:00 a.m.–noon
Contact: Lynn Trogdon, *LynnWTrogdon@gmail.com*
Membership fee: $45/year
Affiliation: Word Weavers

WORD WEAVERS CHARLOTTE
www.facebook.com/WordWeaversCharlotte
> **Meetings:** Sonesta Hotel, 5700 Westpark Dr., Charlotte; first Saturday
> of the month
> **Contact:** Kim Dent, *cltwordweavers@yahoo.com*
> **Members:** 15
> **Membership fee:** $45/year
> **Affiliation:** Word Weavers

WORD WEAVERS HICKORY-NEWTON
www.facebook.com/groups/2328785447421711
> **Meetings:** Vertical Life Church, 111 W. 8th St., Newton; first Saturday
> of each month, 9:30 a.m.-noon
> **Contact:** Shannon Ratcliffe, 336-420-6213, *Shannonparkerratcliffe@gmail.com*
> **Members:** 9
> **Membership fee:** $45/year
> **Affiliation:** Word Weavers

WORD WEAVERS PIEDMONT TRIAD
> **Meetings:** Wellspring Community Church, 600 May Rd., Thomasville;
> third Saturday of the month, 10:00 a.m.-noon
> **Contact:** Renee Kennedy, *reneelk3588@icloud.com*
> **Membership fee:** $45/year
> **Affiliation:** Word Weavers

WORD WEAVERS WILMINGTON
> **Meetings:** Calvary Baptist Church, 423 23rd St., Wilmington; second
> Monday of the month, 6:30-8:30 p.m.
> **Contact:** Angie Mojica, *ms_a_2000@yahoo.com*
> **Membership fee:** $45/year
> **Affiliation:** Word Weavers

OHIO

ACFW OHIO
www.facebook.com/groups/220166801456380
> **Meetings:** Etna United Methodist Church, 500 Pike St., Etna; first
> Saturday of the month, noon-3:00 p.m.
> **Contact:** Rebecca Waters, *ohio@acfwchapter.com*
> **Members:** 65

Membership fee: national fee

Affiliation: American Christian Fiction Writers

COLUMBUS CHRISTIAN WRITERS ASSOCIATION

minaraulston.com/columbus_christian_writers_association

Meetings: Zoom, second Sunday of each month, 3:00-5:00 p.m.

Contact: Mina R. Raulston, 614-507-7893, *m_raulston@hotmail.com*

Members: 5

Membership fee: none

Affiliation: American Christian Writers

DAYTON CHRISTIAN SCRIBES

www.facebook.com/groups/1000432386797105

Meetings: Kettering Seventh-Day Adventist Church, 3939 Stonebridge Rd., Kettering; second Thursday of the month, 7:00-9:00 p.m.

Contact: Kim D. Villalva, 512-680-8729, *Kdanisk@yahoo.com*

Members: 20

Membership fee: $15/year

DAYTON CHRISTIAN WRITERS GUILD

www.facebook.com/ChristianAuthorToles

Meetings: Corinthian Baptist Church, 700 S. James McGhee Blvd., Dayton; second Saturday of the month, 2:00 p.m.

Contact: Tina Tole

MIDDLETOWN AREA CHRISTIAN WRITERS (MAC WRITERS)

middletownwriters.blogspot.com

Meetings: Healing Word Assembly of God, 5303 S. Dixie Hwy., Franklin; second Tuesday of each month, 7:00-8:30 p.m.

Contact: Donna J. Shepherd, 513-373-5671, *donna.shepherd@gmail.com*

Members: 25

Membership fee: $30/year or $5/meeting

WORD WEAVERS HUDSON

Meetings: River of Life Church, 5649 Stow Rd., Hudson; second Tuesday of each month, 6:45 p.m.

Contact: Stephanie Pavlantos, 330-671-4200, *stephaniep.oh@netzero.net*

Members: 3

Membership fee: $45/year

Affiliation: Word Weavers

WORD WEAVERS NORTHEAST OHIO

Meetings: Ashland Church of the Brethren, 122 E. 3rd St., Ashland; first Thursday of each month, 6:30-8:30 p.m.
Contact: Cherie Martin, *kitties395@yahoo.com*
Members: 10
Membership fee: $45/year
Affiliation: Word Weavers

OKLAHOMA

ACFW OKLAHOMA CITY

www.okchristianfictionwriters.com

Meetings: The Oklahoma Student Loan Authority, classroom A, 525 Central Park Dr., Oklahoma City; third Saturday of each month, 1:00-3:00 p.m.
Contact: Chris Tarpley, *OCFWchapter@gmail.com*
Members: 35
Membership fee: $20/year plus national fee
Affiliation: American Christian Fiction Writers

FELLOWSHIP OF CHRISTIAN WRITERS

www.facebook.com/FCWwriters

Meetings: Kirk of the Hills Presbyterian Church, 4102 E. 61st St., Tulsa, and Zoom, second Tuesday of each month, 6:30 p.m.
Contact: Mike Moguin, 918-704-1244, *mwmog68@gmail.com*
Members: 40
Membership fee: $30

WORDWRIGHTS (OKC)

www.wordwrights-okc.com

Meetings: The Last Drop Coffee Shop, 5425 N. Lincoln Blvd., Oklahoma City; second Saturday of the month, 10:00 a.m.–noon
Contact: Donna Le, 405-501-2522, *dkle45@hotmail.com*
Members: 30
Membership fee: none

OREGON

OREGON CHRISTIAN WRITERS
www.oregonchristianwriters.org

Meetings: Portland metro area, two or three all-day Saturday
  conferences, summer coaching conference
Contact: President, 503-393-3356, *president@oregonchristianwriters.com*
Membership fee: $60/year; couples, $75; students and seniors (62+), $35

WORDWRIGHTS (OR)

Meetings: Gresham/east Multnomah County; two times a month,
  Thursday afternoons
Contact: Susan Thogerson Maas, 503-663-7834, *susan.maas@frontier.com*
Members: 5
Affiliation: Oregon Christian Writers

PENNSYLVANIA

CHRISTIAN WRITERS GUILD

Meetings: Perkin's Restaurant, 505 Galleria Dr., Johnstown; last
  Tuesday of each month, 1:00 p.m.
Contact: Betty Rosian, 814-255-4351, *wordsforall@hotmail.com*
Members: 12
Membership fee: $1/meeting

GREATER PHILLY CHRISTIAN WRITERS FELLOWSHIP
writehisanswer.com/cwfsmorningcritiquegroup

Meetings: online; every other Thursday, 10 a.m.–noon
Contact: Marlene Bagnull, 484-991-8581, *mbagnull@aol.com*
Members: 10
Membership fee: none

LANCASTER CHRISTIAN WRITERS
lancasterchristianwriters.com

Meetings: Lancaster Mennonite School, 2176 Lincoln Hwy. E,
  Lancaster, and online; third Saturday of each month, 9:30 a.m.–
  noon
Contact: JP Robinson, 717-341-8457, *lancasterwrites@gmail.com*
Members: 400

Membership fee: free and $15/year for extra benefits

LANSDALE WOMEN'S CRITIQUE GROUP
writehisanswer.com/cwfseveningcritiquegroup
> **Meetings:** 951 Anders Rd., Lansdale; every other Thursday,
> 7:30-10:00 p.m.
> **Contact:** Marlene Bagnull, 484-991-8581, *mbagnull@aol.com*
> **Members:** 12
> **Membership fee:** none

SOUTH CAROLINA

ACFW SOUTH CAROLINA
www.scwritersacfw.com
> **Meetings:** North Anderson Baptist Church, 2308 N. Main St.,
> Anderson; fourth Saturday of the month, 2:00-5:00 p.m.
> **Contact:** Elva Martin, 864-226-7024, *elvacmartin@gmail.com*
> **Members:** 20+
> **Membership fee:** $21/year plus national fee
> **Affiliation:** American Christian Fiction Writers

ACFW SOUTH CAROLINA LOWCOUNTRY
www.facebook.com/groups/ACFWSCLowCountry
> **Meetings:** Seacoast Church, 750 Long Point Rd., Mt. Pleasant; fourth
> Saturday of each month, 10:00 a.m.–noon
> **Contact:** Laurie Larsen, *sclowcountry@acfwchapter.com*
> **Members:** 12
> **Membership fee:** $20/year plus national fee
> **Affiliation:** American Christian Fiction Writers

WORD WEAVERS AIKEN
www.AikenWordWeavers.com
> **Meetings:** Trinity United Methodist Church, 2724 Whiskey Rd., Aiken;
> monthly
> **Contact:** Lee Russ, 864-608-5530, *AikenWordWeavers@gmail.com*
> **Members:** 5
> **Membership fee:** $45/year
> **Affiliation:** Word Weavers

WORD WEAVERS CHARLESTON

www.facebook.com/groups/2112701302307131

> **Meetings:** St. John's Parish Church, 3673 Maybank Hwy., John's Island; third Saturday of the month, 10 a.m.–noon
> **Contact:** Bonnie Anderson, 843-559-4775, *bonnieanderson0706@gmail.com*
> **Members:** 15
> **Membership fee:** $45/year
> **Affiliation:** Word Weavers

WORD WEAVERS HARTSVILLE

> **Meetings:** Coker College Library, 300 E. College Ave., Hartsville; first Monday of the month, 6:30-9:00 p.m
> **Contact:** Barbara Arthur, *barbaraarthur@barbaraarthur.com*
> **Membership fee:** $45/year
> **Affiliation:** Word Weavers

WORD WEAVERS LEXINGTON SC

www.LexingtonWordWeavers.com

> **Meetings:** Trinity Baptist Church, 2003 Charleston Hwy., Cayce; second Monday of each month, 6:45-9:00 p.m.; members-only bonus training time, 6:15-6:45 p.m.
> **Contact:** Jean Wilund, *wilund5@sc.rr.com*
> **Members:** 30
> **Membership fee:** $45/year
> **Affiliation:** Word Weavers

WORD WEAVERS UPSTATE SC

> **Meetings:** Fountain Inn First Baptist Church, 206 N. Weston St., Fountain Inn; second Thursday of each month, 9:30 a.m.
> **Contact:** Tammy Karasek, *wwupstatesc@yahoo.com*
> **Members:** 12
> **Membership fee:** $45/year
> **Affiliation:** Word Weavers

WRITING 4 HIM

> **Meetings:** First Baptist Church, 250 E. Main St., Spartanburg; second Thursday of the month, 9:45 a.m.
> **Contact:** Linda Gilden, *linda@lindagilden.com*
> **Members:** 50
> **Membership fee:** none

TENNESSEE

ACFW KNOXVILLE
www.facebook.com/groups/341397182924371
> **Meetings:** Parkway Baptist Church, 401 S. Peters Rd., Knoxville; second Tuesday of the month
> **Contact:** Debra Jenkins, *knoxville@acfwchapter.com*
> **Members:** 20
> **Membership fee:** national fee
> **Affiliation:** American Christian Fiction Writers

ACFW MEMPHIS
facebook.com/groups/699561666820044
> **Meetings:** Collierville; third Saturday of the month except December, 10 a.m.–noon
> **Contact:** Lynn Watson
> **Members:** 30
> **Membership fee:** national fee
> **Affiliation:** American Christian Fiction Writers

ACFW MID-TENNESSEE
acfwmidtn.org
> **Meetings:** Nashville
> **Contact:** Suzie Waltner, *midtennessee@acfwchapter.com*
> **Members:** 25
> **Membership fee:** $24/year plus national fee
> **Affiliation:** American Christian Fiction Writers

WORD WEAVERS KNOXVILLE
www.facebook.com/groups/336414403544597
> **Meetings:** Pleasant Grove Baptist Church, 3736 Tuckaleechee Pike, Maryville; third Saturday of the month, 9:30 a.m.–noon
> **Contact:** Beth Boring, 865-679-3370, *boringb@bellsouth.net*
> **Members:** 12
> **Membership fee:** $45/year
> **Affiliation:** Word Weavers

WORD WEAVERS NASHVILLE
> **Meetings:** Mortgage Company Office, 327 Caldwell Dr., Ste. 500, Goodlettsville; second Saturday of each month, 10:00 a.m.
> **Contact:** Kim Aulich, 615-848-4831, *KAAfterGodsOwnHeart@gmail.com*

Members: 10
Membership fee: $45/year
Affiliation: Word Weavers

WORD WEAVERS SOUTH MIDDLE TENNESSEE
www.facebook.com/groups/323376445183667

> **Meetings:** Edgemont Baptist Church, 150 Fairfield Pike, Shelbyville; third Saturday of the month, 10:00–noon
> **Contact:** Anita Heath, 931-619-0259, *sweets_719@hotmail.com*
> **Members:** 5
> **Membership fee:** $45/year
> **Affiliation:** Word Weavers

TEXAS

ACFW ALAMO CITY
www.facebook.com/groups/243114107289

> **Meetings:** San Antonio; second Saturday of the month, 10 a.m.–noon
> **Contact:** Jessica Alvarado
> **Members:** 15
> **Membership fee:** national fee
> **Affiliation:** American Christian Fiction Writers

ACFW CENTRAL TEXAS
www.centexacfw.com

> **Meetings:** Georgetown Public Library, room 211, 402 W. 8th St., Georgetown; third Saturday of the month, 9:30-11:30 a.m.
> **Contact:** Rhonda Beckman, *Rhonda.Beckman@hotmail.com*
> **Members:** 20
> **Membership fee:** national fee
> **Affiliation:** American Christian Fiction Writers

ACFW DFW
acfwdfwtx.com

> **Meetings:** second Saturday of every month, 10:00 a.m.
> **Contact:** Stacy Simmons
> **Members:** 40
> **Membership fee:** national fee
> **Affiliation:** American Christian Fiction Writers

ACFW EAST TEXAS

Meetings: Longview; third Saturday of the month
Contact: Joy K. Massenburge, *easttexas@acfwchapter.com*
Membership fee: national fee
Affiliation: American Christian Fiction Writers

ACFW THE WOODLANDS
wotsacfw.blogspot.com

Meetings: place varies, The Woodlands; third or fourth Saturday of
the month
Contact: Linda Kozar, *lindakozar@gmail.com*
Members: 40
Membership fee: $5/year plus national fee; $10/session, nonmembers
Affiliation: American Christian Fiction Writers

CENTRAL HOUSTON INSPIRATIONAL WRITERS ALIVE!
www.centralhoustoniwa.com

Meetings: Houston's First Baptist Church, 7474 Katy Fwy., Houston;
second Thursday of each month except July and December, 7:00 p.m.
Contact: Diana Battista, 832-315-8430, *loveeternal@comcast.net*
Members: 16
Membership fee: $25; associate, $15; senior (55+), $20

CHRISTIAN WRITERS WORKSHOP
www.facebook.com/groups/374145049720167

Meetings: First Woodway Baptist Church, 101 Ritchie Rd., Woodway;
beginning in January each year, we meet for eleven consecutive
Wednesday evenings; four critique groups meet year round once a
month
Contact: Reita Hawthorne, 254-339-3060, *reitahawthorne2@gmail.com*
Members: 50
Membership fee: none

CROSS REFERENCE WRITERS
sites.google.com/site/crossreferencewriters

Meetings: first Thursday of the month, 7:00-8:30 p.m.
Contact: Tammy Hensel, 979-204-0674, *CrossRefWriters@yahoo.com*
Members: 10

ROARING WRITERS

roaringwriters.org

Meetings: various locations in Dallas/Fort Worth area; check the website
Contact: Jan Johnson
Members: 250

ROCKWALL CHRISTIAN WRITERS GROUP

www.facebook.com/groups/rockwallchristianwritersgroup

Meetings: Lake Pointe Church, 701 E. I-30, Rockwall; second Wednesday of each month except December, 7:00 p.m.
Contact: Leslie Wilson, 214-505-5336, *leslieporterwilson@gmail.com*
Members: 15-20
Membership fee: none

WORD WEAVERS NORTH TEXAS

Meetings: 3807 Vinecrest Dr., North Dallas; third Monday of the month, 6:30-8:30p.m.
Contact: Suzanne Reeves, *suzreeves@comcast.net*
Members: 8
Membership fee: $45/year
Affiliation: Word Weavers

VIRGINIA

ACFW VIRGINIA

acfwvirginia.com

Meetings: Leesburg and Virginia Beach; first Saturday of each month
Contact: Kelly Goshorn, *acfwvirginia@gmail.com*
Membership fee: $15/year plus national fee
Affiliation: American Christian Fiction Writers

CAPITAL CHRISTIAN WRITERS FELLOWSHIP

capitalchristianwriters.org

Meetings: Centreville Presbyterian Church, 15450 Lee Hwy., Centreville, and virtual webinars, Wednesdays, 8:00 p.m., six times yearly; quarterly in-person meetings, Saturday morning
Contact: CCWF president, *president@ccwritersfellowship.org*
Members: 40
Membership fee: $49

WORD WEAVERS HAMPTON ROADS

www.facebook.com/groups/244135990554237

> **Meetings:** Great Bridge Baptist Church, 604 S. Battlefield Blvd., Chesapeake; first Tuesday of every month, 6:30 p.m.
> **Contact:** Amy L. Harden, 757-699-1118, *AmyL@AmyLHarden.com*
> **Members:** 12+
> **Membership fee:** $45/year
> **Affiliation:** Word Weavers

WORD WEAVERS MIDLOTHIAN

www.facebook.com/groups/827114188095928

> **Meetings:** Winfree Memorial Baptist Church, 13617 Midlothian Turnpike, Midlothian; second Saturday of each month, 10:30 a.m.–noon
> **Contact:** Carla Pollard, 804-512-8795, *Carlajoe102@gmail.com*
> **Members:** 4
> **Membership fee:** $45/year
> **Affiliation:** Word Weavers

WORD WEAVERS RICHMOND

www.facebook.com/groups/80930348

> **Meetings:** West End Assembly of God, 401 N. Parham Rd., Henrico; first Monday of each month, 7:00 p.m.
> **Contact:** Sue Schlesman, 804-586-4078, *sueschlesman@gmail.com*
> **Members:** 20
> **Membership fee:** $45
> **Affiliation:** Word Weavers

WORD WEAVERS WOODBRIDGE

> **Meetings:** Chinn Library Community Room, 13065 Chinn Park Dr., Woodbridge; last Saturday of the month, 10:00 a.m.–noon
> **Contact:** Lauren Craft
> **Membership fee:** $45/year
> **Affiliation:** Word Weavers

WASHINGTON

VANCOUVER CHRISTIAN WRITERS
Meetings: Vancouver, first Monday of the month, 9:00 a.m.
Contact: Jon Drury, 510-909-0848, *jondrury2@yahoo.com*
Members: 9
Membership fee: none
Affiliation: Oregon Christian Writers

WALLA WALLA CHRISTIAN WRITERS
Meetings: SonBridge, 1200 S.E. 12th St., College Place; first and third
Tuesday of each month, 3:00 p.m.
Contact: Helen Heavirland, 541-938-3838, *hlh@bmi.net*
Members: 5

WISCONSIN

ACFW WISCONSIN SOUTHEAST
www.facebook.com/wiseacfw
Meetings: first Thursday of the month, 6:30-8:30 p.m.
Contact: Laura DeNooyer Moore, *nancyr@wi.rr.com*
Members: 25
Affiliation: American Christian Fiction Writers
Membership fee: national fee

PENS OF PRAISE CHRISTIAN WRITERS
www.susanmarlene.com/writers-pens
Meetings: Manitowoc Public Library, 707 Quay St., Manitowoc, and
online; third Tuesday of each month except December and holidays,
6:00-7:30 p.m.
Contact: Susan Marlene, 920-242-3631, *susanmarlenewrites@gmail.com*
Members: 10
Membership fee: none

WESTERN WISCONSIN CHRISTIAN WRITERS GUILD
www.wwcwg.com
Meetings: Bethesda Lutheran Church, 123 W. Hamilton, Eau Claire;
second Tuesday of each month, 7:00 p.m.
Contact: Sheila Wilkinson, 715-839-1207, *wwcwg.info@gmail.com*

Members: 20
Membership fee: $30/year

WORD AND PEN CHRISTIAN WRITERS

wordandpenchristianwriters.com

> **Meetings:** Zoom; second Monday each month except December,
> 7:00-9:00 p.m.
> **Contact:** Christine Stratton, 920-739-0752, *gcefsi@new.rr.com*
> **Members:** 15
> **Affiliation:** American Christian Writers

AUSTRALIA AND NEW ZEALAND

AUSTRALASIAN CHRISTIAN WRITERS

australasianchristianwriters.com

> **Meetings:** Tuesday book chats on website and in Facebook group
> **Contact:** Narelle Atkins, Jenny Blake, Iola Goulton; contact through the
> website
> **Members:** 700

CHRISTIAN WRITERS DOWNUNDER

christianwritersdownunder.blogspot.com

> **Meetings:** Facebook discussions, occasional physical meetings
> **Contact:** Jeanette O'Hagan, *CWDBloggers@gmail.com*
> **Members:** 1,000+

NEW ZEALAND CHRISTIAN WRITERS

www.nzchristianwriters.org

> **Meetings:** various places; see website
> **Contact:** Justin St. Vincent, *president@nzchristianwriters.org*
> **Members:** 210+

OMEGA WRITERS

www.omegawriters.org

> **Contact:** Adele Jones, *secretary@omegawriters.org*
> **Services:** Australian group with local and online chapters across
> the country and New Zealand. See the website for locations.
> Also sponsors an annual conference and the CALEB Award to
> recognize the best in Australasian Christian writing, published and
> unpublished.

Members: 125
Membership fee: $60/year

CANADA

InSCRIBE CHRISTIAN WRITERS' FELLOWSHIP
inscribe.org

Contact: *president@inscribe.org*
Services: Canadian group with chapters across the country. See the website for locations. Also sponsors workshops, a fall conference, and contests and produces the quarterly magazine *FellowScript* that is included with membership.
Members: 160
Membership fee: varies; see website

MANITOBA CHRISTIAN WRITERS ASSOCIATION

Meetings: Bleak House, 1637 Main St., Winnipeg; first Saturday of the month except July and August, 1:00 p.m.
Contact: Frieda Martens, 204-770-8023, *friedamartens1910@gmail.com*
Members: 23
Membership fee: $30
Affiliation: InScribe Christian Writers' Fellowship

THE WORD GUILD
www.thewordguild.com

Contact: 800-969-9010, *info@thewordguild.com*
Services: Regional writers chapters across Canada. Sponsors contests and awards for Canadian Christian writers.
Members: 325
Membership fee: $65/year; professional, $105; student, $30

19

EDITORIAL SERVICES

Entries in this chapter are for information only, not an endorsement of editing skills. Before hiring a freelance editor, ask for references if they are not posted on the website; and contact two or three to help determine if this editor is a good fit for you. You may also want to pay for an edit of a few pages or one chapter before hiring someone to edit your complete manuscript.

A LITTLE RED INK | BETHANY KACZMAREK
Jarrettsville, MD | 443-608-4013
editor@bethanykaczmarek.com | *www.bethanykaczmarek.com/little-red-ink2*
> **Contact:** email
> **Services:** copyediting, manuscript evaluation, proofreading, substantive editing and rewriting
> **Types of manuscripts:** adult, novels, short stories, teen/YA
> **Charges:** hourly rate
> **Credentials/experience:** "An ACFW Editor of the Year finalist (2015), Bethany enjoys working with both traditional and indie authors. Several of her clients are award-winning and best-selling authors, though she does work with aspiring authors as well. She has edited for speculative fiction publishing houses Enclave Publishing and Brimstone Fiction."

A LITTLE RED INK | ERYNNE NEWMAN
41 Barclay Dr., Travelers Rest, SC 29690
ErynneNewman@gmail.com | *www.ALittleRedInk.com*
> **Contact:** website
> **Services:** back-cover copy, copyediting, manuscript evaluation, proofreading
> **Types of manuscripts:** adult, novels, short stories, teen/YA
> **Charges:** hourly rate
> **Credentials/experience:** "I am a writer of Romantic Suspense and a

researcher of things that probably have me on several government watch lists. I have been editing professionally since 2014 and, in addition to my own, I have seen over a hundred of my authors' stories published, even won a Rita Award and a few best seller ribbons. I love story, and I think that's what makes me a great editor. I can see the diamond in your rough and help make it sparkle while keeping your voice your voice. My specialty is characters. I want to help you deepen your point of view and make readers fall in love with your hero . . . and maybe even your villain. I'm an unapologetic grammar nerd, and I hope we can laugh our way through learning the rules (and learning when and where to break them) together."

A WAY WITH WORDS WRITING AND EDITORIAL SERVICES | RENEE GRAY-WILBURN
waywords@earthlink.net | *awaywithwordswriting.wordpress.com*

Contact: email

Services: back-cover copy, coauthoring, copyediting, discussion questions for books, ghostwriting, proofreading, résumés, substantive editing and rewriting, transcription, write children's manuscripts

Types of manuscripts: adult, articles, Bible studies, curriculum, devotionals, easy readers, gift books, middle grade, nonfiction books, novels, picture books, query letters, short stories, technical material, teen/YA

Charges: custom, hourly rate

Credentials/experience: "More than twenty years of freelance writing and editing. Wrote five children's books for Capstone Press; extensive curriculum writing for David C. Cook and Group Publishing; wrote children's articles/activities and parenting articles for Focus on the Family; developed online study guides for Wallbuilders; extensive copyediting and proofreading for NavPress (including the Remix Message Bible), David C. Cook, WaterBrook, and major international ministries, as well as numerous independent authors. Coauthored nonfiction book and wrote dozens of articles and devotions. Writing and editing experience for both fiction and nonfiction manuscripts in children, YA, and adult markets."

A WORD IN SEASON | SAMANTHA HANNI
3400 Windsor Ter., Oklahoma City, OK 73122 | 405-642-7855
samantha.hanni@mrshanni.com | *mrshanni.com/work-with-me*

Contact: email, website

Services: copyediting, manuscript evaluation, substantive editing and rewriting

Types of manuscripts: adult, articles, Bible studies, curriculum, devotions, nonfiction books, teen/YA

Charges: flat fee, word rate

Credentials/experience: "I am passionate about wielding words for good, whether it be writing my own or refining the words of others. For the past decade, I've had the privilege of writing and editing, helping individuals and businesses share the content that's most important to them. As a freelance writer and editor, I have self-published four books for Christian teens and edited dozens of manuscripts for Christian authors, many of them debut authors. I have provided copy editing services for two Christian publishing houses and for The Odyssey Online. Specialty: non-fiction."

AB WRITING SERVICES, LLC | ANN BYLE

3149 Boyes Ave. NE, Grand Rapids, MI 49525 | 616-389-4436
annbyle@gmail.com | *www.annbylewriter.com*

Contact: email

Services: back-cover copy, consulting, copyediting, discussion questions for books, ghostwriting, manuscript evaluation

Types of manuscripts: adult, articles, book proposals, devotions, nonfiction books, novels, query letters

Charges: hourly rate

Credentials/experience: "Ann's experience includes years as a newspaper copy editor, freelance journalist for newspapers and magazines including *Publishers Weekly,* writing her own books including *Christian Publishing 101*, and co- and ghost-writing book projects."

ABOVE THE PAGES EDITORIAL SERVICES | PAM LAGOMARSINO

abovethepages@gmail.com | *www.abovethepages.com*

Contact: email

Services: back-cover copy, copyediting, discussion questions for books, manuscript evaluation, proofreading

Types of manuscripts: adult, articles, Bible studies, book proposals, curriculum, devotions, easy readers, gift books, middle grade, nonfiction books, novels, picture books, query letters, scripts, short stories, teen/YA

Charges: custom, flat fee, word rate

Credentials/experience: "Over five years of experience editing, proofreading, or beta-reading Christian nonfiction books, devotionals, sermons, Bible studies, homeschool curriculum, children's books, and Christian fiction. AA in English, as well as certificates in Children's Books, Essential Skills for Editing Nonfiction, Devotionals, Proofreading, and Young Adult Fiction from the Christian PEN, and Keys to Effective Editing from Sandhills Community College."

ACEVEDO WORD SOLUTIONS, LLC | JENNE ACEVEDO
editor@jenneacevedo.com | www.jenneacevedo.com

Contact: email

Services: back-cover copy, coauthoring, copyediting, discussion questions for books, project management, proofreading, substantive editing and rewriting, writing coach

Types of manuscripts: adult, articles, Bible studies, book proposals, curriculum, devotions, easy readers, gift books, middle grade, nonfiction books, query letters, teen/YA

Charges: hourly rate, word rate

Credentials/experience: "Consultant for private and corporate clients, cofounder of Christian Editor Network LLC, former director of The Christian PEN, former director of PENCON, member of Christian Editor Connection, editing/proofreading instructor for The PEN Institute, founder and director of Chandler Writers' Group."

ACW CRITIQUE SERVICE | REG A. FORDER
4854 Aster Dr., Nashville, TN 37211 | 615-331-8668
ACWriters@aol.com | www.ACWriters.com

Contact: email

Services: copyediting, manuscript evaluation, proofreading, substantive editing and rewriting

Types of manuscripts: adult, articles, book proposals, curriculum, devotions, easy readers, gift books, middle grade, nonfiction books, novels, picture books, poetry, query letters, scripts, short stories, technical material, teen/YA

Charges: flat fee, hourly rate, page rate, word rate

Credentials/experience: "Established almost 40 years ago. Staff of experienced editors."

AM EDITING AND FREELANCE WRITING | ANGELA MCCLAIN
amediting35@gmail.com | www.amediting.webs.com

Contact: email

Services: back-cover copy, coauthoring, copyediting, discussion questions for books, ghostwriting, manuscript evaluation, proofreading, writing coach

Types of manuscripts: adult, articles, Bible studies, devotions, easy readers, gift books, middle grade, nonfiction books, novels, picture books, poetry, short stories, teen/YA

Charges: page rate

Credentials/experience: "As an editor, Angela is a communications professional who assists writers with writing tasks. Angela is an experienced editor and writer with thorough knowledge of grammar, composition, and other fields relating to the written word. Angela works as a freelance contractor who assists writers with the creation and presentation of written material. Angela works on written material in various capacities, from simple proofreading of internal documents to the creation, presentation, and sometimes even publication of mass-printed material. In addition to the general requirements of written language, she ensures the material conforms to the needs of the author. Angela pays close attention to detail. Angela possesses these traits as well as an overall talent for written communication."

AMBASSADOR COMMUNICATIONS | CLAIRE HUTCHINSON

13733 West Gunsight Dr., Sun City West, AZ 85375 | 812-390-7907
clairescreenwriter@gmail.com | *www.clairehutchinson.net*

Contact: email

Services: copyediting, ghostwriting, manuscript evaluation, proofreading, substantive editing and rewriting, writing coach

Types of manuscripts: academic, adult, articles, Bible studies, board/picture books, book proposals, curriculum, devotions, easy readers, gift books, middle grade, nonfiction books, novels, poetry, query letters, scripts, short stories, teen/YA

Charges: flat fee, word rate

Credentials/experience: "Claire Hutchinson (M.A. English, Manitoba; Cert. Feature Film Writing, Cert. Professional Program in Screenwriting, UCLA) is a produced and award-winning screenwriter, script analyst, producer, film festival judge, speaker, and teacher. As a script consultant for over 15 years, Claire has consulted for companies such as Du More Films, Living Water Media, Visual Productions, CV Films, and Abel Company. Claire's credits include 'The Christmas Coat' (pending, 2021), 'Tomorrow' (2018), 'The Thought of You' (2018), 'Living the Dream' (2018, co-producer, director, writer), 'Lucky's Treasure' (2017) and 'Waves' (2015).

Claire also judges ICVM Scene Shop, 168 Film Festival, 168 Write of Passage Screenwriting Competition, Great Lakes Christian Film Festival, Life Fest Film Festival, and WR2R Film Festival."

AMI EDITING | ANNETTE IRBY
editor@AMIediting.com | *www.AMIediting.com*

Contact: email

Services: copyediting, critiquing, manuscript evaluation, proofreading, substantive editing and rewriting

Types of manuscripts: novels, short stories

Charges: hourly rate

Credentials/experience: "Annette spent five years working in acquisitions with a CBA publisher. She has almost twenty years of experience editing in the CBA marketplace and has worked with several well-known authors and publishers. She's an award-winning author and book reviewer. See her website for testimonials."

AMY BOEKE'S EDITING SERVICE
3149 Sandy Hollow Rd., Rockford, IL 61109
abboeke@gmail.com

Contact: email

Services: copyediting, proofreading

Types of manuscripts: adult, articles, nonfiction books, novels, teen/YA

Charges: word rate

Credentials/experience: "English degree, master's level secondary English teaching degree, several years of experience freelance editing for multiple book genres."

AMY DROWN
editing@amydrown.com | *www.amydrown.com/editing*

Contact: email

Services: back-cover copy, copyediting, manuscript evaluation, proofreading, substantive editing and rewriting

Types of manuscripts: adult, novels, one sheets, teen/YA

Charges: flat fee, word rate

Credentials/experience: "Internationally recognized freelance editor specializing in inspirational fiction writing and editing since 2009. I contract with publishers, as well as directly with authors, both published and prepublished, and offer highly competitive rates."

ANDREA MERRELL

60 McKinney Rd., Travelers Rest, SC 29690 | 864-616-5889
AndreaMerrell7@gmail.com | *www.AndreaMerrell.com*

Contact: email, website
Services: back-cover copy, copyediting, proofreading
Types of manuscripts: adult, articles, devotions, nonfiction books, novels, short stories
Charges: hourly rate
Credentials/experience: "Professional freelance editor. Associate editor for LPC Books and Christian Devotions Ministries. Member of The Christian PEN: Proofreaders and Editors Network."

ANN KROEKER, WRITING COACH

ann@annkroeker.com | *annkroeker.com/writing-coach*

Contact: email, website
Services: writing coach
Types of manuscripts: adult, articles, Bible studies, book proposals, devotions, gift books, nonfiction books, poetry, query letters
Charges: flat fee, hourly rate
Credentials/experience: "I leverage over 25 years of experience in the publishing industry to equip clients to reach their writing goals. A published author and coauthor, corporate and freelance writer, book editor, and poet, I've served on the editorial teams of two large online organizations and focused on serving others in my role as a writing coach. My clients have signed book contracts, won awards, been accepted into prestigious MFA programs, launched their own freelance writing businesses, and landed articles and essays in national publications. I stay up-to-date with best practices and refine skills through professional development that builds on a B.A. in English (Creative Writing emphasis), Indiana University."

ANNE RAUTH

3120 Karnes Blvd., Kansas City, MO 64111 | 913-710-8484
anne@annerauth.com

Contact: email
Services: blog posts, newsletters
Types of manuscripts: blog posts, websites
Charges: hourly rate
Credentials/experience: "Anne Rauth has been working in the marketing field for over twenty years at Fortune 500 Companies, nonprofit organizations as well as assisting individuals to promote their books."

ARMOR OF HOPE WRITING AND PUBLISHING
SERVICES | DENISE M. WALKER

info@armorofhopewritingservices.com | *www.armorofhopewritingservices.com*

Contact: email

Services: copyediting, proofreading, writing coach

Types of manuscripts: Bible studies, board/picture books, devotions, easy readers, nonfiction books

Charges: flat fee, word rate

Credentials/experience: "I have been in business for over five years and have copyedited and/or proofread 100+ nonfiction, children's picture books, and easy readers. In addition, I serve as a writing coach, assisting nonfiction authors with organizing and developing their thoughts. I am also a full-service nonfiction self-publishing coach and an author of middle grades/YA fiction, women's Christian fiction, and Bible literacy journals. I have attended several book writing and editing workshops. I am also certified in middle grades English language arts and have taught English for over 20 years."

AUTHOR GATEWAY | CALEB BREAKEY

424 W. Bakerview Rd., Ste. 105, Bellingham, WA 98226

team@authorgateway.com | *www.authorgateway.com*

Contact: email

Services: book proposals, writing coach

Types of manuscripts: books of all kinds and all ages

Charges: $3,500-$5,500

Credentials/experience: "Backed by more than 200 years of experience, HarperCollins Christian Publishing's Author Gateway provides the best team in the country dedicated to helping men and women of faith land a prominent literary agent and sign with a major Christian publisher. We serve authors who are looking to up their game when it comes to pitching to literary agents and acquisition editors."

AUTHORIZEME | SHARON NORRIS ELLIOTT

PO Box 1816, South Gate, CA 90280 | 310-508-9860

AuthorizeMeNow@gmail.com | *lifethatmatters.net/authorizeme*

Contact: email

Services: back-cover copy, book-contract evaluation, coauthoring, copyediting, discussion questions for books, ghostwriting, manuscript evaluation, proofreading, substantive editing and rewriting, writing coach

Types of manuscripts: academic, adult, articles, Bible studies, board/
picture books, book proposals, curriculum, devotions, easy readers,
gift books, middle grade, nonfiction books, poetry, teen/YA

Charges: custom, page rate, word rate

Credentials/experience: "Sharon's credentials/experience as an
editor include her 35-year career as a high school English teacher,
years as a managing editor of several magazines, functioning as a
freelance editor for major publishing houses, and being a sought-
after keynote and seminar instructor at major Christian writers'
conferences nationwide. Sharon is a multi-published author herself,
and is a member of ACE (Academy of Christian Editors), SCBWI
(Society of Children's Book Writers and Illustrators), and AWSA
(Advanced Writers and Speakers Association). Because of her
growing positive reputation as an editor and book developer in the
publishing arena, she started AuthorizeMe in 2008 to be able to
help others enter the publishing world. Sharon's personal, hands-on
assistance is what sets AuthorizeMe apart as special and unique."

AUTHORS WHO SERVE | RACHEL HILLS

1290 Crafton Ct., Mooresville, IN 46158 | 317-443-0019
rachelhills619@protonmail.com | *authorswhoserve.com*

Contact: email, website

Services: ghostwriting, manuscript evaluation, substantive editing and
rewriting, writing coach

Types of manuscripts: academic, adult, nonfiction books, novels,
query letters, sermons to books

Charges: custom, packages for coaching, word rate

Credentials/experience: "I believe in the power of the written word.
I help authors clarify the content of their writing to produce a
book sought by readers. I assist pastors and leaders to transition
their spoken words to the written word. I coach writers from early
formation of a concept to final production of their book. My abilities
stem from 19 years' experience editing, multiple certifications in the
industry, and a passion to see Jesus represented in excellence."

AVODAH EDITORIAL SERVICES | CHRISTY DISTLER

www.avodaheditorialservices.com

Contact: website

Services: copyediting, manuscript evaluation, proofreading,
substantive editing and rewriting

Types of manuscripts: adult, devotions, easy readers, nonfiction books, novels, picture books, poetry, short stories

Charges: word rate

Credentials/experience: "Educated at Temple University and University of California–Berkeley. Thirteen years of editorial experience, both as an employee and a freelancer. Currently works mostly for publishing houses but accepts freelance work as scheduling allows."

BANNER LITERARY | MIKE LOOMIS

mike@mikeloomis.co | www.MikeLoomis.co

Contact: email, website

Services: back-cover copy, book-contract evaluation, coauthoring, copyediting, discussion questions for books, ghostwriting, manuscript evaluation, proofreading, substantive editing and rewriting, writing coach

Types of manuscripts: articles, book proposals, devotions, nonfiction books, query letters

Charges: custom, flat fee

Credentials/experience: "I'm a book developer, ghostwriter, and editor. I also coach authors on planning the best book for their goals. Because of my more than twenty years of experience in publishing, I help authors refine their idea, polish their work, and reach their audience. I've worked with *New York Times* bestselling authors, publishers (Simon and Schuster, Multnomah, Zondervan, Random House, Nelson, NavPress, and Penguin) but am most energized by helping first-time authors."

BARBARA KOIS

7135 W. Amber Burst Ct., Tucson, AZ 85743 | 630-532-2941
barbara.kois@gmail.com

Contact: email, phone

Services: back-cover copy, coauthoring, copyediting, ghostwriting, manuscript evaluation, proofreading, substantive editing and rewriting, writing coach

Types of manuscripts: adult, Bible studies, devotions, easy readers, gift books, middle grade, nonfiction books, novels, teen/YA

Charges: word rate

Credentials/experience: "I have edited more than 200 books (both fiction and nonfiction) for several well-known publishers and I have had eight of my own books published as well. I have been a writing teacher and coach for many authors and I provide most types of edits from ghostwriting to substantive, content, and copy edits, with most everything in between."

BBH LITERARY | DAVID BRATT
david@bbhliterary.com | bbhliterary.com

> **Contact:** email, website
> **Services:** manuscript evaluation, substantive editing and rewriting
> **Types of manuscripts:** academic, articles, book proposals, nonfiction books, query letters
> **Charges:** hourly rate
> **Credentials/experience:** "Twenty-one years editing for Eerdmans Publishing; Ph.D. in American religion (Yale University, 1999)."

BLACK DOG EDITING | TORI MERKIEL
blackdogeditor@gmail.com | blackdogediting.info

> **Contact:** email, website
> **Services:** copyediting, manuscript evaluation, proofreading, substantive editing and rewriting
> **Types of manuscripts:** adult, middle grade, novels, query letters, short stories, teen/YA
> **Charges:** flat fee
> **Credentials/experience:** "Tori Merkiel has been on both sides of the publishing world as an author, acquisitions editor, and literary agency intern. She now takes on clients through Black Dog Editing to help them discover their voice and create the stories of their heart."

BOOK WHISPERS
Australia
info@bookwhispers.com.au | www.bookwhispers.com.au

> **Contact:** email
> **Services:** back-cover copy, copyediting, manuscript evaluation, marketing copy, proofreading, substantive editing and rewriting
> **Credentials/experience:** "The team has more than ten years of experience in traditional publishing."

BOOKOX | THOMAS WOMACK
165 S. Timber Creek Dr., Sisters, OR 97759 | 541-788-6503
Thomas@BookOx.com | www.BookOx.com

> **Contact:** email
> **Services:** copyediting, discussion questions for books, manuscript evaluation, substantive editing and rewriting, writing coach

Types of manuscripts: Bible studies, book proposals, devotions, nonfiction books, novels

Charges: word rate

Credentials/experience: "My four decades of editing experience have centered on Christian books published by Crossway, Zondervan, Multnomah, WaterBrook, NavPress, Harvest House, David C. Cook, and other publishing houses. I've had the great privilege of working on projects by gifted and godly authors such as Jerry Bridges, J. I. Packer, Henry Blackaby, Randy Alcorn, Os Guinness, Tony Evans, Larry Osborne, Christopher Yuan, Bob Kauflin, Kay Arthur, Larry Crabb, Jeramy Clark, Dave Harvey, Greg Laurie, Richard Blackaby, Ruth Myers, C. J. Mahaney, Andy Stanley, Thelma Wells, David Jeremiah, Norm Wright, James Kennedy, Richard Halverson, Carolyn Castleberry, and a great many others. These have included numerous titles especially in the categories of spiritual nurture and care, spiritual disciplines and devotion, Bible study and theology, and marriage and family, as well as memoirs, fiction, and business and leadership books."

BREAKOUT EDITING | DORI HARRELL

doriharrell@gmail.com | www.doriharrell.wix.com/breakoutediting

Contact: email

Services: copyediting, proofreading, substantive editing and rewriting, website text

Types of manuscripts: adult, articles, devotions, middle grade, nonfiction books, novels, picture books, query letters, short stories, teen/YA

Charges: word rate

Credentials/experience: "Dori is a multiple-award-winning writer and a highly experienced editor who freelance edits full time and has edited more than 300 novels and nonfiction books. Breakout authors final in awards or win awards almost every year! She edits for publishers, including Gemma Halliday Publishing and Kregel Publications, and as an editor, she releases more than twenty books annually."

BROOKSTONE CREATIVE GROUP | SUZANNE KUHN

100 Missionary Ridge, Birmingham, AL 35242 | 302-514-7899

www.brookstonecreativegroup.com

Contact: website

Services: book proposals, copyediting, ghostwriting, one-sheets, proofreading, substantive editing and rewriting, writing coach

Types of manuscripts: books of all kinds and all ages
Charges: flat fee
Credentials/experience: Suzanne has more than thirty years of book-specific experience. Brookstone is an expansion of her business, SuzyQ, with a team of almost two dozen professionals who bring a wide range of knowledge and experience to help you get published.

BUTTERFIELD EDITORIAL SERVICES | DEBRA L. BUTTERFIELD
4810 Gene Field Rd., Saint Joseph, MO 64506 | 816-752-2171
deb@debralbutterfield.com

Contact: email
Services: copyediting, substantive editing and rewriting, writing coach
Types of manuscripts: adult, book proposals, nonfiction books, novels
Charges: word rate
Credentials/experience: "Former copywriter for Focus on the Family. Eleven years experience as freelance editor. Seven years editorial experience with traditional publisher with book layout and cover design experience as well. Author of eight books, nonfiction and fiction. I have been blogging on the craft of writing since 2012."

byBRENDA | BRENDA WILBEE
4631 Quinn Ct. #202, Bellingham, WA 98226 | 360-389-6895
Brenda@BrendaWilbee.com | *www.BrendaWilbee.com*

Contact: email
Services: writing coach
Types of manuscripts: academic, adult, nonfiction books, novels
Charges: hourly rate
Credentials/experience: "Brenda Wilbee is an award-winning and best-selling author of 10 books, dozens of articles, short stories, and radio scripts with over 30 years of publishing experience as a writer, editor, and book designer, and she's taught in the public school system, specializing in homeschool connections—and has 7 years' experience teaching university and college composition. Her books have sold over 700,000 copies. MA: Professional Writing."

C. S. LAKIN COPYEDITOR AND WRITING COACH
335 Casa Loma Rd., Morgan Hill, CA 95037 | 530-200-5466
cslakin@gmail.com | *www.livewritethrive.com*

Contact: email, website
Services: copyediting, critiquing, manuscript evaluation, proofreading,

substantive editing and rewriting, writing coach

Types of manuscripts: adult, articles, Bible studies, book proposals, devotions, easy readers, gift books, middle grade, nonfiction books, novels, picture books, poetry, query letters, short stories, teen/YA

Charges: hourly rate, page rate

Credentials/experience: "Professional copyeditor, writing coach, workshop instructor with 16 years professional experience. Has worked with literary agents and publishers, and critiques more than 200 manuscripts a year for clients in six continents."

CALLED WRITERS CHRISTIAN PUBLISHING, LLC |
CHRIS McKINNEY

1922 37th St. NE, Tuscaloosa, AL 35406 | 205-286-2057
shannon@calledwriters.com | *calledwriters.com*

Contact: website

Services: back-cover copy, coauthoring, copyediting, ghostwriting, manuscript evaluation, proofreading, substantive editing and rewriting

Types of manuscripts: nonfiction books

Charges: word rate

Credentials/experience: "Chris McKinney is the founder and managing editor of Called Writers Christian Publishing. He was formerly the executive editor of *GODSPEED Magazine*, where he had the pleasure of serving editor-in-chief David Aikman, a legendary Christian journalist. In addition to *GODSPEED Magazine*, Chris's articles have been featured by CBN, Crosswalk, *Engage Magazine*, and many other publications and websites. Chris is the author and co-author of several notable Christian books. He has also been a featured guest on various Christian radio, internet, and television shows."

CARLA ROSSI EDITORIAL SERVICES
carla@carlarossi.com | *www.carlarossi.com*

Contact: email

Services: back-cover copy, copyediting, manuscript evaluation, substantive editing and rewriting, writing coach

Types of manuscripts: adult, novels, short stories, teen/YA

Charges: word rate

Credentials/experience: "Professional editor since 2014. Member of writing and editing organizations. Specialize in romance and fantasy fiction."

CATHY STREINER

South Carolina

Cathy@thecorporatepen.com

Contact: email

Services: back-cover copy, coauthoring, copyediting, discussion questions for books, proofreading, substantive editing and rewriting, writing coach

Types of manuscripts: academic, adult, articles, Bible studies, devotions, easy readers, gift books, middle grade, nonfiction books, novels, scripts, short stories, technical material, teen/YA

Charges: custom, flat fee, hourly rate, word rate

Credentials/experience: "Author of a Christian novel, I have experience with the start-to-finish self-publishing process. I also have extensive experience working with writers who need editing and proofreading services as well as limited coaching with constructive feedback."

CELTICFROG EDITING | ALEX MCGILVERY

Kamloops, BC, Canada | 250-819-4275

thececlticfrog@gmail.com | celticfrogediting.com

Contact: email, website

Services: manuscript evaluation, writing coach

Types of manuscripts: adult, articles, devotionals, middle grade, nonfiction books, novels, short stories, teen/YA

Charges: word rate

Credentials/experience: "I have been reviewing and critiquing books for more than three decades, and editing since 2014. One client compared my work favourably with the editors at a traditional publisher."

CHERI FIELDS EDITING

1232 Garfield Ave. NW, Grand Rapids, MI 49504 | 269-953-4271

Cherifieldsediting@gmail.com | Cherifields.com

Contact: email, website

Services: back-cover copy, coauthoring, discussion questions for books, manuscript evaluation, substantive editing and rewriting, writing coach

Types of manuscripts: articles, Bible studies, curriculum, devotions, easy readers, middle grade, nonfiction books, picture books, short stories, teen/YA

Charges: custom, flat fee, word rate

Credentials/experience: "Cheri Fields is a gold member of the Christian PEN for nonfiction and children's editing. She is a graduate of the Institute of Children's Literature and a published author. She works daily to polish the message of the biblical science community for a lay audience and she is a homeschool mom with decades of experience in children's books from board books to YA."

CHRISTIAN COMMUNICATOR MANUSCRIPT CRITIQUE SERVICE | SUSAN TITUS OSBORN

3133 Puente St., Fullerton, CA 92835 | 714-313-8651
susanosb@aol.com | *www.christiancommunicator.com*

Contact: email, phone, website
Services: back-cover copy, book-contract evaluation, coauthoring, copyediting, discussion questions for books, ghostwriting, manuscript evaluation, proofreading, writing coach
Types of manuscripts: academic, adult, articles, Bible studies, book proposals, curriculum, devotionals, easy readers, gift books, middle grade, nonfiction books, novels, picture books, poetry, query letters, scripts, short stories, technical material, teen/YA
Charges: hourly rate, page rate
Credentials/experience: "Our critique service, comprised of 14 professional editors, has been in business for 37 years. We are recommended by ECPA, the Billy Graham Association, and a number of publishing houses and agents."

CHRISTIAN EDITING SERVICES | IOLA GOULTON

New Zealand
igoulton@christianediting.co.nz | *www.christianediting.co.nz*

Contact: website
Services: copyediting, manuscript evaluation, writing coach
Types of manuscripts: adult, novels, teen/YA
Charges: custom
Credentials/experience: "Iola is a member of The Christian PEN: Proofreaders and Editors Network, American Christian Fiction Writers, Romance Writers of New Zealand, and Omega Writers. She has completed fiction editing courses with The Christian PEN and Lawson Writers Academy, and won the 2016 ACFW Genesis Award (Novella), and edited the 2018 RITA Award winner (Romance with Religious or Spiritual Elements)."

CHRISTIAN EDITOR CONNECTION | IRENE CHAMBERS
director@ChristianEditor.com | www.ChristianEditor.com

Contact: website

Services: back-cover copy, coauthoring, copyediting, ghostwriting, indexing, manuscript evaluation, proofreading, substantive editing and rewriting, writing coach

Types of manuscripts: academic, adult, articles, book proposals, curriculum, devotions, easy readers, gift books, middle grade, nonfiction books, novels, picture books, poetry, query letters, short stories, technical material, teen/YA

Charges: custom

Credentials/experience: "Christian Editor Connection has established, professional editors who have been extensively screened and tested. Fill out the website form to Request an Editor and you will be personally matched with members who best fit your needs. Those editors who are interested and available will contact you with detailed quotes so you can choose the right one for you."

CHRISTIANBOOKPROPOSALS.COM | CINDY CARTER
ccarter@ecpa.org | www.ChristianBookProposals.com

Contact: website

Service: "Operated by the Evangelical Christian Publishers Association (ECPA), it is the only manuscript service created by the top Christian publishers looking for unsolicited manuscripts in a traditional, royalty-based relationship. It allows authors to submit their manuscript proposals in a secure, online format for review by editors from publishing houses that are members of ECPA."

Types of manuscripts: books of all kinds and all ages

Charges: $98 for six months

COLLABORATIVE EDITORIAL SOLUTIONS | ANDREW BUSS
info@collaborativeeditorial.com | collaborativeeditorial.com

Contact: email

Services: copyediting, proofreading

Types of manuscripts: academic, adult, articles, Bible studies, devotionals, nonfiction books, technical material

Charges: hourly rate, page rate

Credentials/experience: "I'm a professional editor with more than five years of full-time experience working with authors and scholarly publishers such as InterVarsity Press, Reformation Heritage, P&R Publishing, Georgetown University Press, and Baylor University

Press. Although I primarily work in the genre of scholarly nonfiction, I'm always keen to work with creative and thoughtful authors, whatever the topic or genre. I'm a member of the Editorial Freelancers Association and the Society of Biblical Literature."

COMMUNICATION ASSOCIATES | KEN WALKER

729 Ninth Ave. #331, Huntington, WV 25701 | 304-525-3343
kenwalker33@gmail.com | *www.KenWalkerWriter.com*

Contact: email
Services: back-cover copy, coauthoring, copyediting, discussion questions for books, ghostwriting
Types of manuscripts: adult, articles, Bible studies, devotionals, nonfiction books
Charges: flat fee, hourly rate
Credentials/experience: "Started freelancing in 1983 and fulltime in 1990. Experienced in ghostwriting, substantive editing, and book editing. Written or edited more than 85 books."

CORNERSTONE-INK EDITING | VIE HERLOCK

vherlock@yahoo.com | *www.cornerstone-ink.com*

Contact: email
Services: copyediting, manuscript evaluation, substantive editing and rewriting
Types of manuscripts: adult, articles, book proposals, devotionals, gift books, middle grade, nonfiction books, novels, query letters, short stories, teen/YA
Charges: word rate
Credentials/experience: "Vie Herlocker provides 'Tough-Love Editing with a Tender Touch.' She is a member of Christian Editor Connection, Christian Proofreaders and Editors Network, ACFW, and Word Weavers, Int. Her experience includes: editing for a small Christian publisher (10 years), editing for a regional magazine, judging a national writing contest, and freelance editing. She uses *The Chicago Manual of Style, Christian Writers' Manual of Style,* and *Merriam-Webster 11th.*"

CREATIVE EDITORIAL SOLUTIONS | CLAUDIA VOLKMAN

13128 Silver Thorn Loop, North Fort Myers, FL 33903 | 203-645-5600
cvolkman@mac.com

Contact: email
Services: back-cover copy, copyediting, discussion questions for books,

ghostwriting, manuscript evaluation, proofreading, substantive editing and rewriting, writing coach

Types of manuscripts: adult, Bible studies, devotions, gift books, nonfiction books, novels

Charges: custom

Credentials/experience: "I have over thirty-five years of publishing experience, much of it working with Christian and Catholic publishers. Now, as the owner of Creative Editorial Solutions, I have a team of editors skilled in a variety of editorial services. From book coaching to copyediting and proofreading, we can find the right editorial solution for your book publishing needs."

CREATIVE ENTERPRISES STUDIO | MARY HOLLINGSWORTH

1507 Shirley Way, Ste. A, Bedford, TX 76022-6737 | 817-312-7393
ACreativeShop@aol.com | *CreativeEnterprisesStudio.com*

Contact: email

Services: coauthoring, copyediting, discussion questions for books, ghostwriting, manuscript evaluation, proofreading, substantive editing and rewriting

Types of manuscripts: adult, book proposals, curriculum, devotionals, easy readers, gift books, middle grade, nonfiction books, novels, picture books, short stories, teen/YA

Charges: custom

Credentials/experience: "CES is a publishing services company, hosting more than 150 top Christian publishing freelancers. We work with large, traditional Christian publishers on books by best-selling authors. We also produce custom, first-class books on a turnkey basis for independent authors, ministries, churches, and companies."

CREWS AND COULTER EDITORIAL SERVICES | KAY COULTER

806 Hopi Trl., Temple, TX 76504 | 254-778-6490
bkcoulter@sbcglobal.net | *crewscoultereditorialservices.com*

Contact: email, phone, website

Services: coauthoring, copyediting, ghostwriting, manuscript evaluation, proofreading, substantive editing and rewriting, writing coach

Types of manuscripts: academic, adult, Bible studies, book proposals, devotionals, gift books, nonfiction books, novels, short stories, teen/YA

Charges: custom, hourly rate

Credentials/experience: "Kay is a published author and has been an editor since 2002, having worked with authors on over three hundred projects. Kay has been a Christian for more than fifty years and also served in a speaking/singing ministry for twenty-five years. She loves words and the Word and helping authors realize their dreams."

CROSS & DOT EDITORIAL SERVICES | KATIE VORREITER

Katie@CrossAndDot.net | *www.CrossAndDot.net*

Contact: email, website

Services: copyediting, proofreading

Types of manuscripts: adult, articles, curriculum, devotionals, gift books, middle grade, nonfiction books, novels, short stories, technical material, teen/YA

Charges: flat fee

Credentials/experience: "Certificate in professional sequence in editing, U.C. Berkeley; MA in international management; BA in English and Spanish."

DILLER DESIGNS | LILA DILLER

128 Teak Dr., Statesville, NC 28625

liladiller78@gmail.com | *www.liladiller.com/editingservices*

Contact: email

Services: copyediting, proofreading

Types of manuscripts: adult, Bible studies, devotionals, middle grade, nonfiction books, novels

Charges: word rate

Credentials/experience: "As a life-long reader and lover of grammar, I love to help new authors turn their book babies into professional and gripping prose."

DONE WRITE EDITORIAL SERVICES | MARILYN A. ANDERSON

127 Sycamore Dr., Louisville, KY 40223 | 502-244-0751

shelle12@aol.com

Contact: email, phone

Services: copyediting, proofreading, substantive editing and rewriting, writing coach

Types of manuscripts: academic, adult, articles, Bible studies, book proposals, children, curriculum, devotionals, gift books, nonfiction books, novels, poetry, query letters, short stories, technical material

Charges: hourly rate

Credentials/experience: "I am qualified by both bachelor's and master's degrees in English. I am also qualified because I have tutored more than thirty English/writing students since 2004. Most of them have been English-language learners. Also, I have taught English/writing as a classroom teacher. I have additionally conducted business-project editing for several corporations over the years. I currently copyedit for nonfiction and fiction independent writers, as well as for publishers and a few Christian ministries and am in the process of mentoring several other writers/editors. I copyedit both books (such as memoirs) and doctoral dissertations, theses, and other academic journal articles and papers.

"I offer a free sample edit, and my rates are both reasonable and competitive. I am a Gold charter member of The Christian PEN proofreaders and editors' network, along with a tested member of the Christian Editor Connection."

ECHO CREATIVE MEDIA | BRENDA NOEL
bnoel@thewordeditor.com | *echocreativemedia.weebly.com*

Contact: email

Services: copyediting, discussion questions for books, ghostwriting, proofreading, substantive editing and rewriting

Types of manuscripts: adult, articles, book proposals, curriculum, devotionals, easy readers, gift books, nonfiction books, picture books, short stories, teen/YA

Charges: flat fee, hourly rate

Credentials/experience: "Sixteen years of experience in the Christian publishing industry."

EDIT RESOURCE, LLC | ERIC STANFORD
19265 Lincoln Green Ln., Monument, CO 80132 | 719-290-0757
info@editresource.com | *www.editresource.com*

Contact: email

Services: back-cover copy, book proposals, coauthoring, copyediting, discussion questions for books, ghostwriting, indexing, manuscript evaluation, proofreading, substantive editing and rewriting, writing coach

Types of manuscripts: adult, Bible studies, book proposals, curriculum, devotions, middle grade, nonfiction books, novels, query letters, teen/YA

Charges: depends on the service

Credentials/experience: "Owners Eric and Elisa have a combined 40

years of experience and have worked with numerous bestselling authors and books. They also represent a team of other top writing and editing professionals."

EDITING BY LUCY | LUCY CRABTREE
editingbylucy@gmail.com | *editingbylucy.com*

Contact: email
Services: copyediting, proofreading
Types of manuscripts: adult, articles, book proposals, nonfiction books, novels, query letters, short stories
Charges: word rate
Credentials/experience: "Polished writer and editor with nine years of professional experience in the publishing industry (seven years) and educational settings (two years). Well-versed in Microsoft Office and Adobe Creative Suite. Familiarity with Associated Press, American Psychological Association, and *Chicago Manual* style books. Experience with Drupal, WordPress, and Blogger."

EDITING GALLERY, LLC | CAROL CRAIG
2622 Willona Dr., Eugene, OR 97408 | 541-735-1834
kf7orchid@gmail.com | *www.editinggallery.com*

Contact: email
Services: back-cover copy, coauthoring, copyediting, manuscript evaluation, proofreading, substantive editing and rewriting, writing coach
Types of manuscripts: adult, board/picture books, book proposals, easy readers, middle grade, nonfiction books, novels, query letters, teen/YA
Charges: hourly rate
Credentials/experience: "University of Oregon/English Major—I have edited for many well-known fiction authors and have over thirty years of experience as an editor."

eDITMORE EDITORIAL SERVICES | TAMMY DITMORE
501-I S. Reino Rd. #194, Newbury Park, CA 91320 | 805-630-6809
tammy@editmore.com | *www.editmore.com*

Contact: email
Services: copyediting, discussion questions for books, manuscript evaluation, proofreading, substantive editing and rewriting
Types of manuscripts: academic, adult, articles, Bible studies, curriculum, devotions, nonfiction books, teen/YA

Charges: flat fee, hourly rate, word rate

Credentials/experience: "Tammy Ditmore has worked as an editor and writer for daily newspapers, academic journals, books, magazines, and individual authors for more than three decades. She specializes in nonfiction and offers critiques, consultations, developmental editing, copyediting, and proofreading services. Contact eDitmore Editorial Services to find out how you can get the most out of your words."

EDITOR FOR YOU | MELANIE RIGNEY

4201 Wilson Blvd. #110328, Arlington, VA 22203 | 703-863-3940
editor@editorforyou.com | *www.editorforyou.com*

Contact: email

Services: manuscript evaluation

Types of manuscripts: adult, book proposals, devotionals, nonfiction books, novels

Charges: flat fee

Credentials/experience: "Melanie has decades of professional editing experience, including time as editor of *Writer's Digest* magazine and a publishing manager for what was Hayden Books. Since 2003, her consultancy, Editor for You, has helped hundreds of publishers, agents, and authors. Melanie knows what it's like on the other side of the desk; she's authored several books for Catholic publishers."

EDITOR WORLD: ENGLISH EDITING AND PROOFREADING SERVICES | PATTI FISHER

11815 Fountain Way, Ste. 300, Newport News, VA 23606 | 614-500-3348
info@editorworld.com | *www.editorworld.com*

Contact: website

Services: copyediting, proofreading

Types of manuscripts: academic, adult, articles, Bible studies, book proposals, curriculum, devotions, easy readers, gift books, middle grade, nonfiction books, novels, poetry, query letters, scripts, short stories, technical material, teen/YA

Charges: word rate

Credentials/experience: "Editor World provides a marketplace for writers to find their own personal editor and have their work edited within a specific time period. Clients choose a professional editor based on the editor's profile, such as qualifications, skills, number of pages edited through Editor World, and previous client ratings. Writers, particularly academic writers, need editing services but do not know of a convenient, reliable place to find them. Editor World responds to this need. Our editing panel includes university faculty, professional editors, published authors, and retired professionals who love words more than anything else. Our editors are tested on their editing skills before being accepted to provide editing services through Editor World."

EDITORIAL SERVICES | KIM PETERSON

1114 Buxton Dr., Knoxville, KY 37922

petersk.ktp@gmail.com | *naturewalkwithgod.wordpress.com/about-kim*

Contact: email

Services: back-cover copy, copyediting, discussion questions for books, manuscript evaluation, proofreading, writing coach

Types of manuscripts: academic, adult, articles, blog posts, book proposals, curriculum, devotionals, easy readers, gift books, middle grade, nonfiction books, novels, picture books, poetry, query letters, short stories, technical material, teen/YA

Charges: hourly rate

Credentials/experience: "Freelance writer; college writing instructor; conference speaker. MA in print communication from Wheaton College."

ELOQUENT EDITS, LLC | DENISE ROEPER

PO Box 291003, Port Orange, FL 32129 | 386-290-4117

denise.eloquentedits@gmail.com | *www.eloquentedits.com*

Contact: email, website

Services: copyediting, proofreading

Types of manuscripts: adult, easy readers, gift books, middle grade, nonfiction books, novels, short stories, teen/YA

Charges: word rate

Credentials/experience: "Whether your creation is fiction or nonfiction, you can be assured that it will receive my full attention and service, resulting in a crisp and clear document at an affordable price."

EMH INDEXING SERVICES | ELISE HESS

emhess5@gmail.com

Contact: email

Services: indexing

Charges: page rate

Credentials/experience: "I have experience in subject, Scripture, and name indexes, as well as index updates. I have written indexes for Moody Publishers, Wiley Publishers, and many more. My husband and I are pastors, and I have a Biblical Studies degree so I am very familiar with Christian materials."

EXEGETICA PUBLISHING | CATHY CONE

312 Greenwich #112, Lee's Summit, MO 64082

editor@exegeticapublishing.com | exegeticapublishing.com/editing

Contact: website

Services: copyediting, manuscript evaluation, proofreading, substantive editing and rewriting

Types of manuscripts: academic, articles, Bible studies, curriculum, devotions, nonfiction books

Charges: page rate

Credentials/experience: "Exegetica editorial staff have more than 30 years editing experience with diverse media and publishers."

EXTRA INK EDITS | MEGAN EASLEY-WALSH

Ireland

Megan@ExtraInkEdits.com | www.ExtraInkEdits.com

Contact: email

Services: back-cover copy, discussion questions for books, manuscript evaluation, proofreading, writing coach

Types of manuscripts: adult, articles, devotions, easy readers, middle grade, nonfiction books, novels, picture books, poetry, query letters, short stories, teen/YA

Charges: flat fee, word rate

Credentials/experience: "Megan Easley-Walsh is an Amazon international multi-bestselling author of historical fiction, a researcher, and a writing consultant and editor at Extra Ink Edits. She is an award-winning writer and has taught college writing in the UNESCO literature city of Dublin, Ireland. Her degrees are in history-focused International Relations. Megan is a professional member of the Irish Writers Centre and a member of the Historical Novel Society. She has over 10 years of experience with Extra Ink Edits, helping writers with everything from query critiques to full manuscript critiques."

FAITH EDITORIAL SERVICES | REBECCA FAITH

PO Box 184, Novelty, OH 4072 | 216-906-0205

rebecca@faitheditorial.com | *www.faitheditorial.com*

Contact: email, website

Services: copyediting, manuscript evaluation, proofreading

Types of manuscripts: academic, adult, articles, Bible studies, book proposals, curriculum, devotions, medical, nonfiction books, technical material

Charges: hourly rate

Credentials/experience: "My experience editing in the Christian market includes six years as managing editor for a Christian nonprofit, another eight years editing/transcribing content for a global Christian ministry, and copyediting nonfiction Christian books and devotionals. In addition I have eleven years experience editing technical, engineering, medical, and educational material for university presses, journal publishers, and independent clients. I hold membership in the EFA, the Christian PEN (Gold), and the Christian Editor Connection."

FAITHFULLY WRITE EDITING | DAWN KINZER

dawnkinzer@comcast.net | *www.faithfullywriteediting.com*

Contact: email

Services: copyediting, manuscript evaluation, proofreading, substantive editing and rewriting

Types of manuscripts: novels, short stories

Charges: flat fee, page rate

Credentials/experience: "Dawn Kinzer launched Faithfully Write Editing in 2010. She is currently focusing on editing fiction: full-length novels, novellas, and short stories. She is a member of the Northwest Christian Writers Association, American Christian Fiction Writers, The Christian PEN, and the Christian Editor Connection. Four of her own novels have been published, and her work has also been included in devotionals and magazines. Dawn co-hosts and writes for the Seriously Write blog, which is dedicated to encouraging and equipping Christian writers."

FAITHWORKS EDITORIAL & WRITING, INC. | NANETTE THORSEN SNIPES

PO Box 1596, Buford, GA 30518 | 770-945-3093

nsnipes@bellsouth.net | *www.faithworkseditorial.com*

Contact: email, website

Services: copyediting, manuscript evaluation, proofreading, work-for-hire projects

Types of manuscripts: adult, articles, business materials, devotions, easy readers, gift books, memoir, middle grade, nonfiction books, picture books, poetry, query letters, short stories

Charges: hourly rate, page rate

Credentials/experience: "Member: The Christian PEN (Proofreaders and Editors Network), Christian Editor Connection, Christian Editor Network. Proofreader for corporate newsletters, thirteen years. Published writer for more than twenty-five years. Published hundreds of articles in magazines and stories in more than sixty compilation books, including Guideposts, B&H, Regal, and Integrity. Twelve years of editorial experience in both adult and children's short fiction and books, memoirs, short stories, devotions, articles, business. Rates are generally by page but, under specific circumstances, by the hour. Editorial clients have published with such houses as Zondervan, Tyndale, and Revell."

FINAL TOUCH PROOFREADING & EDITING | HEIDI MANN
mann.heidi@gmail.com | *www.FinalTouchProofreadingAndEditing.com*

Contact: email, website

Services: copyediting, proofreading

Types of manuscripts: adult, articles, Bible studies, curriculum, devotionals, easy readers, middle grade, nonfiction books, novels, picture books, teen/YA

Charges: flat fee, hourly rate

Credentials/experience: "Fourteen years of experience as a seminary-trained Lutheran pastor; excellent understanding of writing mechanics and style, honed through years of higher education and professional use; freelance editor since 2007 serving authors, publishers, and other entities; have completed multiple educational courses to enhance my knowledge and skills; passionate about writing that intersects with Christian faith. Member of The Christian PEN."

THE FOREWORD COLLECTIVE | MOLLY HODGIN
1726 Charity Dr., Brentwood, TN 37027 | 615-497-4322
molly.hodgin@theforewordcollective.com | *www.theforewordcollective.com*

Contact: email, website

Services: back-cover copy, book-contract evaluation, coauthoring, discussion questions for books, ghostwriting, manuscript evaluation, substantive editing and rewriting, writing coach

Types of manuscripts: adult, apps, board/picture books, book proposals, cookbooks, devotions, easy readers, gift books, middle grade, nonfiction books, novels, query letters, style books, teen/YA

Charges: flat fee, hourly rate

Credentials/experience: "Molly Hodgin, founder and CEO of The Foreword Collective, has over twenty years of publishing experience. Before founding The Foreword Collective, Molly served as the Associate Publisher for the Specialty Division of HarperCollins Christian Publishing. She has also served as the Editorial Director for Zondervan Gift, Thomas Nelson Gift Books, Tommy Nelson Kids Books, and The Thomas Nelson New Media Division, a Senior Editor for Scholastic Inc. and an editor for Penguin Young Readers Group. Molly has extensive experience in acquiring and editing gift books, cookbooks, style books, devotionals, trade nonfiction books, YA and middle grade fiction, and children's picture books and board books. Her specialty is helping authors craft a book proposal that will stand out to land them an agent or publishing deal. She has also written, ghost written, and co-authored over seventy-five books.

"If Molly isn't the right fit for your book, well, The Foreword Collective also employs a number of highly experienced industry professionals from all areas of Christian publishing. Whether you are an experienced author looking for editorial help or brand building or a new author who wants to make the leap into traditional publishing, The Foreword Collective is here to help!"

FREELANCE WRITING & EDITING SERVICES | ROBIN SCHMITT

schmitt.freelancer@sbcglobal.net | robinschmitt.com

Contact: email, phone

Services: back-cover copy, coauthoring, copyediting, discussion questions for books, ghostwriting, manuscript evaluation, substantive editing and rewriting, writing coach

Types of manuscripts: adult, articles, Bible studies, curriculum, devotionals, easy readers, gift books, middle grade, nonfiction books, novels, picture books, scripts, short stories, teen/YA

Charges: flat fee, hourly rate, page rate, word rate

Credentials/experience: "More than 20 years of experience as a writer and editor in Christian publishing. I've edited many books, both fiction and nonfiction, for adults, teens, and children. In every project I take on, I always strive for the highest standard of excellence."

FRENCH AND ENGLISH COMMUNICATION SERVICES |
DIANE GOULLARD

3104 E. Camelback Rd., PMB 124, Phoenix, AZ 85016-4502 | 602-870-1000
RequestFAECS2008@cox.net | *frenchandenglish.com*

Contact: email, mail, phone, website

Services: coauthoring, copyediting, French to English translation, proofreading

Types of manuscripts: academic, adult, articles, back-cover copy, Bible studies, board/picture books, book proposals, curriculum, devotions, easy readers, gift books, middle grade, nonfiction books, novels, poetry, query letters, scripts, short stories, technical material, teen/YA

Charges: custom, flat fee, hourly rate, page rate, word rate

Credentials/experience: "Experienced professional French to English and English to French translator, proofreader, interpreter, voiceover-narrator. Extremely detail oriented. Log on my website and contact me. Looking forward to serving you."

GINA KAMMER, THE INKY BOOKWYRM

1054 Deer Ridge Ct. NW, Lonsdale, MN 55046 | 507-381-1887
ginalkammer@gmail.com | *ginakammer.com*

Contact: website

Services: copyediting, manuscript evaluation, proofreading, substantive editing and rewriting, writing coach

Types of manuscripts: adult, easy readers, middle grade, novels, picture books, teen/YA

Charges: word rate

Credentials/experience: "Gina Kammer specializes in editing and book coaching for science fiction and fantasy. She is a former Capstone editor and Bethany Lutheran College writing/journalism instructor with 10+ years of experience in fiction and children's nonfiction. Using brain science hacks, hoarded craft knowledge, and solution-based direction, this book dragon helps science-fiction and fantasy authors get their stories—whether on the page or still in their heads—ready to enchant their readers."

GINA MUSHYNSKY

8400 Transit Ln., Baldwinsville, NY 13027 | 315-289-9470
ginamushynsky@gmail.com

Contact: email

Services: copyediting, proofreading, substantive editing and rewriting

Types of manuscripts: adult, Bible studies, devotions, nonfiction books

Charges: custom, word rate

Credentials/experience: "Since 2016 I've edited or proofread over two dozen titles for Pearson, Crossroad Publishing, Anaiah Press, and 5 Fold Media in addition to numerous self-publishing authors. My prior editing experience includes eight years as a newspaper editor and over four years as an assistant editor for an e-commerce web content provider. I hold a Bachelor of Arts in English from the University at Buffalo (NY)."

GINGER KOLBABA

ginger@gingerkolbaba.com | www.gingerkolbaba.com

Contact: email

Services: coauthoring, copyediting, discussion questions for books, ghostwriting, manuscript evaluation, proofreading, substantive editing and rewriting, writing coach

Types of manuscripts: adult, articles, Bible studies, book proposals, devotionals, gift books, nonfiction books, novels, query letters, short stories, teen/YA

Charges: flat fee, hourly rate

Credentials/experience: "More than twenty-five years in the industry. Former editor of *Today's Christian Woman* and *Marriage Partnership* magazines and *Kyria.com*, all national, award-winning publications of Christianity Today International. Best-selling author; written or contributed to more than forty books and one thousand articles, both in print and online. Clients include many publishing houses and best-selling authors."

GRACE NOTES, LLC | GALADRIEL GRACE

galadriel@galadrielgrace.com | galadrielgrace.com

Contact: email, website

Services: back-cover copy, consulting, copyediting, discussion questions for books, manuscript evaluation, proofreading, writing coach

Types of manuscripts: adult, articles, Bible studies, book proposals, curriculum, middle grade, nonfiction books, novels, query letters, short stories, teen/YA

Charges: custom, flat fee, word rate

Credentials/experience: "Over 15 years experience working with authors, personal branding and creative marketing."

HANEMANN EDITORIAL | NATALIE HANEMANN
nathanemann@gmail.com | www.nataliehanemannediting.com

Contact: email, website

Services: copyediting, manuscript evaluation, substantive editing and rewriting

Types of manuscripts: adult, book proposals, middle grade, nonfiction books, novels, teen/YA

Charges: flat fee

Credentials/experience: "Eleven years in-house at publishing houses, eight of those at Thomas Nelson in the fiction division under the tutelage of Allen Arnold. Since 2012, I've been freelance editing fiction and nonfiction (substantive and line), as well as helping authors get their synopses ready to submit to agents. I've edited more than three hundred manuscripts and particularly love working with newer authors or authors who are unsure if they should publish traditionally or indie. Certified by the Christian Editors Connection."

HAYHURST EDITORIAL, LLC | SARAH HAYHURST
1441 Haynescrest Ct., Grayson, GA 30017 | 470-825-2905
sarah@sarahhayhurst.com | www.sarahhayhurst.com

Contact: email

Services: copyediting, proofreading, substantive editing and rewriting, website text, writing coach

Types of manuscripts: adult, articles, Bible studies, devotions, nonfiction books

Charges: word rate

Credentials/experience: "Sarah graduated *cum laude* with a bachelor's degree in Communication Arts in 2014. She has enjoyed a variety of positions, such as editor/online teacher for a publishing company, managing editor for a university, computer/ESL teacher for a school, marketing manager for a law firm and an engineering firm, and communications director for a school. Sarah is a gold-level member of The Christian PEN and Christian Editor Network with whom she passed extensive testing and demonstrated expertise in the substantive editing, copyediting and proofreading of both fiction and nonfiction manuscripts as well as other nonfiction content. Sarah has over ten years of experience in editing and started her own editorial company in 2014."

HEATHER PUBOLS

heather.pubols@gmail.com | *heatherpubols.com/editing-services*

Contact: email, website
Services: copyediting, substantive editing and rewriting
Types of manuscripts: academic, articles, Bible studies, nonfiction books, technical material
Charges: hourly rate
Credentials/experience: "More than 20 years of editorial experience working in corporate communications for Christian missions organizations. Freelance editor since 2018."

HENRY MCLAUGHLIN

henry@henrymclaughlin.org | *www.henrymclaughlin.org*

Contact: email
Services: coauthoring, copyediting, ghostwriting, manuscript evaluation, substantive editing and rewriting, writing coach
Types of manuscripts: adult, nonfiction books, novels, short stories
Charges: custom
Credentials/experience: "Award winning author, teacher at conferences, editing, coaching, mentoring for several years."

HONEST EDITING | BILL LELAND

PO Box 310, Sisters, OR 97759
bill@writersedgeservice.com | *www.honestediting.com*

Contact: email, website
Services: book proposals, copyediting, substantive editing and rewriting
Types of manuscripts: academic, adult, Bible studies, book proposals, devotions, gift books, middle grade, nonfiction books, novels, teen/YA
Charges: flat fee
Credentials/experience: "Work done by professional freelance editors with years of experience who have worked with or been employed by major Christian Publishers."

HONEYCOMB HOUSE PUBLISHING, LLC | DAVID E. FESSENDEN

dave@fessendens.net | *www.davefessenden.com/writing-speaking-agenting*

Contact: email
Services: back-cover copy, book-contract evaluation, coauthoring, copyediting, discussion questions for books, manuscript evaluation,

substantive editing and rewriting, writing coach

Types of manuscripts: academic, adult, Bible studies, book proposals, devotionals, gift books, middle grade, nonfiction books, novels, teen/YA

Charges: flat fee

Credentials/experience: "David E. Fessenden, publisher for Honeycomb House Publishing, LLC, has degrees in journalism and theology, and over 30 years of experience in writing, editing, and editorial management for Christian book publishers."

IEDIT.INK | BOBBIE TEMPLE

3328 Flagstaff Ln., Knoxville, TN 37931 | 954-559-9587
editingbox@outlook.com | iedit.ink

Contact: website

Services: manuscript evaluation, substantive editing and rewriting, writing coach

Types of manuscripts: adult, easy readers, graphic novels, middle grade, picture books, teen/YA

Charges: page rate, word rate

Credentials/experience: "I have several years of publishing, writing, editing, and graphic design experience as well as multiple certifications. Currently working as a middle-grade editor at Elk Lake."

IMMORTALISE | BEN MORTON

PO Box 656, Noarlunga Centre, SA 5168, Australia
info@immortalise.com.au | www.immortalise.com.au

Contact: email

Services: copyediting, manuscript evaluation, proofreading, writing coach

Charges: page rate

Credentials/experience: "Published author, creative writing teacher, experienced editor and publisher, MA fiction writing supervisor."

INKSMITH EDITORIAL SERVICES | LIZ SMITH

liz@inksmithediting.com | www.inksmithediting.com

Contact: email

Services: copyediting, indexing, proofreading, sermon transcription

Types of manuscripts: academic, adult, articles, Bible studies, devotions, nonfiction books

Charges: page rate, word rate

Credentials/experience: "Liz edits primarily Christian nonfiction. She works with self-publishing authors as well as writers preparing a manuscript for submission to traditional publishers. Her other services include general and Scripture indexes, sermon transcription, typesetting (interior design), and e-book formatting."

INKSNATCHER | SALLY HANAN

429 S. Avenue C, Elgin, TX 78621 | 512-351-5869
inkmeister@inksnatcher.com | *www.inksnatcher.com*

Contact: email

Services: back-cover copy, coauthoring, copyediting, discussion questions for books, ghostwriting, proofreading, substantive editing and rewriting, website text

Types of manuscripts: adult, articles, Bible studies, curriculum, devotions, gift books, middle grade, nonfiction books, novels, short stories, teen/YA

Charges: hourly rate, word rate

Credentials/experience: "Certified nonfiction copy editor by the Christian Editor Connection."

INSPIRATION FOR WRITERS, INC. | SANDY TRITT

1527 18th St., Parkersburg, WV 26101 | 304-428-1218
IFWeditors@gmail.com | *www.InspirationForWriters.com*

Contact: email

Services: copyediting, ghostwriting, manuscript evaluation, proofreading, substantive editing and rewriting, writing coach

Types of manuscripts: academic, adult, articles, Bible studies, book proposals, curriculum, devotions, easy readers, gift books, middle grade, nonfiction books, novels, query letters, scripts, short stories, technical material, teen/YA

Charges: word rate

Credentials/experience: "More than 75 percent of Inspiration for Writers, Inc.'s business is repeat business, and we relish establishing long-term relationships with our writers. As per our mission statement, we believe in treating our writers exactly as we would want to be treated—with respect and compassion. Yet, we also believe in being honest. We want our writers to be happy with us ten years from now, so we tell you the truth about your writing. We just make sure all our criticism is of the constructive sort. After all, our purpose is to improve your writing, not destroy your confidence.

"The best way to get started is to request a no obligation, free sample edit. That allows us to see the level of your writing and recommend a service to you, as well as match you up with the editor who is best suited to your specific genre, writing level and personality. It also allows you to see what to expect from us before any money changes hands."

JAMES WATKINS
jim@jameswatkins.com | jameswatkins.com/editing

> **Contact:** email
> **Services:** discussion questions for books, manuscript evaluation, substantive editing and rewriting, writing coach
> **Types of manuscripts:** adult, articles, devotions, nonfiction books
> **Charges:** word rate
> **Credentials/experience:** "Award-winning author and editor (two industry book awards; four Evangelical Press Association awards for editing); served with American Bible Society as editor and Wesleyan Publishing house as editor, editorial director, acquisitions editor; taught writing for 15 years at Taylor University. Ordained minister who has edited several commentaries."

JAMI'S WORDS | JAMI BENNINGTON
jami@jamiswords.com | jamiswords.com

> **Contact:** email, website
> **Services:** copyediting, manuscript evaluation, proofreading, beta reading, substantive editing and rewriting
> **Types of manuscripts:** adult, middle grade, novels, short stories, teen/YA, articles, nonfiction books, devotions, book proposals
> **Charges:** word rate
> **Credentials/experience:** "1999 BA Education, emphasis Fine Arts/Humanities. 2010 launch of Jami's Words, a website geared to sharing my opinions on books, reviewing Christian authors' novels, and helping authors expand readership. 2020 UC San Diego Copyediting Certificate. Silver Member of The Christian PEN."

JAMIE CHAVEZ, EDITOR
3035 Argyle Ave., Murfreesboro, TN 37127 | 615-948-4430
jamie.chavez@gmail.com | www.jamiechavez.com

> **Contact:** email
> **Services:** copyediting, manuscript evaluation, substantive editing and rewriting

Types of manuscripts: adult, devotionals, easy readers, gift books, middle grade, nonfiction books, novels, picture books, teen/YA

Charges: flat fee

Credentials/experience: "Jamie Chavez worked for more than ten years in the Christian publishing industry and twenty as a professional copywriter before becoming a freelance editor in 2004. Books she's edited have become *New York Times* best sellers, won Christy and Carol Awards, and been finalists for many other awards and honors. She enjoys the collaborative nature of editing and finds long-term relationships especially rewarding— bring on the second, third, fourth book in the series! Jamie counts many national publishing houses as clients, many authors as friends, and spends her days making good books better."

JANIS WHIPPLE

9608 Regiment Ct., Land O Lakes, FL 34638 | 954-579-8545
janiswhipple@gmail.com

Contact: email

Services: coauthoring, copyediting, discussion questions for books, manuscript evaluation, proofreading, substantive editing and rewriting, writing coach

Types of manuscripts: adult, articles, book proposals, curriculum, devotionals, gift books, nonfiction books, query letters, teen/YA

Charges: flat fee, hourly rate

Credentials/experience: "Thirty years of editing, ten years as an in-house editor with B&H Publishers in acquisitions and managing editing, fifteen years as a freelance editor and writing coach."

JAY K. PAYLEITNER & ASSOCIATES

629 N. Tyler Rd., Saint Charles, IL 60174 | 630-377-7899
jaypayleitner@gmail.com | *www.jaypayleitner.com*

Contact: email, phone, website

Services: back-cover copy, coauthoring, ghostwriting

Types of manuscripts: adult, devotionals, gift books, nonfiction books

Charges: flat fee

Credentials/experience: "Author of 30 books with Harvest House, Broadstreet, DaySpring, Tyndale, Multnomah, Bethany House, and Worthy."

JEANETTE GARDNER LITTLETON, PUBLICATION SERVICES

3706 N.E. Shady Lane Dr., Gladstone, MO 64119-1958 | 816-459-8016
jeanettedl@earthlink.net | *www.linkedin.com/in/jeanette-littleton-b1b790101*

Contact: email

Services: back-cover copy, book-contract evaluation, copyediting, discussion questions for books, indexing, manuscript evaluation, proofreading, substantive editing and rewriting

Types of manuscripts: adult, articles, Bible studies, book proposals, curriculum, devotionals, gift books, nonfiction books, novels, query letters, short stories, technical material, teen/YA

Charges: flat fee, hourly rate, page rate

Credentials/experience: "I've been a full-time editor and writer for more than thirty years for a variety of publishers. I've written five thousand articles and edited thousands of articles and dozens of books. Please see my profile at LinkedIn."

JEANETTE HANSCOME

jeanettehanscome@gmail.com | *jeanettehanscome.com*

Contact: email

Services: back-cover copy, coauthoring, discussion questions for books, ghostwriting, manuscript evaluation, substantive editing and rewriting, writing coach

Types of manuscripts: adult, articles, book proposals, devotions, gift books, middle grade, nonfiction books, novels, query letters, short stories, teen/YA

Charges: flat fee, hourly rate

Credentials/experience: "Jeanette Hanscome has written five books and hundreds of articles, devotions and stories, as well as contributing to over a dozen devotionals and story collections. As a freelance editor and coach, Jeanette has experience in a variety of genres including devotionals, women's contemporary fiction, historical romance, YA, memoirs, and general non-fiction. She is also a speaker and regularly teaches workshops at writers conferences. She is currently on the board of the West Coast Christian Writers Conference."

JENNIFER EDWARDS COMMUNICATIONS

mail.jennifer.edwards@gmail.com | *www.jedwardsediting.net*

Contact: email, website

Services: back-cover copy, copyediting, discussion questions for books, manuscript evaluation, proofreading, writing coach

Types of manuscripts: academic, adult, Bible studies, book proposals, curriculum, nonfiction books, query letters

Charges: hourly rate

Credentials/experience: "Jennifer Edwards is an established professional nonfiction editor, writer, and publishing coach serving Christian authors and publishers. She has worked with 40+ authors and numerous Christian publishers and ministries, including Penguin Random House, Faithlife (Lexham Press), Principles to Live By Publishing, BMH Books, Compel/She Speaks, FDM.World, Redemption Press, Gospel Advocate, The Sophos Group, and more. Her master's degree in Biblical and Theological Studies from Western Seminary has proven invaluable in helping Christian authors with their manuscripts by providing a critical eye for content, a thorough understanding of Scripture, and insightful theological thinking."

JENWESTWRITING | JENNIFER WESTBROOK

14030 Connecticut Ave. #6813, Silver Spring, MD 20916

support@jenwestwriting.com | *www.jenwestwriting.com*

Contact: email, website

Services: back-cover copy, copyediting, ghostwriting, manuscript evaluation, substantive editing and rewriting

Types of manuscripts: Bible studies, devotions, nonfiction books, novels

Charges: custom

Credentials/experience: "I've been editing books for over 20 years and have worked with over 40 authors. My clients' books run the gamut of genres, including non-fiction, novels, self-help, devotionals, Bible studies, and children's books. My approach to editing is goal-oriented, keeping my clients' desires in mind so I can help them create a book that meets their needs."

JHWRITING+ | NICOLE HAYES

jhwritingplus@yahoo.com | *www.jhwritingplus.com*

Contact: email, website

Services: coauthoring, copyediting, discussion questions for books, ghostwriting, manuscript evaluation, proofreading, substantive editing and rewriting, writing coach

Types of manuscripts: adult, articles, curriculum, devotionals, gift books, nonfiction books, novels, poetry, short stories, technical material, teen/YA

Charges: flat fee, word rate

Credentials/experience: "Bachelor's degree in English; PhD in education. Although I do most writing, editing, and proofreading projects, my niche is creative nonfiction (engaging, dramatic, factual prose). I have been writing and editing for more than twenty-five years."

JLC SERVICES | JODY L. COLLINS

1403 Newport Ct. SE, Renton, WA 98058 | 425-260-0948
heyjode70@yahoo.com | *www.jodyleecollins.com*

Contact: email

Services: back-cover copy, copyediting, proofreading, writing coach

Types of manuscripts: Bible studies, book proposals, curriculum, devotionals, nonfiction books, picture books

Charges: custom

Credentials/experience: "BA in liberal studies, English major. Teaching credential, 1991. Twenty-five years of experience writing online and in print. Author of *Living the Season Well: Reclaiming Christmas*. Coach/consultant for multiple clients from editing to self-publishing."

JOHN SLOAN, LLC

830 Grey Eagle Cir. N, Colorado Springs, CO 80919 | 719-888-0365
jsjohnsloan@gmail.com | *sloanhinds.com*

Contact: email

Services: coauthoring, substantive editing and rewriting, writing coach

Types of manuscripts: academic, adult, Bible studies, devotions, easy readers, gift books, nonfiction books, short stories, teen/YA

Charges: flat fee, hourly rate, word rate

Credentials/experience: "I have worked in publishing and editorial roles for 40 years, with Multnomah Press and HarperCollins Christian Publishing, Zondervan. I am offering my services for freelance work in the areas of book development, collaboration, writer coaching, book doctoring, macro editing, content editing. I have worked with a broad spectrum of book and author types: I have edited the literary and general market works of authors like Philip Yancey and Frederick Buechner; the popular issues volumes of writers like Chuck Colson; the high visibility authors like Lee Strobel and Ben Carson; the broader market authors and pastors like John Ortberg and Mark Batterson; and I've worked in the area of the popular academic works. For 4 years my partner Meredith Hinds and I have operated a successful freelance business."

JOT OR TITTLE EDITORIAL SERVICES | SAMUEL RYAN KELLY

sam@jotortittle.com | jotortittle.com

Contact: email

Services: copyediting, manuscript evaluation, proofreading, substantive editing and rewriting, writing coach

Types of manuscripts: academic, adult, articles, Bible studies, devotionals, nonfiction books, novels, short stories

Charges: hourly rate

Credentials/experience: "Sam has a double BA in English and biblical and religious studies and an MA in theology. He specializes in academic writing and has a background in biblical languages, but he likes to bring his expertise to a variety of projects. In addition to his freelance work, Sam does research for pastors and churches at Docent Research Group and serves as an associate editor with Wordsmith Writing Coaches."

JOY MEDIA | JULIE-ALLYSON IERON

PO Box 413, Mt. Prospect, IL 60056

j-a@joymediaservices.com | www.joymediaservices.com

Contact: email

Services: back-cover copy, copyediting, discussion questions for books, ghostwriting, manuscript evaluation, proofreading, substantive editing and rewriting, writing coach

Types of manuscripts: adult, articles, Bible studies, book proposals, devotions, gift books, nonfiction books, novels

Charges: flat fee, hourly rate

Credentials/experience: "Master's degree in journalism with more than thirty years in Christian publishing management, writing, and editing. Fourteen years as a mentor/master craftsman with the Jerry B. Jenkins Christian Writers Guild."

JR'S RED QUILL EDITING | JUDITH ROBL

PO Box 802, Lyons, KS 67554 | 620-257-3143

jrlight620@yahoo.com | www.judithrobl.com/editing-2

Contact: email, website

Services: back-cover copy, copyediting, discussion questions for books, manuscript evaluation, proofreading, writing coach

Types of manuscripts: adult, Bible studies, devotions, gift books, novels, query letters, short stories

Charges: custom

Credentials/experience: "Educated as a secondary English teacher decades ago, I've edited for people for many years. My first major accomplishment in editing was published in 2010. I use *The Chicago Manual of Style* unless another style guide is provided. No project is undertaken without a sample edit to see if we are a good fit. I believe the relationship between author and editor is second only to competence."

KACI LANE CREATIONS, LLC | KACI LANE HINDMAN
kacilane@kacilane.com | www.kacilane.com

Contact: email

Services: coauthoring

Types of manuscripts: devotions, gift books

Charges: custom

Credentials/experience: "BA in Communications/Journalism from The University of Alabama, 16 years experience as a published writer, author of clean and inspirational romances, guest blogger."

KAREN APPOLD
kappold@msn.com

Contact: email

Services: copyediting, proofreading

Types of manuscripts: academic, articles, curriculum

Charges: flat fee, hourly rate, word rate

Credentials/experience: "I am an award-winning journalist with a BA from Penn State University in English (Writing). I have more than 25 years of professional editorial experience. I mainly write on healthcare/medical and retail, but welcome Christian-themed work."

KATHY IDE BOOK SERVICES
Kathy@KathyIde.com | www.KathyIde.com

Contact: email, website

Services: copyediting, manuscript evaluation, proofreading, writing coach

Types of manuscripts: adult, Bible studies, book proposals, devotions, gift books, nonfiction books, novels, query letters, short stories

Charges: hourly rate

Credentials/experience: "Kathy is the author of *Proofreading Secrets of Best-Selling Authors, Editing Secrets of Best-Selling Authors,* and the *Capitalization Dictionary.* She is also the editor-compiler of the Fiction Lover's Devotional series. She has been a professional freelance editor since 1998, offering a full range of editorial services for aspiring writers, established authors, and book publishers. She has spoken and taught at writers' conferences across the country for several years, as well as directing three. Kathy is owner of Christian Editor Network, parent company to The Christian PEN: Proofreaders and Editors Network, the Christian Editor Connection, the PEN Institute, and PENCON."

KATIE PHILLIPS CREATIVE SERVICES

1500 E. Tall Tree Rd. #33202, Derby, KS 67037-6033 | 316-293-9202
morford.katie@gmail.com | *www.katiephillipscreative.com*

Contact: email, phone

Services: back-cover copy, manuscript evaluation, writing coach

Types of manuscripts: adult, book proposals, novels, query letters, short stories, teen/YA

Charges: custom, hourly rate, word rate

Credentials/experience: "Katie Phillips is a developmental editor, as well as a writing, branding, and business coach for women authors of YA sci-fi/fantasy looking to take their career to the next level. Her clients include multiple award winners and finalists, and have gone on to sign book deals, find agents, and profitably self-publish. She has a BA in Journalism and Mass Communications and worked over ten years as an editor for newspapers and in non-profit communications. She helped found indie publishing house Crosshair Press (now Uncommon Universes) and studied writing under agent Les Stobbe and author DiAnn Mills. She was an AWSA Editor of the Year finalist and studied business and branding strategies under coach Michelle Knight."

KEELY BOEVING EDITORIAL

keely.boeving@gmail.com | *www.keelyboeving.com*

Contact: website

Services: coauthoring, copyediting, ghostwriting, manuscript evaluation, substantive editing and rewriting

Types of manuscripts: adult, book proposals, middle grade, nonfiction books, novels, query letters, teen/YA

Charges: hourly rate

Credentials/experience: "Experienced editor and copy editor, formerly worked in editorial for Oxford University Press. Have worked with independent clients, literary agencies, and publishers as a freelancer for the past several years."

KELLY KAGAMAS TOMKIES
kellytomkies@gmail.com

Contact: email

Services: copyediting, ghostwriting, proofreading, substantive editing and rewriting, writing coach

Types of manuscripts: adult, articles, book proposals, devotionals, easy readers, middle grade, nonfiction books, novels, picture books, query letters, short stories, teen/YA

Charges: flat fee

Credentials/experience: "I have nearly twenty years of editorial experience, including authoring seven books for different publishers, contributing chapters to two National Geographic books, serving as editor of three major business magazines, and years of experience writing and editing for publishers and individual authors. My client list includes HarperCollins, John Wiley and Sons, McGraw-Hill, Kirkus Editorial, Fountainhead Press, Barbour Books, Vantage Press, and Gadfly, LLC, as well as individual authors who wish to find publishers or self-publish."

KRISTEN STIEFFEL
PO Box 593549, Orlando, FL 32859 | 407-928-7801
kristen@kristenstieffel.com | *www.kristenstieffel.com*

Contact: email

Services: copyediting, ghostwriting, manuscript evaluation, substantive editing and rewriting, writing coach

Types of manuscripts: adult, novels, short stories, teen/YA

Charges: word rate

Credentials/experience: "Kristen Stieffel is a writer and freelance editor specializing in science fiction and fantasy. She serves on the organizing committee for Realm Makers, the only conference for Christians writing speculative fiction. For several years Kristen was the copyeditor for *Havok*, a flash fiction magazine specializing in the speculative genres. Kristen is the author of two published books—one fantasy and one steampunk—and has published multiple novellas and short stories. Before freelancing she was a newspaper copyeditor, but nevertheless values the importance of preserving each author's voice."

LEE WARREN COMMUNICATIONS

leewarrenjr@outlook.com | *www.leewarren.info/editing.html*

Contact: email, website

Services: copyediting, manuscript evaluation, proofreading

Types of manuscripts: adult, articles, Bible studies, curriculum, devotionals, gift books, nonfiction books, novels

Charges: flat fee, word rate

Credentials/experience: "Lee Warren has more than twenty years of experience in the Christian publishing industry (both traditional and indie). He has been a contract editor for Barbour Publishing, Electric Moon Publishing, and Bold Vision Books, as well as editing manuscripts through his own service."

LESLIE H. STOBBE

201 E. Howard St. #E-46, Tryon, NC 28782 | 828-808-7127

lhstobbe123@gmail.com | *www.stobbeliterary.com*

Contact: email

Services: back-cover copy, book-contract evaluation, coauthoring, ghostwriting, manuscript evaluation, substantive editing and rewriting, writing coach

Types of manuscripts: adult, book proposals, curriculum, devotionals, nonfiction books

Charges: hourly rate

Credentials/experience: "I've been writing articles, church materials, and curriculum; ghostwriting for prominent authors; editorial director at three publishers and president of one; literary agent for 25 years; mentor at hundreds of writers conferences; and book writer coach for many years. I can take a book idea development through rewrites and editing to book proposal for agents and editors."

LESLIE L. MCKEE EDITING

lmckeeediting@gmail.com | *lmckeeediting.wixsite.com/lmckeeediting*

Contact: email

Services: back-cover copy, copyediting, discussion questions for books, proofreading, substantive editing and rewriting

Types of manuscripts: adult, articles, devotions, easy readers, middle grade, nonfiction books, novels, picture books, poetry, short stories, teen/YA

Charges: flat fee, page rate, word rate

Credentials/experience: "Freelance editor and proofreader with various publishing houses (large and small) since 2012, working with traditionally published and self-published authors. Also an editor with Havok Publishing. Member of The Christian PEN and American Christian Fiction Writers. See website for details on services offered, as well as testimonials and a portfolio."

LESLIE SANTAMARIA

leslie@lesliesantamaria.com | lesliesantamaria.com

Contact: email

Services: back-cover copy, copyediting, manuscript evaluation, proofreading, writing coach

Types of manuscripts: book proposals, easy readers, middle grade, nonfiction books, picture books, query letters

Charges: flat fee, page rate

Credentials/experience: "Published author, freelance editor, and writing coach, with more than 200 pieces published in periodicals, specializing in children's literature."

LIBBY GONTARZ

libbygontarz@gmail.com | libbygontarz.com

Contact: email, phone

Services: copyediting, discussion questions for books, substantive editing and rewriting

Types of manuscripts: adult, articles, Bible studies, curriculum, devotions, middle grade, nonfiction books

Charges: custom, page rate, word rate

Credentials/experience: "After a career of teaching and nationwide educational training, I accepted a curriculum development position at an educational publishing company. Writing lessons and assessments gradually led into editing. Since 2015, I have focused on Christian nonfiction, editing for various publishers and individuals. Your project deserves professional editing!"

LIFE LAUNCH ME | JANE RUBIETTA

jane@lifelaunchme.com | www.LifeLaunchMe.com

Contact: email

Services: back-cover copy, book-contract evaluation, coauthoring, copyediting, discussion questions for books, ghostwriting, manuscript evaluation, proofreading, writing coach

Types of manuscripts: adult, articles, Bible studies, book proposals, devotions, nonfiction books, novels, query letters

Charges: hourly rate

Credentials/experience: "Jane Rubietta has written 22 books, 100s of articles, helped train writers and speakers for more than 20 years, and co-authored three books. Jane speaks internationally and also trains writers and speakers at conferences around the globe."

LIGHTHOUSE EDITING | DR. LON ACKELSON

13326 Community Rd. #11, Poway, CA 92064 | 858-748-9258
Isaiah68la@sbcglobal.net | *lighthouseedit.com*

Contact: website

Services: back-cover copy, book-contract evaluation, coauthoring, copyediting, ghostwriting, manuscript evaluation, substantive editing and rewriting

Types of manuscripts: adult, Bible studies, book proposals, curriculum, devotionals, nonfiction books, query letters

Charges: flat fee, hourly rate, page rate

Credentials/experience: "A professional editor for thirty-four years and a published writer for forty years."

LIGHTNING EDITING SERVICES | DENISE LOOCK

699 Golf Course Rd., Waynesville, NC 28786 | 908-868-5854
denise@lightningeditingservices.com | *www.lightningeditingservices.com*

Contact: email

Services: coauthoring, copyediting, discussion questions for books, ghostwriting, manuscript evaluation, proofreading, substantive editing and rewriting

Types of manuscripts: adult, articles, Bible studies, book proposals, devotions, nonfiction books, teen/YA

Charges: flat fee, hourly rate

Credentials/experience: "Former high school English teacher and college instructor Denise Loock is a general editor for Iron Stream Media and also accepts freelance projects. With thirty years' experience in the academic world coupled with ten years in the publishing industry, she helps writers produce books that attract publishers and engage readers."

LILA DILLER

dillerdesigns@gmail.com | *www.liladiller.com/editingservices*

Contact: website
Services: coauthoring, copyediting, ghostwriting, proofreading
Types of manuscripts: adult, articles, Bible studies, devotions, nonfiction books, novels
Charges: word rate
Credentials/experience: "Are you struggling to self-edit or finding an affordable professional editor? You're in the right place! Because I want to help independent writers (Indies) avoid some of the mistakes I made with my first book, I'm offering editing and proofing services. If you don't have the time or technical know-how to figure out how to do these necessary tasks for yourself, I can help you save time and much frustration. Believe me, it took me several tries and much frustration trying to figure it all out. Now that I know what I'm doing and have helped several authors, I can help you, too. For editing and proofreading services, I offer 5 pages (or the first chapter, whichever is shortest) as a free sample of my work and to see if we would work well together."

LINDSAY A. FRANKLIN

Lindsay@LindsayAFranklin.com | *lindsayafranklin.com*

Contact: website
Services: coauthoring, copyediting, ghostwriting, manuscript evaluation, proofreading, substantive editing and rewriting, writing coach
Types of manuscripts: adult, easy readers, middle grade, nonfiction books, novels, picture books, short stories, teen/YA
Charges: hourly rate, word rate
Credentials/experience: "Award-winning, published author; member of The Christian PEN."

LISA BARTELT

lmbartelt@gmail.com | *lisabartelt.com*

Contact: email, website
Services: back-cover copy, coauthoring, manuscript evaluation, proofreading
Types of manuscripts: adult, articles, nonfiction books, novels
Charges: custom
Credentials/experience: "Ten years of writing and editing for daily newspapers in the Midwest followed by more than 10 years of

freelance writing and editing, including as a judge for both fiction and non-fiction writing contests."

LISSA HALLS JOHNSON EDITORIAL

13926 Double Girth Ct., Matthews, NC 28105 | 479-220-8662
lissahallsjohnson@gmail.com | *lissahallsjohnson.com*

Contact: email, website
Services: manuscript evaluation, substantive editing and rewriting, writing coach
Types of manuscripts: memoir, novels, teen/YA
Charges: hourly rate
Credentials/experience: "Editor for fiction, nonfiction narrative, memoir for 20+ years. Some writers have received Christy Award finalist awards or nominations, on bestselling lists, *Publishers Weekly* starred reviews."

LOGOS WORD DESIGNS, LLC | LINDA NATHAN

PO Box 735, Maple Falls, WA 98266-0735 | 360-599-3429
editor@logosword.com | *www.logosword.com*

Contact: email
Services: back-cover copy, copyediting, discussion questions for books, ghostwriting, manuscript evaluation, proofreading, substantive editing and rewriting
Types of manuscripts: academic, adult, articles, Bible studies, book proposals, devotionals, gift books, nonfiction books, novels, query letters, short stories, technical material, teen/YA
Charges: custom, flat fee, hourly rate, page rate, word rate
Credentials/experience: "Linda Nathan has over 30 years of experience as a professional independent freelance writer, editor, and publishing consultant, working with authors and institutions on a wide range of projects. She is a published author with 10 years of experience in the legal field and has spoken on the radio and at conferences and seminars. Since 1992 she has run her own company, Logos Word Designs, LLC. Linda has a B.A. in Psychology from the University of Oregon and master's level work. She is a freelance staff editor with Redemption Press, a Gold member of the Christian Editor Connection, and a member of four other professional writers' and editors' associations."

LOUISE M. GOUGE, COPYEDITOR

900 Jamison Loop #105, Kissimmee, FL 34744 | 407-694-5765

Louisemgouge@aol.com | *louisemgougeauthor.blogspot.com*

Contact: email

Services: back-cover copy, copyediting, manuscript evaluation, substantive editing and rewriting

Types of manuscripts: book proposals, novels, short stories

Charges: word rate

Credentials/experience: "Louise M. Gouge is a retired college English professor and the author of twenty-five novels. For editing, she utilizes CMOS and MLA. Copyediting includes checking grammar, punctuation, spelling, and phrasing. Substantive editing includes making sure character arcs are balanced, the story is well paced, and the conclusion is satisfying. Checking a client's research will raise the cost, the amount depending upon how much research is required. Novel editing $1,000-3,000."

LUCIE WINBORNE

116 Hickory Rd., Longwood, FL 2750-2708 | 321-439-7743

lwinborne704@gmail.com | *www.bluetypewriter.com*

Contact: email

Services: copywriting, proofreading

Types of manuscripts: adult, devotionals, middle grade, nonfiction books, novels, poetry, short stories, teen/YA

Charges: hourly rate

Credentials/experience: "Conversant with *Chicago Manual of Style, Merriam-Webster Collegiate Dictionary*, Google Docs and Microsoft Word, with experience in fiction, nonfiction, educational, and business documents. Demonstrated adherence to deadlines and excellent communication and organizational skills."

LYNNE TAGAWA

5606 Onyx Way, San Antonio, TX 78222 | 210-544-4397

lbtagawa@gmail.com | *www.lynnetagawa.com/editing*

Contact: email

Services: copyediting, proofreading

Types of manuscripts: novels, short stories

Charges: word rate

Credentials/experience: "Educator, writer, and editor serving as proofreader for Chapel Library literature ministry for many years. Member, Christian PEN. Experience copyediting historical fiction."

MANYESHA BATIST INC.

4071 Orleans Ct., Denver, CO 80249 | 303-253-0424

mybatistinc@gmail.com | *mybatistinc.journoportfolio.com*

Contact: email

Services: back-cover copy, coauthoring, copyediting, discussion questions for books, ghostwriting, proofreading, substantive editing and rewriting

Types of manuscripts: articles, devotions, nonfiction books

Charges: flat fee, hourly rate, page rate, word rate

Credentials/experience: "Manyesha Batist is a seasoned journalist with more than 17 years of experience as both an editor and writer."

MARCY WEYDEMULLER

marcy@sowinglightseeds.com

Contact: email

Services: discussion questions for books, manuscript evaluation, substantive editing and rewriting, writing coach

Types of manuscripts: adult, articles, curriculum, devotionals, easy readers, middle grade, nonfiction books, novels, picture books, short stories, teen/YA

Charges: hourly rate

Credentials/experience: "I have worked on more than forty published novels, and four of the authors I work with have published three or more series. My current edits have included historical fiction, historical Christmas novella, YA contemporary, middle-readers both historical and contemporary, suspense/mystery, woman's romance, and memoir. I have more than twenty-five years of experience writing, mentoring, and teaching, both in fiction and nonfiction, including Bible studies and college composition. I have completed a BA in history and sociology and an MFA in writing, with a special focus on fantasy, poetry, and children's literature."

MARTI PIEPER, COLLABORATIVE WRITER AND EDITOR

246 Maple Grove Rd., Seneca, SC 29678 | 352-409-3136

marti@martipieper.com | *www.martipieper.com*

Contact: email, website

Services: coauthoring, copyediting, discussion questions for books, ghostwriting, manuscript evaluation, proofreading, writing coach

Types of manuscripts: adult, articles, Bible studies, book proposals, curriculum, devotions, gift books, nonfiction books, query letters, teen/YA

Charges: custom

Credentials/experience: "Marti Pieper's eclectic publishing career includes ghostwriting a young adult memoir that made the ECPA bestseller list and traveling to six Latin American countries to share stories of teen mission trips and an award-winning missionary memoir. She has written seven traditionally published nonfiction books and edited several more, written and edited for both print and digital publications, and taught at multiple writers conferences."

MEGHAN BIELINSKI PROFESSIONAL WRITING AND EDITING SERVICES

mbielinski34@gmail.com | www.the-efa.org/membershipinfo/meghan-bielinski-21154

Contact: website

Services: copyediting, proofreading

Types of manuscripts: adult, nonfiction books, novels, short stories, teen/YA

Charges: word rate

Credentials/experience: "Writing and editing are my passions. Since graduating with a bachelor's in English literature, I have gained five years of experience offering professional editing services. I work with both fiction and nonfiction, most notably self-help, lifestyle, personal finance, YA novels, Christian, and historical fiction."

MENTOR ME CAREER NETWORK | CHERYL ROGERS

cheryl@mentormecareernetwork.com | linkedin.com/in/cherylarogers

Contact: email, phone

Services: coauthoring, copyediting, ghostwriting, manuscript evaluation, proofreading, substantive editing and rewriting, writing coach

Types of manuscripts: adult, articles, middle grade, nonfiction books, teen/YA

Charges: flat fee, hourly rate, word rate

Credentials/experience: "BA in journalism and sociology; more than five years of book editing/freelancing; one year of newspaper copyediting; eleven years of newspaper reporting; four years of desktop design, including brochures, booklets, and flyers."

MISSION AND MEDIA | MICHELLE RAYBURN

info@missionandmedia.com | www.missionandmedia.com

Contact: email

Services: copyediting, discussion questions for books, ghostwriting, proofreading, substantive editing and rewriting

Types of manuscripts: Bible studies, nonfiction books

Charges: flat fee, hourly rate, word rate

Credentials/experience: "Michelle Rayburn has been a freelance writer for more than 20 years and has edited for Christian publishers as well as for indie authors. Has also worked in the marketing and public relations industry. Michelle has an MA in ministry leadership and has published hundreds of articles and Bible studies as well as five books. She specializes in Christian living, Bible study, humor, and self-help."

MONICA SHARMAN EDITING

2930 Coldwater Dr., Colorado Springs, CO 80919 | 719-357-6910
monicasharman@gmail.com | *www.monicasharman.wordpress.com/ monica-sharman-editing*

Contact: email

Services: copyediting, proofreading

Types of manuscripts: academic, adult, articles, Bible studies, curriculum, devotionals, easy readers, gift books, middle grade, nonfiction books, novels, picture books, poetry, short stories, technical material, teen/YA

Charges: flat fee, hourly rate

Credentials/experience: "An engineer-turned-editor, Monica is known for her technical accuracy, her light touch preserving and enhancing the author's voice, and her encouragement. She has edited memoirs, essays, devotionals, fiction, children's fiction, poetry, and Bible studies for traditional publishers as well as self-publishing authors."

NATALIE NYQUIST

nyquist.n.m@gmail.com | *natalienyquist.com/editor*

Contact: email

Services: bibliographies, citations, copyediting, fact-checking, proofreading, research, substantive editing and rewriting

Types of manuscripts: academic, adult, Bible studies, book proposals, cookbooks, curriculum, devotions, gift books, middle grade, nonfiction books, novels, teen/YA

Charges: custom, flat fee, hourly rate

Credentials/experience: "I primarily work for traditional publishers. For private authors I edit only nonfiction for an hourly rate.

Freelance editing since 2012 and training editors through UC Berkeley's editing program since 2018. Earned U of C editing certificate in 2014. Specialties: cites and bibliographies, detail consistency across long projects, biblical studies, and celebrity memoir. 800+ projects completed for publishers, including New York Times, *Publisher's Weekly*, and ECPA bestsellers. Project portfolio: *pathbrite.com/natalienyquist/Icne*."

NEXT INDEX SERVICES | JESSICA MCCURDY CROOKS
jessica@JessicaCrooks.com | www.next-index.com

> **Contact:** email, website
> **Services:** indexing, proofreading, website text
> **Types of manuscripts:** adult, articles, devotionals, middle grade, nonfiction books, novels, teen/YA
> **Charges:** flat fee, hourly rate, page rate, word rate
> **Credentials/experience:** "My training as a librarian and records manager gives me an eye for detail and finding information. I also know how readers tend to search for information, a skill that helps me arrive at keywords and phrases for the indexes I write. I have more than twenty years of indexing experience."

NEXT LEVEL EDITING AND TRANSCRIPTION | DARLENE OAKLEY
248 Oakdale Ave., St. Catharines, ON L2P 2K6, Canada | 289-696-2382
nextleveleditingandt@gmail.com | www.darscorrections.com

> **Contact:** email
> **Services:** copyediting, manuscript evaluation, proofreading, substantive editing and rewriting, transcription
> **Types of manuscripts:** adult, articles, Bible studies, devotionals, nonfiction books, novels, short stories, technical material, teen/YA
> **Charges:** custom, page rate, word rate
> **Credentials/experience:** "15+ years editing fiction/non-fiction, inspirational and mainstream; also urban fiction/non. 15+ transcription experience (interviews, videos, telecons). Past Acquisitions Editor, Project Manager, Social Media for 2 publishing companies. Go-to Editor for many clients."

NOBLE CREATIVE, LLC | SCOTT NOBLE
PO Box 131402, St. Paul, MN 55113 | 651-494-4169
snoble@noblecreative.com | www.noblecreative.com

> **Contact:** email

Services: copyediting, ghostwriting, manuscript evaluation, proofreading, substantive editing and rewriting, writing coach

Types of manuscripts: adult, articles, book proposals, curriculum, devotionals, nonfiction books, query letters

Charges: flat fee

Credentials/experience: "Nearly twenty years of experience as an award-winning journalist, writer, editor, and proofreader. More than 1,000 published articles, many of them prompting radio and television appearances. Won several awards from Evangelical Press Association. Worked with dozens of published authors and other public figures, as well as first-time authors and small businesses. Have a BA and MS from St. Cloud State University and an MA from Bethel Seminary."

NOVEL IMPROVEMENT EDITING SERVICES | JEANNE MARIE LEACH

PO Box 552, Hudson, CO 80642

jeanne@novelimprovement.com | *novelimprovement.com*

Contact: email, website

Services: back-cover copy, copyediting, ghostwriting, manuscript evaluation, substantive editing and rewriting, writing coach

Types of manuscripts: adult, book proposals, novels, poetry, query letters, short stories, teen/YA

Charges: flat fee, page rate

Credentials/experience: "Multi-published author, past coordinator and current gold member of The Christian PEN: Proofreaders and Editors Network; member of Christian Editor Network; and member of the American Christian Fiction writers, where I received the 2012 Member Service Award. I teach online courses through my website on editing fiction to editors and authors. I've been editing, mentoring, and critiquing for thirteen years and over a dozen of my clients have gone on to win numerous writing awards and have made various bestsellers' lists."

OASHEIM EDITING SERVICES, LLC | CATHY OASHEIM

Central Florida | 202-389-8207

cathy@cathyoasheim.com | *www.cathyoasheim.com*

Contact: email, website

Services: copyediting, discussion questions for books, manuscript evaluation, proofreading, substantive editing and rewriting, writing coach

Types of manuscripts: academic, articles, Bible studies, curriculum, devotionals, devotions, doctoral dissertations/theses, nonfiction books, novels, query letters, short stories, technical material

Charges: custom, flat fee, hourly rate, page rate, word rate

Credentials/experience: "Cathy is the author of a memoir and many psychoeducational articles. She is a professional freelance editor since 2012, blogger, and writing coach who specializes in nonfiction, true fiction, and fiction for Indy authors. She has judged over 1,000 Indie books for the Next Generation Indie Book Awards since 2016. Her services also include academic editing and fact checking for doctoral candidates (all have passed their boards), and blogs. A BS degree in Applied Psychology from Regis University allows Cathy to 'Refine Your Masterpiece.' Earlier engineering and military experiences support highly technical work and complex storytelling to get the rough draft manuscript out of the head, to the heart, and out of the plume to a polished product for the readers.

"Organizations: Author Alliance of Independent Authors, Journal Storage, National Association of Independent Writers and Editors, Nonfiction Authors Association, Toastmasters International–Distinguished Toastmaster, and The Christian PEN Proofreaders and Editors Network–Silver Member. She volunteers as an interviewer at the Library of Congress' Veteran Oral History Project."

ODD SOCK PROOFREADING AND COPYEDITING | STEVE MATHISEN

807 Maple St., Hoquiam, WA 98550 | 425-741-8392
scmathisen98037@hotmail.com | oddsock.me

Contact: email, website

Services: copyediting, proofreading, substantive editing and rewriting

Types of manuscripts: adult, devotions, nonfiction books, novels, scripts, short stories, teen/YA

Charges: page rate, word rate

Credentials/experience: "Thoughtful editing at reasonable prices. Join my award-winning clients and allow me to help you put your best foot forward."

OFFSCRIPT EDITING | SHERRY CHAMBLEE

chambleeservices@gmail.com | www.offscript.weebly.com

Contact: email

Services: copyediting, proofreading

Types of manuscripts: adult, articles, devotionals, easy readers, gift books, middle grade, nonfiction books, novels, picture books, poetry, short stories, technical material, teen/YA

Charges: word rate

Credentials/experience: "I am a freelance editor, working directly with authors for the past four years. I have edited both fiction and nonfiction, including works ranging from illustrated children's picture books and middle-grade chapter books, to young adult and adult Christian fiction."

OUR WRITTEN LIVES | RACHAEL HARTMAN

publisher@owlofhope.com | *www.OurWrittenLives.com*

Contact: email, website

Services: book-contract evaluation, coauthoring, copyediting, discussion questions for books, ghostwriting, manuscript evaluation, proofreading, substantive editing and rewriting, writing coach

Types of manuscripts: articles, curriculum, devotionals, nonfiction books

Charges: hourly rate

Credentials/experience: "Member of Christian Small Publisher Association. MS in human services, specialization in counseling; BA in liberal studies with a minor in writing; and certified life coach; ten years in the writing and publishing industry; established Our Written Lives in 2013; author of three books."

PAGE & PIXEL PUBLICATIONS | SUSAN MOORE

pageandpixelpublications@gmail.com | *pageandpixelpublications.com*

Contact: email

Services: back-cover copy, coauthoring, copyediting, ghostwriting, manuscript evaluation, proofreading, substantive editing and rewriting

Types of manuscripts: academic, adult, articles, Bible studies, book proposals, devotions, nonfiction books, novels, query letters, short stories, technical material, teen/YA

Charges: hourly rate

Credentials/experience: "Over thirty-five years experience editing for Christian publishers and independent authors. Offering individual attention, taking into consideration the client's preferences. Familiar with *Chicago Manual of Style*. Attention to detail. Satisfaction guaranteed. Also offer interior design service, e-book formatting, cover design. Your one-stop shop for the independent author."

PAMELA GOSSIAUX

pam@pamelagossiaux.com | *BestsellingBookShepherd.com*

Contact: email, phone, website

Services: back-cover copy, coauthoring, consulting, copyediting, discussion questions for books, ghostwriting, manuscript evaluation, proofreading, substantive editing and rewriting, writing coach

Types of manuscripts: adult, articles, Bible studies, blog posts, book proposals, devotionals, easy readers, gift books, middle grade, nonfiction books, novels, picture books, poetry, query letters, short stories, teen/YA

Charges: custom, flat fee, hourly rate, packages

Credentials/experience: "Pamela Gossiaux is an international bestselling author, an Associated Press award-winning journalist, speaker, editor, ghostwriter and author consultant. Her clients are bestselling authors on the *USA TODAY, Wall Street Journal*, Barnes and Noble and Amazon bestsellers list, and she also loves working with new and unpublished authors and entrepreneurs. Fiction and non-fiction."

PERFECT WORD EDITING SERVICES | LINDA HARRIS

lharris@perfectwordediting.com | *www.perfectwordediting.com*

Contact: email

Services: copyediting, proofreading, substantive editing and rewriting

Types of manuscripts: adult, articles, board/picture books, book proposals, curriculum, devotions, easy readers, middle grade, nonfiction books, query letters

Charges: page rate, word rate

Credentials/experience: "Linda Harris has been a freelance editor and writer for over 40 years. She is a gold member of The Christian PEN (Proofreaders and Editors Network). She teaches a class on editing children's books for The PEN Institute."

PERPEDIT PUBLISHING INK | BECKY LYLES

PO Box 190246, Boise, ID 83719 | 208-562-1592

beckylyles@beckylyles.com | *www.beckylyles.com*

Contact: email

Services: copyediting, ghostwriting, manuscript evaluation, proofreading, writing coach

Types of manuscripts: adult, articles, Bible studies, book proposals, devotionals, nonfiction books, novels, query letters, short stories, teen/YA

Charges: flat fee, hourly rate, word rate

Credentials/experience: "15 years creating/proofing/editing articles, newsletters and magazines for government and corporate entities and 15 years freelance-editing fiction and nonfiction, including Bible studies, white papers, résumés, novels and short stories."

PICKY, PICKY INK | SUE MIHOLER

1075 Willow Lake Rd. N, Keizer, OR 97303

suemiholer@comcast.net

Contact: email

Services: copyediting, proofreading

Types of manuscripts: articles, Bible studies, devotionals, nonfiction books

Charges: hourly rate

Credentials/experience: "In business since 1998, I have edited at least 100 manuscripts for publishers but mostly for authors preparing their manuscripts for publication."

PRATHER INK LITERARY SERVICES | VICKI PRATHER

107 Billy Byrd Dr., Clinton, MS 39056 | 601-573-4295

pratherINK@gmail.com | pratherink.wordpress.com

Contact: email

Services: coauthoring, copyediting, discussion questions for books, manuscript evaluation, proofreading, substantive editing and rewriting

Types of manuscripts: adult, articles, Bible studies, curriculum, devotionals, nonfiction books, novels, poetry, short stories, teen/YA

Charges: custom, flat fee, hourly rate, word rate

Credentials/experience: "I've been freelance editing since 2014. I've worked with around twenty authors on short, long, and repeat projects. My clients praise me for taking their work and making them shine!"

PROFESSIONAL PUBLISHING SERVICES | CHRISTY CALLAHAN

PO Box 461, Waycross, GA 31502

professionalpublishingservices@gmail.com | professionalpublishingservices.us

Contact: email, website

Services: copyediting, discussion questions for books, French to English translation, French-language editing, manuscript evaluation, proofreading, substantive editing and rewriting, writing coach

Types of manuscripts: academic, adult, articles, Bible studies, curriculum, devotionals, easy readers, gift books, nonfiction books, novels, picture books, poetry, short stories, technical material, teen/YA

Charges: flat fee, hourly rate, word rate

Credentials/experience: "Christy graduated Phi Beta Kappa from Carnegie Mellon University and then earned her MA in Intercultural Studies from Fuller Seminary. A gold member of The Christian PEN: Proofreaders and Editors Network and certified by the Christian Editor Connection and Reedsy, she also completed the 40-hour Foundational Course (Christian track) with the Institute for Life Coach Training."

PROVISION EDITING | NINA HUNDLEY

mrshundley14@gmail.com | ninahundley.com

Contact: email, website

Services: copyediting, manuscript evaluation, substantive editing and rewriting

Types of manuscripts: adult, articles, Bible studies, book proposals, devotionals, middle grade, nonfiction books, novels, query letters, teen/YA

Charges: flat fee, word rate

Credentials/experience: "Freelance editor with a focus on fiction manuscripts. Member of the Editorial Freelancers Association and silver member of The Christian Pen: Proofreaders and Editors Network."

PURPOSEFUL AUTHOR SUPPORT | MARSHA MALCOLM

PO Box 115, Savanna-la-mar PO, Westmoreland, Jamaica | 876-823-2092

purposefulnitpicker@gmail.com | www.purposefulauthorsupport.com

Contact: email

Services: copyediting, discussion questions for books, proofreading

Types of manuscripts: Bible studies, devotions, gift books, nonfiction books, novels, short stories

Charges: word rate

Credentials/experience: "I have received the following certificates: Centre of Excellence Proofreading and Editing Diploma (2021, with Distinction), Expert Rating Certificate in Editing (2014). I have been doing freelance editing since 1998 and currently specialize in clean and Christian nonfiction manuscripts. I have also edited novels, articles, course manuals, essays, and more."

PWC EDITING | PAUL W. CONANT

527 Bayshore Pl., Dallas, TX 75217-7755 | 214-289-3397
pwcediting@gmail.com | *PWC-editing.com*

Contact: email
Services: copyediting, proofreading
Types of manuscripts: academic, adult, articles, Bible studies, business materials, devotions, nonfiction books, novels, poetry, short stories, technical material, textbooks
Charges: hourly rate, word rate
Credentials/experience: "Book editor since '94; textbook editor for 1.5 years; Academic editor since 2001; Silver member of The Christian PEN (Proofreaders and Editors Network); contract editor for Holy Fire Publishing; copyeditor for Christian Editing and Design, Redemption Press, and Creative Enterprises Studio."

REBECCA LUELLA MILLER'S EDITORIAL SERVICES

rluellam@yahoo.com | *rewriterewordrework.wordpress.com*

Contact: email, website
Services: back-cover copy, copyediting, manuscript evaluation, proofreading, substantive editing and rewriting, writing coach
Types of manuscripts: academic, adult, articles, devotionals, middle grade, nonfiction books, novels, query letters, short stories, teen/YA
Charges: page rate, word rate
Credentials/experience: "I became an editor as a direct result of my work as a critique partner. Behind that were the thirty years I spent as an English teacher evaluating student writing. Since 2004 I have had the privilege of working with numerous traditionally published authors, self-published authors, and aspiring authors alike."

THE RED LOUNGE FOR WRITERS | CECILY PATERSON

19 Coora Ave., Belrose, NSW 2085, Australia | +61410760271
cecilyapaterson@gmail.com | *www.redloungeforwriters.com*

Contact: website
Services: writing coach
Types of manuscripts: memoir
Credentials/experience: "A published author of 12 books and a prize-winning memoirist, Cecily Paterson helps experienced writers as well as novice scribblers with memoirs."

REFINE SERVICES, LLC | KATE MOTAUNG

kate@refineservices.com | www.refineservices.com

Contact: email

Services: copyediting, proofreading

Types of manuscripts: adult, articles, Bible studies, board/picture books, book proposals, curriculum, devotions, easy readers, gift books, middle grade, nonfiction books, novels, poetry, query letters, scripts, short stories, teen/YA

Charges: word rate

Credentials/experience: "I have over six years of experience offering copy editing and proofreading services for writers. I work with all types of projects including nonfiction and fiction, book proposals, full-length manuscripts, children's picture books, and everything in between. Feel free to visit the review page on my website to read reviews from past clients."

REVISIONS BY RACHEL, LLC | RACHEL E. BRADLEY

Editor@RevisionsbyRachel.com | www.RevisionsbyRachel.com

Contact: email

Services: back-cover copy, coauthoring, copyediting, ghostwriting, indexing, manuscript evaluation, proofreading, substantive editing and rewriting, writing coach

Types of manuscripts: adult, Bible studies, novels, teen/YA

Charges: custom, word rate

Credentials/experience: "Rachel holds a bachelor of science from Northeastern State University in Oklahoma, she is a gold member of the Christian PEN: Proofreaders and Editors Network, is an established freelance editor with the Christian Editor Connection, is an instructor with the PEN Institute, and has served as a judge for the Excellence in Editing Award and as faculty for PENCON, the only conference for editors in the Christian market."

RICK STEELE EDITORIAL SERVICES

26 Dean Rd., Ringgold, GA 30736 | 706-937-8121

rsteelecam@gmail.com | steeleeditorialservices.myportfolio.com

Contact: website

Services: back-cover copy, book-contract evaluation, copyediting, manuscript evaluation, proofreading, substantive editing and rewriting, writing coach

Types of manuscripts: academic, adult, articles, Bible studies, book proposals, curriculum, devotions, middle grade, nonfiction books, novels, query letters, short stories, teen/YA

Charges: flat fee

Credentials/experience: "To fulfill your dream to be that great author, you may find you need some professional publishing help. Rick Steele Editorial Services has the experience and know-how to provide the attention you need, whether it involves coaching or more hands-on editing. Can help with all aspects of both traditional and custom publishing, including editorial critiques, query letter and proposal coaching services, developmental editing, and copyediting."

ROBIN'S RED PEN | ROBIN PATCHEN

robinpatchen9@gmail.com | robinpatchen.com/editing

Contact: email

Services: copyediting, manuscript evaluation, substantive editing and rewriting, writing coach

Types of manuscripts: adult, articles, devotions, nonfiction books, novels, teen/YA

Charges: page rate

Credentials/experience: "Nominated for ACFW's Editor of the Year three years in a row, Robin Patchen is a multi-published, award-winning author and freelance editor specializing in Christian fiction. She is one of the authors of *Five Editors Tackle the 12 Fatal Flaws of Fiction Writing*, an in-depth guide to self-editing. Patchen loves mentoring new authors and helping established authors polish their books. She enjoys reading and editing almost every clean YA and adult genre."

SARA LAWSON

423 N. Monterey St., Alhambra, CA 91801 | 530-933-9838

sarareneelawson@gmail.com | www.sarasbooks.com

Contact: email, website

Services: back-cover copy, copyediting, discussion questions for books, proofreading, substantive editing and rewriting

Types of manuscripts: academic, adult, articles, Bible studies, devotions, middle grade, nonfiction books, novels, scripts, short stories, teen/YA

Charges: custom

Credentials/experience: "Sara Lawson has over 10 years of freelance editing experience working with fiction and nonfiction books, magazine articles, television scripts, and academic papers of all lengths. She has also served at both predominantly white and Asian American churches, so she understands a variety of ministry contexts. She loves to help writers because she believes that everyone has a story to tell and no one should have to let technical writing abilities get in the way of telling that story."

SARAH HAMAKER

sarah@sarahhamaker.com | *www.sarahhamaker.com/editorial-services*

Contact: email, website

Services: coauthoring, copyediting, ghostwriting, proofreading, substantive editing and rewriting, writing coach

Types of manuscripts: adult, nonfiction books, novels

Charges: custom

Credentials/experience: "As an experienced writer and editor, Sarah has edited magazine publications, fiction and nonfiction books for both adult and children. In addition, she's ghostwritten articles and *Out of the Shadows: A Journey of Recovery from Depression.* As an experienced editor, she can take your book (both fiction and nonfiction) from start to finish, providing project management and guidance along the indie publishing route. On her website you can book a free, 15-minute consultation with her to discuss bringing your idea into a published book."

SCRIVEN COMMUNICATIONS | KATHIE NEE-SCRIVEN

22 Ridge Rd. #220, Greenbelt, MD 20770 | 240-542-4602

KathieScriven@yahoo.com

Contact: email, phone

Services: copyediting, manuscript evaluation, writing coach

Types of manuscripts: adult, articles, Bible studies, book proposals, devotions, middle grade, nonfiction books, poetry, query letters, short stories, teen/YA

Charges: flat fee

Credentials/experience: "I have edited more than eighty Christian nonfiction books and countless shorter pieces. Former editor of four Christian publications and freelance writer. Bachelor's degree in mass communication with a concentration in journalism from Towson University. My services include coaching and helping authors with their marketing and publicity strategies. I can email a document that goes over my background and experience in greater detail to anyone interested."

SHARMAN EDITS | SHARMAN J. MONROE

3431 S. Dakota Ave. NE, Washington, DC 20018 | 240-353-8000
myjourneytome@gmail.com | *www.sharmansedits.com*

Contact: website

Services: book coach, copyediting, proofreading, substantive editing and rewriting

Types of manuscripts: adult, devotions, nonfiction books, novels, teen/YA

Charges: flat fee, hourly rate

Credentials/experience: "I have over 25 years of experience writing, editing and proofreading. Since starting my business in 2011, I have edited and proofed over 50 manuscripts, fiction and non-fiction, and of different genres ranging from Christian to devotionals, entrepreneurship, motivational, mystery, self-help/personal development, urban to young adult to name a few. The majority of my clients are first-time authors and their books can be found on Amazon and Barnes and Noble."

SHARON HINCK

sharon@sharonhinck.com | *www.sharonhinck.com*

Contact: email

Services: substantive editing and rewriting, writing coach

Types of manuscripts: novels

Charges: word rate

Credentials/experience: "As an adjunct professor for MFA writing students, I bring a teacher's heart to the work of editing. As an award-winning author, I share from experience and offer suggestions with a spirit of encouragement and mentoring. I've edited for dozens of first-time novelists in a variety of genres but also for many experienced best-selling authors."

SHERRY MADDEN

madden58sheryl@gmail.com

Contact: email

Services: back-cover copy, copyediting, discussion questions for books, proofreading

Types of manuscripts: adult, articles, Bible studies, devotionals, nonfiction books, novels, short stories

Charges: page rate

Credentials/experience: "Certificate in professional editing, freelancing since 2015."

SHIRL'S EDITING SERVICES | SHIRL THOMAS

9379 Tanager Ave., Fountain Valley, CA 92708 | 714-968-5726
shirlth@verizon.net

Contact: email, phone
Services: copyediting, manuscript evaluation, proofreading, substantive editing and rewriting, writing coach
Types of manuscripts: adult, articles, book proposals, devotionals, gift books, nonfiction books, novels, poetry, query letters, short stories
Charges: custom, hourly rate
Credentials/experience: "Shirl has been a successful freelance writer/editor since 1973 and has had 165 clients and students. Last published book: *My 36 Years in Space* (2018) has 5 stars on Amazon and has excellent reviews. Another: *Making My Way* is mandatory reading for the 9th grade."

SO IT IS WRITTEN | TENITA JOHNSON

5172 Aintree Rd., Rochester, MI 48306 | 313-999-6942
info@soitiswritten.net | *www.soitiswritten.net*

Contact: website
Services: back-cover copy, coauthoring, copyediting, ghostwriting, manuscript evaluation, proofreading, substantive editing and rewriting, writing coach
Types of manuscripts: adult, Bible studies, curriculum, devotionals, easy readers, gift books, middle grade, nonfiction books, novels, poetry, scripts, short stories, teen/YA
Charges: page rate
Credentials/experience: "Authors worldwide write better thanks to editorial guru and authorpreneur, Tenita C. Johnson. Perfecting manuscripts for hundreds of best-selling authors, she's on a mission to end the prominent everyday abuse of the English language and rectify punctuation pet peeves. Tenita collaborates with industry professionals to take manuscripts to the marketplace, positioning authors for success in the literary world."

SPLASHDOWN BOOKS | GRACE BRIDGES

New Zealand
gracebridges1@gmail.com | *www.gracebridges.kiwi/hire-me*

Contact: website
Services: copyediting, manuscript evaluation, proofreading, substantive editing and rewriting

Types of manuscripts: adult, middle grade, novels, short stories, teen/YA

Charges: word rate

Credentials/experience: "Editor of dozens of published books; anthology editor of multiple short-story collections, including award-winning publications. Specialist in word flow, rhythm, clarity, and reader satisfaction. International perspective."

STARCHER DESIGNS | KARA STARCHER

kara@starcherdesigns.com | *www.starcherdesigns.com*

Contact: email

Services: ghostwriting, manuscript evaluation, substantive editing and rewriting, writing coach

Types of manuscripts: adult, memoir, nonfiction books, novels

Charges: word rate

Credentials/experience: "I have a BA in Publishing and have worked as a freelance editor for over 20 years."

STICKS AND STONES | JAMIE CALLOWAY-HANAUER

snsedits@gmail.com | *www.snsedits.com*

Contact: email

Services: book-contract evaluation, coauthoring, copyediting, discussion questions for books, ghostwriting, manuscript evaluation, proofreading, substantive editing and rewriting, writing coach

Types of manuscripts: adult, articles, book proposals, curriculum, devotionals, easy readers, middle grade, nonfiction books, novels, poetry, query letters, short stories, teen/YA

Charges: flat fee

Credentials/experience: "Jamie has eighteen years of experience in the editing field. Previously a full-time public interest attorney who also edited part-time, she is now the owner/operator of Sticks and Stones, where she specializes in academic, legal, and faith-based fiction and nonfiction for adults and teens; ghostwriting; and proposal and query review and development."

SUE A. FAIRCHILD, EDITOR

512 Elm St., Watsontown, PA 17777 | 570-939-0318

sueafairchild74@gmail.com | *www.sueafairchild.wordpress.com*

Contact: email, website

Services: back-cover copy, coauthoring, copyediting, proofreading, substantive editing and rewriting, writing coach

Types of manuscripts: adult, Bible studies, devotions, gift books, middle grade, nonfiction books, novels, short stories, teen/YA

Charges: word rate

Credentials/experience: "Editor/Writing Coach Elk Lake Publishing, Redemption Press; proofreader Iron Stream Media and Zeitgeist, a division of Penguin Random House LLC; Gold Member editor of The Christian Pen."

SUPERIOR EDITING SERVICE | JAN ACKERSON

611 S. Elm, Three Oaks, MI 49128 | 269-756-9912

jan_ackerson@yahoo.com | *www.superioreditingservice.com*

Contact: website

Services: copyediting, substantive editing and rewriting, writing coach

Types of manuscripts: adult, easy readers, gift books, middle grade, novels, picture books, poetry, short stories, teen/YA

Charges: word rate

Credentials/experience: "Seven years editing (both freelance and for Breath of Fresh Air Press), author of *Stolen Postcards*, short stories in multiple anthologies."

SUSAN J. BRUCE

Australia

Susan@susanjbruce.com | *www.susanjbruce.com*

Contact: email

Services: copyediting, manuscript evaluation, proofreading

Types of manuscripts: adult, devotions, nonfiction books, novels, short stories, teen/YA

Charges: flat fee, hourly rate

Credentials/experience: "Master of Arts in Creative Writing. For more details see *www.susanjbruce.com/Editing.*"

SUSAN KING EDITORIAL SERVICES

susan@susankingedits.com | *susankingedits.com*

Contact: email, website

Services: coauthoring, copyediting, discussion questions for books, ghostwriting, proofreading, substantive editing and rewriting, writing coach

Types of manuscripts: academic, adult, articles, Bible studies, book proposals, devotions, gift books, nonfiction books, novels, poetry, query letters, short stories, teen/YA

Charges: hourly rate

Credentials/experience: "During my more than 29 years in the industry, I served over 20 years as an editor for *The Upper Room*, the world's premier daily devotional guide reaching 3 million subscribers in over 100 countries and published in 35 languages. For the past 23 years, I have trained writers at more than one hundred Christian writers' conferences in the U.S. and Canada. My professional life has also included teaching freshman English, American literature, and feature-writing classes at Lipscomb University, Biola University, and Abilene Christian University for a total of 27 years. Currently, I am the compiler and editor of the Short and Sweet book series."

SUSAN R. EDITORIAL | SUSAN RESCIGNO
PO Box 473, Crompond, NY 10517 | 914-844-5217
SusanR.Edit@gmail.com | *srescigno7.wixsite.com/mysite*

Contact: website
Services: copyediting, indexing, project management, proofreading
Types of manuscripts: academic, adult, nonfiction books
Charges: hourly rate, page rate
Credentials/experience: "30 years' experience in publishing industry. Copyedit using MS Word track changes. Create indexes using Sky Index Pro. Clients have included CLC Publications, Orbis Books, Twenty-third Publications."

TANDEM SERVICES | JENNIFER CROSSWHITE
PO Box 220, Yucaipa, CA 92399 | 414-465-2567
jennifer@tandemservicesink.com | *www.tandemservicesink.com*

Contact: email, website
Services: copyediting, manuscript evaluation, substantive editing and rewriting, writing coach
Types of manuscripts: adult, devotionals, nonfiction books, novels
Charges: custom, flat fee, hourly rate
Credentials/experience: "We empower authors to improve their effective commerce around their books. With twenty years' experience spanning both sides of the publishing desk, from author to former managing editor, we've worked with authors for Barbour, Zondervan, Thomas Nelson, Concordia, B&H, and others. Member of The Christian PEN professional editors association."

THREE FATES EDITING | SARAH GRACE LIU
28 Close Hollow Dr., Hamlin, NY 14464
sarah.grace@threefatesediting.com | *www.threefatesediting.com*

Contact: email, website

Services: copyediting, ghostwriting, manuscript evaluation, proofreading, substantive editing and rewriting

Types of manuscripts: academic, adult, Bible studies, middle grade, nonfiction books, novels, poetry, short stories, teen/YA

Charges: word rate

Credentials/experience: "I have an MA in Creative Writing and have run my own editing business since 2012. My true specialization is speculative fiction. For nonfiction, I am more comfortable with progressive texts."

TISHA MARTIN EDITORIAL

tisha@tishamartin.com | www.tishamartin.com

Contact: email, website

Services: back-cover copy, copyediting, discussion questions for books, manuscript evaluation, proofreading, substantive editing and rewriting, writing coach

Types of manuscripts: adult, articles, devotions, gift books, memoir, nonfiction books, novels, scripts, short stories, teen/YA

Charges: flat fee, hourly rate, word rate

Credentials/experience: "Committed to partnering with you to create a resilient story that empowers and delights readers. You write what is burning inside you; I edit to let the fire show through the smoke. My background consists of working with 250 manuscripts. Since 2014, I have judged in premier national contests (including Writer's Digest), guiding and encouraging authors with story techniques, and since 2017, have written back-cover copy and evaluated, edited, and developed a variety of fiction and memoir. Visit my website and contact me for an assessment and introductory conversation. Let's do this together!"

TRAILBLAZE WRITING & EDITING | SARAH BARNUM

sarah@trail-blazes.com | trail-blazes.com

Contact: email, website

Services: copyediting, manuscript evaluation, proofreading, substantive editing and rewriting, writing coach

Types of manuscripts: adult, articles, devotionals, gift books, nonfiction books, novels, short stories

Charges: flat fee, word rate

Credentials/experience: "Sarah Barnum is a member of Inspire Christian Writers and the Christian PEN (Proofreaders and Editors

Network), and she serves on the board, leadership team, and faculty for the West Coast Christian Writers Conference. Sarah holds a bachelor's degree with highest honors and edits for both publishers and freelance authors."

TUPPANCE ENTERPRISES | JAMES PENCE

PO Box 99, Greenville, TX 75403 | 469-730-6478

james@pence.com | *jamespence.com*

>   **Contact:** email, phone, website
>   **Services:** coauthoring, copyediting, ghostwriting, manuscript evaluation, proofreading, substantive editing and rewriting, writing coach
>   **Types of manuscripts:** adult, articles, Bible studies, book proposals, devotions, middle grade, nonfiction books, novels, query letters, short stories, technical material, teen/YA
>   **Charges:** flat fee, hourly rate, word rate
>   **Credentials/experience:** "James has been writing and editing professionally since 2000, and is a traditionally published author of ten books. Publishers include Osborne/McGraw-Hill, Tyndale, Kregel, Baker (co-author), Thomas Nelson (ghostwriter), and Mountainview Books. Published works include textbooks, how-to, novels (adult and YA), Christian living, and memoir."

TURN THE PAGE CRITIQUES | CINDY THOMSON

PO Box 298, Pataskala, OH 43062 | 614-354-3904

cindyswriting@gmail.com | *cindyswriting.com/index.php/critique-service*

>   **Contact:** email
>   **Services:** critiquing, manuscript evaluation, proofreading
>   **Types of manuscripts:** articles, book proposals, novels, query letters
>   **Charges:** flat fee
>   **Credentials/experience:** "Published author both traditionally and independently of fiction and non-fiction, author of numerous magazine articles, and a former mentor with the Jerry B. Jenkins Christian Writers Guild, I can help you get a solid footing as you prepare to publish."

THE VERSATILE PEN | CHRISTY PHILLIPPE

8816 S. 73rd East Ave., Tulsa, OK 74133 | 918-284-7635

christy6871@aol.com | *www.theversatilepen.com*

>   **Contact:** email
>   **Services:** copyediting, discussion questions for books, manuscript

evaluation, proofreading, substantive editing and rewriting

Types of manuscripts: adult, articles, curriculum, devotionals, gift books, nonfiction books, novels, short stories, teen/YA

Charges: hourly rate, word rate

Credentials/experience: "More than twenty years of experience as managing editor, senior editor, and editorial director of various publishing companies and as the owner of The Versatile Pen."

VINEMARC COMMUNICATIONS | MARCIA LAYCOCK

PO Box 637, Blackfalds, AB T0M 0J0, Canada | 403-885-9828

marcia@marciafeelaycock.com | *www.marcialeelaycock.com*

Contact: email

Services: copyediting, proofreading

Types of manuscripts: adult, novels, short stories, teen/YA

Charges: hourly rate

Credentials/experience: "I have edited several books, both fiction and non-fiction, currently working with Siretona Creative."

WHALIN & ASSOCIATES | W. TERRY WHALIN

9457 S. University Blvd., Ste. 621, Highlands Ranch, CO 80129 | 720-708-4953

terry@terrywhalin.com | *terrywhalin.blogspot.com*

Contact: email

Services: coauthoring, discussion questions for books, ghostwriting, substantive editing and rewriting

Types of manuscripts: adult, book proposals, devotionals, gift books, nonfiction books

Charges: flat fee

Credentials/experience: "Terry has written more than sixty books for traditional publishers, including one book that has sold more than 100,000 copies. He has written for more than fifty publications and worked in acquisitions at three publishing houses."

WHITE PENCIL PRODUCTIONS, INC. | KARLA DIAL

620 Dee Ct., Redding, CA 96002 | 719-930-3094

Karladial.com

Contact: email

Services: coauthoring, copyediting, ghostwriting, proofreading, substantive editing and rewriting

Types of manuscripts: adult, articles, nonfiction books, novels, short stories, teen/YA

Charges: retainer

Credentials/experience: "I am an award-winning journalist with more than 20 years of experience as a reporter, writer, managing editor, and editor in chief at both daily and monthly, local and national publications. You have something to say; I can help you say it the best way possible."

WILDCAT WRITING SERVICES | JEFF ADAMS

3675 N. Verdugo Rd., Kingman, AZ 86409 | 928-716-9673
jeffadams@frontiernet.net | *wildcatwritingservices.com*

Contact: email
Services: back-cover copy, book proposals, discussion questions for books, manuscript evaluation, substantive editing and rewriting, writing coach
Types of manuscripts: adult, Bible studies, book proposals, curriculum, devotions, gift books, nonfiction books, query letters
Charges: custom
Credentials/experience: "I'm a substantive editor certified by Christian Editor Connection. I've contributed to more than 25 books. I create, evaluate, and prepare book proposals, including chapter-by-chapter synopsis and sample chapters, for presentation to editors, publishers, and agents. I help writers write better."

WORD MARKER EDITS | KATHRESE MCKEE

8765 Spring Cypress, Ste. L219, Spring, TX 77379 | 281-787-6938
kmckee@kathresemckee.com | *www.wordmarkeredits.com*

Contact: website
Services: copyediting, ghostwriting, manuscript evaluation, proofreading, substantive editing and rewriting
Types of manuscripts: adult, middle grade, novels, short stories, teen/YA
Charges: hourly rate, page rate, word rate
Credentials/experience: "Kathrese is an editor, fiction author, former middle-school reading and ESL teacher, speaker, and blogger. She specializes in editing speculative fiction written from a Christian worldview but is also available to edit other genres and fiction for the general market. She is a silver member of The Christian PEN: Proofreaders and Editors Network."

WORDMELON, INC. | MARGOT STARBUCK

308-A Northwood Cir., Durham, NC 27701 | 919-321-5440
wordmelon@gmail.com | *www.wordmelon.com*

Contact: email

Services: coauthoring, discussion questions for books, ghostwriting, manuscript evaluation, substantive editing and rewriting, writing coach

Types of manuscripts: articles, Bible studies, book proposals, nonfiction books, query letters

Charges: flat fee

Credentials/experience: "Margot Starbuck, a *New York Times* bestselling collaborator and an award-winning author of over 20 books, is a graduate of Westmont College and Princeton Seminary. Margot has had a hand in over 100 major publishing projects, serving publishers as a writer, collaborator, ghostwriter, editor, and writing coach. Passionate about effective communication, she teaches at writing conferences across the country and delights in equipping writers to craft winning book proposals at *wordmelon.com.*"

WORDPOLISH EDITORIAL SERVICES | YVONNE KANU

1 Massey Sq., Toronto, ON M4C 2I2, Canada

yvonnei@wordpolish.net | www.wordpolish.net

Contact: email, website

Services: copyediting, manuscript evaluation, proofreading, writing coach

Types of manuscripts: academic, adult, articles, Bible studies, book proposals, devotions, easy readers, nonfiction books, novels, short stories, teen/YA

Charges: word rate

Credentials/experience: "A professional editor with nine years of experience in publishing, communications and technical writing."

WORDS FOR WRITERS | GINNY L. YTTRUP

PO Box 1651, Lincoln, CA 95648

ginny@wordsforwriters.net | wordsforwriters.net

Contact: email, website

Services: manuscript evaluation, substantive editing and rewriting, writing coach

Types of manuscripts: adult, articles, book proposals, devotions, nonfiction books, novels, query letters, short stories

Charges: custom, word rate

Credentials/experience: "Award-winning author, developmental editor, member of The Christian Pen, and Reedsy."

WRITE AWAY EDITING | JEFFREY PEPPLE

15317 Laurel Ridge, Leo, IN 46765 | 260-627-3003
jlepepple@gmail.com

Contact: email

Services: copyediting, manuscript evaluation, proofreading, substantive editing and rewriting

Types of manuscripts: academic, adult, articles, Bible studies, curriculum, devotionals, easy readers, gift books, middle grade, nonfiction books, novels, picture books, short stories, technical material, teen/YA

Charges: flat fee, hourly rate, page rate

Credentials/experience: "BA in professional writing, Taylor University. Have edited manuscripts and websites."

WRITE BY LISA | ELIZABETH (LISA) R. THOMPSON

200 Laguna Dr. S, Litchfield Park, AZ 85340 | 623-258-5258
writebylisa@gmail.com | www.writebylisa.com

Contact: email

Services: back-cover copy, citations, coauthoring, copyediting, discussion questions for books, ghostwriting, manuscript evaluation, proofreading, substantive editing and rewriting, writing coach

Types of manuscripts: adult, Bible studies, board/picture books, curriculum, devotions, easy readers, gift books, middle grade, nonfiction books, novels, short stories, teen/YA

Charges: flat fee, hourly rate, word rate

Credentials/experience: "I have been writing and editing full-time since May 2009. I have a BA in elementary education with a minor in English. I have edited about 300 books to date. On Facebook, I also admin an editing group and a Christian writing group and am the mod for a proofreading group and a second Christian writing group."

WRITE CONCEPTS, LLC | ALICE CRIDER

590 Highway 105 #107, Monument, CO 80132 | 719-651-0160
editoralicecrider@gmail.com | www.alicecrider.com

Contact: website

Services: back-cover copy, ghostwriting, substantive editing and rewriting, writing coach

Types of manuscripts: adult, book proposals, nonfiction books

Charges: flat fee

Credentials/experience: "With more than twenty years of experience in traditional Christian publishing, Alice Crider has edited many bestselling books by top-level authors such as Kyle Idleman, Tricia Goyer, and Lisa Bevere. She specializes in nonfiction developmental, content, and line editing. She is skilled at analyzing a manuscript's strengths and weaknesses as well as suggesting improvements, clarifications, and revisions. As a certified life coach, Alice is brilliant at helping authors get in touch with the heart of their message in order to communicate powerfully. She is also a certified marketing copywriter and a competent collaborator on projects that need more than editing."

THE WRITE EDITOR | ERIN K. BROWN

510 Adirondac Ave., Hamilton, MT 59840 | 406-239-5590
thewriteeditor@gmail.com | *www.writeeditor.net*

Contact: email, website
Services: copyediting, manuscript evaluation, proofreading, substantive editing and rewriting
Types of manuscripts: academic, adult, articles, Bible studies, book proposals, devotionals, gift books, nonfiction books, novels, query letters, short stories
Charges: custom
Credentials/experience: "Erin Brown is a professional freelance editor, proofreader, and writer. Erin's formal training in editorial practices and procedures, ten years in Christian retailing, twenty-six years in education, and many years as a Christy Award judge afford her a wide knowledge and experience base. She combines her love of editing and teaching by mentoring new writers and teaching nonfiction editing skills to professional editors. She is the director of The PEN Institute, the premiere online educational institute for Christian editors."

THE WRITE FLOURISH | TIM AND NOLA PASSMORE

Toowoomba, Australia
nola@thewriteflourish.com.au | *www.thewriteflourish.com.au*

Contact: email
Services: copyediting, manuscript evaluation, mentoring, proofreading, substantive editing and rewriting
Types of manuscripts: academic, adult, articles, book proposals, devotionals, memoir, nonfiction books, novels, poetry, short stories, teen/YA
Charges: hourly rate

Credentials/experience: "Tim and Nola Passmore each have more than 20 years' experience as university academics. Nola also has a degree in creative writing. They founded The Write Flourish in 2014 and have edited a wide range of manuscripts across a variety of styles and genres. They have also had many of their own short pieces published including fiction, poetry, devotions, memoir, nonfiction and academic articles. They would love to help you add the right flourish to your manuscript."

WRITE HIS ANSWER MINISTRIES | MARLENE BAGNULL

951 Anders Rd., Lansdale, PA 19446 | 484-991-8581
mbagnull@aol.com | *writehisanswer.com/editingmentoring*

Contact: email

Services: copyediting, manuscript evaluation, proofreading, substantive editing

Types of manuscripts: adult, articles, devotionals, nonfiction books, novels

Charges: flat fee, hourly rate

Credentials/experience: "More than thirty-five years of experience in publishing, leading critique groups, and directing writers conferences; author of twelve books and more than a thousand sales to Christian periodicals; editor, typesetter, and publisher of eleven Ampelos Press books."

WRITE NOW EDITING | KARIN BEERY

PO Box 31, Elk Rapids, MI 49629
karin@karinbeery.com | *writenowedits.com*

Contact: email

Services: back-cover copy, copyediting, ghostwriting, manuscript evaluation, substantive editing and rewriting, writing coach

Types of manuscripts: adult, novels, teen/YA

Charges: page rate, word rate

Credentials/experience: "Member of The Christian Proofreaders and Editors Network and the Christian Editor Network; PEN Institute instructor."

WRITE PATHWAY EDITORIAL SERVICES | ANN KNOWLES

annknowles03@aol.com | *write-pathway.blogspot.com*

Contact: email

Services: coauthoring, copyediting, ghostwriting, proofreading, Spanish translation, transcription, writing coach

Types of manuscripts: adult, articles, book proposals, curriculum, devotionals, easy readers, gift books, middle grade, nonfiction books, novels, picture books, poetry, query letters, short stories, teen/YA

Charges: custom

Credentials/experience: "Retired educator, MA in education, certified ESL and Spanish; ESL training consultant for public schools and community colleges. I joined The Christian PEN: Proofreaders and Editors Network in 2005 and started Write Pathway in 2007. I have taken numerous courses from The Christian PEN, American Christian Fiction Writers, Write Integrity Press, and Christian Writers International."

THE WRITE STAGE | RONNELL GIBSON AND KENZI NEVINS
ainfo@thewritestage.com | TheWriteStage.com

Contact: website

Services: consulting, manuscript evaluation, writing coach

Types of manuscripts: adult, book proposals, easy readers, middle grade, novels, picture books, query letters, short stories, teen/YA

Charges: flat fee, word rate

Credentials/experience: "Editor and former literary agent turned social media specialist, Ronnell and Kenzi have published hundreds of articles, devotions, and stories and won multiple awards. They both teach at various conferences, writers groups, and classrooms and are members of The Christian PEN and Realm Makers. They specialize in story coaching and social media branding."

WRITE WAY | PEGGYSUE WELLS
3419 E 1000 N, Roanoke, IN 46783 | 260-433-2817
peggysuewells@gmail.com | www.PeggySueWells.com

Contact: email, website

Services: back-cover copy, coauthoring, copyediting, discussion questions for books, ghostwriting, manuscript evaluation, substantive editing and rewriting, writing coach

Types of manuscripts: adult, articles, Bible studies, board/picture books, book proposals, curriculum, easy readers, gift books, middle grade, nonfiction books, novels, query letters, scripts, short stories, teen/YA

Charges: custom, hourly rate

Credentials/experience: "Bestselling author, dream driver, and great connector, PeggySue Wells is the writing sherpa for your project."

WRITE WAY COPYEDITING, LLC | DIANA SCHRAMER
diana@writewaycopyediting.com | *www.writewaycopyediting.com*

> **Contact:** email
> **Services:** copyediting, manuscript evaluation
> **Types of manuscripts:** Bible studies, devotionals, gift books, memoir, nonfiction books, novels
> **Charges:** hourly rate
> **Credentials/experience:** "I started my business in 2010 and have copyedited 100+ book-length manuscripts and have reviewed 200+ manuscripts. In addition, I have copyedited and reviewed front- and back-cover copy as well as business-related documents and blogs."

WRITER JUSTIFIED | JUDY HAGEY
judy.hagey@gmail.com | *judyhagey.com*

> **Contact:** email, website
> **Services:** back-cover copy, copyediting, proofreading, substantive editing and rewriting
> **Types of manuscripts:** academic, adult, articles, devotions, nonfiction books, novels
> **Charges:** word rate
> **Credentials/experience:** "I have filled various roles in Christian higher education and the nonprofit world, including ten years as the writing director of a ministry producing small-group discipleship materials. Editing credits include theological dissertations, fiction, and nonfiction manuscripts. I currently freelance for traditional publishers as well as individual clients. I have a BA degree in education from Dordt University and am a (certified) Gold Member of the Christian Professional Editors Network."

THE WRITER'S EDGE | BILL CARMICHAEL
info@writersedgeservice.com | *www.writersedgeservice.com*

> **Contact:** website
> **Service:** "Professional editors with many years of experience in working with major Christian publishers evaluate, screen, and expose potential books to traditional Christian publishing companies."
> **Types of manuscripts:** books of all kinds and all ages
> **Charges:** $99

WRITER'S TABLET AGENCY | TERRI WHITMIRE
4371 Roswell Rd #315, Marietta, GA 30062 | 770-648-4101
Writerstablet@gmail.com | *www.Writerstablet.org*

Contact: email, phone

Services: back-cover copy, copyediting, discussion questions for books, manuscript evaluation, proofreading, substantive editing and rewriting, writing coach

Types of manuscripts: adult, articles, Bible studies, curriculum, devotionals, easy readers, middle grade, nonfiction books, novels, picture books, short stories, technical material, teen/YA

Charges: flat fee, hourly rate, word rate

Credentials/experience: "Owner, Terri Whitmire, and her team of skilled writers, editors, and marketers are diverse and prepared to fulfill your content needs. At the Writer's Tablet Agency, we believe that words are critical in communicating your unique message. Together, we will develop or edit your content to tailor fit your individual objectives. Whether you need to write a novel, perfect a presentation, or build an e-commerce website, Writer's Tablet will provide expertise and scrupulous attention to detail every step of the way.

"A seasoned author and successful writing consultant, Mrs. Whitmire earned a bachelor's degree in Information Technology from North Carolina's A&T State University. She pursued a writing certification from the Institute of Children's Literature. She is the author of five published books and passionately provides inspired written solutions to businesses and aspiring authors. Some of her clients have gone on to be best-selling authors, public speakers, and leaders in their industry."

YO PRODUCTIONS, LLC | YOLONDA SANDERS

1543 Reynoldsburg, Columbus, OH 43068 | 614-452-4920
info_4u@yoproductions.net | *www.yoproductions.net*

Contact: email, phone, website

Services: back-cover copy, coauthoring, copyediting, discussion questions for books, ghostwriting, manuscript evaluation, proofreading, substantive editing and rewriting, writing coach

Types of manuscripts: academic, adult, articles, Bible studies, book proposals, curriculum, devotions, nonfiction books, novels, poetry, query letters, scripts, style books, technical material, teen/YA

Charges: custom, flat fee, hourly rate, word rate

Credentials/experience: "More than thirteen years of professional editing and writing experience, editor and writer for a national publication."

20

PUBLICITY AND **MARKETING SERVICES**

THE ADAMS GROUP PUBLIC RELATIONS | GINA ADAMS
Brentwood, TN | 888-253-3622
gina@adamsprgroup.com | *www.adamsprgroup.com*

Contact: phone, website form
Services: social-media management, press kits, contributed content, branding, media coaching, videos, broadcast appearances
Books: all faith-based genres
Charges: flat fee
Credentials/experience: "Gina Adams has served in the Christian marketplace for over 30 years representing singers, bands, films, authors, speakers, and major conference events. In 1994, Gina formed The Adams Group, an independent PR and marketing firm dedicated to working with Christian communicators who need assistance with promoting their products and increasing their national exposure. Her clients have appeared on a variety of Christian and mainstream media outlets, including Focus on the Family, TBN, *Fox News, 60 Minutes,* American Family Radio, *The 700 Club, The New York Times,* CBN, Daystar, and *CBS This Morning,* among a myriad of other broadcast and print outlets. Gina holds a BS in business and marketing from Murray State University and a certificate of achievement in Christian apologetics from Biola University. She has also earned an Expert Rating Certification in Social Media Marketing."

ANNE RAUTH
Kansas City, MO | 913-710-8484
anne@annerauth.com | *www.annerauth.com*

Contact: email
Services: marketing, public relations, strategic planning
Books: nonfiction

Charges: hourly rate

Credentials/experience: "Over 20 years of experience in marketing, public relations, and strategic planning for Fortune 500 companies, small businesses, nonprofit organizations, as well as individual authors."

AUDRA JENNINGS PR

Corsicana, TX | 903-874-8363

ajenningspr@gmail.com | *www.audrajennings.com*

Contact: email

Services: publicity, blog tours, social-media management, graphics packages

Specialty: Christian books to Christian media

Books: nonfiction, fiction, children's

Charges: flat fee, hourly rate

Credentials/experience: "I have worked as a publicist in the Christian market since 2002. For 16 years, I worked for two different agencies before going freelance on my own and have worked with every major Christian publisher over the years. I currently work part-time on staff for New Growth Press but also take on projects on my own."

AUTHOR MEDIA | THOMAS UMSTATTD JR.

Austin, TX | 512-582-7290

thomas@authormedia.com | *authormedia.com*

Contact: website form

Services: marketing consulting, web development, branding, web design

Books: fiction, nonfiction, children's

Charges: flat fee, hourly rate

Credentials/experience: More than ten years of experience. Included in "101 Best Websites for Authors" by *Writer's Digest*.

AUTHOR SUPPORT SERVICES | RUSSELL SHERRARD

Carmichael, CA | 916-967-7251

russellsherrard@reagan.com | *www.sherrardsebookresellers.com/Word-Press/author-support-services-the-authors-place-to-get-help*

Contact: email

Services: Twitter and Facebook marketing, submitting URL to search engines, blog administration

Books: ebooks, fiction, nonfiction

Charges: flat fee
Credentials/experience: "Writing and editing since 2009; currently providing freelance services for multiple clients."

BANNER CONSULTING | MIKE LOOMIS
mike@mikeloomis.co | www.mikeloomis.co

Contact: email, website form
Services: book-launch planning, branding, article curation and placement, web development, PR
Specialty: branding and marketing strategy
Books: nonfiction
Charges: custom
Credentials/experience: "I've worked with internationally known brands and *New York Times* bestsellers. I've helped clients get breakthrough PR, speaking engagements, and bestseller lists."

BBH LITERARY | LAURA BARDOLPH HUBERS
616-319-1641
laura@bbhliterary.com | bbhliterary.com
David Bratt, david@bbhliterary.com

Contact: email, website form
Services: book publicity
Books: nonfiction
Charges: flat fee
Credentials/experience: "Nine years on staff in the marketing department at Eerdmans Publishing, with roles that included publicist, publicity manager, and director of marketing and publicity."

BLUE RIDGE READER CONNECTION | HEATHER KREKE
brreaderconnection@gmail.com | www.blueridgereaderconnections.com
Debb Hackett, brreaderconnection@gmail.com
Darlene L. Turner, brreaderconnection@gmail.com

Contact: email
Services: "Blue Ridge Reader Connections (BRRC) is a website that helps authors connect to readers. All authors will be provided with an author page that showcases up to three of their books. Authors will have the opportunity to add links for purchasing books and connecting with readers through newsletter sign-ups and their websites. Authors will be featured on the BRRC Facebook group and will be invited to participate in Facebook Live events. BRRC

also offers authors a searchable database of reviewers, marketing experts, and book-club recourses."

Books: any: fiction, nonfiction, young adult, middle grade, children's

Charges: flat fee

Credentials/experience: "BRRC falls under the Blue Ridge Mountains Christian Writers Conference, which is directed by DiAnn Mills and Edie Melson."

THE BLYTHE DANIEL AGENCY, INC. | BLYTHE DANIEL

www.theblythedanielagency.com

Blythe Daniel, publicist

Stephanie Alton, marketing manager

Contact: website form

Services: range of publicity campaigns utilizing broadcast and print media and the Internet, including blogs, podcasts, articles, TV and radio interviews, book reviews, and book launches

Books: primarily adult and young-adult nonfiction

Charges: custom

Credentials/experience: "We have personal relationships with hundreds of media outlets that we have developed over the past twenty years in the business. Through our relationships, understanding of the changing media landscape, and careful selection of content we promote, we are able to provide our clients more opportunities to bring recognition to their books." Blythe worked five years as the publicity director and two years as the marketing director for Thomas Nelson.

BROOKSTONE CREATIVE GROUP | SUZANNE KUHN

Birmingham, AL | 302-514-7899

www.brookstonecreativegroup.com

Contact: website form

Services: Amazon optimization, social-media assessment and consulting, video interviews, email and digital marketing, search-engine optimization, Facebook and Google ad management

Books: all

Charges: custom, flat fee

Credentials/experience: Suzanne has more than thirty years of book-specific experience. Brookstone is an expansion of her promotion business, SuzyQ, with a team of almost two dozen professionals who bring a wide range of knowledge and experience to help you get published.

CHOICE MEDIA & COMMUNICATIONS | HEATHER ADAMS

404-423-8411

hello@choicemediacommunications.com | www.choicemediacommunications.com
Grace Burke, senior publicist, Grace@ChoiceMediaCommunications.com
Olivia Parven, senior publicist, Olivia@ChoiceMediaCommunications.com
Allie Ellis, publicist, Allie@ChoiceMediaCommunications.com
Brittany Battista, associate publicist, Brittany@ChoiceMediaCommunications.com
Hannah Harter, associate publicist, Hannah@ChoiceMediaCommunications.com

Contact: website form
Services: media relations, branding and strategy, social media, events
Books: nonfiction
Charges: flat fee, retainer-based partnership
Credentials/experience: "Choice Media & Communications is a boutique media and communications business dedicated to providing clients with quality public relations. Choice helps authors create a clear communications plan, gain media coverage, and receive guidance they won't get anywhere else. With more than two decades of high-level professional communications experience across varying industries and with many of today's tastemakers and thought leaders, Choice founder Heather Adams created a public relations business marked with warmth and enthusiasm, strategic development, clear communication, detailed execution, and thorough reporting."

CHRISTIAN INDIE PUBLISHING ASSOCIATION | SUSAN NEAL

Charlotte, NC | 704-277-7194

cspa@christianpublishers.net | www.christianpublishers.net

Contact: email
Services: resources and tools for publishing and marketing for independent authors
Specialty: marketing services
Books: all genres
Credentials/experience: "Our mission is to support, strengthen, and promote independent authors and small publishers in the Christian marketplace. We have been doing this since 2004."

EABOOKS PUBLISHING | CHERI COWELL

407-712-3431

Cheri@eabookspublishing.com | www.eabookspublishing.com

Contact: website form
Services: marketing coaching is one-on-one for three to four months to lay a foundation

Specialty: websites, social media, e-newsletters, and marketing plan
Books: all genres
Charges: flat fee
Credentials/experience: "We don't believe marketing should be about you or your book; it should be about meeting readers' needs. Our websites, social media, and newsletter plan is reader focused and not author focused. Books sell when you meet readers' needs."

EPIC—A RESULTS AGENCY

Murfreesboro, TN | 615-829-6441
hello@epic.inc | epic.inc

Contact: email, phone, website form
Services: social-media management, email marketing, publicity campaigns, press materials, media training, platform development
Credentials/experience: Group of PR and marketing specialists with years of experience.

JONES LITERARY | JASON JONES

Murfreesboro, TN | 512-720-2996
jason@jonesliterary.com | jonesliterary.com

Contact: email
Services: publicity, digital marketing strategy, podcast production
Specialty: areas of Christian faith, apologetics, persecution of the church, religious liberty, American history, conservative politics, culture, marriage/family
Books: nonfiction
Charges: custom
Credentials/experience: "Previously, Jason led one of the industry's premier Christian public relations firms, SERVE Literary & Media. Prior to that, he spent five years with Thomas Nelson Publishers. He has led campaigns for eleven *New York Times* bestselling titles and has managed some of the industry's most successful authors. He frequently works with producers and editors at *FOX News,* CNN, *Huckabee,* CBS, NBC, Moody Radio, Salem Radio, CBN, *Christianity Today,* and numerous other national outlets."

KATIE BELL COMMUNICATIONS | KATIE BELL

Jackson, TN | 731-803-9056
hello@katiebellcommunications.com | katiebellcommunications.com

Contact: website form
Services: publicity campaigns, press materials, blog and social-media

posts, media training

Credentials/experience: "I jumped into the publishing world headfirst at HarperCollins Publishers in 2012. I single-handedly led publicity efforts for both the Gift and Children's Book Divisions, where I launched bestselling books for media personalities, top music artists, ministry leaders, reality television personalities, pastors, inspiring mamas, and new authors. Later I joined ICON as a book publicist. As publicity director, I led publicity campaigns for major publishing clients, launching several *New York Times* bestsellers, and assisting with some film and nonprofit work. Five years later, I began to feel the pull to embark on a new adventure with Katie Bell Communications, recognizing a need in the industry for a seasoned publicity partner to offer more attention to each campaign to deliver outstanding results."

MCCLURE/MUNTSINGER PUBLIC RELATIONS | PAMELA MCCLURE AND JANA MUNTSINGER

Franklin, TN | 615-595-8321

info@mmpublicrelations.com | *www.mmpublicrelations.com*

Contact: email

Services: customized publicity campaigns, including radio, TV, Internet, and social media

Books: any book they like

Charges: custom

Credentials/experience: "After more than 40 combined years of book publicity, we have long and strong relationships with dozens of editors, writers, and producers. We specialize in knowing how to place religious books in Christian and general-market media, traditional outlets, and online."

MEDIA CONNECT | SHARON FARNELL

New York City, NY | 212-593-6337

sharon.farnell@finnpartners.com | *www.media-connect.com*

Contact: email

Services: full-service book publicity firm with TV and radio campaigns, print, online, book tours, etc.

Books: primarily nonfiction but also children's and some fiction

Charges: flat fee

Credentials/experience: "Since joining the company in 1997, Sharon has been instrumental in helping faith-based authors and publishers reach both the Christian and mainstream audience. She has successfully placed her clients in a variety of top media outlets."

SIDE DOOR COMMUNICATIONS | DEBBIE LYKINS
224-234-6699

deb@sidedoorcom.net | *www.sidedoorcom.net*

Contact: email

Services: media relations, press-kit creation, consulting, publicity-plan development

Books: primarily nonfiction, also children's and fiction but highly selective

Charges: custom

Credentials/experience: "Side Door Communications is a national publicity agency that connects faith-based publishers and personalities with national and local media outlets as well as bloggers, with the goal of obtaining coverage in newspapers and magazines, and on radio, television, and the Internet. Based in the Milwaukee area, founder Debbie Lykins has more than two decades of experience in marketing, publicity, and communications."

VERITAS COMMUNICATIONS | DON S. OTIS
Sandpoint, ID | 719-275-7775

don@veritasincorporated.com | *www.veritasincorporated.com*

Contact: email

Services: schedule radio and television interviews, write and distribute media releases, author training, website representation, travel tracking, select convention representation

Specialty: author training and media promotion

Books: prefers nonfiction and issues-related titles

Charges: flat fee

Credentials/experience: "Thirty years of publicity experience, scheduled more than 30,000 interviews and articles, author of five books, former host and producer for both radio and television."

WHO ARE YOU TRYING TO SERVE? | BRIAN ALLAIN
brian@writingforyourlife.com | *writingforyourlife.com*

Contact: email

Services: marketing plans, platform development, courses, conferences

Specialty: marketing plans for authors

Books: all books for the Christian or general market

Charges: custom, flat fee, hourly rate

Credentials/experience: "Who Are You Trying To Serve? is led by Brian Allain, producer of Writing for Your Life, Publishing in Color, and Compassionate Christianity, and formerly Founding Director of the Frederick Buechner Center. At the Buechner Center he launched and managed Mr. Buechner's online presence, established strategic partnerships around the world, and launched new workshops and books. Brian has supported several additional spiritual authors with their online marketing. He has also supported Drew Theological Seminary, Princeton Theological Seminary, Western Theological Seminary, and other companies on various marketing projects. His strengths are creating business transformation through innovation and high-trust relationships, with positive influence and great dedication."

WILDFIRE MARKETING | ROB EAGAR

Suwanee, GA | 770-887-1462

Rob@StartaWildfire.com | *www.StartaWildfire.com*

Contact: email

Services: all facets of book marketing, including book launches, author websites, email marketing, social media, public speaking, and author-revenue growth

Specialty: book marketing

Books: all genres

Charges: flat fee

Credentials/experience: "Rob Eagar is the founder of Wildfire Marketing, a consulting practice that has coached more than 450 authors and helped books hit *The New York Times* best-seller list in three different categories: new fiction, new nonfiction, and backlist nonfiction. His company has attracted numerous best-selling authors, including Dr. Gary Chapman, Lysa TerKeurst, DeVon Franklin, Wanda Brunstetter, and Dr. John Townsend."

21

LEGAL AND ACCOUNTING SERVICES

CAROL TOPP CPA

10288 Amberwood Ct., Cincinnati, OH 45241 | 513-290-4730

Carol@TaxesforWriters.com | *TaxesForWriters.com*

Contact: email, website form
Services: accounting, consultations, tax questions
Charges: hourly rate
Credentials/experience: "I am a CPA (Certified Public Accountant) and author of 15 books both self-published and small publishers. I am the author of *Business Tips and Taxes for Writers.* I have given presentations at numerous writers conferences and to writers groups both live and virtual. I also do one-on-one consultations via phone or Zoom with writers to discuss their business set-up, operation, and taxes. I am no longer accepting clients for individual tax preparation."

CHRIS MORRIS CPA, LLC

11209 N. 161st Ln., Surprise, AZ 85379 | 623-451-8182

cmorris@chrismorriscpa.com | *chrismorriscpa.com/cwmg*

Contact: website form
Services: accounting, contract review, taxes
Charges: custom, flat fee
Credentials/experience: "Chris Morris CPA is a firm that has focused its resources on developing a deep understanding of the creative entrepreneur space. We have the privilege of counting photographers, authors, publishing presses, editors, virtual assistants, and bloggers among our clients. In other words, we live and breathe the world of the creative entrepreneur."

TOM UMSTATTD CPA

13276 Research Blvd., Austin, TX 78750 | 512-250-1090

tom@taxmantom.com | *www.taxmantom.com*

> **Contact:** email, phone, website form
> **Services:** accounting, taxes
> **Charges:** flat fee, hourly rate

22

SPEAKING SERVICES

ADVANCED WRITERS AND SPEAKERS ASSOCIATION (AWSA)
PO Box 6421, Longmont, CO 80501
ReachOut2Linda@gmail.com | awsa.com

Director: Linda Evans Shepherd

Contact: email, mail

Services: website directory, online prayer group, coaching, online training and community, conference prior to the opening of Christian Product Expo, fall retreat at the Christian Booksellers Expo at Munce

Membership: Main membership qualifications: two major forms of communication from this list: national media (column, blog, podcast, radio or TV show), published book, speaking more than twice a year outside your community, making movies, acting; protégé membership for beginning to intermediate communicators

Fee: women only, $40/year

CHRISTIAN COMMUNICATORS CONFERENCE
contact@christiancommunicators.com | www.ChristianCommunicators.com

Directors: Tammy Whitehurst, Lori Boruff

Contact: website form

Services: annual conference to educate, validate, and launch speakers to the next level for beginning or seasoned speakers; speaker directory listing on website

CHRISTIAN SPEAKER NETWORK
christianspeaker.net

Contact: website form

Services: web page that is listed in the online database

Fee: $39.95/year

CHRISTIAN WOMEN SPEAKERS

womenspeakers.com

Director: Marnie Swedberg
Contact: website form
Services: web page that is listed in the online database
Fees: free; $29.99/month or $299/year for higher ranking, extra
features and benefits; $899/lifetime for highest level of promotion

DECLARE

info@wearedeclare.com | wearedeclare.com

Directors: Eryn Hall, Megan Fish
Contact: email, website form
Services: annual conference in October to equip women to be
effective communicators, blog, podcasts, community events

MOUNTAINSIDE SPEAKING RETREAT

See entry in "Writers Conferences and Seminars."

NEXT STEP COACHING SERVICES

info@nextstepcoachingservices.com | nextstepcoachingservices.com

Directors: Amy Carroll, Melanie Chitwood
Contact: website form
Services: coaching for women speakers to sharpen messages, develop
marketing, and gain organizational tools; weekly speaking tips via
email

NORTHWEST CHRISTIAN SPEAKERS

Bellingham, WA | 360-966-0203
Coordinator@NWSpeakers.com | www.christianspeakersnw.com

Director: Christie Miller
Contact: website form
Services: speakers bureau, not limited to the Northwest
Qualifications/requirements: attend training workshops/evaluation
session

SHE SPEAKS CONFERENCE
See entry in "Writers Conferences and Seminars."

SPEAK UP SPEAKER SERVICES
3141 Winged Foot Dr., Lakeland, FL 33803 | 586-481-7661
gene4speakup@aol.com | *speakupspeakerservices.com*
>**Director:** Carol Kent
>**Contact:** mail
>**Services:** speakers bureau, fee negotiation, contracts for services, speech and TV-interview coaching, SpeakUp Conference (see listing in "Writers Conferences and Seminars")
>**Qualifications/requirements:** at least two books or CDs currently available in the Christian market and regularly speaking nationally; see list of application details to mail
>**Representation:** exclusive, nonexclusive

ULTIMATE CHRISTIAN COMMUNICATORS CONFERENCE
ultimatechristiancommunicatorsconference.com
>**Contact:** website form
>**Services:** annual conference for women to train, coach, and provide networking for beginning and advanced speakers

23

WRITING EDUCATION RESOURCES

A WRITER'S DAY

podcasts.apple.com/us/podcast/a-writers-day/id1472104073

Type: podcast

Host: R. A. Douthitt

Description: "A helpful podcast to help writers learn more about the craft, talk with published authors, and learn more about the publishing industry in order to have a competitive edge. Today, it takes more than just a good story to become a successful writer. You must know about marketing strategies, publishing options, and platforms that will help you stand out from the millions of writers out there. This podcast will help you."

ANN KROEKER, WRITING COACH

annkroeker.com/podcasts

Type: podcast

Host: Ann Kroeker

Description: "These writing podcast episodes offer practical tips and motivation for writers at all stages. . . . Tune in for solutions addressing anything from self-editing and goal-setting . . . to administrative and scheduling challenges."

AUTHOR SCHOOL

authorschool.com

Type: courses

Director: Rachelle Gardner

Description: Pen to Published: Giving you the tools you need while pursuing publishing. Every week, you will receive a new lesson jam-packed with information and resources to help you take the next step toward publishing. Live online sessions with replays.

CHRISTIAN EDITOR NETWORK, LLC

www.ChristianEditorNetwork.com

> **Type:** organization
> **Director:** Kathy Ide
> **Description:** "Our goal is to equip, empower, and encourage editors in the Christian market. Join our community of like-minded professionals in The Christian PEN. Advance your knowledge and skills through The PEN Institute. Attend the PENCON editors conference. Once you're established, apply to join Christian Editor Connection to get more job leads."

CHRISTIAN PUBLISHING SHOW

christianpublishingshow.com

> **Type:** podcast
> **Host:** Thomas Umstattd Jr.
> **Description:** "The Christian Publishing Show is a podcast to help Christian authors change the world. We talk about how to improve in the craft of writing, how to get published, and how to market effectively. Get expert advice from industry insiders."

THE CHRISTIAN SPECULATIVE FICTION PODCAST

podcasts.apple.com/us/podcast/the-christian-speculative-fiction-podcast/ id1463468309

> **Type:** podcast
> **Host:** Paul Regnier
> **Description:** "Author interviews and topic discussions about speculative fiction and how faith intersects with stories. Discussions cover writing craft, publishing, promotion, and everything related to the life of a speculative fiction author. Join us as we talk about storytelling in the genres of science fiction, fantasy, paranormal, superhero, and everything in between."

CHRISTIAN WRITERS INSTITUTE

christianwritersinstitute.com

> **Type:** organization, courses
> **Director:** Steve Laube
> **Description:** "The Christian Writers Institute was created to help Christians become proficient in the skills, craft, and business of writing. To build the Kingdom of God word-by-word. It does so by providing audio, video, and pdf courses taught by some of the industry's best teachers. In addition, the Institute publishes a

number of books on writing for writers, including *The Christian Writers Market Guide*. Originally founded in 1945, it is estimated that over 30,000 students have been trained by the Christian Writers Institute."

CREATE IF WRITING

createifwriting.com/podcast-and-show-notes

Type: podcast

Host: Kirsten Oliphant

Description: "Create If Writing is a weekly podcast for writers and bloggers dealing with authentic platform building online. You will hear from experts on list-building, connecting through Twitter, and how to utilize Facebook. But tools for building an audience would feel empty without a little inspiration, so these training episodes are balanced with inspirational interviews with writers who share their creative process, ups and downs, and how they have dealt with success or failure."

DECLARE PODCAST

podcasts.apple.com/us/podcast/declare/id867933809

Type: podcast

Host: Anne Watson

Description: "The mission of Declare is to equip women to walk in their callings as Christian communicators."

FIGHTWRITE PODCAST

fightwrite.net/podcast

Type: podcast

Host: Carla Hoch

Description: "A writer's resource for writing action and fight scenes."

THE GATECRASHERS PODCAST

www.stitcher.com/show/the-gatecrashers-podcast

Type: podcast

Hosts: Amanda Luedeke, Charis Crowe

Description: "Teaming up to talk about both sides of publishing (self-publishing and traditional), Amanda and Charis share their combined twenty years of experience in the industry from both sides of the desk. They offer a glimpse behind the 'gates' as they share the realities, opportunities, and difficulties of the publishing world."

THE HABIT
thehabit.co/the-habit-podcast

Type: podcast
Host: Jonathan Rogers
Description: "Conversations about writing with writers."

HOME ROW: JUST KEEP WRITING
homerowpod.com

Type: podcast
Host: J. A. Medders
Description: "Get inspired to write from some of today's best writers. Listen. Learn. Just keep writing. You might learn how to get a book deal, write a best-seller, or quit your day job. Maybe you'll get that nudge you need to . . . write the blog, article, or book you've been thinking on for far too long. As Christians, our aim is to write in such a way that Jesus is made much of and the Church is encouraged to follow our risen Lord."

THE JERRY JENKINS WRITERS GUILD
www.JerrysGuild.com

Type: organization
Director: Jerry Jenkins
Description: "The Writers Guild is like a writing conference you can access from anywhere 24/7. Instant access to video training on any writing topic. Additionally, several times each month Jerry answers your questions live, hosts new writing workshops, interviews industry experts, and so much more." Membership is open only periodically; join the waitlist for the next open period. Jerry also offers individual online courses at *jerryjenkins.com*.

KICK-START YOUR AUTHOR PLATFORM MARKETING CHALLENGE
christianediting.co.nz/kick-start

Type: courses
Director: Iola Goulton
Description: "Forty-day email challenge, with an email each day with a series of tasks to complete. Ongoing support is available via a private Facebook group. Topics: What is Marketing?; Understanding Your Brand; Know Your Genre; Know Your Target Reader; Design Your Visual Brand: fonts, colors, author photo, website logo; Create and Brand Social Media: Facebook,

Instagram, Pinterest, Twitter; Create a Social Media Plan; To Blog or Not to Blog?; Create a Mailing List; Set Up, Design, and Configure Your Website."

KINGDOM WRITERS
authors.libsyn.com/podcast

> **Type:** podcast
> **Hosts:** CJ and Shelley Hitz
> **Description:** "CJ and Shelley Hitz are passionate about equipping and empowering Christian writers of all genres to share their unique gifts with the world. This podcast is filled with spiritual encouragement as well as prayers to help you overcome the resistance you face as a writer. Your story matters! We believe that you have a specific role to play in the kingdom of heaven to impact lives for eternity. And because of this, we will pour out our lives encouraging writers like you to not only tell your stories but to take the courageous step of self-publishing your stories in books that will outlive you and leave behind a powerful legacy."

NOVEL MARKETING PODCAST
authormedia.com/novel-marketing

> **Type:** podcast
> **Host:** Thomas Umstattd Jr.
> **Description:** "This is the show for writers who want to build their platform, sell more books, and change the world with writing worth talking about. Whether you self-publish or are with a traditional house, this podcast will make book promotion fun and easy. Thomas Umstattd Jr. interviews publishers, indie authors and best-selling traditional authors about how to get published and sell more books."

PASTOR WRITER
pastorwriter.com/episodes

> **Type:** podcast
> **Host:** Chase Replogle
> **Description:** "Join me as I interview pastors, authors, and writing experts in my journey to better understand the calling and the craft of writing, reading, and living the Christian life."

THE PEN INSTITUTE
PENInstitute.com

> **Type:** organization, courses

Director: Erin Brown

Description: "Lesson Packs, Group Instruction, One-on-One Instruction, and Individual Mentoring for aspiring and established freelance and in-house editors. Instructors are all experienced industry professionals. Established in 2004. Whether you are just beginning your editing career or are looking for an advanced class to update your skills, The PEN Institute has courses for you."

THE PORTFOLIO LIFE WITH JEFF GOINS

podcasts.apple.com/us/podcast/the-portfolio-life-with-jeff-goins/ id844091351

Type: podcast

Host: Jeff Goins

Description: "Jeff Goins shares thoughts & ideas that will help you to pursue work that matters, make a difference with your art & discover your true voice!"

THE PROLIFIC CREATOR

theprolificwriter.libsyn.com

Type: podcast

Host: Ryan Pelton

Description: "The Prolific Creator is about writing fast, often, and well. Follow writer and publisher Ryan Pelton as he discusses processes and strategies for writing, editing, publishing, and marketing your books. TPC podcast also interviews some of the most prolific writers in the world. Be inspired as they discuss their journey into writing, explore tips and tricks on the craft, and learn about the latest trends in publishing today."

SERIOUS WRITER, INC.

seriouswriter.com

Type: organization, courses

Directors: Cyle Young, Bethany Jett

Description: "Serious Writer's mission is to set the industry standard for excellence for the clean and Christian writing markets through online courses, one-day book camps, and writers conferences. The Serious Writer Academy offers recorded classes and workshops. The Serious Writer Club offers various levels of membership, so you can take your writing journey to the next level with hundreds of hours of training, live calls, networking opportunities, and more."

THE STORY BLENDER PODCAST

www.thestoryblender.com

> **Type:** podcast
> **Host:** Steven James
> **Description:** "We are passionate about well-told, impactful stories. We love to listen to them. Watch them. Create them. So, we decided to talk with premier storytellers from around the country. Hear their stories and get their insights. From novelists to comedians to film makers to artists. Stories are told through a variety of people in a variety of ways. And here they are. The secrets of great storytelling from great storytellers."

THE STORY EMBERS PODCAST

storyembers.org/podcast

> **Type:** podcast
> **Host:** Grace Livingston
> **Description:** "A discussion-based podcast where Story Embers staff members explore how to glorify God through storytelling. New episodes are released every third Monday of the month and cover all areas of story craft, including plot, theme, characters, and more."

THE STORYTELLER'S MISSION

www.buzzsprout.com/872170

> **Type:** podcast
> **Host:** Zena Dell Lowe
> **Description:** "Zena Dell Lowe is a seasoned and engaging teacher with a passion for writers and storytellers. Her focused, concise, and practical episodes (all under 20 minutes) not only explore the nuts and bolts of the craft, but also dive deep into the inner life of the artist and the 'why' behind creativity. If you believe that story matters, you'll want to give this podcast a listen."

WRITE FROM THE DEEP

writefromthedeep.com/write-from-the-deep-podcast

> **Type:** podcast
> **Hosts:** Karen Ball, Erin Taylor Young
> **Description:** "Encouragement, refreshment, and truth from writers, for writers. Every writer, at some point, faces the deep places of crushing trials and struggles. But the deep is also a place where we can learn to abide in God as never before. This podcast reminds

writers they're not alone, and equips and helps them to embrace the deep, to discover their truest voice and message, and to share it with refined craft and renewed passion."

THE WRITE HOUR

thewritecoach.biz/the-write-hour-podcast

Type: podcast

Host: Joyce Glass

Description: "How do I start writing a book? Why do I need to write a book? What is the process to write a book? What is next after I have written my book? Are you a personal development leader ready to expand your business with a book? Have your questions answered by Joyce Glass, The Write Coach For Personal Development Leaders. Learn from leaders in the publishing world and begin your writing journey or take your writing career to the next level. Dig deeper with step-by-step instructions and miniworkshops. Joyce's strong point is breaking down the overwhelm and guides you to the next step in your journey. In every episode, she gives practical advice you can implement immediately. Join The Write Hour each week for your dose of writing motivation!"

THE WRITERLY LIFE

podcasts.apple.com/us/podcast/the-writerly-life/id914574328

Type: podcast

Host: Clarissa Moll

Description: "Are you ready to take the next step in your writing life? Whether you're a beginner stumped about what to do first or an experienced writer who's ready for new growth, you'll find what you're looking for here at The Writerly Life, brought to you by hope*writers, the most encouraging place on the internet for writers to make progress.

"Each episode of The Writerly Life offers you practical tips and interviews with publishing pros to help you skip the long learning curve and put you ahead of the game. The Writerly Life is all about balancing the art of writing with the business of publishing so that you can hustle without losing heart. Listen in and be inspired to keep putting your pen to the page. We'll help you find clarity to take the next step in your writing journey. 'You have words, and your words matter. Let's get them out into the world!'"

WRITING AT THE RED HOUSE

www.writingattheredhouse.com/podcast-2

Type: podcast

Host: Kathi Lipp

Description: "Writing at the Red House offers training for upcoming speakers and authors through . . . a podcast to help equip you with the tools you need to get your message out."

WRITING FOR YOUR LIFE

writingforyourlife.com

Type: organization

Director: Brian Allain

Description: "Writing for Your Life is committed to offering a wide variety of useful resources and services to support spiritual writers. We offer online and in-person conferences featuring leading spiritual writers and publishing industry experts. We also provide a host of services and free resources to support your spiritual writing. We cannot guarantee that you will become a best-selling author, but we will help you take your best shot. Learn to tell your own story; write for your life!"

WRITING FOR YOUR LIFE PODCAST

writingforyourlife.com/writing-for-your-life-podcast

Type: podcast

Host: Brian Allain

Description: "If you write, or read, books that matter—books with substance and soul—then this is the place for you. We are here to help you gain inspiration and knowledge to empower your writing. Join us weekly for interviews and presentations from our author partners and industry professionals."

YOUR BEST WRITING LIFE

www.buzzsprout.com/1127762

Type: podcast

Host: Linda Goldfarb

Description: "Christian writing industry experts share weekly content for all levels of Christian writers. Whether you're a beginner or bestseller, you receive practical information and how-to application you can use to grow your writing career as a faith-based author. Each week, Linda Goldfarb and her guests cover various topics, including the craft of writing, fiction topics, nonfiction topics, self-care for writers, and the business of writing to name a few. If you're an aspiring Christian writer, we have content to help you grow. Published writers, we have current content to make your next book proposal, manuscript editing, speaking event, and writer's conference worth your time and energy."

24

CONTESTS

A listing here does not guarantee endorsement of the contest. For guidelines on evaluating contests, go to *www.sfwa.org/other-resources/for-authors/writer-beware/contests*.

> **Note:** Dates may not be accurate since many sponsors had not posted their 2022 dates before press time.

CHILDREN AND TEENS

CORETTA SCOTT KING BOOK AWARD
www.ala.org/awardsgrants/awards/24/apply

> **Description:** Sponsored by Coretta Scott King Task Force, American Library Association. Annual award for children's books published the previous year by African-American authors and/or illustrators. Books must promote an understanding and appreciation of the "American Dream" and fit one of these categories: preschool to grade 4, grades 5–8, grades 9–12.
> **Deadline:** December 1
> **Entry fee:** none
> **Prizes:** $1,000 and plaque

SOCIETY OF CHILDREN'S BOOK WRITERS AND ILLUSTRATORS
www.scbwi.org/awards/grants/for-authors

> **Description:** Sponsors a variety of contests, scholarships, and grants.
> **Deadline:** varies
> **Entry fee:** none
> **Prizes:** ten awards for published authors and five for unpublished authors plus grants for emerging voices and student writers

WORDS AND MUSIC WRITING COMPETITION
wordsandmusic.org/contest

> **Description:** Sponsored by The Pirate's Alley Faulkner Society, Inc. Seven categories: novel, novella, book-length narrative fiction, novel-in-progress, short story, essay, poetry, and short story by a high-school student. For previously unpublished work only.
> **Deadline:** May 15
> **Entry fee:** varies by category
> **Prizes:** $250-$7,500, depending on category

FICTION

AMERICAN CHRISTIAN FICTION WRITERS CONTESTS
acfw.com/acfw-contests

> **Description:** Genesis Contest for unpublished Christian fiction writers in a number of categories/genres. First Impressions award for unpublished writers. Carol Awards for best Christian fiction published the previous year.
> **Deadline:** varies by contest
> **Entry fee:** varies by category and membership

BARD FICTION PRIZE
www.bard.edu/bfp

> **Description:** Sponsored by Bard College. Awarded to a promising, emerging young writer of fiction, 39 years or younger and an American citizen. Entries must be previously published.
> **Deadline:** June 15
> **Entry fee:** none
> **Prize:** $30,000 and appointment as writer-in-residence for one semester at Bard College, Annandale-on-Hudson, New York

BOSTON REVIEW AURA ESTRADA SHORT STORY CONTEST
www.bostonreview.net/contests

> **Description:** Previously unpublished short stories no longer than 5,000 words.
> **Deadline:** June 30
> **Entry fee:** $20
> **Prize:** $1,000 plus publication

BULWER-LYTTON FICTION CONTEST
www.bulwer-lytton.com

> **Description:** Sponsored by San Jose State University English Department. For the worst opening line to a novel. Each submission must be a single sentence; multiple entries allowed. Entries will be judged by categories: general, detective, western, science fiction, romance, etc. Overall winners, as well as category winners.
> **Deadline:** June 30
> **Entry fee:** none
> **Prizes:** publication on the website

FLANNERY O'CONNOR AWARD FOR SHORT FICTION
www.ugapress.org/index.php/series/FOC

> **Description:** Sponsored by University of Georgia Press. For collections of short fiction. Length: 40,000–75,000 words. Contestants must be residents of North America.
> **Deadline:** submit between April 1 and May 31
> **Entry fee:** $30
> **Prize:** $1,000 plus publication under royalty book contract

GET PUBBED
scriveningspress.com/get-pubbed

> **Description:** Sponsored by Scrivenings Press. Entries will be divided among four broad categories: speculative, historical, contemporary, and mystery/suspense. Submit the first ten pages.
> **Deadline:** November 30
> **Entry fee:** $25
> **Prizes:** grand prize: publishing contract, paid registration for annual author retreat, thorough critique of up to 25 pages of your manuscript, and $75 Amazon gift card; entry with the highest score in each genre: critique of up to 25 pages of your manuscript and $25 Amazon gift card

GRACE PALEY PRIZE FOR SHORT FICTION
www.awpwriter.org/contests/overview

> **Description:** Sponsored by Association of Writers and Writing Programs. Short-story collections. May contain stories previously published in periodicals. Length: 150-300 pages.
> **Deadline:** submit between January 1 and February 28
> **Entry fee:** $25
> **Prize:** $5,500 and publication

HAVOK

gohavok.com/submission-guidelines

> **Description:** Sponsored by Havok Publishing. For flash fiction under 1,000 words. Havok operates as an ongoing publishing contest, with monthly themes and deadlines, seasonal awards, and smaller prizes randomly throughout the year ("Best Story Title," "Most Prolific Author," etc.). Publishes stories in five major genres (mashups allowed): science fiction, fantasy, mystery, thriller, and comedy. Each month, 20 stories win the website publication round. Then each six-month season, 30 of those published stories win their way into our print and ebook anthologies (with payment varying upon season as we continue growth as a company; we paid $30 to each anthology winner in 2020). Top two stories in each six-month season are awarded $100 each.
>
> **Deadline:** monthly
>
> **Entry fee:** free
>
> **Prizes:** $100 Readers' Choice Award, $100 Editors' Choice Award, and more

JACK DYER FICTION PRIZE

craborchardreview.siu.edu/submissions-annual-lit.html

> **Description:** Sponsored by Southern Illinois University Department of English. Annual competition for short stories twenty pages or fewer on a theme.
>
> **Deadline:** submit between December 1 and January 31
>
> **Entry fee:** $2
>
> **Prize:** $500 each and publication in *Crab Orchard Review*

JAMES JONES FIRST NOVEL CONTEST

tinyurl.com/v8ee2t8v

> **Description:** Sponsored by Wilkes University. For a first novel or novel-in-progress by a US writer who has not published a novel. Submit a two-page outline and the first fifty pages of an unpublished novel.
>
> **Deadline:** March 15
>
> **Entry fee:** $30 plus $3 processing fee
>
> **Prizes:** first place, $10,000; two runners-up, $1,000 each; a selection from the winning work is published in *Provincetown Arts*

KATHERINE ANNE PORTER PRIZE FOR FICTION

untpress.unt.edu/authors/porter-prize-submissions

> **Description:** Sponsored by University of North Texas Press. Quality

unpublished fiction by emerging writers of contemporary literature. Can be a combination of short-shorts, short stories, and novellas from 100 to 200 pages (27,500-50,000 words). Material should be previously unpublished in book form.

Deadline: submit between May 1 and June 30

Entry fee: $25

Prize: $1,000 and publication by UNT Press

NATIONAL WRITERS ASSOCIATION NOVEL-WRITING CONTEST

www.nationalwriters.shoppingcartsplus.com/f/Novel_Form4.pdf

Description: To encourage development of creative skills and recognize and reward outstanding ability in the area of novel writing. Any genre or category of novel manuscript may be entered. Only unpublished works in the English language. Maximum length: 100,000 words. Must be submitted via USPS.

Deadline: postmarked by April 1

Entry fee: $35

Prizes: first place, $500 and possible representation; second place, $250; third place, $150; fourth through tenth places, book of the winner's choice; honorable mentions, certificate

NATIONAL WRITERS ASSOCIATION SHORT-STORY CONTEST

www.nationalwriters.shoppingcartsplus.com/f/Short_Story_Contest1.pdf

Description: Any genre of story. Length: 5,000 words maximum. Submit only unpublished works in the English language via mail.

Deadline: postmarked by July 1

Entry fee: $15

Prizes: first place, $250; second place, $100; third place, $50; fourth through tenth places: recognition

NOVEL STARTS

scriveningspress.com/novel-starts

Description: Sponsored by Scrivenings Press. For an unfinished novel in four genres: speculative, historical, contemporary, and mystery/suspense. Submit the first five pages.

Deadline: September

Entry fee: $25

Prizes: grand prize: author retreat, invitation to submit novel for consideration by Scrivenings Press once it is finished, thorough critique of up to 25 pages of your manuscript, and $75 Amazon gift card; entry with the highest score in each genre: critique of up to 25 pages of your manuscript and $25 Amazon gift card

REALM AWARD: READER'S CHOICE

www.realmmakers.com/realm-award-readers-choice-alliance-award

Description: Sponsored by The Faith and Fantasy Alliance to give readers their say in what speculative fiction novels they enjoyed most in the preceding year. Only readers may nominate books in this contest. Books may be traditionally published or self- published.
Deadline: submit between April 5 and 22
Entry fee: none
Prize: certificate of recognition

REALM MAKERS AWARDS

www.realmmakers.com

Description: Sponsored by The Faith and Fantasy Alliance. Realm Makers Genre Awards in these categories: debut, science fiction, fantasy, young adult, supernatural/horror, and other (for those who don't feel other categories accurately characterize their speculative work). Realm Award recognizes the most excellent speculative novel written by a Christian author in the previous calendar year. Length: 60,000 words minimum; 50,000 words minimum for young adult. Parable Award for Excellence in Cover Design is awarded to the best overall cover for a speculative novel written by a Christian author.
Deadline: submit between January 1 and 20
Entry fee: $35
Prizes: cash

SERENA MCDONALD KENNEDY AWARD

www.snakenationpress.org/submission-guidelines

Description: Sponsored by Snake Nation Press. Novellas up to 50,000 words or short-story collections up to 200 pages, published or unpublished.
Deadline: August 31
Entry fee: $25
Prize: $1,000 and publication

TOBIAS WOLFF AWARD FOR FICTION

www.bhreview.org/contest-submissions-guidelines

Description: Sponsored by Western Washington University's

Bellingham Review. Length: 5,000 words maximum.
Deadline: submit between December 1 and March 15
Entry fee: $20
Prize: $1,000 plus publication

ZOETROPE: ALL-STORY SHORT FICTION COMPETITION

www.zoetrope.com/contests

Description: For all genres of literary fiction. Entries must be unpublished and strictly 5,000 words or fewer. More than one entry allowed.
Deadline: October 1
Entry fee: $30
Prizes: first place, $1,000; second place, $500; third place, $250; plus publication of winning story and consideration for agency representation

MULTIPLE GENRES

BLUE RIDGE MOUNTAINS CHRISTIAN WRITERS CONFERENCE CONTESTS

www.blueridgeconference.com/contest-info

Description: Sponsors three book contests for fiction or nonfiction: Foundation Awards, Directors' Choice, and The Selahs. Look for details about guidelines, deadlines, and entry fees on the website after January 1.
Deadline: varies by contest
Entry fee: $35-$40

THE BRAUN BOOK AWARDS

wordalivepress.ca/pages/the-braun-book-awards

Description: Sponsored by Word Alive Press. For unpublished Christian books written by Canadian citizens and permanent residents in Canada. Categories: nonfiction and fiction.
Deadline: March 15
Entry fee: none
Prize: One fiction and one nonfiction manuscript will each receive a royalty-based book publishing contract. A select number of secondary winners will also receive prizes, including credit towards publishing.

CALEB AWARD
www.omegawriters.org/caleb-award

> **Description:** Sponsored by Omega Writers. CALEB stands for Christian Authors Lifting Each other's Books and recognizes the best in Australasian Christian writing, published and unpublished.
> **Deadline:** April 30
> **Entry fee:** AUD $40
> **Prize:** AUD $400 (services in kind)

CHRISTIAN INDIE REWARDS
www.christianaward.com

> **Description:** Sponsored by Christian Indie Publishing Association. This award is designed to promote and bring recognition to quality Christian books by small publishers and independently published authors. Books must be printed in English, for sale in the United States, and promote the Christian faith. Awards are offered in eighteen categories. Publishers and authors may nominate titles, and Christian readers vote to determine the winners.
> **Deadline:** November 15
> **Entry fee:** $77-$97, depending on submission date
> **Prize:** promotion

COLUMBIA JOURNAL CONTESTS
columbiajournal.org/submit/winter-contest

> **Description:** Fiction and nonfiction: 7,500 words maximum; poetry: five pages maximum.
> **Deadline:** February 15
> **Entry fee:** $10
> **Prizes:** $250 in each category plus publication

ERIC HOFFER BOOK AWARD
www.hofferaward.com

> **Description:** Eighteen categories for books from small, academic, and micro presses, including self-published, ebooks, and older books. The prose category is for creative fiction and nonfiction fewer than 10,000 words.
> **Deadline:** January 21
> **Entry fee:** varies by category
> **Prizes:** $2,500 grand prize, other prizes awarded in categories

EUPLE RINEY MEMORIAL AWARD

www.thestorytellermagazine.com/contests

> **Description:** Sponsored by *The Storyteller*. Open-genre contest but must be about family—good or bad. Can be fiction or nonfiction (indicate which). Length: 3,000 words maximum. No pornography, graphic anything, New Age, or children's stories will be accepted.
>
> **Deadline:** June 30
>
> **Entry fee:** $5
>
> **Prizes:** first place, $50; second place, $25; third place, $15; honorable mention, $10; plus editor's choice award

EVANGELICAL PRESS ASSOCIATION CONTEST

www.evangelicalpress.com/contest

> **Description:** Higher Goals awards in a variety of categories for periodical manuscripts published in the previous year. Although most submissions are made by publication staff members, associate EPA members may also submit their articles.
>
> **Deadline:** January 17
>
> **Entry fee:** $50
>
> **Prizes:** certificates

EXCELLENCE IN EDITING AWARD

ChristianEditor.com/eie

> **Description:** Sponsored by Christian Editor Connection. This award celebrates newly released books that are superbly written, well edited, and published by a CBA publisher or self-published by a Christian author. It is open to all books published in hardcover or paperback in 2021. Books must be written in English, have been released in North America, and contain a Christian worldview.
>
> **Deadline:** December 31
>
> **Entry fee:** $35 for members, $40 for nonmembers before November 15, $40 and $45 after that date
>
> **Prizes:** winning authors and editors will each receive an award plaque, emblem stickers for marketing, and one selection from an array of Christian Editor Network benefits

INSCRIBE CHRISTIAN WRITERS' FELLOWSHIP CONTEST

inscribe.org/contests

> **Description:** Sponsors contests for InScribe members: Fall Contest, Winter Contest, Word Challenge, FellowScript Contests, Barnabas

Award, Janette Oke Award.
Deadline: varies with each contest
Entry fee: varies with each contest
Prizes: vary by category

NARRATIVE MAGAZINE 30 BELOW CONTEST
www.narrativemagazine.com/node/345528

Description: For writers ages 18-30. Fiction, nonfiction, poetry (up to five poems), essays, memoirs. Length: 15,000 words maximum. Restrictions on previously published works.
Deadline: November 19
Entry fee: $25 per entry
Prizes: $1,500, $750, $300, plus ten finalists will receive $100 each

NARRATIVE MAGAZINE CONTESTS
www.narrativemagazine.com/submit-your-work

Description: Biannual contests in a variety of categories, including short stories, essays, memoirs, poetry, and literary nonfiction. Entries must be previously unpublished. Length: varies by category.
Deadline: varies
Entry fee: varics
Prizes: vary by category

NATIONAL WRITERS ASSOCIATION CONTESTS
www.nationalwriters.com/page/page/2734945.htm

Description: Sponsors six contests: nonfiction, novel, young writers, poetry, short short, and David Raffelock Award for Publishing Excellence.
Deadline: varies by contest
Entry fee: varies by contest
Prizes: vary by contest

NEW MILLENNIUM AWARDS
newmillenniumwritings.submittable.com/submit

Description: Sponsored by New Millennium Writings. Fiction and nonfiction, 6,000 words maximum; flash fiction (short-short story), 1,000 words maximum; poetry, three poems to five pages total. No restrictions as to style or subject matter.
Deadline: November 30
Entry fee: $20, $45 for three entries, $72 for five entries
Prizes: $1,000 plus publication for each category

OREGON CHRISTIAN WRITERS CASCADE AWARDS

oregonchristianwriters.org

> **Description:** Contests for novels; nonfiction books; memoir; young adult/middle grade fiction and nonfiction books; poetry; children's chapter and picture books; articles, columns, and blog posts; short stories/flash fiction; and devotions. Separate divisions for published and unpublished authors. Awards are presented at the summer conference in Portland, Oregon.
>
> **Deadline:** submit between February 15 and March 15
>
> **Entry fee:** $30-$35 for members, $40-$45 for nonmembers
>
> **Prizes:** certificates

SERIOUS WRITER BOOK OF THE DECADE CONTEST

www.seriouswriter.com/contests

> **Description:** Sponsored by Serious Writer, Inc. Open to books published between January 1, 2011 and December 31, 2020, in all genres except horror and erotica.
>
> **Deadline:** March 5
>
> **Entry Fee:** $45 early bird
>
> **Prize:** grand prize: two-day, one-night stay plus dinner event for awards ceremony; engraved award; $300 of Serious Writer Academy classes; free registration to one Serious Writer in-person or online event; special feature on Serious Writer blog; customized press release to send to local newspapers

SERIOUS WRITER BOOK OF THE YEAR CONTEST

www.seriouswriter.com/contests

> **Description:** Sponsored by Serious Writer, Inc. For books published in January–December 2021. Open to books of all genres except horror and erotica.
>
> **Deadline:** March 5
>
> **Entry Fee:** $45 early bird
>
> **Prize:** grand prize: two-day, one-night stay plus dinner event for awards ceremony; engraved award; $300 of Serious Writer Academy classes; free registration to one Serious Writer in-person or online event; special feature on Serious Writer blog; customized press release to send to local newspapers

SERIOUS WRITER WRITER OF THE YEAR CONTEST

www.seriouswriter.com/contests

> **Description:** Sponsored by Serious Writer, Inc. Open to unpublished

417

works in all genres except horror and erotica.

Deadline: March 5

Entry Fee: $45 early bird

Prize: grand prize: two-day, one-night stay plus dinner event for awards ceremony; engraved award; $300 of Serious Writer Academy classes; free registration to one Serious Writer in-person or online event; special feature on Serious Writer blog; customized press release to send to local newspapers

SOUL-MAKING KEATS LITERARY COMPETITION

www.soulmakingcontest.us

Description: Sponsored by National League of American Pen Women, Nob Hill, San Francisco Branch. Categories include flash fiction, short story, memoir vignette, humor, novel excerpt, intercultural essay, creative nonfiction, religious essay, young-adult poetry, and young-adult prose.

Deadline: November 30

Entry fee: $5

Prizes: first place, $100; second place, $50; third place, $25 in each category

TENNESSEE WILLIAMS/NEW ORLEANS LITERARY FESTIVAL

tennesseewilliams.net/contests

Description: Tennessee Williams gained some early recognition by entering a writing contest. The festival that bears his name now sponsors writing contests in poetry, fiction, very short fiction, and one-act playwriting.

Deadline: varies according to genre

Entry fee: varies

Prizes: vary by category

THE WORD GUILD CHRISTIAN WRITING AWARDS

thewordguild.com/contests

Description: The Word Awards recognize the best work published in the previous year in 35 categories of writing, including novels, nonfiction books, articles, columns, poems, song lyrics, scripts, and screenplays. Fresh Ink Student Writers Contest for never-before-published student writers. In the Beginning for unpublished novice and emerging writers. The Grace Irwin Prize for Canadian writers who are Christians recognizes the best book published in the previous year. The Leslie K. Tarr Award celebrates a major career contribution to Christian writing and publishing in Canada. The Partnership Award recognizes an individual or organization that has shown exceptional support and encouragement for Canadian writers and editors who are Christians.

Deadline: varies according to the award
Entry fee: varies according to the award
Prizes: vary according to the award

WRITER'S DIGEST COMPETITIONS

www.writersdigest.com/writers-digest-competitions

Description: Every other month, *Writer's Digest* presents a creative challenge for fun and prizes, providing a short, open-ended prompt for short-story submissions based on that prompt. Winner receives publication in *Writer's Digest*. Also sponsors annual contests for feature articles, short stories (multiple genres), poetry, personal essays, and self-published books (categories vary).

Deadline: varies according to contest
Entry fee: varies
Prizes: first place, $500; second place, $500; and more places for each contest; grand prize, $2,500

WRITERS-EDITORS NETWORK ANNUAL INTERNATIONAL WRITING COMPETITION

www.writers-editors.com/Writers/Contests/contests.htm

Description: Nonfiction and fiction: 4,000 words maximum; children's literature (story, fiction-book chapter, poem, magazine article, or nonfiction-book chapter targeted to a specific age group): 4,000 words maximum. Poetry may be traditional or free verse. All entries must be unpublished or self-published and not accepted for publication by a traditional publisher at the time they are entered in the contest.

Deadline: March 15
Entry fee: poetry, $5 for members, $15 for nonmembers; prose: $10 for members, $20 for nonmembers
Prizes: vary per contest

THE WRITERS' UNION OF CANADA AWARDS & COMPETITIONS

www.writersunion.ca/content/awards

Description: Short Prose Competition for Developing Writers:

fiction or nonfiction by an author who has not yet published a book. Length: 2,500 words maximum. Danuta Gleed Literary Award for the best first collection of short fiction.

Deadline: Short Prose, March 1; Danuta, January 31

Entry fee: $29

Prizes: Short Prose, $2,500; Danuta, $10,000 plus two finalist awards for $500 each

NONFICTION

ANNIE DILLARD AWARD IN CREATIVE NONFICTION
bhreview.org/contest-submissions-guidelines

Description: Sponsored by Western Washington University's *Bellingham Review*. Unpublished essays on any subject. Length: 5,000 words maximum.

Deadline: submit between December 1 and March 15

Entry fee: $20 for first submission; $10 each additional one

Prize: $1,000

AWP PRIZE FOR CREATIVE NONFICTION
bhreview.org/contest-submissions-guidelines

Description: Sponsored by Association of Writers and Writing Programs. Open to published and unpublished authors. Book collection of nonfiction manuscripts. Length: 150–300 pages.

Deadline: submit between January 1 and February 28

Entry fee: $15 for members, $30 for nonmembers

Prize: $2,500 and publication with the University of Georgia Press

THE BECHTEL PRIZE
www.twc.org/publications/bechtel-prize

Description: Sponsored by Teachers & Writers Collaborative. For unpublished essays that explore themes related to creative writing, arts education, and/or the imagination. Length: 2,500 words maximum.

Deadline: January 15

Entry fee: $20

Prize: $1,000 and publication

EVENT NON-FICTION CONTEST
www.eventmagazine.ca/contest-nf

Description: Unpublished creative nonfiction. Length: 5,000 words maximum.

Deadline: October 15
Entry fee: $34.95, includes a one-year subscription to *EVENT*
Prizes: first place, $1,500; second place, $1,000; third place, $500 plus publication

GUIDEPOSTS WRITERS WORKSHOP CONTEST
www.guideposts.org/enter-the-guideposts-writers-workshop-contest

Description: Contest is held in even years. Submit an original, unpublished, true, first-person story (your own or ghostwritten for another person) in 1,500 words or fewer about an experience that changed your life. Show how faith made a difference.
Deadline: mid-June
Entry fee: none
Prizes: twelve all-expenses-paid, weeklong writers workshop in New York to learn about inspirational storytelling and writing for Guideposts publications

INTREPID TIMES TRAVEL WRITING COMPETITION
intrepidtimes.com/competitions

Description: Sponsored by Exisle Publishing. Intrepid Times has a proud history of running narrative, travel-writing contests that focus on stories, places, and people.
Deadline: July 31
Entry fee: free
Prizes: first place, $150, publication on website, possible publication in anthology; runners up, $50

JOHN GUYON LITERARY NONFICTION
craborchardreview.siu.edu/submissions-annual-lit.html

Description: Sponsored by Southern Illinois University Department of English. Annual competition. Literary nonfiction, 6,500 words.
Deadline: submit between December 1 and January 31
Entry fee: $2
Prize: $500 and publication online

NEW LETTERS EDITOR'S CHOICE AWARD
www.newletters.org/editors-choice-award

Description: For unpublished essays. Length: 8,000 words maximum.
Deadline: October 18
Entry fee: $20
Prize: $1,000 and publication in magazine

RICHARD J. MARGOLIS AWARD

www.margolisaward.org

> **Description:** Sponsored by Blue Mountain Center. Given annually to a promising young journalist or essayist whose work combines warmth, humor, wisdom, and concern with social justice. Submit at least two examples of published or unpublished work and a short biographical note, including a description of current and anticipated work. Length: 30 pages maximum.
>
> **Deadline:** July 1
>
> **Entry fee:** none
>
> **Prize:** $5,000 plus a one-month residency at the Blue Mountain Center in Blue Mountain Lake, New York

PLAYS/SCRIPTS/SCREENPLAYS

ACADEMY NICHOLL FELLOWSHIPS IN SCREENWRITING

www.oscars.org/nicholl/about

> **Description:** International contest open to any writer who has not optioned or sold a treatment, teleplay, or screenplay for more than $25,000. May submit up to three scripts. Length: 70-160 pages.
>
> **Deadline:** submit between March 3 and May 3
>
> **Entry fee:** $45-$85, depending on submission date
>
> **Prizes:** up to five $35,000 fellowships; recipients will be expected to complete at least one original feature-film screenplay during the fellowship year

AMERICAN ZOETROPE SCREENPLAY CONTEST

www.zoetrope.com/contests

> **Description:** To find and promote new and innovative voices in cinema. For screenplays and television pilots. No entrant may have earned more than $5,000 as a screenwriter for theatrical films or television or for the sale of, or sale of an option to, any original story, treatment, screenplay, or teleplay. Prizes, fellowships, awards, and other contest winnings are not considered earnings and are excluded from this rule. Length: film scripts, 70-130 pages; one-hour television pilot scripts, 45-65 pages; half-hour television scripts, 22-34 pages.
>
> **Deadline:** September 19
>
> **Entry fee:** $35-$50, depending on submission date

Prizes: first place, $5,000, plus consideration for film option and development; ten finalists will also get this consideration

AUSTIN FILM FESTIVAL SCREENWRITERS COMPETITION
austinfilmfestival.com/submit

Description: Offers a number of contest categories, including narrative feature, narrative short, documentary feature, documentary short for screenplay, teleplay, and scripted digital competition.
Deadline: varies by type
Entry fee: $35-$70, varies by type and submission date
Prizes: $1,000- $5,000

KAIROS PRIZE FOR SPIRITUALLY UPLIFTING SCREENPLAYS
www.kairosprize.com

Description: Sponsored by Movieguide. For feature-length screenplays. Judges consider not only a script's entertainment value and craftsmanship, but also whether it is uplifting, inspirational, and spiritual and if it teaches lessons in ethics and morality. Length: 87-130 pages; will accept scripts up to 150 pages (not counting the title page) for an additional $20.
Deadline: October
Entry fee: varies, depending on submission date
Prizes: $15,000 each for first-time and professional screenwriters

MILDRED AND ALBERT PANOWSKI PLAYWRITING COMPETITION
www.nmu.edu/forestrobertstheatre/playwritingcompetition

Description: Sponsored by Forest Roberts Theatre, Northern Michigan University. Unpublished, unproduced, full-length plays. Award to encourage and stimulate artistic growth among educational and professional playwrights. Provides students and faculty members the opportunity to mount and produce an original work on the university stage.
Deadline: submit between October 1 and November 1
Entry fee: none
Prize: $2,000, a summer workshop, a fully mounted production, and transportation to Marquette, Michigan

MOONDANCE INTERNATIONAL FILM FESTIVAL COMPETITION

www.moondancefilmfestival.com

>**Description:** Offers a variety of awards for films, screenplays, librettos, and features that raise awareness about social issues.
>**Deadline:** October 31
>**Entry fee:** $25-$50
>**Prizes:** promotion to film companies for possible option

SCRIPTAPALOOZA SCREENPLAY COMPETITION

www.scriptapalooza.com/competition/how-to-enter

>**Description:** Any screenplay from any genre considered; must be the original work of the author (multiple authorship acceptable). Shorts competition: screenplays fewer than 40 pages.
>**Deadline:** submit between September 13 and April 4
>**Entry fee:** $30-$70
>**Prizes:** first place, $10,000; each genre winner, $500 (action, adventure, comedy, drama, family, science fiction, thriller/horror, historical), plus access to more than 50 producers through Scriptapalooza's network

SCRIPTAPALOOZA TV COMPETITION

www.scriptapaloozatv.com/competition

>**Description:** Scripts for television pilots, one-hour dramas, reality shows, and half-hour sitcoms. Length: pilots, 30-60 pages; one-hour program, 50-60 pages; reality show, one- to five-page treatment; half-hour sitcom, 25-35 pages.
>**Deadline:** October and April
>**Entry fee:** $45-$50, varies with deadline
>**Prizes:** first place, $500; second place (4), $200; third place (3), $100, plus access to more than 50 producers through Scriptapalooza's network

POETRY

49TH PARALLEL POETRY AWARD

bhreview.org/contest-submissions-guidelines

>**Description:** Sponsored by Western Washington University's *Bellingham Review*. Up to three poems in any style or on any subject.

Deadline: submit between December 1 and March 15
Entry fee: $20; international entries, $30
Prize: $1,000 and publication

ACADEMY OF AMERICAN POETS

poets.org/academy-american-poets/american-poets-prizes

Description: See the website for a list of multiple contests and prizes.

ANHINGA-ROBERT DANA PRIZE FOR POETRY

www.anhingapress.org/anhinga-robert-dana-prize

Description: Sponsored by Anhinga Press. For poets trying to publish a first or second book of poetry. Length: 48–80 pages.
Deadline: submit between February 15 and May 31
Entry fee: $28 per manuscript
Prize: $2,000, a reading tour, and publication by Anhinga Press

BALTIMORE REVIEW POETRY CONTEST

baltimorereview.submittable.com/submit

Description: All styles and forms of poetry, directed toward an announced theme. Maximum of three entries.
Deadline: November 30
Entry fee: $10
Prize: $100-$500 and publication

BARBARA MANDIGO KELLY PEACE POETRY AWARDS

www.peacecontests.org/#poetry

Description: Sponsored by Nuclear Age Peace Foundation. Awards to encourage poets to explore and illuminate positive visions of peace and the human spirit. Poems must be original, unpublished, and in English. May submit up to three poems for one entry fee.
Deadline: July 1
Entry fee: adults, $15; youth ages 13-18, $5; none for ages 12 and under
Prizes: adult winner, $1,000; youth winner, $200; ages 12 and under, $200

BLUE MOUNTAIN ARTS POETRY CARD CONTEST

www.sps.com/contest-3

Description: Biannual contest. Poems may be rhymed or unrhymed, although unrhymed is preferred. Poems also considered for greeting cards or anthologies. No limit to number of entries.

Deadline: June 30 and December 31
Entry fee: none
Prizes: $350, $200, $100

BOSTON REVIEW ANNUAL POETRY CONTEST

www.bostonreview.net./contests

> **Description:** Submit up to five unpublished poems; no more than ten pages total. Submit manuscripts in duplicate with cover note.
> **Deadline:** May 31/June 30
> **Entry fee:** $20, includes a subscription to *Boston Review*
> **Prize:** $1,000 plus publication

CAVE CANEM POETRY PRIZE

cavecanempoets.org/prizes/cave-canem-poetry-prize

> **Description:** Sponsored by Cave Canem Foundation. Supports the work of black poets of African descent with excellent manuscripts and who have not found a publisher for their first book. Offered every other year. Length: 48-75 pages.
> **Deadline:** varies, with a spring season date
> **Entry fee:** none
> **Prize:** $1,000 plus publication by a national press and copies of the book, with a feature reading in New York City

COMSTOCK REVIEW CHAPBOOK CONTEST

comstockreview.org/comstock-writers-group-chapbook-award-for-2014

> **Description:** Submissions must be unpublished as a collection, but individual poems may have been published previously in journals. Length: 25-34 pages. Poems may run longer than one page.
> **Deadline:** submit between August 1 and October 31
> **Entry fee:** $30
> **Prize:** $1,000 plus publication and author copies

FLO GAULT STUDENT POETRY PRIZE

www.sarabandebooks.org/flo-gault

> **Description:** Sponsored by Sarabande Books. For full-time Kentucky undergraduate students. Submit up to three poems.
> **Deadline:** submit between October 1 and December 1
> **Entry fee:** none
> **Prize:** $500 and publication

HOLIDAY POETRY CONTEST

www.thestorytellermagazine.com/contests

> **Description:** Sponsored by *The Storyteller*. Poems may be rhyming or nonrhyming and must be about any holiday. Length: 40 lines maximum. Multiple entries accepted.
> **Deadline:** postmarked by August 31
> **Entry fee:** $5 per three poems
> **Prizes:** first place, $25 plus publication; second place, $15; third place, $10

HOLLIS SUMMERS POETRY PRIZE

www.ohioswallow.com/poetry_prize

> **Description:** Sponsored by Ohio University Press. For an unpublished collection of original poems, 60–95 pages. Open to both those who do not have a published book-length collection and to those who do.
> **Deadline:** December 1
> **Entry fee:** $30
> **Prize:** $1,000 plus publication in book form by Ohio University Press

JAMES LAUGHLIN AWARD

www.poets.org/academy-american-poets/james-laughlin-award-guidelines

> **Description:** Sponsored by Academy of American Poets. To recognize a second full-length print book of original poetry by a US citizen, permanent resident, or person who has DACA/TPS status, forthcoming within the next calendar year. Author must have published one book of poetry in English in a standard edition (48 pages or more) in the United States or under contract and scheduled for publication during the current calendar year; publication of chapbooks (less than 48 pages) does not disqualify. Length: 48-100 pages.
> **Deadline:** submit between August 1 and October 1
> **Entry fee:** none
> **Prize:** $5,000 plus publication

KATE TUFTS DISCOVERY AWARD

www.cgu.edu/tufts

> **Description:** Sponsored by Claremont Graduate University. Award presented annually for a first poetry volume published in the preceding year by a poet of genuine promise.
> **Deadline:** June 30
> **Entry fee:** none
> **Prize:** $10,000

KINGSLEY TUFTS POETRY AWARD
www.cgu.edu/pages/6422.asp

Description: Sponsored by Claremont Graduate University. Presented annually for a published book of poetry by a midcareer poet to both honor the poet and provide the resources that allow artists to continue working toward the pinnacle of their craft.

Deadline: June 30

Entry fee: none

Prize: $100,000 and one week residence at Claremont Graduate University

MURIEL CRAFT BAILEY MEMORIAL POETRY AWARD
comstockreview.org/annual-contest

Description: Sponsored by *Comstock Review*. Unpublished poems up to 40 lines. No limit on number of submissions.

Deadline: submit between April 1 and July 15

Entry fee: postal, $5 per poem for up to five poems; online, $27.50 for five poems

Prizes: first place, $1,000; second place, $250; third place, $100

NEW LETTERS PRIZE FOR POETRY
www.newletters.org/writers-wanted/writing-contests

Description: A single poetry entry may contain up to six poems, and the poems need not be related.

Deadline: May 18

Entry fee: $20 for first entry; $15 for every subsequent entry. If entering online, add a $5 service charge to entry fee. One-year subscription to *New Letters* included in price of first entry.

Prize: $1,500 for best group of three to six poems

PATRICIA CLEARY MILLER AWARD
www.newletters.org/patricia-cleary-miller-award-for-poetry

Description: Sponsored by *New Letters*. A single poetry entry may contain up to six poems, and the poems need not be related.

Deadline: May 18

Entry fee: $24 each entry; if entering online, add a $5 service charge to entry fee; includes a one-year subscription to *New Letters*

Prize: $2,500 for best group of three to six poems

PHILIP LEVINE PRIZE FOR POETRY
www.fresnostate.edu/artshum/english/levineprize

Description: Sponsored by California State University Department of English. An annual book contest for original, previously unpublished, full-length poetry manuscripts. Length: 48-80 pages with no more than one poem per page.
Deadline: submit between July 1 and September 30.
Entry fee: $28 online, $25 postal
Prize: $2,000 and publication by Anhinga Press

POETRY SOCIETY OF VIRGINIA POETRY CONTESTS
poetrysocietyofvirginia.org

Description: More than twenty-five categories for adults and students. Form and length limit of entries vary according to the contests. All entries must be unpublished, original, and not scheduled for publication before the winners of the competition are announced.
Deadline: submit between November 1 and January 19
Entry fee: $4 per poem for nonmembers
Prizes: $100, $50, $30, $20, varying according to specific competition

SLIPSTREAM ANNUAL POETRY CHAPBOOK COMPETITION
www.slipstreampress.org/contest.html

Description: Sponsored by Slipstream Press. Entries may be any style, format, or theme. Length: 40 pages maximum.
Deadline: December 1
Entry fee: $20
Prize: $1,000 plus 50 published copies of chapbook

SOUL-MAKING KEATS LITERARY COMPETITION: JANICE FARRELL POETRY PRIZE
soulmakingcontest.us/guidelines-rules

Description: Sponsored by National League of American Pen Women. Three poems per entry. One poem per page; one-page poems only. Free verse, blank verse, and prose poems.
Deadline: November 30
Entry fee: $5 per entry
Prizes: first place, $100; second place, $50; third place, $25

TOI DERRICOTTE & CORNELIUS EADY CHAPBOOK PRIZE
cavecanempoets.org/prizes/toi-derricotte-cornelius-eady-chapbook-prize

Description: Sponsored by Cave Canem Foundation. Dedicated to the discovery of exceptional chapbook-length manuscripts by black poets. Presented in collaboration with the O, Miami Poetry Festival and The Center for the Humanities at the CUNY Graduate Center.

Deadline: September 15

Entry fee: donations optional

Prize: $1,000, publication, ten copies of the chapbook, and a feature reading

TOM HOWARD/MARGARET REID POETRY CONTEST

winningwriters.com/our-contests/tom-howard-margaret-reid-poetry-contest

Description: Sponsored by Winning Writers. Poetry in any style or genre. Published poetry accepted. Length: 250 lines maximum.

Deadline: submit between April 15 and September 30

Entry fee: $12 per poem

Prizes: Tom Howard Prize, $3,000 for poem in any style or genre; Margaret Reid Prize, $3,000 for poem that rhymes or has a traditional style; $200 each for ten honorable mentions in any style

UTMOST NOVICE CHRISTIAN POETRY CONTEST

www.utmostchristianwriters.com/poetry-contest/poetry-contest-rules.php

Description: Sponsored by Utmost Christian Writers Foundation. Unpublished poems may be rhymed or free verse, up to 60 lines. Need not be religious in content. Maximum of five entries.

Deadline: February 28

Entry fee: $20 per poem

Prizes: $1,000, $500, $300; ten honorable mentions, $100; best rhyming poem, $300; honorable mention rhyming poem, $200

VIOLET REED HAAS PRIZE FOR POETRY

www.snakenation.press/contests

Description: Sponsored by Snake Nation Press. Length: 75-100 pages. Previously published eligible.

Deadline: December 31

Entry fee: $25

Prize: $1,000 plus publication

WERGLE FLOMP HUMOR POETRY CONTEST

winningwriters.com/our-contests/wergle-flomp-humor-poetry-contest-free

Description: Sponsored by Winning Writers. Submit one published or unpublished humor poem up to 250 lines.

Deadline: April 1

Entry fee: none

Prizes: first place, $2,000; second place, $250; ten honorable
mentions, $100; plus the top twelve entries will be published
online

RESOURCES FOR CONTESTS

These websites are sources for announcements about other contests.

DAILY WRITING TIPS

www.dailywritingtips.com/25-writing-competitions

FREELANCE WRITING

www.freelancewriting.com/writingcontests.php

FUNDS FOR WRITERS

fundsforwriters.com/contests

NEW PAGES

www.newpages.com/classifieds/big-list-of-writing-contests

POETS & WRITERS

www.pw.org/grants

TETHERED BY LETTERS

tetheredbyletters.com/resources/contest-list

THE WRITE LIFE

thewritelife.com/writing-contests

DENOMINATIONAL PUBLISHERS

Note: Not all of these houses and publications are owned by denominational publishing companies, and some publish for a broader audience than the denomination.

ANGLICAN
Anglican Journal

ASSEMBLIES OF GOD
God's Word for Today
Influence
LIVE
My Healthy Church
Take Five Plus

BAPTIST
B&H Kids
B&H Publishing
The Brink
CommonCall
HomeLife
Judson Press
Light Magazine
Mature Living
Parenting Teens
ParentLife
Point

Randall House
The Secret Place

BRETHREN
GraceConnect

CATHOLIC
America
American Catholic Press
The Arlington Catholic Herald
Ave Maria Press
Catholic Book Publishing Corp.
Catholic New York
Catholic Sentinel
Celebrate Life Magazine
Christ Is Our Hope
Columbia
Commonweal
Franciscan Media
Image Books
LEAVES
Liturgical Press

Living Faith
Living Faith for Kids
Loyola Press
Our Sunday Visitor, Inc.
Our Sunday Visitor Newsweekly
Paraclete Press
Parish Liturgy
Pauline Books & Media
Paulist Press
Resurrection Press
Scepter Publishers
St. Anthony Messenger
U.S. Catholic

CHARISMATIC

Charisma
Charisma House
Charisma Leader
Chosen
Emanate Books
Whitaker House

CHRISTIAN CHURCH/ CHURCH OF CHRIST

Christian Standard
College Press Publishing
Leafwood Publishers

CHURCH OF GOD

Bible Advocate
Gems of Truth
Now What?
Pathways–Moments with God
Warner Christian Resources

EPISCOPAL

Church Publishing Incorporated
Forward Day by Day
Forward Movement

EVANGELICAL COVENANT

The Covenant Companion

LUTHERAN

Beaming Books
Broadleaf Books
Canada Lutheran
The Canadian Lutheran
Christ in Our Home
Fortress Press
Lutheran Forum
The Lutheran Witness
Northwestern Publishing House
The Word in Season

MENNONITE

Canadian Mennonite
The Messenger
Rejoice!

MESSIANIC

The Messianic Times

METHODIST

Abingdon Press
Light + Life Magazine
Methodist History Journal
The Upper Room

NAZARENE

The Foundry Publishing
Holiness Today
Reflecting God
Standard

ORTHODOX

Ancient Faith Publishing

PENTECOSTAL

testimony/ENRICH

PRESBYTERIAN

byFaith
Flyaway Books
Presbyterians Today
*These Days: Daily Devotions for
    Living by Faith*
Westminster John Knox Press

QUAKER/FRIENDS

Friends Journal
Fruit of the Vine

REFORMED

Christian Courier
P&R Publishing
Tulip Publishing

THE SALVATION ARMY

Faith & Friends
New Frontier Chronicle
Peer
SAConnects
The War Cry

SEVENTH-DAY ADVENTIST

Guide
The Journal of Adventist Education
Ministry
Our Little Friend
Pacific Press
Primary Treasure
Vibrant Life

WESLEYAN

Light from the Word

PUBLISHING LINGO

My first week working in a bookstore I learned a valuable lesson. I had a stack of books in my arms that I had taken from a shipment in the back room. My boss walked by; said, "Steve, please put those in the dump"; and kept walking.

I paused and thought, *Why should I throw these away? They are brand new books!* To my chagrin, I discovered that, in bookstore lingo, a dump was a cardboard display in the front of the store.

The lesson I learned is that knowing the lingo can keep you from being confused or potentially misunderstanding some instructions. Like bookstores, writing and publishing have their own lingo. The following definitions will acquaint you with some of the more important terms.

ABA: American Booksellers Association. This acronym has come to mean the general market, as opposed to CBA, the Christian market.

Advance: Money a publisher pays to an author up front, against future royalties. The amount varies greatly from publisher to publisher and is often paid in two or three installments (on signing the contract, on delivery of the manuscript, and on publication).

AE: An abbreviation for Acquisitions Editor. Not all publishing houses use this abbreviation, but they all have people who acquire in their editorial departments.

All rights: An outright sale of a manuscript. The author has no further control over any subsidiary rights or reusing the piece.

Anecdote: A short, poignant, real-life story, usually used to illustrate a single thought. It need not be humorous.

ARC: Advance Reader Copy. An early paperback (or ebook) version of a book sent out for reviews around four to six months prior to publication.

Assignment: When an editor asks a writer to create a specific manuscript for an agreed-on price.

As-told-to story: A true story you write as a first-person account about someone else.

Audience: The people who are expected to be reading your manuscript, in terms of age, life experience, knowledge of and interest level in the story or subject. Editors want to be sure writers understand their assumed audiences well.

Audiobooks: Spoken-word books available by streaming via the Internet, on compact disc, or MP3 file.

Backlist: A publisher's previously published books that are still in print a year or more after publication.

Bible versions:
AMP—*Amplified Bible*
ASV—*American Standard Version*
CB—*Confraternity Bible* (Catholic)
CEB—*Common English Bible*
CEV—*Contemporary English Version*
CJB—*Complete Jewish Bible*
CSB—*Christian Standard Bible*
ESV—*English Standard Version*
GNB—*Good News Bible*
GW—*GOD'S WORD Translation*
HCSB—*Holman Christian Standard Bible* (replaced by CSB)
ICB—*International Children's Bible*
KJV—*King James Version*
KJV21—*21st Century King James Version*
MEV—*Modern English Version*
MSG—*The Message*
NAB—*New American Bible*
NABRE—*New American Bible Revised Edition*
NASB—*New American Standard Bible*
NCV—*New Century Version*
NEB—*New English Bible*
NET—*New English Translation*
NIrV—*New International Reader's Version*
NIV—*New International Version*

NJB—*New Jerusalem Bible*
NKJV—*New King James Version*
NLT—*New Living Translation*
NRSV—*New Revised Standard Version*
PHILLIPS—*J.B. Phillips New Testament*
RSV—*Revised Standard Version* (replaced by NRSV)
TEV—*Today's English Translation* (aka *Good News Bible*)
TLB—*The Living Bible*
TNIV—*Today's New International Version*
VOICE—*The Voice Bible Translation*
WEB—*World English Bible*

Bio: Brief information about the author.

Bluelines: The last printer's proofs used to catch errors before a book or periodical is printed. May be physical pages or digital proofs in PDF.

BOB: Back-of-Book ad for the author's previous book(s) or a similar book released by the publisher. It uses the blank pages in the back of a book or extra pages at the end of an ebook.

Book proposal: Submission of a book idea to an agent or editor. It usually includes a hook, summary and purpose of the book, target market, uniqueness of the book compared to similar ones in the marketplace, chapter-by-chapter summaries or plot synopsis, marketing and promotion information, your credentials, and delivery date, plus one to three sample chapters, including the first one.

Byline: Author's name printed below the title of a story, article, etc.

Camera-ready copy: The text and artwork for a book that are ready for the press.

Category romance: Novels of around 50,000-60,000 words that are published in categories and according to strict guidelines. For example, Love Inspired novels, the Christian division of Harlequin.

CBA: Christian Booksellers Association. The acronym has come to describe the Christian market as opposed to ABA, the general market. As an entity, the CBA folded in 2019, but the acronym still applies when referring to the Christian publishing industry.

Chapbook: A small book or pamphlet containing poetry, religious readings, etc.

Circulation: The number of copies sold or distributed of a periodical.

Clips: Copies of articles you have had published in newspapers or magazines.

Colophon: The publisher's emblem or imprint used on the title page or spine of a book or a statement at the end of a book with information about its production, such as the type of font used.

Column: A regularly appearing feature, section, or department in a periodical with the same heading. It's written by the same person or a different freelancer each time.

Comp copies: Complimentary copies given to the author by the publisher on publication.

Comps: Shorthand for "comparable." The publisher may have comps on cover designs or titles to help position the book in the marketplace.

Concept statement: A 50- to 150-word summary of your proposed book.

Contributing editor: A freelance writer who has a regular column or writes regularly for the periodical.

Contributor's copy: Copy of an issue of a periodical sent to an author whose work appears in it.

Copyedit: The editor checks grammar, punctuation, and citations to make sure the work is accurate. More detailed than a developmental edit. Some publishers refer to this as the line edit.

Copyright: Legal protection of an author's work. A manuscript is automatically copyrighted in your name when you produce it. You don't need to register it with the Copyright Office unless you are self-publishing a book or other publication since a traditional publisher registers it for you.

Cover copy: Or "copy." The text on the back cover of a book, in the online description, or in marketing materials. For a hardcover, it can also include flap copy, the text on the inside dust-jacket flaps.

Cover letter: A letter that accompanies some article submissions. Usually it's needed only if you have to tell the editor something specific, to give your credentials for writing a manuscript of a technical nature, or to remind the editor that the manuscript was requested or expected. Often used as the introduction to a book proposal.

Credits, list of: A listing of your previously published works.

Critique: An evaluation of a manuscript.

Defamation: A written (libel) or spoken (slander) injury to the reputation of a living person or organization. If what is said is true, it cannot be defamatory, but that does not prevent the injured party from bringing a lawsuit.

Derivative work: A work derived from another work, such as a condensation or abridgment. Contact the copyright owner for permission before doing the abridgment, and be prepared to pay that owner a fee or royalty.

Developmental edit: Usually the first round of editing done on a manuscript. The editor helps "develop" the book by shaping its content and structure. Also called a substantive edit or line edit.

Devotion: A short manuscript based on a Scripture verse or passage that shares a personal spiritual discovery, inspires to worship, challenges to commitment or action, or encourages. A book or periodical of devotions is called a devotional.

Ed board: Editorial board meeting. The editors meet to discuss the new proposals they received to determine which ones should go to the pub board.

Editorial guidelines: See "Writers guidelines."

Em dash (—): Used to create a break or set off material in a sentence instead of using a comma. *The Chicago Manual of Style* calls this punctuation mark "the most versatile of the dashes."

En dash (–): An en dash is longer than a hyphen but shorter than an em dash. Often used in-between numbers and dates to show a range. It was called the "en" dash because in the early days of typesetting it was same width as the capital letter N.

Endorsements: Flattering comments about a book, usually printed on the back cover or in promotional material.

Epub: Term for a specific file format used for ebooks. Mobi is used for Kindle (Amazon). Epub is used by everyone else (Nook, Kobo, Apple, Google Play, etc.).

Essay: A short composition expressing the author's opinion on a specific subject.

Evangelical: A person who believes that one receives God's forgiveness for sins through Jesus Christ and believes the Bible is the authoritative Word of God. This is a broad definition for a label with broad application. Often mistakenly used as a synonym for "Christian."

Exegesis: Interpretation of a Scripture passage.

Feature article: In-depth coverage of a subject, usually focusing on a person, an event, a process, an organization, a movement, a trend, or an issue. It's written to explain, encourage, help, analyze, challenge, motivate, warn, or entertain, as well as to inform.

Filler: A short item used to "fill" a page of a periodical. It could be a joke, anecdote, light verse, short humor, puzzle, game, etc.

First rights: A periodical editor buys the right to publish a manuscript that has never been published and to do so only once.

Foreign rights: Selling or giving permission to translate or reprint published material in another country.

Foreword: Opening remarks in a book to introduce the book and its author. Often misspelled as *forward*.

Freelance: Supplied by freelance writers.

Freelancer or freelance writer: A writer who is not on salary but sells his or her material to a number of different periodicals and publishers.

Galley proof: A typeset copy of a book or magazine used to detect and correct errors before printing.

General editor: Usually, the person who oversees a large work that has multiple authors writing individual chapters for a book or a series of books. This person is not an employee within a publishing house.

General market: Non-Christian market, sometimes called secular market.

Genre: Refers to a type or classification, as in fiction or poetry. For instance, westerns, romances, and mysteries are fiction genres.

Glossy: A photo with a shiny, rather than matte, finish. Also, a publication printed on such paper.

Go-ahead: When an editor tells you to write or submit your article.

Hard copy: A printed manuscript, as opposed to one sent via email.

Independent book publisher: A book publisher who charges authors to publish their books or buy a certain number of copies, as opposed to a royalty house that pays authors. Some independent publishers also pay a royalty. Sometimes called a subsidy, vanity, self, or custom publisher.

ISBN: International Standard Book Number, an identification code needed for every version of a book.

Journal: A periodical presenting information in a particular area, often for an academic or educated audience.

Kill fee: A fee paid for a completed article done on assignment that is subsequently not published. The amount is usually 25-50 percent of the original payment.

Libel: A published false statement that is damaging to another person's reputation; a written defamation.

Line edit: See "Developmental edit" and "Copyedit." Check to see how your editor defines each process.

Little/literary: Small-circulation periodicals whose focus is providing a forum for the literary writer, rather than on making money. Often they do not pay or pay in copies.

Mainstream fiction: Other than genre fiction (such as romance, mystery, or fantasy). Stories of people and their conflicts handled on a deeper level.

Mass market: Books intended for a wide, general market, produced in a smaller format, usually with smaller type and sold at a lower price. The expectation is that their sales will be higher.

Matte finish: A nonglossy, nonreflective finish on a book cover. Has a textured feel.

Mobi: Term for a specific file format used for ebooks. Mobi is used for Kindle (Amazon). Epub is used by everyone else.

Ms: Abbreviation for manuscript.

Mss: Abbreviation for more than one manuscript.

NASR: Abbreviation for North American Serial Rights. Permission for a periodical targeting readers in the US and Canada to publish a manuscript.

New-adult fiction: A developing fiction genre with protagonists ages 18-25. In the general market, these novels often explore sexual themes considered too "adult" for the YA or teen market. They tend to be marketed to older teen readers.

Novella: A short novel, usually 20,000–35,000 words. The length varies from publisher to publisher.

On acceptance: Editor pays a writer at the time the manuscript is accepted for publication.

On assignment: Writing a manuscript at the specific request of an editor.

On publication: Publisher pays a writer when his or her manuscript is published.

On speculation/spec: Writing something for a periodical editor with the agreement that the editor will buy it only if he or she likes it.

Onetime rights: Selling the right to publish a manuscript one time to more than one periodical, primarily to nonoverlapping audiences, such as different denominations.

Over the transom: Unsolicited manuscripts sent to a book editor. Comes from the old transom, which was a window above the door in office buildings. Manuscripts could be pushed "over the transom" into the locked office.

Overrun: The extra copies of a book printed during the initial print run.

Pen name/pseudonym: A name other than your legal name used on a manuscript to protect your identity or the identities of people included or when you wish to remain anonymous. Put the pen name in the byline under the title and your real name with your contact information.

Perfect binding: When pages of a paperback are glued together (bound) on the spine and the cover is then attached.

Periodical: A magazine, newsletter, or newspaper.

Permissions: Asking permission to use text or art from a copyrighted source.

Personal experience: An account based on a real-life experience.

Personality profile: A feature article that highlights a specific person's life or accomplishments.

Plagiarism: Stealing and using the ideas or writing of someone else as your own, either as is or rewriting slightly to make it sound like your own.

POD/Print-on-demand: A printing process where books are printed one at a time or in small numbers instead of in quantity. The production cost per book is higher, but no warehousing is necessary.

POV: Point-of-view. A fiction term that describes the perspective of the one telling the story, such as first person or third person.

Press kit: A compilation of promotional materials for a book or author, used to publicize a book.

Pub board: A formal meeting where people from editorial, marketing, sales, finance, and management meet to discuss whether or not to publish a book.

Public domain: Work for which copyright protection has expired. Copyright laws vary from country to country; but in the US, works published more than 95 years ago have entered the public domain. Because the US copyright law has changed several times, check with the Copyright Office (*copyright.gov*) to determine if a work is in public domain or not. Generally, since 1978, copyright endures for the author's life plus seventy years.

Query letter: A letter sent to an editor about an article or book you propose to write and asking if he or she is interested in seeing it.

Recto: The right-hand page in printing.

Reprint rights: Selling the right to reprint an article that has already been published. You must have sold only first or onetime rights originally and wait until it has been published the first time.

Response time: The number of weeks or months it takes an editor or agent to get back to you about a query, proposal, or manuscript you sent.

Review copies: Books given to reviewers or buyers for bookstore chains and online sellers.

Royalty: The percentage an author is paid by a publisher on the sale of each copy of a book.

Running head: The text at the top of each page that can show the author's name, book title, chapter, or page number.

SASE: Self-addressed, stamped envelope. Always send it with a hard-copy manuscript or query letter.

SASP: Self-addressed, stamped postcard. May be sent with a hard-copy manuscript to be returned by the editor to indicate it arrived safely. Rarely used.

Satire: Ridicule that aims at reform.

Second serial rights: See "Reprint rights."

Secular market: An outdated term for the non-Christian publishing market.

Self-publisher: See "Independent book publisher."

Serial: Refers to publication in a periodical, such as first serial rights.

Sidebar: A short feature that accompanies an article and gives additional information about the topic, such as a recommended reading list. It is often set apart by appearing within a box or border.

Signature: All books are printed in 16-page increments or signatures (occasionally in 32-page increments for large books like Bibles). A large sheet of paper is printed, then folded multiple times. Three sides are cut (top, side, and bottom). The fourth side holds eight double-sided pages. The signatures are compiled and bound into the finished book.

Simultaneous submissions: Sending the same manuscript to more than one editor at the same time. Usually this action is done with nonoverlapping periodical markets, such as denominational publications or newspapers in different cities, or when you are writing on a timely subject. Most periodical editors don't accept simultaneous submissions, but they are the norm in the book market. Be sure to state in a cover letter or on the first page that it is a simultaneous submission.

Slander: The verbal act of defamation.

Slanting: Writing an article to meet the needs of a particular market.

Slush pile: The stack of unsolicited manuscripts that arrive at an editor's desk or email inbox.

Subsidiary rights: All the rights, other than book rights, included in a book contract, such as translations, audiobooks, book clubs, and movies.

Subsidy publisher: See "Independent book publisher."

Substantive edit: See "Developmental edit."

Synopsis: A brief summary of a work, ranging from one paragraph to several pages.

Tabloid: A newspaper-format publication about half the size of a regular newspaper.

Take-home paper: A small periodical given to Sunday-school students, children through adults. These minimagazines are published with the curriculum.

Think piece: A magazine article that has an intellectual, philosophical, or provocative approach to a subject.

Trade book: Describes a 5½" x 8½" paperback book (sometimes 6" x 9"). This is a typical trim size for a paperback. Mass-market books are smaller, around 4" x 6".

Trade magazine: A magazine whose audience is in a particular business.

Trim size: The size of a book after being trimmed in the printing process. (See "Signature" for more information.)

Unsolicited manuscript: A manuscript an editor did not specifically ask to see.

Vanity publisher: See "Independent book publisher."

Verso: The left-hand page in printing.

Vignette: A short, descriptive literary sketch of a brief scene or incident.

Vita: An outline of one's personal history and experience.

Work-for-hire: A manuscript you create for an agreed payment, and you give the publisher full ownership and control of it. You must sign a contract for this agreement to be legal.

Writers guidelines: Information provided by an editor that gives specific guidance for writing for the publication or publishing house. If the information is not offered online, email or send an SASE with your request for printed guidelines.

INDEX

NOTES

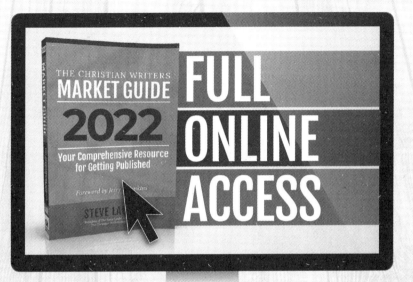